W9-AJN-537

SOMERVILLE'S 100 BEST BRITISH WALKS

Somerville's
100 Best British Walks

Christopher Somerville

with illustrations by Claire Littlejohn

First published by Haus Publishing Ltd in 2009

This revised edition published in 2012 by
The Armchair Traveller at the bookHaus
70 Cadogan Place, London SW1X 9AH
www.thearmchairtraveller.com

A CIP catalogue record for this book is available from the British Library

ISBN 978-1-907973-72-7

Designed and typeset in Garamond by MacGuru Ltd
info@macguru.org.uk

Printed in India by Replika Press Pvt Ltd

Contents

Acknowledgements

So many lovely people have given me so much help over the years in arranging and carrying out more than 200 Daily Telegraph Walks of the Month that it would take a book just to list and thank them all. I am grateful to Bernice Davidson, Gill Charlton and Graham Boynton, successive Travel Editors at the Daily Telegraph, who have encouraged me to contribute these walks to the newspaper each month since September 1990. Illustrators of the series have come and gone over the years, but I would especially like to thank John Montgomery (1996–2004) and Claire Littlejohn (2004–2009) for their beautiful work, which has so greatly enhanced what I have written.

Individual friends and fellow walkers who lightened my footsteps in many and varied settings on the walks featured in this collection include Vanessa Lawrence through the valleys of South Gloucestershire; the Circuit of Bath Sponsored Walkers; Chris Fenwick, Dave Bronze and others of the Dr Feelgood 'family' around Canvey Island; John Francis, Tony Aldous and Marcus Elsegood of Anglia TV, with whom I did over a hundred walks in East Anglia; the gentlemen of Northamptonshire's Ten Foot Club; Peter Hewlett around the cliffs of the Llŷn Peninsula in North Wales; John McNally of The Searchers, who gave me a top-table glimpse into Merseybeat-era Liverpool; Meg Peacocke on her wonderful Poetry Path near Kirkby Stephen; the Rossendale Round-the-Hills walkers; Darren Whitaker of Natural England across the restored South Yorkshire peatlands of Thorne Moors; the inspirational Marc Woods in Wharfedale; Mark Reid, 'Mr Inn Way', in Arkengarthdale; Chris McCarty of Natural England among the spring flowers and birds of Upper Teesdale; long-term friend and 'music teacher' Andy Lyddiatt in the Durham Dales; Dorothy Breckenridge, Lindsey Mowat and Jenny Glumoff up Ben Lomond; Barry Meatyard in the wilds of Ardmeanach; Steve Duncan and Irvine Butterfield on the Road to the Isles across Rannoch Moor; Jane Jowitt, Alexa and John Dewar, Elspeth Turner and Stewart Asquith for good cheer in Glen Esk; Andrew Bateman through the wintry Forest of Abernethy; Jean Stewart high above Glen Carron.

A special thanks, too, to the Daily Telegraph readers who turned out in force to help me celebrate 'significant numbers': the 100th Walk of the Month at Henley-on-Thames in Oxfordshire (on a bloody awful day), the 150th at Ravenglass in West Cumbria, and the 200th around Greywell and the ancient Harroway track on the Hampshire/Berkshire border.

As always, my wife Jane and my family have supported and encouraged me all the way, and have joined me whenever they could.

Dedication

THIS BOOK is dedicated with respect and affection to my friend Dave Richardson – a music, bird and plant man in his heart and bones – who has been my companion on many memorable hikes in Scotland.

Introduction

AUGUST 1990, and my teenage daughter Ruth was not exactly ecstatic about the idea of spending her birthday walking in the Black Mountains. Who could blame her? It was soaking wet, freezing cold and foggy. But she came along anyway, and we had a great time striding the hillsides, talking nonsense, singing our heads off and eating blackberries out of the hedges. I banged out a piece about the day's ramble on my typewriter, sent it off (keeping a carbon duplicate – yes, it was like that back then!) to Bernice Davidson at the Telegraph's travel desk, and more or less thought that would be the last I'd hear of it. But that walk on the wet slopes between Llanthony Abbey and Capel-y-ffin turned out to be the first of a series which grew and flourished under the banner of 'Walk of the Month'.

It has really been a huge pleasure to do these walks, and to try to catch their essence month by month. Choosing a place to set each walk has never given me the slightest headache. We live in an archipelago of islands which boasts, for its size, the most varied selection of landscapes in the world, and the most accessible and well-maintained network of public footpaths. In Ordnance Survey's incomparable Explorer maps, we possess a key to exploring and enjoying our countryside which walkers of other lands can only envy.

I have been inspired by what these landscapes have brought out of writers, painters, musicians, poets; by the way that naturalists, bird-watchers and wildflower experts can open your eyes; by the chance to walk with conservationists and see their vitally important work at first hand; by the enthusiastic recommendations and the good company of friends. Into the rich stew of these walks I have tried to stir all the forementioned elements, and many more – the wildly changing weather of these islands, the beautiful and absorbing manifestations of our four distinct seasons, the nature and composition of the rocks and shores, snatches of elation and fear from the 'skull cinema' films that constantly unreel while one is out walking, and the countless workers, idlers and walkers I have met along the way and what they've had to say about a thousand things.

At the turn of 2009, 'Walk of the Month' is well past its bicentenary. It is high time to get round to producing what Telegraph readers have been requesting for some time now – a collection of the best Walks of the Month. I have had enormous difficulty picking a 'Hundred Best'. What about the trek in the snow beside the River Severn? Yes, and how about that amazing one along the Firth of Forth with all those pink-footed geese in the sky? That was wonderful – but aren't you forgetting summer in the Forest of Bowland, and autumn among the oaks and chestnuts of Savernake Forest?

In the end it has been largely a case of picking the walks with a pin, and spreading them out as evenly as possible. Here are Cornish cliff paths and Sussex downlands, moody Essex marshes and Birmingham canals, seldom-walked corners of Lakeland, jewel-like spring flowers of Teesdale, heart-stopping views from the tops of Munros, lonely estuaries haunted by curlews and winter geese. If I have missed out any of your favourites, I'm sorry. If I've chosen walks that grab you by the ear and tug you outdoors, then I'll be delighted.

See you out there … somewhere, some time soon!

Christopher Somerville

WEST COUNTRY

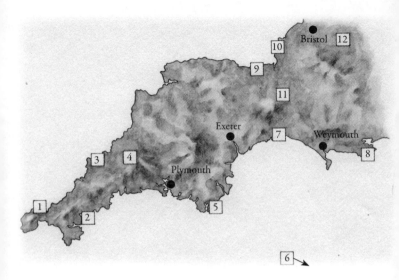

St Ives, Zennor and the old Coffin Road, Penwith, West Cornwall

Summer walk along the cliffs and through the ancient fields of Penwith

AT SEVEN O'CLOCK on a beautiful Cornish morning we gathered in the cool basement kitchen of Penayr house – Jane and I, our son George and his partner Katy back from their home in Australia for an English summer holiday, our daughters Elizabeth and Mary, and Elizabeth's friend Pip – to eat George's special scrambled eggs. 'Perfect,' sighed Jane, looking round the table at her reassembled family, then out across the harbour of St Ives, already splashed gold with early sunshine out of the bluest of skies.

Six of us were due to set out – it was Elizabeth's turn for dinner duty, and with the creation of home-made gnocchi and tomato sauce on her mind she had elected to stay behind. 'Slip, Slop and Slap,' said Katy the sun-aware Aussie, looking up at the cloudless sky. We duly slipped on T-shirts, slopped on the sun-screen and slapped on a hat apiece.

Herring gulls are a lot more ruthless with their offspring than humans. As we went down through the narrow streets of the town to the waterfront, we passed this year's hatch sitting disconsolately on the lichen-stained roofs in shabby suits of half-fledged brown, wheezing plaintively in vain hope that their parents might start feeding them once more. On Porthmeor Beach a line of crumpled sleeping bags yielded a row of crumpled faces – young members of our own species, just waking up after a cold and lumpy night on the sand. Above their frowsy heads, beds of pink and blue hydrangeas blazed in the clear Cornish sunlight, and the stone walls of the lanes sprouted red and white brush-heads of valerian from the crevices between the blocks of granite.

Five hundred spectacularly beautiful miles form the South-West

ST IVES, ZENNOR
& THE OLD COFFIN ROAD
PENWITH · CORNWALL

CARN
NAUN
POINT

LITTLE
CARRACKS

THE
CARRACKS

TREVEGA
CLIFF

CORNISH

CHRISTOPHER AT
TREGERTHEN
CLIFF

MUSSEL POINT

WICCA
POOL

TREGERTHEN
CLIFF

GALA
ROCKS

ZENNOR
HEAD

WICCA

BOSCUBBEN

TREGERTHEN
TREMEDDA

PENDOUR
COVE

GIANT'S
ROCK

HIGHER
TREGERTHEN

CARN
COBBA

ST SENARA'S
CHURCH

ZENNOR

B3306

ZENNOR
MERMAID,
ST SENARA'S
CHURCH

PANORAMA OF ST IVES

CLODGY POINT

THE ISLAND

PEN ENYS POINT

PORTHMEOR BEACH

PORTH-GWIDDEN BEACH

TATE ST IVES

HARBOUR (START OF WALK)

TROWAN

OLD COFFIN ROAD

VENTON VISION FARM

ST IVES

TREVALGAN

B3306

RAILWAY STATION

HYDRANGEAS

HEATHER & ANCIENT FARMING LANDSCAPE

Coast Path, and the stretch that lies just west of St Ives is an absolute peach – a succession of headlands crowned with extravagantly weathered grey granite tors, interspersed with rocky coves where seals swim and cormorants fish from the barnacled rocks. Today the sea was the luminescent blue of a mussel shell, the headlands covered with drifts of purple heather in full bloom, the heather itself twined with nets of honeysuckle, madder and bindweed.

We took the path in our individual styles, the younger walkers forging ahead, Jane and I daundering behind. As a habitual tramper of the smoking-boots persuasion, I got great delight out of being made to slow down and take things in. We watched kittiwakes sailing the air currents of the cliffs on black-tipped wings. We stuck our noses into clumps of wild thyme and pale butterwort. We stopped to look at linnets with their pink breast-patches, and listened to blackcaps warbling on the thorn bushes. A peregrine came tumbling out of the sky and shot out of sight behind the cliffs. I found a silk purse of spider eggs tethered to a clump of heather by gossamer cables. Without Jane's observant eyes and mind alongside, I don't suppose I would have seen one tenth of all this.

We caught up with the others in the green cleft above River Cove, under a sky pale with heat. 'When it's roasting in Western Australia,' Katy told us, 'my dad dunks his hat in the water and sticks it straight on his head.' We took her advice, and walked on refreshed and gasping.

On Zennor Head we turned our backs on the Coast Path and made for Zennor, the remote granite-built village that has supplied Cornwall with some of its best tall tales. The best-known concerns Matthew Trewhella of the golden voice, who enchanted a mermaid with his singing. She came for him after evensong one Sunday night, and lured him away to her lair beneath the waters of Pendour Cove. Wanderers there on calm summer nights report hearing the lovers singing duets below the waves.

In the transept of St Senara's Church I found the mermaid, stiff and stark after 600 years as a carved bench end, saucily displaying her belly-button above a scaly tail. In her left hand she held the comb of vanity. In her right was a round object that joyless folk identify as the mirror of heartlessness; but I prefer its older and more generous interpretation as a quince, the fruit whose beautiful alternative name is love-apple.

After our ploughman's lunch in the Tinner's Arms, the party

divided along gender lines. The ladies opted to take the bus back into St Ives, while the gentlemen struck out along the ancient Coffin Road through the fields. This former route for bodies borne to Christian burial passes through a farming landscape that remembers its Bronze Age origins in the tiny size of the fields and the immense sturdiness and thickness of their walls. Each field is linked to its neighbour by a Cornish stile, a row of four or five well-spaced bars of granite set over a pit. It forms a grid barrier that baffles cattle and sheep – but not the sagacious local pigs, apparently.

Zennor became the focus of a bohemian arty set in the early years of the 20th century. At Tregerthen we passed below the row of cottages where DH Lawrence and his wife Frieda lived, loved and squabbled in poverty and misery during the First World War. Lawrence with his straggly ginger beard, Midlands accent and reputation for writing outlandish filth proved too odd for the locals, while his wife's German nationality engendered suspicions of spying. They were ejected humiliatingly in 1917.

High above the cottages rises the ridge of Higher Tregerthen, crowned with a couple of large houses set among wild rocks. Here lived a disreputable acquaintance of the Lawrences, the occultist Aleister Crowley, 'the wickedest man in the world', much given to midnight cavortings with more or less willing maidens in the stone circles of the Cornish moors. Rupert Brooke's ex-lover Ka Cox met her death here, some say as a result of Crowley exerting his nefarious powers.

We shook off the chill of haunted Tregerthen and walked on in the afternoon sunlight. In the hamlet of Trevega a jolly lunch party sat under a tree finishing their wine. 'You look very comfortable,' I ventured as we went by. 'Oh, we are!' they chorused. 'Beats walking, anyway!' I couldn't agree – not with a couple of miles more of this delectable Cornish countryside in prospect, topped off with the promise of an evening dip in that glittering, sun-warmed sea.

STEPPING OUT – *Walk 1*

MAP: OS 1:25,000 Explorer 102; 1:50,000 Landranger 203

TRAVEL: By train to St Ives station (*www.thetrainline.co.uk*)

By road – A30, A3074

WALK DIRECTIONS: From St Ives railway station (OS ref SW519401), ahead through car park. Before reaching A3074, right down steps (Coast Path sign); left past Pedn Olva hotel along The Warren. Keep to waterfront along harbour. Sharp left by Beach Restaurant (519408) up High Street for 50 yd, then right up The Digey; at end, left along Porthmeor Beach. Follow Coast Path waymarks (acorn symbols and signposts) for 5 miles. Cut across the neck of Zennor Head to rejoin Coast Path (450390). Left here; then where Coast Path swings right in 100 yd, keep ahead over granite stile and on into Zennor.

By St Senara's Church (455385), 'Field path St Ives' notice points to path across fields. Follow yellow arrow waymarks on posts past Tremedda, Tregerthen and Wicca. Just past Boscubben (473395) bear left past 'Residents Vehicles Only' sign down lane for 40 yd, then right across granite stile and on past Trendrine. At Trevessa (481396), granite stile ('public footpath' sign) leads to lane; left for 25 yd, then right ('public footpath' sign) and on. Beyond Trevega Wartha, keep to right of house and on for 2 fields to bear left into lane (486399). Right along lane for 130 yd; where left verge widens, bear left down green lane, past metal gate. In 20 yd, left over stile and on to Trevalgan (489402). Cross stile here at left end of building; on past caravan park to Trowan (494403). Cross yard to lane; cross stone stile ('To St Ives' sign); continue for ¾ mile to tarred lane near Venton Vision Farm (506407). Turn right for 400 yd to road; left to Porthmeor Beach and St Ives.

LENGTH: 11 miles (allow 4 hours or more for St Ives to Zennor, 2–3 hours for return)

CONDITIONS: Parts of Coast Path stony and slippery; some short sections are steep. Not to be done in sandals! No shade along Coast Path.

REFRESHMENTS: Tinners Arms (tel 01736-796927; *www. tinnerarms.com*) or Old Chapel Café, Zennor (tel 01736-798307; *www.backpackers.co.uk/zennor*)

WAYSIDE MUSEUM, ZENNOR: tel 01736-796945

Roseland Peninsula, South Cornwall

Round the margins of a beautiful, back-of-beyond corner of Cornwall

FLYING THE STARS AND STRIPES and a tattered Jolly Roger, the primrose-yellow ferry dodged out of Falmouth. Up in the bows, braving the spray, I admired the skipper's skill as he threaded the little boat between the freighters and sailing dinghies in Carrick Roads. I was heading across the water on this cloudy morning to join my wife and two youngest daughters, Elizabeth (14) and Mary (10), in St Mawes, the one and only town in Roseland.

The sea has gnawed the granite flank of south-west Cornwall into a tatter of peninsulas separated by mazily winding inlets. Roseland is the remotest and the most beautiful of these, uncrowded even at the height of summer, a neck of land half drowned in greenery where you can walk without the world's boots grazing your heels.

Roseland is itself cut into two ragged mini-peninsulas by the northward wriggle of the Percuil River. At the quay in St Mawes the four of us scrambled on board a diminutive tug-like boat, and ten minutes later were decanted at the tiny jetty of St Anthony-in-Roseland on the south side of St Mawes Harbour, under the palatial turrets and windows of Place Manor.

The Spry family have lived at Place since 1649. Their memorials line the transepts of St Anthony's Church, sunk among trees just behind the manor. 'Come and have a look, Dad – it's beautiful!' chirped Mary, framed in the round-arched doorway of the church. Fulsome sculptures commemorated two Sprys who became admirals in the Royal Navy. A stricken figure of Britannia grieved over eighteenth-century Sir Richard Spry; his nephew Sir Thomas was mourned by a young Jack Tar and a scantily clad maiden.

Mossy gravestones lurched and leaned in a jungle of grass beside the churchyard footpath. We paused to read the memorial inscription to Charles and William Edger, brothers in their early twenties who were drowned at sea in the autumn of 1889 – all too common a fate for Roseland fishermen down the ages. In this back-of-beyond knuckle of coast, young men who did not farm the sloping fields between their hedgebanks were destined to brave the seas.

The travel writer H.V. Morton happened upon St Anthony-in-Roseland shortly after the First World War, while taking the sentimental journey that crystallised into his best-selling *In Search of England*. 'I took the map,' he wrote, 'and one name curled itself round my heart. I do not think that in the whole length and breadth of England there is a more beautiful name … St Anthony-in-Roseland!'

Morton overnighted in a Roseland farm labourer's pink thatched cottage, and fell deeply and romantically in love with the area. 'A deserted Eden,' he gushed, ' … incredible, unspoilt beauty.' Roseland is still pretty close to that – one of Cornwall's most delectable places, much of it watched over by the National Trust.

We topped a swell of cornfield outside the village and found ourselves looking out over a misty panorama of river, inlet and sea coast. The path rambled up and down along the clifftops between fields and sea, edging round deep coves with sandy floors. White bells of convolvulus hung in the hedges; montbretia poked tiny orange tongues out of the field walls. Blue buttons of scabious studded the rabbit-burrowed turf banks. In a freshwater dell we found marsh marigolds, bullrushes and spearblade leaves of wild mint.

'What colour are my eyes?' enquired Elizabeth, pausing in mid-scramble across a stone-stile. Yesterday they had looked sea-green; today, seen under cloudy skies, they were spray-grey. 'Mine, too,' said Mary, out of a curtain of hair tangled and sticky from a week's sea bathing.

Down on St Anthony Head the lighthouse blinked its own sleepy eye. Early afternoon lethargy began to weigh on my daughters' will. They set off with Jane for a slow walk back along the lane to Place ferry, while I went on round the steep curve of the headland.

'Drake's Downs' said the OS map, proudly. It was from here in 1588 that Cornish coast watchers spotted the Spanish Armada, and sent word hurriedly westward by beacon to Plymouth, that foreign city across the River Tamar. St Anthony Head was always a handy eyrie above the Western Approaches; so much so that during the 19th century it was heavily ramparted and armed with a gun battery, fortifications that still frown over the sea.

Below the battery I found a little bird hide built above a rocky cove. 'Come and share my perch,' invited its solitary incumbent, offering a pair of binoculars and patting the bench beside her. 'There's a bit of a treat sitting on that ledge over there.'

A magnificent peregrine was hunched against the dark rock, his back the colour of dry slate, his head a brilliant blob of black and white. Around him kittiwakes, fulmars and gulls wheeled on the cliff thermals or huddled on ledges, oblivious to the pair of humans concealed a few yards away. But the peregrine knew exactly where we were, and kept his eyes fixed on us with unwinking attention while we stared back entranced.

The coast path led on through bracken and buckthorn, a switch-back highway between sky and sea. A row of black cormorants stood on a black rock a hundred yards from shore, heads lifted together like a choir. Porthbeor Beach opened at my feet, a long yellow bar of pristine sand backed by sloping cliffs and topped with a smooth dull gold thatch of cornfields.

I took to the road through the hamlet of Bohortha, and went on down the spine of Roseland along a flowery sunken lane. This was National Trust land, its herringbone walls and small fields beautifully kept. From the crest of the peninsula there were far views over the water to the neat white houses on St Mawes Harbour, where Jane and the girls might already be spreading clotted cream on their teatime scones. Further up the Percuil River, estuarine mud gleamed at the bends.

A well-beaten path ran south through woods above the river. I followed it back towards Place, dropping down steps to a rocky beach spread with orange wrack as fine as mermaids' hair. Out in the creek the little ferryboat lay moored above its own reflection. 'Wait there,' the calm voice of the ferryman called across the water. 'With you in a minute or two... plenty of time...'

STEPPING OUT – *Walk 2*

MAP: OS 1:25,000 Explorer 105; 1:50,000 Landranger 204

TRAVEL: By rail (www.thetrainline.co.uk) or road (A30/A39) to Falmouth. Ferry to St Mawes and on to Place (*www. kingharryscornwall.co.uk*)

WALK DIRECTIONS: From Place Quay (855323), walk up the road past Place Manor entrance gates. In 200 yd turn right over a stile (857320 – fingerpost 'Coast Path; St Anthony Head). Pass St Anthony's Church (855320); NT acorns and yellow arrows on wooden posts point the way to the Coast Path. Follow it anticlockwise around the peninsula. 100 yards short of the lighthouse (846311), bear sharp left up steps; turn right at the top to explore the ramparts, observation post and bird hide.

Return to the top of the steps; continue for 10 yards, then bear right up steps (yellow arrow) to a car park. Turn right to pass St Anthony Battery (847312), and continue on along the coast path for 1 mile. Pass a silver painted NT Porthbeor sign; in 150 yards, bear left across a field to turn right along a road (861320). In 50 yards turn left (Bohortha sign) into Bohortha hamlet. By Bohurrow farmhouse bear right (860323 – fingerpost 'Lowlands, Froe Creek') past Manor Farm into a lane between tall hedgebanks. In ¼ mile you'll pass a double fingerpost; keep ahead here ('Froe Creek').

The lane ends at a stile and gate (862328). Continue along the field edge; in 50 yards dogleg right, then left through a gate/stile into another lane between hedgebanks, then follow a field edge to cross a stile (864332). A yellow arrow on a post points left along the path to the Percuil River. At a fingerpost walk down through the trees; then turn left through the woods above the river for ¾ mile. Bear right at a silver painted NT 'Ferry to St Mawes' sign (855324), and turn down steps to a tiny rocky beach. Here you can hail the St Mawes ferry (moored offshore).

LENGTH OF WALK: 5½ miles – allow 2–3 hours.

CONDITIONS: Some steps and stiles.

REFRESHMENTS: Ice-cream van (perhaps) in St Anthony Head car park; otherwise, bring all you need with you

Padstow, Rock and the Camel Estuary, Cornwall

A classic seaside walk through John Betjeman's beloved seaside landscape

RAIN CLOUDS were jostling low over North Cornwall. But the two little girls in shorts, their ribboned plaits swinging below yellow sou'westers, didn't seem to mind. They went scooting past me hand-in-hand along the cliff path above Padstow, singing 'Raindrops Keep Falling On My Head' in breathy trebles. It could have been Peggy Purey-Cust and her best friend, I thought as I watched them skip; two adorable mites, straight out of *Summoned By Bells*.

The L-shaped estuary of the River Camel, where the clustered houses of Padstow look across half a mile of water to the tree-cradled villas of Rock, is John Betjeman country to the core, the foundation of a million seaside holiday memories and dreams. In *Summoned By Bells*, the poet's blank-verse hymn to nostalgia, the Cornwall chapters had always captivated me with their evocation of the sights, sounds and smells of seaside holidays. Now I was setting out through a windy grey morning to walk cliffs, bays and lanes that seemed more real, bathed in their early 20th-century Betjeman-glow, than they did in my own memories of childhood holidays here in the 1950s.

Since those days the South West Peninsula Coast Path has become established, a beautifully waymarked rollercoaster walk that took me up the Padstow shore of the estuary towards the long vulture's-neck promontory of Stepper Point. The barley fields along the cliffs were rustling their beards stiffly in a sharp northerly breeze, and it was an eye-watering push against the wind until I reached the gaunt old light tower on the headland. The prow of Pentire Point on the far side of the estuary sported a white bow wave of spray, and slate-grey water was heaving round the black crown-shaped rock of Newland a mile offshore. It was a rough weather view, wild and mesmerising, and I lingered over it in the shelter of the granite tower before letting the wind push me back south across the fields towards Padstow.

Down on Padstow harbour I waited for the ferry to buzz me over the water to Rock on the far bank of the Camel estuary. Rock is a different world. Over here in 'Hampstead-on-Sea', holidaymakers wear battered deck shoes and dinghy club sweaters. Walking north from the ferry slipway through the shaggy-backed dunes I met a hearty crowd of pink-necked teenage girls fresh from bathing at Daymer Bay, larking about as they jogged home wrapped in towels – a sight that John Betjeman would have loved.

On the sands of Daymer Bay young John would scamper early on the first morning of the holiday:

> *'Then before breakfast down toward the sea*
> *I ran alone, monarch of miles of sand,*
> *Its shining stretches satin-smooth and vein'd.'*

In *Summoned By Bells* Betjeman caught the feeling of warm rock pools and sand between the toes, the mingled smells of honeysuckle, drains and pipe smoke, the sense of holiday freedom. There was also the other side of the coin, the troubled holidays in later teenage summers, overshadowed by fear of his tense, irascible father and his own self-consciousness:

> *'An only child, deliciously apart,*
> *Misunderstood and not like other boys,*
> *Deep, dark and pitiful I saw myself*
> *In my mind's mirror ...'*

From the coast path in the dunes I crossed the golf links where John would dam the stream and caddy unwillingly for his father. I was aiming for the endearingly crooked spire of St Enodoc's, the 'sinkininny church'. St Enodoc's was sunk in sand drifts and all but buried until the Rev Hart Smith took on its restoration in 1863. Nowadays, lovingly looked after and still innocent of electricity, it is both a living church and a shrine for devotees of John Betjeman. The poet lies in the churchyard, his grey slate tombstone incised with his name and dates, 1906–1984, in wonderfully florid rococo style that Betjeman himself would surely have smiled over. His view is of the round green tump of Bray Hill, and the haze of surf in Daymer Bay.

Two sounds tremendously evocative of Cornish holidays – the hollow slap of a spade on an upturned sandcastle bucket, and the plaintive scream of seagulls – followed me as I walked on along the cliffs under clearing skies to Polzeath. Playing on Polzeath beach as a child I used to thrill to the sound of the Kelly's ice-cream van chiming and roaring out on to the sands. Kelly's was the best, the creamiest and most clotted of all Cornish ice-creams. There was a Kelly's van on the beach today. I bought a cornet for auld lang's syne, and let nostalgia persuade me that it hadn't dropped its creaminess quota since 1955.

A gauze of surf spray hung over the long narrow beach at Polzeath. Surfers in their hundreds were riding inshore on successive ranks of white wind-driven rollers. There was a crowd on the clifftops, too, where men in yellow rescue jackets were coiling up ropes. 'Guy got cut off by the tide in the cove down there,' said one. 'We put a rope over the cliff and he hauled himself up OK.' The rescuee grinned and shivered as his friends led him away.

Walking back over the fields to Rock and the ferry, I pictured young John Betjeman stuck on a lonely cliff:

> *'A sea-pink clump the only thing to clutch,*
> *Cold wave-worn slate so mercilessly smooth*
> *And no-one near and evening coming on ...'*

Help arrived, of course, and everything came all right by bedtime – as it always would do, on those safe seaside holidays in the dream Cornwall of long ago.

STEPPING OUT – *Walk 3*

MAP: OS 1:25,000 Explorer 106; 1:50,000 Landranger 200

TRAVEL: By road: A30 or A38 to Bodmin; A389 to Wadebridge and Padstow. Park in Padstow Link Car Park on A389 at top of town.

WALK DIRECTIONS: From car park (OS ref SR917753) steps by public lavatories lead into town. Left around harbour. Opposite Padstow Rowing Club (920756), Coast Path (CP) sign points up incline. Follow CP signs north along coast for 3 miles to old light tower on Stepper Point (910784). 100 yds beyond tower, stone wall bends inland and CP goes straight on; take path that bisects the angle, to corner of wall on skyline. Keep ahead on clear path to right of gorse patch; in 150 yds bear left to cross 2 wall stiles (910779, 911778) and descend to coastguard cottages (912776).

Retrace CP for ½ mile to south side of bay; where CP bends left (911769), keep ahead up slope, passing Tregirls farm on your right. Just above Tregirls (912764), right through gate and left along walled lane for ½ mile to pass Prideaux Place (914756). In 20 yds, left along Fentonluna Lane to Padstow harbour. Take ferry from pier (921755) across Camel Estuary to Rock.

From landing slip (927757), left by car park and along CP, keeping to higher inland edge of dunes. Just before dark trees around Brea House go right (928768), following white stone markers across golf links to cross footbridge. Bear left along stream to St Enodoc's Church (931772). Follow white markers back to CP in Daymer Bay (929776); follow CP north along cliff for 1½ miles to Polzeath.

Opposite post office turn right (937789; 'Valley Caravan Park 100 yd' sign) down lane, passing caravan park. In ½ mile cross stream at Shilla Mill (940783). At 3-way fingerpost, left over stile; up slope on grassy path across golf course (yellow arrow waymarks) to hedge. Left; in 150 yds, right past Llangollan (945778). Ahead over wall stile, following white stones diagonally right across fairway to cross stile in hedge (944775). Left around field edge; in 150 yds, left over stile (yellow arrow); across field and cross stile (943773), right of barns of Trewiston Farm. Aim ahead for fence posts, then left around field edge and farm. Over stile, across narrow field and following stile; across camping field to cross road by stiles (945770).

Cross narrow field and stile; across next field to cross footbridge halfway along hedge on far side (945767). Diagonally right across next field to cross stile; across next field to cross stile in far top corner (944765). In 25 yds, right on gravelled lane; in 50 yds, right ('Manor Cottage' sign; yellow arrow) along track for ⅓ mile, crossing two roads. At little island of trees (940759), left to road; right for ¾ mile to ferry.

LENGTH OF WALK: 11½ miles.

REFRESHMENTS: Many pubs/cafés in Padstow, Rock and Polzeath

PADSTOW-ROCK FERRY: Daily, continuously

READING: *Summoned By Bells* by John Betjeman (John Murray)

Walk 4

Rough Tor and Brown Willy, Bodmin Moor, Cornwall

Into the wild heart of Jamaica Inn country

IT WAS JUST ONE MORE in a string of grey, stormy mornings in this blusterous North Cornwall summer. I didn't want another day of huddling in the lee of beach rocks or checking the local papers for museums. If the weather was going to play the wild card, I'd go out and meet it halfway. But where should I walk? I'd already done the coast path, and had had my fill of wind-tossed waves yeastily boiling round granite cliffs.

Somewhere inland, then; somewhere high and wild; somewhere I'd never yet been. How about Bodmin Moor? Our holiday cottage possessed a dog-eared paperback copy of *Jamaica Inn*, which I'd idly picked up at the start of the holiday and had raced through at the speed of knots. Daphne du Maurier's rattling smuggler yarn had young Mary Yellan as its innocent heroine, and creepy Francis Davey, albino vicar of Altarnun, for a sinister villain. But the chief protagonist of the tale had been Bodmin Moor, 'a silent, desolate country, vast and untouched by human hand.'

I didn't fancy going to Jamaica Inn itself, a tourist site these days. Better to leave 'the grey slate inn with its tall chimneys' as du Maurier had lodged it firmly in my imagination, lonely and forbidding beside a dusty white ribbon of road. But the map showed me a better prospect only three miles from the inn as the raven flew: the peaks of Rough Tor (1,311 ft) and Brown Willy (1,375 ft), the highest summits on Bodmin Moor, with a great swathe of open moorland all round them. Better still, this was the setting for the climax of *Jamaica Inn*, the rescue of Mary Yellan from the clutches of the fiendish clergyman.

'Rough Tor?' echoed the man in the lane beyond Tregoodwell. 'Oh – you mean *Row-ter*, that's how we say it. Yes, just keep on down there and you won't miss it.' He wasn't wrong. Only a thick Bodmin Moor mist could keep Rough Tor out of view in this northern sector of the moor. It rose dead in front of me, a great dark piling of naked granite. Lesser tors outcropped in a line along the ridge – Little Rough Tor's grey pimples of rock, the stacked slabs of Showery Tor – but it was Rough Tor that riveted me, a cold and hard height that beckoned irresistibly. No wonder it had fixed itself as a dramatic location in Daphne du Maurier's fertile imagination.

On the grassy banks of a stream near the car park I found the lichen-bearded granite column of the Charlotte Dymond monument. Unlike lucky Mary Yellan, nobody stepped in to save poor Charlotte, a young domestic maid, on the springtime Sunday morning in 1844 when her fellow servant Matthew Weeks brought her to this spot and murdered her. Not all the tales of Bodmin Moor have happy endings.

Below the ridge half-wild moor ponies were feeding, their forelocks blowing around their eyes. They cropped the grass among the ring-shaped foundations of the huts of Bronze Age farmers. I paced the dimensions: these primitive stone houses were between seventeen and twenty feet wide. Some of their door jambs still stood in place, aligned south or west away from the bitterest winds. What a hell of a life it must have been, trying to coax a viable harvest from the barley, oats and flax they sowed in their tiny walled fields, half-frozen in winter, always tired and usually hungry, eternally red-eyed and stinking and coughing from turf-smoke. I thought of the breakfast still warm in my belly, the decent boots and coat that were keeping the cold wind from my well-tubbed person, and felt ashamed of my 'ooh, it might rain, don't know if I'll go out' deliberations earlier that morning.

Up the flank of Roughtor Moor I went, wandering where I pleased across this wide slope of Access Land, but aiming for the 'cheese-press' stack on top of Showery Tor. As if on cue, a silvery shower of rain came sparkling out of the north as I reached the ridge, spattering my face and leaving lines of drops like liquid brilliants to sidle along the edges of the tor's granite slabs. I climbed to the top and stood looking out across a tremendous prospect of moors and farmlands. But ahead I could spy a far better viewpoint, the knobbly pyramid of Brown Willy himself, rising on the far side of a deep and marshy valley.

Wheatears skimmed away with their characteristic 'white-arse'

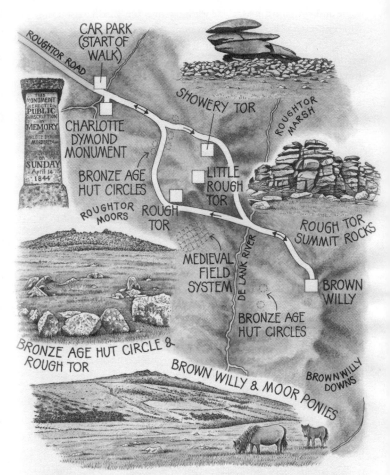

Bronze Age Hut Circle & Rough Tor

Brown Willy & Moor Ponies

ROUGH TOR & BROWN WILLY
BODMIN MOOR, CORNWALL

flash as I made my way down from Showery Tor, passing more moor ponies tugging the grass free with soft tearing noises, working their cuds or just chewing rhythmically and stolidly as they lifted their dreamy brown eyes to watch me go by. One little mare had a tiny foal with her, only a few days old. He hid behind his mother, his eyes and ears just visible over her broad back as he shyly glanced at the intruder.

A bootful of cold stream water and I was up the far bank, climbing the long slope towards the ragged top of Brown Willy through rocks spattered pink and white with the miniature stars of stonecrop. A skylark went up with a trilling burst of ecstatic singing, and under this umbrella of celestial music I stood by the rough old summit cairn, lord of all Bodmin Moor, looking west to where a strip of clear-washed blue sky lay over Port Isaac Bay. The summit of Rough Tor, by contrast, rose into a blanket of wind-shredded mist, as I saw when I had descended from Brown Willy and was climbing through medieval field walls towards the Rough Tor ridge. Now where on earth had that crept up from?

The granite cliffs that rim Rough Tor stand stacked high and cracked into rectangular shapes. The wind, rain, droughts and frosts of millennia have sculpted the summit stones so that they lie like flying saucers one on top of another, some pairs so smoothly shaped and so deeply eroded that their point of contact forms a pivot on which the upper stone – perhaps fifty tons in weight – can be made to rock to and fro. These amazingly delicately balanced rocking stones, called 'logan stones' hereabouts, are a challenge to one and all. Up on the summit I selected a logan stone the size of a small car. After several minutes of purple-faced and fruitless heaving, I suddenly discovered the knack. Click ... clack! Click ... clack! How do you keep a mist-bound walker happy? Give him a logan stone, and a romantic film clip to run in his personal skull cinema, until the murk burns away and a fine afternoon lies spread above the moor.

Through the tatters of fog came striding Vicar Davey, unmasked by now as *éminence grise* of a fearsome smuggling and wrecking gang, murderer of Mary Yellan's Aunt Patience and her husband, Joss Merlyn, the landlord of Jamaica Inn and ringleader of the smugglers. With the villain hurries Mary, his hostage. The bloodhounds of the pursuing forces of law and order are baying behind them, and now they burst out of the mist. The demonic vicar of Altarnun climbs the rocks to escape their teeth; and then a shot rings out.

'He stood for a moment, poised like a statue, his hair blowing in the wind; and then he flung out his arms as a bird throws his wings for flight, and drooped suddenly and fell; down from his granite peak to the wet dank heather and the little crumbling stones.'

STEPPING OUT – *Walk 4*

MAP: OS 1:25,000 Explorer 109; 1:50,000 Landranger 200, 201

TRAVEL: From A39 Bude road on north-east edge of Camelford (OS ref SX110839), minor road to Tregoodwell and on for 2 miles to car park at end of Roughtor Road (138819).

WALK DIRECTIONS: From car park descend to go through gate and cross stream. Bear right over stile and stepping stones to reach Charlotte Dymond monument (138817); then return over stile and bear right uphill. Rough Tor, to the right, is the biggest of several tors on the ridge ahead; Little Rough Tor is 300 yards left of it; another 300 yards left is Showery Tor, which you aim for. From rocks at summit of Showery Tor (149813) aim for upstanding peak of Brown Willy ahead, following obvious track into intervening valley. Cross De Lank River (153805), go through gate and follow track (waymark posts) up left flank of Brown Willy. Cross stile and bear right, aiming for summit (159800)

Return to re-cross De Lank River; from here aim straight ahead for summit of Rough Tor (146808). Return downhill to car park.

LENGTH: 4 miles

CONDITIONS: Three gentle climbs and descents on moorland paths; rough stony ground on the tors.

REFRESHMENTS: None – take a picnic

READING: *Jamaica Inn* by Daphne du Maurier (Penguin paperback)

Start Point & East Prawle, South Devon

Savage coast of dangers by land and sea

FROM THE HEIGHTS above Start Point I looked out through bin-oculars over a South Devon coast painted muted and cloudy. The sea, cliffs, sands, woods and fields of Start Bay lay washed in shades of grey and white, and the sun slipped like a ghost through gauzy layers of mist. The only sounds up here were the cheeping of pipits in the bracken, and the far-off wash of waves on the rocks below – a dreamy sound, as if the sea itself had entered the soft mood of the day.

It was hard to imagine that these gentle waves could ever raise an angry roar. Yet I knew that, in certain circumstances of wind and tide, the sea in Start Bay could grow teeth ferocious enough to devour houses, men and ships. The shore settlements of Slapton Cellars and Strete-Undercliffe were two of those washed away by the sea over the years; Hallsands was another.

The binoculars showed me a little group of houses, broken and roofless, huddled on a rock ledge between Hallsands cliff and beach a mile to the north. Yesterday I'd viewed these derelict houses from a platform in the cliff just above them. Hallsands had been over-whelmed in a tremendous storm in January 1917, the whole shore village literally pounded to pieces by giant waves. Blame was laid at the door of the dredging works which had removed half a million tons of shingle from a bank just off Hallsands. Too late it was real-ised that this shingle bank had formed a natural buffer, shielding the houses on their ledge from the full power of the sea.

Start Point narrows into the sea as a green-backed peninsula, its spine broken by the dark dinosaur plating of mica schist outcrops. I followed the lane down to the stumpy white lighthouse at the tip. It was closed, this early in the morning, but I remembered enjoying the tour of the building the year before – the gleaming instruments, the cylindrical kitchen and bedrooms, the guide's tales of storms and wrecks out in Start Bay.

Below the innocuous surface of the bay lies the Skerries bank, covered by less than a fathom of water at low tide. A tall man could stand on tiptoe out there in the middle of Start Bay. In the days of sail the bank and the bay claimed hundred of ships, many thousands of lives. After a storm and a shipwreck the bay would be covered in flotsam, the shore piled with furniture from ships, ropes, wooden planks and cargo. Dead bodies bobbed in the floating wreckage and lay among the rocks and on the sand. There was nothing the local people could do, except bury the dead and use whatever they could salvage.

Such terrible scenes seemed a long world away today, with the mist dreamily drifting and the waves lapping softly at the Black Stone reef off the point. A cormorant went speeding across the wrinkled sea like a black torpedo bomber. Beneath him a seal put its head out of the water and stayed rocking in the tide, watching a party of youngsters in wetsuits and white helmets jumping one by one from the rocks of Sleaden Point into the waves twenty feet below.

I walked the cliff path above Great Mattiscombe Sands, looking west over the dull gold beach and down the curve of the coast. A tiny star glittered in the dark bulk of Prawle Point – daylight concentrated in the slit of a wave-cut arch. Prawle Point was another deathtrap for ships. In 1873 the tea clipper *Lallah Rhookh* struck the rocks and disgorged its 1300 tons of cargo. Local legend says the tea formed a bank ten feet high which was quarried away by the wives of Prawle, who were accustomed to the taste of sea salt – even in their cuppas.

Round in Lannacombe Bay, lines of low surf were pounding the sand below the old restored limeburner's house. Lannacombe lay as peaceful as a picture, a tiny beach at the foot of a long high-banked lane. On a sunnier day scores of people would be lazing and playing on the beach, but today the gulls and I had it to ourselves as rain began to freckle in from the sea.

Guillemots and cormorants stood in segregated crowds on the slippery black back of Ballsaddle Rock, round whose skirts the waves sluiced and foamed. Buddleia bushes and bracken shed their cold drops on me as I brushed by. But the showers were already easing as I climbed the green lane to East Prawle, where red valerian, foxgloves and pink clumps of sea thrift dashed the walls and rocks with colour.

I stamped off the rain and kicked off my muddy boots in the porch of the Pig's Nose. This is a place to savour, a real country pub where the décor is whatever has settled into place over the years, and the atmosphere is created not by a team of smart theme designers but by whoever happens to be at the bar and in yarn-spinning mood. Stirrups, cane carpet beaters, hayforks, bow saws and hunting crops festoon the ceiling beams. Centuries of beer and tobacco, of music and high old times have soaked themselves into the fabric of the building.

'Fish (if I catch)' said the menu board. The landlord hadn't caught today, but his smoked mackerel was great, and so was the Dartmoor Pride drawn from the barrel.

'The Yardbirds!' promised the bar poster. Sixties psychedelic R&B heroes, live on stage in East Prawle village hall! Really? I quizzed the landlord. He concurred, in a downbeat kind of way. 'Oh, he's got a bit of push in the music business,' confided a local. A great load of push, and a heart full of soul, I'd say. I'll bet it was a brilliant night.

When I emerged from the Pig's Nose, well fed and watered, I saw that the mist had drifted in from the sea to veil the village. But soon the feeble sun strengthened and the cloud cover began to shred way. I followed field paths and green lanes from East Prawle, a network of flowery ways that dipped sharply to funnel me back down to the coast at Woodcombe Sand. The young bullocks who were lazing in the shade of the hazels didn't greatly appreciate my passing, but a couple of sharp swearwords stopped their nonsense.

Walking up the stream valley from Great Mattiscombe Sand to the Start Point car park under clearing skies, I turned round for a last look out to sea. The incoming tide had covered the wicked teeth of rock that I had earlier seen glinting offshore. Now the sea lay still and silent once more, all its menace hidden under a covering of beautiful shot-silk blue.

STEPPING OUT – *Walk 5*

MAP: OS 1:25,000 Explorer OL20; 1:50,000 Landranger 202

TRAVEL: M5, A30, A384 to Totnes; A381, A3122 and minor roads to Strete and Stokenham; minor roads to Start Point car park (OS ref SX821376).

WALK DIRECTIONS: From Start Point car park walk down to lighthouse (829371). Just above, leave road ('Minehead' fingerpost) and follow South West Coast Path (acorn and yellow arrow waymarks) west for 2¾ miles, past Great Mattiscombe Sand, Lannacombe Beach and Woodcombe Sand.

Three fields beyond Maelcombe House (790364), bear right off Coast Path (788361 – 'Public Bridleway East Prawle ½ mile' fingerpost). Climb green lane for 200 yards; emerging from trees, climb steps on right (784360 – yellow arrow), then field slope. Cross stone stile at top (783360); right along stony lane, then right (783361) up tarmac lane, to Pig's Nose pub, East Prawle (781364).

Leaving pub, left down lane, round left bend. Take first right along lane; just before phone box, right (781366) along lane – tarmac, then stones. Cross stream (786369), then climb to skirt field edge with hedge on left. At far side of field, right (787371 – 'Public Bridleway Lannacombe Green 1½' fingerpost) along lane which bends left (blue arrow). In 100 yards it bends right – but keep ahead here (789371 – footpath fingerpost) through gate and along green lane.

In 150 yards bear right at fork ('Footpath Woodcombe Sand ½' fingerpost) down green lane that becomes steep and muddy. Left at the bottom (795369 – 'Coast Path' fingerpost), back to Great Mattiscombe Sand, where Coast Path turns right on cliff at far end of beach. Bear left here (818369 – 'Footpath car park ½ mile' fingerpost) through wicket gate and up path to Start Point car park.

LENGTH: 8 miles

CONDITIONS: Coast Path awkward underfoot in places; path between Woodcombe and Woodcombe Sand is muddy.

REFRESHMENTS: Pig's Nose, East Prawle (01548-511209; *www. pigsnoseinn.co.uk*)

Walk 6

St Aubin to La Corbière, Jersey, Channel Islands

Bunkers and batteries, tides and towers – the historic south coast of Jersey

THE MORNING BUS from St Brelade to St Aubin was packed with chatty, cheery pensioners. Fragments of Jersey lives drifted down the gangway to Jane and me. 'Well! The coach left her behind, so she was well and truly stuck out in the wilds – but *she didn't care one bit*! Glad to have a few hours away from Cyril, *I'd* say!'

The Channel Island of Jersey isn't solely about elderly retirees, as the tourist board is only too keen to point out. But there's no denying that there is an awful lot of them – in remarkably fine shape, too. Is it the clean air and water around the island, the very un-English hours of sunshine, or the laid-back atmosphere of the place? Their banter and backchat followed us as we left the bus in St Aubin and set out past the massive granite jaws of the harbour breakwaters.

A previous visit to the island, and a couple of beautiful coastal walks there in the company of noted walk leaders Remi Couriard and Mike Stentiford, had filled me with longing to return and tackle one of Jersey's most spectacular hikes – the in-and-out, up-and-down coast path of the island's south-western corner. Jersey's granite rock, its numberless bays and heathy headlands, the richness of its wildlife, and the scatter of towers and fortifications that bear witness to its highly-coloured and turbulent history, combine to make it a tiny but tight-packed box of delights for walkers.

You do have to keep an eye on the tide when you are planning to walk the outer coves of St Aubin's Bay, something that Jane and I had not quite taken into account. On the rocky outcrop of La Housse we found ourselves pinched between two inlets. We sat it out for an hour, admiring the rich pink of sea-wetted beach pebbles, the black teeth of the rocks and the brilliant scarlets and oranges of the ribbon

weed along the shore. Out in the bay, islets of rock held the grim outlines of St Aubin's Fort and Elizabeth Castle, reminders of Jersey's situation down the centuries as a valuable plum at the centre of English Channel trade and defence routes – a plum the French, in particular, had many times tried and failed to pluck, from their vantage point only a dozen miles away.

'A clean tideline – what a pleasure,' murmured Jane. 'Beautiful stones, weed, bits of driftwood, shells – no condoms, no plastic nappies. Like West Sussex when I was a child.'

We scrambled through the receding tide, round to Belcroute Bay and a ramp up the cliffs to the woodland paths above. Pine, fir and twisted eucalyptus gave way to the open coastal heath of Noir Mont, a swathe of gorse and heather splashed with buttery yellow and sharp purple. Against these lively colours the wartime bunkers and their long-barrelled guns, when we reached them at the seaward tip of the headland, seemed grey, ominous, and sinister.

Jersey, in common with the other Channel Islands, fell under German occupation in July 1940. Channel Islanders are not British subjects – as they will emphatically tell you – but these self-governing islands have an enduring connection with their northerly neighbour, and they produced some notable defiance of the occupying forces. That didn't prevent the Germans from fortifying the islands as part of Hitler's 'Atlantic Wall' defences. Bunkers, observation towers, gun batteries and barracks still litter their coasts, a wartime legacy that was ignored for decades until minds and perspectives changed and the islanders themselves came to acknowledge the intrinsic fascination and historic importance of the weather-stained and neglected old fortifications.

We scouted round the echoing concrete bunkers before making across the heath to the Old Portelet Inn and a nectarous glass of cold orange juice. Then it was onward along paths cut through the gorse of Portelet Common, a nature reserve where stonechats, linnets and the rare crimson-waistcoated Dartford warbler find rich pickings and safe haven. More than could be said of the woolly mammoths and rhinoceros that roamed here in Ice Age times; they were driven over the cliffs to death and dismemberment by Neanderthal hunters whose own teeth have been excavated from the caves above St Brelade's Bay.

Down at the feet of the cliff we walked the shining half-tide crescent of the bay. Worm casts and rain pocks made miniature sculptures on the sand, and out in the bay a grebe made a smooth incision in the silken grey sea as it broke into the drizzly air from below the waves.

The pink granite Church of St Brelade looks out across the bay from the western side, flanked by the ark-like Chapelle és Pêchears, the Fishermen's Chapel. Here Jane and I waited out the speckly shower, contemplating the chapel's set of beautiful medieval frescoes – extravagantly feathered angels, a Day of Judgement with the dead rising from dinghy-shaped coffins in Sunday-go-to-meeting hats, and a glorious Annunciation in which a solicitous Gabriel humbles himself before a modest and diffident Virgin.

Beyond St Brelade and the diminutive, pristine beach of Beauport, something weird happens to the coast path. Waymarks give enigmatic suggestions, and the path itself turns shy and self-effacing. We hunted about for it in head-high gorse, then gave up the puzzle and headed inland to find the track of a long-disused granite railway – now a footpath – which eased us down to the spectacular conclusion of the walk.

Out at sea, at the tip of a fantastically rocky and rugged promontory, rose the lighthouse of La Corbière. The causeway to it, drowned each high tide, gleamed like an enchanted road. Walking out there towards the smooth white tower among its black rock pinnacles, we felt like a pair of hobbits approaching the fell realm of Mordor in all its gloomy power.

STEPPING OUT – *Walk 6*

MAP: OS 1:25,000 Official Leisure Map of Jersey (widely available locally)

TRAVEL: Flybe (0871-700-2000; *www.flybe.com*) fly to Jersey from 13 UK airports.

From Jersey airport A12/A1 to St Aubin.

End of walk, Corbières – St Aubin: bus service 12, 55.

WALK DIRECTIONS: *NB: First shore section of walk, from Royal Channel Islands Yacht Club to Manoir de Noir Mont, impassable at very high tides. It's best to set off 1 hour after high tide.*

From the north pier of St Aubin harbour (606489), turn south along the harbour. Descend steps by the Royal Channel Islands Yacht Club (607486). Walk round Le Vaû Varin and Le Vaû ès Fontaines bays to climb the ramp below Manoir de Noir Mont in Belcroute Bay (607477). Pass the manoir, to B57 road (Route de Noirmont); left; in 15 yards left again (yellow top post – 604476). Bear immediately right at a fork in the path, through trees, heading generally south, for ¾ mile to Noir Mont headland car park (607466).

Follow the road inland for 200 yd; left along the path around headlands to the Old Portelet pub (603472). Follow the road past the pub car park; ahead past St Meloir house on a tarmac road. In 100 yards, right to a T-junction (601475). Left past a 'Portelet Nature Reserve' sign onto Portelet Common ('La Commune de Haut' on the map). All paths lead to the cliffs, where you bear right to La Cotte headland and battery house (593475). Just beyond, turn left ('Ouaisné Beach' sign), steeply down to the beach. Cross St Brelade's Bay to climb the ramp up to St Brelade's Church (582484).

Left along the lane ('Footpath to Beauport' sign). In 200 yards, right up steps ('Beauport Bay' sign) to cross the gorsey headland of Les Creux. In 10 minutes you pass a stone with green arrows on both sides; keep ahead (right) to cross a tarmac road (side-track: left here to a car park (577481) and a stunning view of Beauport Bay).

NB The coast path runs along the cliffs from the car park to La Corbière, but is poorly waymarked. Alternative: Continue across the road ('Croix' sign) to reach a tarmac path by 'La Moye/St

Brelade' stone sign (575481). Ahead to the T-junction by house No. 68 (572481); right up Rue de la Pointe to the T-junction; left to B83 road (569483). Left for 150 yards; right along a field lane for 400 yards to a T-junction. Right for 50 yards to meet the railway path (566483); left to B83 at La Corbière (555481); out to the lighthouse (507479).

Return to the bus stop at the former railway station (555481); bus back to St Aubin.

LENGTH: 7½ miles

CONDITIONS: Some short, steepish up-and-down sections

REFRESHMENTS: Old Portelet Inn; Corbière Phare hotel.

OTHER WALKS: *Discovering Jersey – 30 circular walks* by John Malletts (available locally).

INFORMATION: Jersey Tourism (01534-500700; *www.jersey.com*)

Lyme Regis to Seaton, Dorset/Devon

A walk through the Undercliff with the French Lieutenant's Woman

'Tina, Tina, come'n look at this big snaky thing!'

The gaggle of Lyme Regis primary school children gazed entranced at the Philpot Museum's fossil collection. Ammonites, belemnites, trilobites and coprolites occupied the whole of their attention, along with the flattened headbones of a fish lizard – 'Cor, Miss, come'n look at the girt big jaws on this!'

A pale, steamy sky hung over a greasily calm sea as I set out from the museum past the bow-windowed old seafront houses of Lyme. The little seaside resort lies where Dorset meets Devon at the inner-most point of the great half circle of Lyme Bay, cradled by steep hills and shielded from storms by the protective arm of the Cobb. This ancient breakwater, its stones studded with fossils, is a beautiful sinuous thing, shaped like an open-mouthed sea beast coiling for a strike to the east.

Strolling along the sloping back of the Cobb I came to 'Granny's Teeth', a set of weatherbeaten stones sticking out of the breakwater wall to form a crude flight of steps leading down to the Cobb's inner promenade. It was up these steps that Louisa Musgrove ran in *Persuasion*, turning at the top to leap down into her lover's arms – or rather, clean through them, knocking herself unconscious on the hard stone walkway.

For me, though, the dominant spirit of the Cobb was not Jane Austen's hapless character, but John Fowles's far tougher and more modern-minded Victorian heroine Sarah Woodruff. The powerful image of a wind-blown woman standing alone at the end of the Cobb and gazing out to sea was the seed that germinated in Fowles's imagination to produce his 1969 masterpiece *The French Lieutenant's Woman* – my personal Desert Island choice.

Out at the seaward tip of the Cobb I idled, gazing inland at the remarkable collapsing landscape of Lyme. To the west of the town rose the tottering grey cliffs of Ware Cleeves, to the east the muddled slopes and ledges of Black Ven, Stonebarrow and Golden Cap. The names tell the story. The cliffs of golden greensand and stony white chalk, resting precariously on dark slippery clays, periodically become weighed down by water from rainfall and underground springs. Their footings start to skid seaward on the slick mat of clay, causing land-slips that can vary in severity from hardly noticeable to catastrophic. The faces of the cliffs, their colours faded by weathering, are forever shearing away in showers of rock, mud and hitherto-hidden fossils, revealing the bright yellow, reds and whites of freshly-exposed strata.

Back on the seafront again I paused at Wason's Seafood Bar on the corner of Ozone Terrace; then, chewing on a handful of crab sticks, I climbed a stepped path up the green cliff face. Shouts of children on the sand faded below as I walked in among the overgrown chasms and deep silences of what John Fowles calls 'the nearest this country can offer to a tropical jungle ... an English Garden of Eden'.

The Undercliff – a savagely tumbled and fissured, wildly over-grown no-man's-land brought into being by the landslips of centu-ries – stretches for five miles from Lyme westward to Seaton, over the county border in Devon. Underhill Farm, the house where Fowles was living when he wrote *The French Lieutenant's Woman*, totters drunkenly below the path at the entrance to the Undercliff, its walls riven with cracks, the ground beneath corrugated into wave-like ripples.

There are no dwellers in the Undercliff these days (though swine-herds and woodmen lived there until the early 1900s) because of the continuing landslips. The five-mile jungle is a National Nature Reserve, threaded by a single narrow, undulating and tricky section of the South West Coast Path. Trees, plants, birds, animals, butter-flies: they thrive on the absolute isolation of the Undercliff, where cliff falls have created canyons, bluffs, rock towers and marshy pools smothered in vegetation and inaccessible to walkers.

The steamy threat of rain had cleared, and strong sunlight filtered greenly through a skylight of ash, field maple, beech and sycamore tops as I followed the broken, root-seamed path among the trees. Far-off waves at the feet of the unseen cliffs round Pinhay Bay sent up a faint sigh to compete with the rustle of countless millions of leaves, but far louder was an explosion of piercingly sweet birdsong from an elder bush as I passed through a sunny clearing. Blackcap or nightingale? I couldn't spot the singer hidden in the leaves.

Somewhere in the broken land round Pinhay Cliffs I spied a tiny grassy natural garden just off the path, a suntrap studded with blue dots of eyebright. Charles Smithson, the quizzical hero of *The French Lieutenant's Woman*, was lost in the Undercliff when he came upon Sarah Woodruff lying 'in the complete abandonment of deep sleep' in a sunny bower such as this. Poor Charles – he was bewitched on the spot. I lingered, picturing the dry Victorian gentleman hesitating on the brink of his plunge into dark pools of obsessive love.

There are one or two signs of the hand of man in the Undercliff – ilex trees planted by Victorian landowners, the cracked skin of their trunks now wrapped in hairy ropes of ivy, and crumbling sections of the flint walls built in the 1840s by John Ames of Pinhay to funnel those he regarded as 'trespassers' through land he considered his own private domain. But ivy, brambles, water and earth movements are steadily obliterating them.

At Dowlands near the western end of the Undercliff I passed the high rampart walls of Goat Island. It was formed on Christmas Eve 1839 during a monumental slip when eight million tons of land dropped 200 feet downwards, leaving a chasm half a mile wide and a twenty-acre 'island' standing in isolation. Next summer the crops left marooned on the top of Goat Island were harvested, while onlookers celebrated with a fête and band music.

Down in Seaton I boarded a scarlet vintage trolleybus ('Crickle-wood' said the destination board) and rode the Seaton & District Electric Tramway up to Colyford, where I could catch a bus back to Lyme. From the road the Undercliff seemed just like any other stretch of woodland, its secrets and wonders hidden away beneath the green cover of trees.

STEPPING OUT – *Walk 7*

MAP: OS 1:25,000 Explorer 116; 1:50,000 Landranger 193

TRAVEL: By rail – Axminster station (6 miles); taxi (*http://www. britinfo.net/taxis/TCUGP28050.htm*) to Lyme Regis.

By road – M5 (Jct 25); A358 to Axminster; A35 east for 1½ miles; B3165 to Lyme Regis. Car park on Pound Street.

WALK DIRECTIONS: Visit the Philpot Museum (OS ref SY343921); then make for the seaward end of the Cobb (340914) to admire the view. Returning landward, bear left along Ozone Terrace to pass walled green of Lyme Regis Bowling Club. Turn right (fingerpost: 'Coast Path West; Seaton 7¼ miles') up long intermittent flight of steps. Over stile at top, bear left (fingerpost: 'Coast Path Seaton 7') across fields to turn left along a stony lane (330917).

In ¼ mile pass crumbling old Underhill Farm on your left (327914 – NB private property; see below) to enter the Undercliff proper at a Nature Conservancy Council notice. From here continue along Undercliff footpath for next 4 miles. Coast Path fingerposts, and occasional acorn symbol with yellow arrow, make wayfinding simple.

Nearing Seaton, climb steps to emerge from Undercliff Reserve (271895). Bear left along edge of scrub, then right (265897) across fields to turn left down a lane (263902). Cross golf course, descend tarred lane; left along B3712 (253901), over bridge and into Seaton.

Returning To Lyme

(a) Taxi (*http://www.britinfo.net/taxis/TCUGP28050.htm*)

(b) Devon Bus (several a day) from Seaton seafront

(c) Seaton Tramway (3 per hour) to Colyford, where you catch Seaton-Lyme bus

LENGTH OF WALK: 8 miles – allow 4–5 hours

CONDITIONS: Tougher than it looks. Coast Path in the Undercliff is cracked, uneven and constantly climbing and descending, with many steps. Slippery after rain. Wear strong boots with good ankle support; take picnic, water.

NB There are no escape paths from the Undercliff Coast Path. Once committed to the Undercliff you must either complete the traverse or retrace your steps. Do not stray from the Coast Path.

REFRESHMENTS: Royal Standard, Lyme Regis (01297-442637; *www.theroyalstandardlymeregis.co.uk*), or Wason's Seafood Bar on Ozone Terrace, Lyme Regis; White Hart, Colyford (01297-553201).

READING: *The French Lieutenant's Woman* by John Fowles (Vintage paperback); *Persuasion* by Jane Austen (Penguin paperback).

PHILPOT MUSEUM: Bridge Street, Lyme Regis DT7 3QA (01297-443370; *www.lymeregismuseum.co.uk*); small admission fee.

UNDERHILL FARM: Please keep out – this is strictly private property, and in an extremely dangerous state.

Walk 8

Swanage to Corfe, Dorset

With stonemasons and shipwrecks along the cliffs of Purbeck

'YES, SHE'S PROPER PURBECK FREESTONE,' said the construction worker on Swanage seafront, with some pride, as he manhandled a slab of silvery grey stone. 'From one of them quarries up near Worth Matravers. Dozens of little quarries up there, you know, keeping us in business. I call 'em Dorset's Pride.'

With a tremendous clatter and whistle of builders the sea-view flats along Swanage's Parade were being refurbished for the coming season. 'Oh, what a beautiful morning!' one lad carolled from the curlicued balcony he was working on. It could have been ironical, but on such a brisk and sharp blue morning he really seemed to mean it.

Purbeck stone, so workable and durable, brought prosperity to Swanage through the building of medieval cathedrals and the rebuilding of post-Great Fire London. It also made the fortune of local stonemason George Burt in the late 19th century: so much so that he spent 30 years and untold millions laying out a country gentleman's estate on the promontory of Durlston Head, overlooking the town to the south.

Burt's ultimate success symbol, the neo-Gothic castle he built on Durlston Head, was dismissed as possessing 'the architectural features of a refreshment buffet, a tram terminus and a Norman keep'. Quite an efficient summing-up, I thought, as I descended past the castle to view the stonemason squire's outsize stone model of the world. Burt was no 'keep-off-my-land' snob; in fact he opened up his estate to the public, scattering it with improving texts incised in stone, along with choice examples of fine statues and stonework he had salvaged while helping to rebuild Victorian London.

The Dorset Coast Path swooped along the cliffs, a pale grey ribbon of clay in the green turf. Pigeons and fulmars rode the cliff updraughts with nonchalant mastery. Beyond the lighthouse on Anvil Point a tremendous view opened up to the west, the cliffs of Purbeck slanting gently seaward from their crest to a sharply cut edge, from which they plummeted 200 feet vertically into the sea.

Looking back I could see square dark mouths in the Durlston cliffs: Tilly Whim caves, now permanently closed for fear of rock falls. But I could remember entering those echoing and pitch dark old quarry delvings as a ten-year-old, on some foolhardy trespassing expedition from school at Langton Matravers a mile or so inland.

Captain Hill, ex-Royal Marine, our sinewy and perfectionist gym teacher, would march us down to Dancing Ledge to plunge in the tidal swimming pool blasted out of the rock platform at sea level. Here it was, opening below me. I scrambled down. Yes, just as I remembered: yeastily frothing and dark, its sloping bottom thick with seaweed and jelly-red anemones.

Nostalgia is a funny drug. Notwithstanding the rising sea wind and bitter late winter day, I actually considered – momentarily – stripping off and belly-flopping in for old times' sake. Then I thought better of it, and made inland for Worth Matravers and one of the world's truly great pubs.

The day they sanitise the Square & Compass will be a truly tragic day. Not that the Newman family, long-term incumbents, have any such intention. The old pub looked warren-like, dark, firelit, stone-flagged and entirely enticing. 'Beef pasties are just out of the oven,' coaxed my host. Jokey conversation rumbled, the protagonists too dimly lit to see. Out in the back-room museum, locally gathered fossils and archaeological artefacts were beautifully displayed in their glass cases. Is there another pub in the world as crankily characterful as the Square & Compass? I doubt it.

Below Worth Matravers the opposing slopes of East and West Man were striped with dozens of strip lynchets, terraces cut deeply into the hillsides by medieval farmers. Somewhere here, they say, lie buried the victims of the *Halsewell* disaster, the worst wreck of many to plague this coast. The facts are bald enough. The 758-ton *Halsewell*, on passage for Bengal, drove into the cliffs in a wild snow-storm at around 2am on January 6, 1786. Out of a complement of some 250 souls, 168 were lost.

What was it about this appalling event that has kept the memory of the *Halsewell* green for more than 200 years in a place that has seen so much disaster by sea? Perhaps it was the huge loss of life;

perhaps the awful predicament of so many who survived the wreck only to fall or be swept away as they tried to climb the cliffs to safety. The morning after the catastrophe, the Vicar of Worth noted: 'In the different recesses of the rocks, a confused heap of boards, broken masts, chests, trunks, and dead bodies, were huddled together, and the face of the water as far as the eye could extend was disfigured with floating carcasses, tables, chairs, casks, and part of every other article in the vessel.'

Seven 'very respectable' young women were among the dead. Most were on their way out east as fodder for the marriage trade, according to the issue of *The Lady* magazine published shortly after the wreck: 'Not one ship is sailing now without (such) a cargo on board, and they are literally going to market. On their arrival they are shewn as we shew a horse, and are disposed of to the best bidder. This is a coarse description, but does not so indelicate a traffic desire rebuke?'

In the sturdy little vaulted and buttressed Norman chapel of St Aldhelm on the cliffs of St Aldhelm's Head I said a prayer for those wretched victims. Then, driven by a sea wind that shoved me in the back like a bully, I scudded inland over boggy fields and commons where horses were grazing, their manes streaming out in the gale.

Corfe Castle's spectacular ruins stood on their mound, plugging a gap in the Purbeck Downs. One of the bravest defences of the Civil War was conducted by Lady Bankes and her few retainers in Corfe Castle. King Edgar's heir Edward was murdered here in 978. History lies thick on the castle. I climbed the mound and looked out from the ruins. But my inner eye was still too full of the *Halsewell's* drowned and desperate to take in the charms of the Dorset downs and meadows spread below.

STEPPING OUT – *Walk 8*

MAP: OS 1:25,000 Outdoor Leisure 15 'Purbeck & South Dorset'

TRAVEL:

Public transport: Rail (www.thetrainline.co.uk) to Wareham, then frequent Wilts & Dorset buses to Corfe and Swanage. Swanage Railway (www.swanagerailway.co.uk) steam trains run Corfe-Swanage every half-hour or so in summer, every hour-and-a-bit April-June and Sep-Oct.

Car: A35 from Dorchester or Bournemouth; A351 to Wareham, Corfe and Swanage, or park & ride at Norden, on A351 just north of Corfe.

WALK DIRECTIONS: From Swanage railway/bus station (OS ref SZ028789), ahead down Station Road to turn right along seafront. Follow shore to Peveril Point (040787); turn south and follow Coast Path round Durlston Bay through Durlston Country Park (Park Centre 031774, Castle and Globe 034773 – all signposted) to lighthouse on Anvil Point (031770). Continue past two pairs of Mile Indicator Posts (029769 and 012768). Shortly after second pair, don't cross unwaymarked stile over wire fence (quagmire ensues); turn right uphill to continue west past Dancing Ledge rock swimming pool (998768). After Seacombe Cliff (984766), head inland up shallow valley. In ⅓ mile bear left (983771 – 'Footpath to Worth' stone) to Worth Matravers. At road, right to Square & Compass, ahead past pond for tea room and church; left to continue walk.

Bear first left along London Row ('No Through Road'). Twin stiles lead to path down to coast. Just before waymark stone, climb right (976761) to skirt Winspit Quarry. Continue west to pass St Aldhelm's Chapel (961755). In 1 mile Coast Path runs inland (north) from Chapman's Pool, descending to track near hamlet at Hill Bottom (963773). Coast Path bears left here; but continue to right on Purbeck Way (PW – fingerpost) up valley. Follow PW signs and blue bridleway arrows on clear track for 1¼ miles to cross B3069 (969792). PW signs point ahead towards Corfe Castle (in view). In 10 minutes, at direction post in cattle quagmire (967782), bear left (green and white PW arrow); left over stile in 10 yd; in 30 yd, right over stile (no waymark!). Keep woodland belt on left. From here PW signs cross Corfe Common into Corfe.

LENGTH OF WALK: 14 miles – allow a full day.

CONDITIONS: A couple of steep descents/ascents on coast, especially just past St Aldhelm's Chapel; very boggy between B3069 and Corfe Common.

REFRESHMENTS: Square & Compass, Worth Matravers (01929-439229)

DURLSTON COUNTRY PARK: (01929-424443; *www.durlston. co.uk*)

Kilve, East Quantoxhead and the Quantock Hills, Somerset

I T WAS COLD, walking down the beach road from Kilve on a brilliantly sunny winter's morning. The West Somerset field slopes had been frostbitten overnight and sparkled greeny-white, a crisp seasonal setting for today's ramble in the seaward fringes of the Quantock Hills.

Kilve's stumpy church of St Mary the Virgin stood by the lane, and just beyond it rose the tumbledown gables of a 14th-century chantry. In Georgian times the local free-traders, landing contraband on Kilve Beach, found the ruined chapel on lonely Sea Lane an ideal place to store their brandy kegs.

By the time of the Napoleonic Wars, things had gotten pretty cosy between the Somerset smugglers and some of the excisemen. It was not unknown for certain officers to sit in the cabin of a smuggling ship, drinking contraband brandy with the captain, even as the "gentlemen" were unloading the illegal cargo. When the King's Men did mount a raid on the Kilve chantry hideout, the smugglers set fire to the hidden brandy kegs and half destroyed the building.

Down on Kilve Beach it did not take me long to find a good, deeply-printed ammonite among the grey and yellow pebbles. "St Keyna's serpents", local people called the tightly-curled fossils, believing they were snakes turned to stone by saintly intervention. Kilve men of bygone generations would come down to the beach at exceptionally low October tides, bringing their fish-dogs – motley mutts – for a session of "glatting" or hunting stranded conger eels in the rock pools.

Today there was one solitary fisherman in orange overalls, casting into the ice-blue water of the Bristol Channel. The view was enormous, stretching from Exmoor's rolling hills to the Welsh shore, the islands of Steep Holm and Flat Holm evenly spaced in mid-channel like some giant's stepping stones.

Flushed a peachy pink by the flat winter sun, the Court House in East Quantoxhead stood among trees on a low green hill, its face to the sea, the brackeny brown arms of the Quantocks at its back. There have been Luttrells at the Court House since the reign of King John. The family they married into at that time had had the place since the Norman Conquest. Parts of the present Court House must date back to the early Middle Ages, if not earlier still.

House and church together make a tight, homogenous huddle on their little knoll above the village pond. From the hillside above East Quantoxhead I looked back to see the Court House windows catch a wintry fire from the sun. Then I turned south and scrambled up Smith's Combe to the top of the Quantocks Hills.

On the western horizon of the Quantocks looms the long, undulating spine of Exmoor. The Quantock range is often overlooked as a poor relation of lordly Exmoor, land of Lorna Doone and Tarka the Otter. All the better for those in the know, said the young Ranger who stopped his Land Rover for a chat. "We like people to discover the Quantocks for themselves. These hills are a bit special, you know."

Brown heather rolled to the southern horizon, while to the north a breathtaking view unfurled over the Bristol Channel and the distant Welsh hills. I found an ancient droveway, splendidly named The Great Road, and walked east looking out at thirty miles of land and sea.

> *"Upon smooth Quantock's airy ridge we roved*
> *Unchecked, or loitered 'mid her sylvan combs,*
> *Thou in bewitching words, with happy heart,*
> *Didst chaunt the vision of that Ancient Man,*
> *The bright-eyed Mariner ..."*

So William Wordsworth, in *The Prelude*, apostrophised his friend Samuel Taylor Coleridge. The poet, writing at Dove Cottage in his beloved Grasmere, was thinking back to the magical year the two young friends had spent in each other's company among these Quantock hills. William and his sister Dorothy had been living in the West Country for a couple of years when in July 1797 they moved into Alfoxden Park, a mile or so above Kilve, so as to be near Coleridge whom they had recently met and passionately befriended.

Coleridge, a brilliant intellect but at heart a loner, already had a wife and baby son at nearby Nether Stowey. He neglected them for weeks at a time to stay with the Wordsworths and go striding the hills. "Three people, but one soul," said Coleridge. He found Dorothy lively, quick-witted, powerfully sensitive. As for William, he was simply "the Giant Wordsworth, God love him!"

Three wild-looking strangers wandering about the secret places of the hills at all hours and in all weathers, jabbering weird notions, two of them with outlandish accents – in those Napoleonic War days, it was not surprising that the local doctor became convinced that they were spies, and wrote to the Home Secretary to tell him about this "emigrant family who have contrived to get possession of a mansion house at Alfoxden".

Secret Agent James Walsh was sent down from London to spy on the spies. He quickly reported back that they were harmless cranks, but local suspicions were not allayed. At the end of their year's tenancy, the Alfoxden lease was not offered to the Wordsworths for renewal. They left the West Country in the summer of 1798, never to return except in fond and poetical memories.

Tucked down in a combe below The Great Road I found Alfoxden (nowadays Alfoxton) Park, a large, handsomely symmetrical house with pillars and pediment, among whose score of rooms William and Dorothy must have rattled around a bit. They did not find what they were really looking for, a place they could fit into like two peas in a pod, until they settled into snug little Dove Cottage at Grasmere at Christmas time the following year.

Below Alfoxton I dropped into Holford Glen, a wooded combe where William often walked and composed. Descending the glen I looked through a mesh of leafless oak branches, out over Kilve to the sea beyond. "The Giant Wordsworth", happily rooted among the Lakes with his beloved Dorothy, treasured these Quantock scenes in his mind's eye all his long life:

"My thoughts on former pleasures ran;
I thought of Kilve's delightful shore,
Our pleasant house when spring began,
A long, long year before."

STEPPING OUT – *Walk 9*

MAP: OS 1:25,000 Explorer 22; 1:50,000 Landranger 181

TRAVEL: M5 to Jct 24; A38 into Bridgwater; A39 towards
 Minehead. In Kilve (12 miles), Hood Arms PH on right; village
 car park on left.

WALK DIRECTIONS: From car park (OS ref ST148429), right
 along A39; in 30 yd, left by post office down Sea Lane for 1 mile,
 past Kilve Church (147439) and Chantry (146440) to beach
 car park. Through gate to left of Old Retort House (144443).
 Ahead for beach; left (west) along cliffs. In ½ mile, path turns
 inland (137443). At T-jct of paths (138436), right to road at
 pond. Cross into car park; follow path at far right corner, with
 Court House (137437) on your right. Opposite church, go
 through gate in left corner of field; cross next field diagonally,
 arriving right of Court Farm, to gate into lane (134433). Cross
 lane (yellow arrow); keep same direction over next field to stile
 into lane (133431). Left to cross A39 (133428).

 Blue bridleway arrow and "Beacon Hill/Bicknoller Post"
 sign point up track, over fields into Smith's Combe (132423).
 Cross stream here; follow up combe, crossing stream several
 times. In ½ mile, follow stream to right, skirting forestry
 (129416) on steep track across open moor to wooden post, 200
 yd below triangulation pillar (124410). Left on broad track for
 ½ mile. 200 yd short of Bicknoller Post (meeting of 7 tracks
 on saddle of ground), turn left (127406) on The Great Road, a
 clear stony track. Follow for 1 mile to stand of forest fire beaters
 by wood (143412). Down Gut Combe among trees to tarmac
 road (145414); right past Alfoxton Park (148414). In ½ mile
 road enters trees; in 100 yd, on right bend, left (155412 – yellow
 arrow), over stile to cross combe on footbridge to road. Right;
 first left past Holford Church to A39 and Plough PH (158413).

 Left up lane behind Plough; in 100 yd, right through gate
 (blue arrow); through trees, then along field edge. Through trees
 again (156421) to gate (blue arrow); ahead across field to gate
 (2 blue arrows) to sunken lane (156423). Right to A39. Right
 (*take care!*) for 200 yd to right bend; left (159423) along Hilltop
 Lane. In ⅔ mile, pass Wyndham's Farm; in 100 yd, left (154432 –
 bridleway, "Kilve" sign) down hedged lane to Kilve.

LENGTH OF WALK: 8½ miles – allow 4 hours.

REFRESHMENTS: Plough PH , Holford (01278-741232); Hood
 Arms, Kilve (01278-741210; *www.thehoodarms.com*)

Brean Down, Somerset

A windy walk high above the Bristol Channel

Fᴿᴏᴍ ᴛʜᴇ ᴛᴏᴘ ꜰʀᴏɴᴛ ꜱᴇᴀᴛ of a doubledecker bus, even on a misty spring morning, you can see a long way along the caravan-farming coast of the Somerset flatlands. As Service 112 inched her way north from Burnham-on-Sea to Brean in the wake of a nonchalantly road-hogging postman on a sit-up-and-beg black bike, I gazed beyond the roofs of the archipelagos of bungalows and the drifts of immobile homes between Burnham-on-Sea and Brean Down, out into the secret, tangled world of the Berrow and Brean sandhills.

Bounding dogs and bolting rabbits darted down the sandy paths. The dunes undulated like a miniature hill range, some as green and smooth-turfed as sheepwalks, others darkly forested with brambles and sea buckthorn. The stumpy grey church tower at Berrow stood isolated in the sandhills; for centuries it was a marker point for sailors negotiating the treacheries of the Bristol Channel. By the time I had alighted from the bus by St Bridget's Church in Brean village, the early sun had sucked up enough of the mist to disclose a dull gleam of ebb tide in the mighty Severn estuary, fifteen miles wide, that was flowing seaward beyond the dunes.

Out on Brean sandflats, the high spring tide had heaped bottles, nets, sea-smoothed wood and tarry rope at the feet of the dunes. Sharp cries came from the tideline where herring gulls, oystercatchers and black-backed gulls squabbled over titbits among heaps of bladder-wrack. Heavy tidal smells of mud, salt water and weed came drifting in with the mist. A crazed mongrel, its coat spiked with salt, went prancing along the waterline, scattering the gulls with volleys of mock-ferocious barks.

Now the whaleback of Brean Down loomed ahead, a pale blue

barrier across the sands, hardening in outline and brightening to sunlit green as I approached. To the east the thick white blanket of the mist still shrouded the peatlands of the Somerset Levels and hid the Down's parent range of Mendip. But I sensed the hills there, a rolling limestone highland like a bare arm stretching west until it dipped this outermost fingertip of downland into the sea.

Brean Down is really an island, a fact you appreciate once you have climbed the 211 steps from shore level to the top, and have walked past the Iron Age hill fort to the eastern end of the Down. From here the geography of the place is revealed. All that separates the sands and muds of Weston Bay, on the north of Brean Down, from the muds and sands of the Brean Flats to the south, is a neck of green farmland not a mile wide. And those rich grazing fields were made out of land reclaimed from the sea; only a few hundred years ago the Down was a tidal island.

Up here you see instantly how the northward cant of the lime-stone forms a shield against the eternally-blowing south-west winds. You grasp how the sheltered hollows could be farmed, how the 200-ft cliffs on the south and east would secure any inhabitants from a surprise attack by marauders. Brean Down is a natural stronghold, a high and lonely refuge where settlers over thousands of years found protection and the means to sustain life.

Larks sang ecstatically overhead in the strengthening sunlight, and I sang too as I walked in shirtsleeves. Three thousand years of history lay printed in the sheep-nibbled turf of the Down's humped back: the ancient hill fort towards the eastern end, the bramble-smothered site of a Roman temple, a pimpling of Bronze Age burial mounds. Climbing the spine of the more westerly of the Down's two knolls, I crossed the low, stony banks built by Celtic farmers as boundaries for their tiny square fields.

At the summit of the knoll there were more round mounds. Bronze Age mourners believed in giving their departed chiefs some-thing good to look at from the grave, and the top of Brean Down is one of the classic viewpoints of the West Country. I sat down among the chieftains and stared round an immense circle of sea and land now unveiled with the final shredding of the mist.

The dome of Steep Holm and the low wedge of Flat Holm, Brean Down's sister islands, lay halfway to Wales in the throat of the Bristol Channel. Beyond them, backed by the distant rise of the Brecon Beacons, the Welsh coast ran down past the dark smear of Cardiff towards the hazy Gower peninsula. Thirty miles across the water, Exmoor's pale purple heights swam off into the south-west.

It would be worth walking here just to gaze on this stupendous view. But Brean Down, a National Trust property, has more to offer. These couple of miles of limestone hold a spectacular richness of wildlife. Rare white rock rose flourishes on the southern slopes and cliffs. Butterflies thrive; peregrines nest in the clefts; cowslips carpet the northern slopes. I kept an eye out for their sherbet-yellow salute to spring-sunshine as I walked down towards the sea, but only rosettes of dark green wrinkled leaves were on show this early in the year.

Down at the tip of the promontory, the old Victorian fort looked grim and grey. It was one of 'Palmerston's Follies', a string of coastal forts built in the 1860s when the British feared invasion by the French. Not that Brean Down Fort's 7-inch guns, being both rifle-barrelled and muzzle-loading, could have done much to deter Moun-seer if he had decided to come. The shells had to be screwed into the guns down the full length of a hot barrel – a cordon-bleu recipe for jamming or explosion.

I rummaged around the old fort, descending steep steps into dank and airless old magazines, fertile breeding grounds for fantasy and paranoia. Was it mental instability, a brainstorm at sunrise, that caused Gunner Thomas Haines to discharge his carbine down the ventilator shaft of No. 3 Magazine at dawn on 6 July, 1900? Was he unlucky in love, or depressed, or did he just want to see what would happen? Three tons of gunpowder went up, demolishing one wall of the fort and hurling heavy pieces of masonry far and wide. Haines himself was killed outright, the sole casualty of the explosion. His act of folly or desperation ruined the stronghold; the guns were removed and the fort lay out of commission for the next forty years.

On the outbreak of the Second World War, Brean Down Fort was re-armed, fun and games ensued as weird and wonderful experimental weapons were tried out – often with unlooked-for results, as when the splendidly-named 'Expendable Noise-maker' departed from the fort at 900 from its intended course. It landed in a local farmer's chicken-run, and blew it up around his ears.

Coming back over the top of the Down, I lent my heavy old Zeiss binoculars to a falconer out walking his dog. To his intense delight, he had spotted a pair of peregrines. Together we watched them cavorting above the flatlands. A foolish kestrel hovered provocatively directly under them, and all the highly-strung caged inmates of the Tropical Bird Gardens at the foot of the Down swore up at them like troopers. But the peregrines, if they even noticed the stir they were causing, did not deign to acknowledge it. Instead they continued their sublime upward soaring on the thermals of Brean Down, higher and higher above the sand flats and the green Levels, until the misty blue sky claimed them.

STEPPING OUT – *Walk 10*

MAP: OS 1:25,000 Explorer 153; 1: 50,000 Landranger 182

TRAVEL: Rail (www.thetrainline.co.uk) to Highbridge station, 2
   miles from Burnham-on-Sea.

   Bus – First Group (www.firstgroup.com) service 112 from
Burnham to Brean post office; journey takes about half an hour.

   Car – M5 to Jct 22; B3139 to Burnham, B3140 to Berrow; continue ahead to Brean.

WALK DIRECTIONS: From Brean post office and St Bridget's
   Church (OS ref ST296560) continue north up coast road for
   200 yd. Opposite Weston turning, go left up sandy bridleway
   on to Brean Flats beach. Walk north to Brean Down, and climb
   steps to ridge. Turn left to walk to fort at western tip. Return by
   lower path on northern face of Down.

LENGTH OF WALK: 6 miles – allow 3 hours

CONDITIONS: 211 steps up to Brean Down – otherwise
   straightforward. Down can be very windy.

REFRESHMENTS: Brean Down Cove Café, at foot of Brean Down
   (01278-751088) – friendly beach café

READING: *The Story of Berrow and Brean* by William Kemm
   (paperback available in local shops and libraries)
   National Trust's *Brean Down* excellent booklet guide, now out
   of print – time for a reprint, NT!

INFORMATION: Tourist Information Office, South Esplanade,
   Burnham-on-Sea, Somerset TA8 1BB (01278-787852)

Walk 11

Fivehead and Isle Abbots, Somerset

A springtime squelch among the birds and flowers of West Sedgemoor

'SHE'S PATSIE PIE,' the cheery woman chirruped, leaning from the piebald cob's saddle in the lane going north from Fivehead. 'Used to belong to an Irishman, I'm told.' Patsie Pie stamped her pretty feathered hooves on the wet tarmac. 'Pretty feet, yes,' said the rider, 'but a hell of a job to clean, this weather.'

It had been a solid week of rain, and the Somerset Levels were a sodden sponge. But today sunshine was gingerly fingering the lanes and woods. Cow parsley – 'gypsy lace' to Somerset children – was out in the grass verges, along with clumps of violets and late primroses. Cherry and apple blossom filled the gardens and orchards of Fivehead. The lilac buds were still clenched tight against the nip of spring, but putting my nose close to the sprays I got the faintest hint of the fragrance to come in a month or so.

Over the ridge and down on the edge of West Sedgemoor, the air was full of duck cackle and piping of waders. If agricultural plans had come to fruition a few years ago, this great flat saucer of flood-prone moorland would have been a drained and silent corn bowl. Now, under the care of the RSPB, West Sedgemoor has maintained its watery wildness and is a haven for countless thousand wildfowl.

I perched on a gate to watch lapwings tumbling and squeaking over the gunmetal fleets of floodwater. Walking out along one of the grassy old drove roads into the heart of the moor, my boots sank ankle deep. I gasped at the inrush of chilly water. Curlew were walking ankle deep in the floods, too, tough little brown-jacketed survivors probing endlessly in the mud with slim curved bills.

A green drove road curled along the southern rim of the moor, lined with overshot willow pollards standing in flooded ditches. Clutches of teazles grew in the verges, remnants of an industry that once prospered hereabouts. Clothiers would fill their wooden combing frames with the bristly brown seedheads of Somerset-grown teazles, whose minuscule barbs were ideal for plucking up and thickening the nap of their good quality worsteds. I brushed the sleeve of my sweater experimentally across a teazle clump, and the material was instantly caught and held by scores of hooks as fine as hairs.

The path rose from moor level up a shallow wooded rise, making for the tall column of the Pynsent monument up on the crest of the ridge. In among the trees I disturbed a pair of shaggy brown deer. They sprang away over the bluebell carpet and vanished into the shadows without looking back.

Beside the monument I drew breath and looked up at the tapering column sailing against the clouds. It was William Pitt the Elder who raised the monument in memory of Sir William Pynsent. Pitt had reason to be grateful to the Somerset squire, for Pynsent made over his estate in 1765 to the politician he greatly admired. Pitt used Burton Pynsent House as his country retreat from the stresses of public life, and himself drew up designs for landscaping the grounds. I walked the rim of the valley he caused to be scooped out of the hillside. The subtle curves of the landform drew my gaze out north over the dramatic breadth and depth of the moors: an effect intended and cleverly realised by the designer.

Turning my back on the moorland panorama at last, I topped the ridge and began the long descent southwards down grassy droves. Now the view was over the gently rolling fields and woods of south Somerset, out towards a hilly skyline washed out in the dark grey murk of a tremendous oncoming rainstorm. I quickened step, and made it into the farmyard chapel at Swell Court just as the first heavy drops began to smack the mud outside.

Simon Jenkins's *England's Thousand Best Churches* is a great fat tome; not the kind of book a walker can tote about in his pocket. But I'd taken its excellent advice before setting out. The little Norman chapel of St Catherine beside the medieval farmstead at Swell only merits one of Jenkins's coveted stars. It is far from grand, and doesn't even possess a tower. Sitting in one of its knotted elm pews polished with the patina of many centuries' use, I listened as a blackcap sang in the rain outside.

The storm passed as spring storms do, and I walked out to splash on between hedges thick with cowslips. A hare, lolloping towards me up a green lane, shook a spray of water drops from dark-tipped ears as he turned tail and bounded athletically off. Everything seemed rimmed and pearled with rainwater, including the pansies and forget-me-nots in the flowerbeds along the churchyard wall of St Mary's Church in Isle Abbots.

The village churches of south Somerset are famous for their handsome towers, built by medieval wool wealth and beautified with gloriously honey-coloured stone quarried from Ham Hill. St Mary's at Isle Abbots – a Jenkins Four Star – boasts one of the best: not a particularly tall tower, but one whose bell openings and battlements are sculpted like lacework. The 15th-century statues that stand in the pinnacled niches of the tower include a serene Virgin with her stone locks blowing back, St John the Baptist cradling a lamb, and the risen Christ sending diminutive guards tumbling in all directions as he steps impassively from his tomb.

The churchwarden came in as I was admiring the golden stone arcades of the nave. Would I like to climb the tower? Out on the leads I looked down on a clutch of hunkypunks, puff-chested gargoyles silently howling from the tower top. Then out and away through soft rainfall, across a green landscape cut into squares by the gleaming geometry of flooded ditches.

STEPPING OUT – *Walk 11*

MAP: OS 1:25,000 Explorer 1:50,000 Landranger 193

TRAVEL: *By rail* (www.thetrainline.co.uk) to Taunton (10 miles)

By road: M5 to Jct 25, A358 Ilminster road for 2 miles, then left on A378 Langport road; in 4 miles, right to Fivehead. Park at Crown Inn.

WALK DIRECTIONS: From Crown Inn (OS ref ST352229), left along lane to cross A378 (352233). Continue ('No Through Road' sign) up lane, over crest of ridge, past entrance to Smith's Farm (347237) and on. In 300 yd, lane bends left (347239); ahead here on track along edge of woods. Track soon becomes path and crosses stiles. Where wood edge recedes for 20 yd on your right (351241), aim half left across field to gap in hedge; follows stiles and gates above Eastwood Farm to join drove (355245). Continue below Underhill Farm (360245), and on for ⅔ mile to derelict red brick barn (367248). Just above and beyond barn, stile with 2 yellow arrows; aim diagonally right for far corner of next field (371248). Enter woods; in 10 yd, right over plank bridge; left through trees to cross lane by stile (374248 – arrow). Cross field to enter wood (375250), left for 300 yd, then right up through trees to monument (377252).

South-east down ride (arrow); at end, right to gate into lane (377247). Left for 100 yd; right (stile; arrow) across field to cross A378 (376245 – stiles; 'Swell Church' post sign). Cross Burton Farm drive, diagonally right across next field to far corner; through gateway, down green lane for 150 yd. At end (375240), right along hedge to far top corner of field; through hedge; across next field to reach Swell Court farmyard (370237); chapel on left.

From chapel bear left, then right around house to road (368235); left for ⅔ mile. Follow road past Western Farm (360230) as it bends left, then right. In 40 yd, left (bridleway fingerpost 'Swell Drove ½ m') down grassy hedged lane. At end (361222), right to road (356221). Left to cross Fivehead River (358218); immediately after bridge, right through gate (*NB* – careful! Dodgy lower hinge!). Follow river for ½ mile to concrete footbridge (351214). Don't cross! Bear left here through gate, along lane to Isle Abbots church (352210).

Return to cross footbridge; bear right for 200 yd to cross stile in hedge. Diagonally left over next field to bear left through gate 100 yd along (352217). Follow field edge (hedge on left) past house, to gate (352221) into road. Take lane opposite to Fivehead.

LENGTH OF WALK: 8½ miles – allow 4 hours.

CONDITIONS: Drove near Underhill Farm, and drove between 361222 and 356221, very boggy after rain – wellington country!

REFRESHMENTS: Crown Inn, Fivehead (01460-281919; *www.thecrowninn.2day.ws*)

READING: *England's Thousand Best Churches* by Simon Jenkins (Allen Lane/Penguin).

Circuit of Bath – Wiltshire, Gloucestershire and Somerset

Sponsored circuit of the countryside round Britain's finest Georgian town

I T WAS GOING TO BE an absolute peach of a Sunday walk, all 20 miles of it. I'd signed up to take part in a sponsored hike to raise money for Julian House, a charity that does extraordinary work helping homeless men and women in and around the city of Bath. In company with thousands, I'd be wheeling in a great circle round the hills and through the steep valleys where Bath lies like a gracious dowager among plump green cushions.

The city of Jane Austen would be in sight much of the time, but in ever-changing perspective. Better still, my wife Jane and eldest daughter Ruth would be joining me for a stretch of the way, so there would be someone to go hedge-snacking with. Ruth's very first words, yelled from her perch on my shoulder as we raided the bramble bushes nearly thirty autumns ago, had been: 'More bwackb'wy!' There would be purple mouths and finger-ends before this day was out, too.

It was a solo start for me, however, an 8 o'clock-er. I presented myself at the most convenient checkpoint, a house off the long hill of Lansdown to the north of the city. 'Got your sponsor form? Water? Fruit? I'd do the anti-clockwise circuit if I were you,' confided the checker. 'Sun'll be behind you most of the way, and you'll avoid some long uphill slogs at the end. Good luck!'

Most year-to-year participants in the Round Bath walk do the circuit clockwise, so a widdershins walker like me has plenty of hello-ing and good morning-ing to do. 'Oh, you're a backwards person! An anti-clock!' commented the jolly walkers I met in the fields, red-faced and breathless from their early travails on the steep sides of Lansdown. 'It's all downhill for you!'

It was the most peerless of clear September mornings under a sky as celestially blue as a China bowl. Weston village on the west

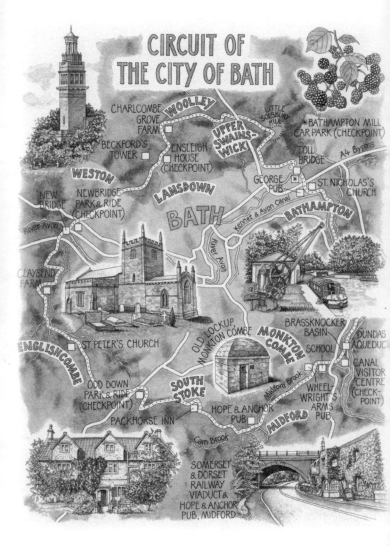

outskirts of Bath lay sprinkled like sugar in its hollow. Rose hips were out in the hedges, blackberries shone in pillarbox red and lustrous black. The sun struck rich gold out of the belvedere crowning Beckford's Tower at the crest of the ridge, and stretched my shadow to immensity along the dew-spangled grass as I walked down to Newbridge and the second of the day's 6 checkpoints.

The lane beyond was blocked by ancient Bedford lorries and superannuated bread vans. Curs snarled and were curbed by a richly tattooed woman. A tiny mite in a glittery fairy dress, a star-tipped wand in one hand and a banana in the other, cast a spell on me with both from her perch on the step of a tottery double-decker bus – a good spell, I hoped.

Between hazel hedges tangled with bryony and old man's beard the path led on to Englishcombe, where people were climbing the steep lane to church for morning service. 'Oh, you should have seen St Peter's yesterday,' said a man with a flower in his buttonhole. 'One of the village lads got married, a most ...' He rummaged for the right phrase: 'Yes, a most *fortunate, beautiful* occasion ...'

In the fields beyond I was brought to bay by three dogs who hackled up and came yelling and dancing at me on their back legs. 'Soft as butter and twice as daft,' smiled their owner, and so they proved, with a blackberry apiece as a negotiating tool.

The Packhorse on the sloping lane in South Stoke is a nice quiet pub. In the front bar two pink-faced old boys sat and yarned in gentle north Somerset voices over their half-pints. Among the brass pots and gleaming settles I found Jane and Ruth toasting their toes at the fire. With a cheddar ploughman's and a glass of bitter in the locker I felt quite snoozy, but soon got back my snap in the fresher air of an afternoon that was beginning to cloud up.

By the Wellow Brook in Midford we passed through the arch of the Somerset & Dorset Railway viaduct. I remembered crossing it on Sunday afternoons in long gone Septembers, inching along behind a clanking and leaky steam engine on the miserable journey back to school at the end of the summer holidays. How the turning colours of the trees, the sun on the Bath stone of the Hope & Anchor and the sparkle of the brook used to mock the prisoner in his sooty cage-on-wheels!

At Brassknocker Basin, where the Somerset Coal Canal meets the Kennet & Avon Canal, we munched on blackberries, as sweet as currants at this season. Ruth and Jane hived off at Bathampton, their fingers satisfactorily empurpled, and I went on alone, climbing to the Iron Age camp on Little Solsbury Hill. A scarlet and gold kite was flying up there, its owner out of sight beyond the slope. Looking back from the last of the day's hills half an hour later, I could still just make out its bobbing shape, a brave splinter of colour against a darkening sky.

STEPPING OUT – *Walk 12*

MAP: OS 1:25,000 Explorer 155; 1:50,000 Landranger 172

TRAVEL: M4 to Jct 18; A46 towards Bath for 2 miles; just past Dyrham Park gates, right for 1⅓ miles to cross A420; continue for 3½ miles to Lansdown. ⅓ mile past Beckford's Tower, left along Granville Road to checkpoint at Ensleigh House.

WALK DIRECTIONS: Full clockwise or anticlockwise directions available at each checkpoint. Do as much or little as you like – there are return buses from each checkpoint. In brief (anticlockwise walk).

Stage 1 (2 miles): From Ensleigh House (OS ref ST742675) cross main road (741673); fork right, then in 150 yd left. From 738671, downhill and through plantation to gate and stile (735668); right downhill to lane (733668). Downhill to road (731667). Left to Weston High Street (728664). Cross by Crown & Anchor; up narrow road opposite; right along larger road, passing school. In ⅓ mile, right into layby (722661); footpath past Oldfield School; cross A431 (720660 – take care!) to reach Newbridge Park & Ride (718658 – Checkpoint).

Stage 2 (5 miles): Cross New Bridge, then A4/A36 at traffic lights. Up track to cross railway (714654); follow lane for ⅓ mile to crossing (711649); left for ¼ mile into caravan park. Right along track; cross road (714645) to follow lane for ⅓ mile to crossroads (709644). Left past Claysend Farm for ⅔ mile; left (711632) on footpath to Englishcombe. Left through village; left at grass triangle (not Washpool Lane!). At top of hill (722629), right on path through Breach Wood and beside Middle Wood to Kilkenny Lane (723615). Left for ½ mile to cross A367, past St Gregory's School into Odd Down Park & Ride (733615 – Checkpoint).

Stage 3 (4½ miles): Left through car park; down Combe Hay Lane for ¼ mile; ahead on right bend (733612), then left for ¾ mile to South Stoke. Downhill past Packhorse pub; in 150 yd left (747611) through fields to lane at Upper Midford (753607). Left for 400 yards; right at left bend (757605) on path to meet B3110 (760606); turn right past Hope & Anchor through Midford. Past brick viaduct, left along Midford Lane for 350 yd; left (764610) along path by Midford Brook for 1 mile. Left across bridges and weirs (774618) into Monkton Combe. Past school, right (775622) through playing fields; under A36 (781621) to Canal Visitor Centre (782622 – Checkpoint).

Stage 4 (3¾ miles): Kennet & Avon Canal north to Bathampton; right at George pub(777665), past church, over railway and A4 to Bathampton Mill car park (775669 – Checkpoint).

Stage 5 (4½ miles): Cross Toll Bridge (774670); up hill; right up steps and path to road (773671); right, then left up Bailbrook Lane for ½ mile. Right beside No 35 (766671); up path to cross Swainswick Lane; climb Little Solsbury Hill to trig pillar (768678). Left round summit; in 400 yards left at waymark; descend WNW. Cross under A46 (761684); lane to Upper Swainswick. Past Hill House, left downhill; through Woodbine Cottage gate and garden into field; cross brook (753685); right uphill to road at Woolley church (750685). Left at T-junction; in 50 yd right; steeply up to Charlcombe Grove Farm (742683); left by Soper's Wood to road (744678); right to Ensleigh House (end).

LENGTH: 20 miles

REFRESHMENTS: Packhorse, South Stoke (01225-832060; www.packhorseinn.com); Wheelwrights Arms, Monkton Combe (01225-722287; *www.wheelwrightsarms.co.uk*); George Inn, Bathampton (01225-425079).

CIRCUIT OF BATH SPONSORED WALK: The walk takes place towards the end of September each year. Information tel 01225-354650; *www.julianhouse.org.uk*

SOUTH

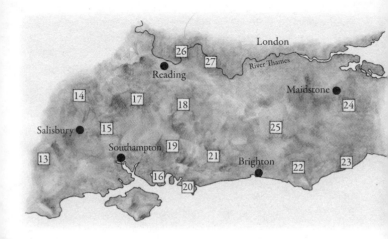

Tollard Royal, Win Green and Ashcombe Valley, Wiltshire

Cranborne Chase and the high South Wiltshire Downs

B ACK IN THE DAYS of Bad King John, it took a speedy horseman two days to ride the bounds of Cranborne Chase. King John loved hunting the deer through the Chase, a dense tangle of woodland that lies at the feet of the South Wiltshire Downs where they roll over into north-east Dorset. The forest always had the character of a wilderness, and enjoyed something of a dark reputation. Thomas Hardy used Cranborne Chase – 'a truly venerable tract of forest land, one of the few remaining woodlands in England of undoubted primeval date' – in *Tess of the d'Urbervilles* as the setting for the rape of Tess by dastardly Alec d'Urberville.

By the early 19th century Cranborne Chase had become a notorious nest of footpads, smugglers and poachers. Wild local squires dressed in quilted coats and beehive helmets of straw would steal the landowners' deer and beat up their gamekeepers for fun. The forest was not brought under control until the 1830s when its owner, Lord Rivers, cut the greater part down and opened up Cranborne's murky depths to the light of day. These days the forest is criss-crossed with open rides and footpaths, and the billowy chalk downs of the Wiltshire/Dorset border rise clear of the trees as an irresistible enticement to walkers.

On a beautiful crisp and cloudless winter's morning Jane and I set off from the picture-book thatched village of Tollard Royal. Various flinty tracks and footpaths run north from the village to the hills. The path we chose brought us up over Rotherley Down, with the bulk of Cranborne Chase a dark dense bar low down in the east.

In Rotherley Wood a sparrowhawk sat in a tree twenty feet above our heads, his ruddy pate gleaming in the sunshine as he turned his head to watch us. In a clump of coppice a nuthatch clung to a hazel trunk. Partridges whirred away explosively across the open plough-lands where thick margins of maize had been left standing to provide food and cover for wildlife. Notices on field gates declared that the land was being farmed in environmentally sensitive fashion – hence the extraordinary richness of bird life in this wintry landscape.

Up on the back of Rotherley Down a stumpy pillar stood on the edge of a complex of grass-grown trenches. 'This Romano-British village,' ran the inscription, slowly fading under wind and weather, 'was excavated and the pits and ditches partly filled back in, by General Pitt Rivers in the years 1886–7.'

Time and weather are gradually smoothing the remnants of the excavated village back into the grassy sward from which the founding father of modern British archaeology raised them. General Pitt-Rivers, owner and excavator of much of the surrounding countryside in late Victorian times, was no amateur treasure-seeker, but an exceedingly serious and systematic student of the historical development of human technology.

The Pitt-Rivers museum in Oxford displays his finds today, but that was only one of three museums he established – the General was a great believer in educating the common man. Precision was his watchword. '92 Pits, 15 human skeletons, 2 British coins, 11 Roman coins and numerous relics of the Roman Age were discovered,' announces the inscription beside the excavation site on Rotherley Down. 'Skulls: 1 was brachycephalic, 3 were mesaticephalic, 6 were dolichocephalic, 3 were hyperdolichocephalic; one was uncertain.'

Our distant ancestors travelled the crests of the downs on track-ways trodden out by feet and hooves over many millennia. The Ox Drove, one of the oldest, loops like a white ribbon along the bare shoulder of the South Wiltshire Downs, high above the tangled trees of Cranborne Chase. 'I love those corduroy ridges on the scarp slopes,' said Jane, stopping on the Ox Drove for a breather. 'They look as if the chalk has curdled into thick waves where the sun catches them just at that low angle.'

Up by the beech clump on Win Green we stood on the very roof of Wiltshire, gazing round over an eighty-mile view from the long blue hump of the Isle of Wight in the south-east to the round brows of the Quantock Hills far in the north-west. Woods, fields, ridges, villages and country houses lay flooded in winter sunshine, a prospect to lift the heart sky-high.

Turning our backs on this stunning panorama we plunged down the footpath into the sycamore woods of the silent, secluded Ashcombe Valley. Suddenly the downs ceased to roll away and downward from under our feet; they rose to hem us in, wrapping us deep into the hidden valley. In the scrubby banks and ragged old hedges, berries clashed colourfully in the afternoon sunlight – deep soft pink of spindle, intense scarlet strings of bryony hanging in loops like carelessly discarded necklaces.

Back in Tollard Royal the cheerful red brick of the King John pub beckoned. We were a little too late for the menu proper, but the landlord obligingly rustled up a brace of bacon rolls that hit the exact spot. Jane was content to sit back and enjoy the bar chat, while I went off for a little fossick around another of General Pitt-Rivers's pet projects, the Larmer Tree Gardens.

The General laid out these pleasure grounds in the 1880s with picnic pavilions, tree-shaded lawns, flowerbeds and a bandstand for the delight and recreation of local people. After their founder's death the gardens decayed and declined, but have recently been revived in all their glory. Within the grounds the Larmer Tree itself, a traditional boundary marker of Cranborne Chase, is a sturdy wych elm sapling. Latest in a line of Larmer Trees stretching back to the days of King John (and maybe much further), it was planted by the great-grandson of General Pitt-Rivers in 1999 to celebrate the new Millennium. That would have pleased the old ethno-archaeologist, a devout believer in rising on stepping-stones of the dead self to higher things.

STEPPING OUT – *Walk 13*

MAP: OS 1:25,000 Explorer 118; 1:50,000 Landranger 184

TRAVEL: Road – M4 to Jct 17, A350 to Shaftesbury, B3081 to Tollard Royal. Park by village pond, or at King John PH if you intend to eat there.

WALK DIRECTIONS: Coming from King John PH (OS ref ST942178), turn left by village pond (944178), then immediately right over stile. Follow path diagonally left up bank. At top bear right; through gate, along grassy headland and over ridge, following yellow arrows. By little spinney on left, keep ahead and down to cross stile (948182). Left (yellow arrow) down slope to Munday's Pond (950184). Beyond gate, three tracks diverge; take middle (grassy) one up slope, following yellow arrows for 1½ miles by Rotherley Wood and Rotherley Down to turn left along Ox Drove road (948206). In ⅔ mile, bear left off road to meeting of 3 trackways (937207). Ahead is gateway marked 'Private Land: No Entry', take track to right of that. In ¾ mile at cattle grid (927208), grass path on left leads past beech clump to panoramic map on Win Green summit (925206).

Ahead to car park; don't go through gates (923205), but turn back left (eastward) along grassy path with fence and dirt road on right. Cross stile (926204); follow National Trust yellow arrows steeply down the hill. Through kissing gate, then through trees to turn right along stony track (930204 – footpath sign). Follow arrow waymarks (white for Rushmore Estate, yellow for Wessex Ridgeway) along valley bottom.

After 1 mile pass chalk quarry on left. In another 250 yds, just before gate across track, reach 2 stiles on left. Cross first one (937187 – Wessex Ridgeway marker in footboard), then stile opposite; left for 30 yd, then bear right through gate and on along grassy trackway, with hedge and fence on right, back to Tollard Royal.

To visit Larmer Tree Gardens: opposite village pond, take road marked 'Rushmore Estate Office'. 150 yd past church, left (943177 – yellow arrow) along fenced path, then through woodland. Emerging by ladder stile (945173), aim across field for lone tree, thence into dip, up grassy ride and through gate (944170) between blocks of woods. Pass brick ruin, then along left side of fenced enclosure to roadway; right to Gardens entrance (943169).

Returning, turn right out of entrance; in 100 yd right down side of Gardens. In 50 yd bear right (941168) along Gardens fence. In 150 yd track bears half left away from fence into dip; right here through gate (941171 – yellow arrow). Aim across field for nearest lone tree; keep half left to ladder stile and path back to village.

LENGTH: 6 miles (8 miles including Larmer Tree Gardens)

REFRESHMENTS: King John PH, Tollard Royal (01725-516207; *www.kingjohninn.co.uk*

LARMER TREE GARDENS AND OTHER WALKS: 01725-516971; *www.larmertreegardens.co.uk*

Vale of Pewsey, Wiltshire

Chalk hills, chalk horse, old waterways and ancient trackways of the Wiltshire Downs

I HADN'T QUITE BARGAINED for the equinoctial realities on tap this early morning – a blustery autumn wind ripping in from the south-west, and a slate-grey dawn sky reeling with driven rain clouds above a sodden Vale of Pewsey.

The hedges along the Kennet & Avon's towpath offered some shelter from the stormy blast. I breakfasted on their blackberries and hazelnuts as I walked west from Wilcot, watching the rooks of the vale tumbling and chasing down the rushing slipstreams of wind. *Prudence, Merlin, Clara Louise* and *Gongoozler* slept on – narrowboats moored nose to tail along the canal's old wharves at Honeystreet.

Under the downland swell of Milk Hill, in the chancel of St Mary's Church at Alton Barnes I found a memorial tablet to Augustus Hare, rector here in the 1830s. Those were desperate times for the agricultural labourers of the district, whose jobs were threatened by technological developments in farm machinery at the same time as the Enclosures Acts were depriving them of the common land where they grazed their own animals. A rioting band of labourers once confronted Hare on his own rectory doorstep, having just shot and wounded his neighbour, Robert Pile of the Manor Farm.

A little window in the north wall of St Mary's looks up to Milk Hill, where Farmer Pile's own peculiar and striking memorial still arches its slender neck and flirts its grass-green hooves – the 180-ft-high White Horse that he caused to be cut out of the turf of the chalk downs in 1812, in order that his native village might boast a mascot to equal the well-known White Horses of neighbouring Cherhill and Marlborough.

Pile seems to have attracted bad luck. He entrusted 20 guineas to a jobbing painter, John Thorne, to organise the cutting of the White

Horse; and Thorne promptly made off with the money. The incumbent of Manor Farm ended up doing most of the work on the horse himself, though he did subsequently have the satisfaction of learning that Thorne had been caught and hanged for various nefarious deeds.

It was the 18th and 19th century land enclosures that finally tamed the Ridgeway, the Bronze Age trackway that climbs the face of the downs above Alton Barnes. For thousands of years the old high road had lurched across the landscape as a wide belt of tracks, among which travellers chose the least boggy according to weather and season. Enclosure, with its emphasis on the value of private property, led landowners to fence, hedge and embank the sprawling old droving track into one course from which beasts and men were not permitted to stray.

I did a fair amount of straying on my way up the Ridgeway to the top of the downs. There were historic monuments to be investigated along side tracks – the White Horse with its flaking white flanks and oddly foreshortened close-to appearance; and the 5,000-year-old neolithic long barrow called Adam's Grave, still proudly standing clear of its eroded ditches. From up here I got a breathtaking view south, across miles of Vale of Pewsey farmland pale mauve after its autumn ploughing, away south and west to the Somerset/Wiltshire border country all blotted out in a milky blur of onrushing rain.

Up on the spine of the downs, among carpets of still-blooming harebells, thistles, scabious and yarrow, I forsook the Ridgeway in favour of a younger but even more striking upland thoroughfare. Exactly what the Dark Ages builders of Wansdyke were up to can only be guessed at. All we know for certain is that some irresistible imperative between the 5th and 7th centuries AD caused them to run a 30-foot-high bank and ditch for sixty miles, from Inkpen Beacon in Hampshire all the way west to the Bristol Channel.

Romano-British warriors of the Arthurian era, defending their adopted Mediterranean culture against barbarian Saxons invading from the north? Saxons from the kingdom of Wessex, laying down a boundary marker? Who can tell? I trod the great green gash, as deep as a modern railway cutting, for a couple of miles, marvelling at its dominance in the downland landscape after so many centuries of existence, staring out at another stunning 30-mile panorama embracing the Marlborough Downs and great swathes of chalk country to the north and east.

The wind blew with increasing force, a battering rain powering in unchecked from the Atlantic with a punch nearly strong enough to knock a walker flat. From the summit of Tan Hill, almost 1,000 feet high, I looked in vain for the spire of Salisbury Cathedral, 25 miles away in the south. The celestial scene-shifter had insinuated an impenetrable gauze of smeared grey, blue and silver, and set it drifting eastwards through the Vale of Pewsey.

Down on the Vale's flat floor, on the way back to Wilcot, the thatched and half-timbered cottages of All Cannings looked too neat and sweet to be real. But appearances are deceptive in rural Wiltshire – as are precise locations. Was it in All Cannings village pond, or in the pond at Bishops Cannings just up the valley, that 18th-century Excisemen found a party of villagers trying to drag the moon out of the water with their hay rakes? Locals are sure about one thing: when the smart Customs men had had a good laugh and gone away, the 'simple' villagers went on with what they had been doing – extracting barrels of contraband brandy from their hiding place in the pond. Not so stupid after all, those Vale of Pewsey peasants.

STEPPING OUT – *Walk 14*

MAP: OS 1:25,000 Explorer 130; 1:50,000 Landranger 173

TRAVEL: By rail to Pewsey (www.thetrainline.co.uk). Wilcot is 1½
miles from Pewsey station, easily walkable; or take a taxi.
By road – M4 to Jct 15; A345 through Marlborough towards
Pewsey; Wilcot signed on right, 1 mile from Pewsey.

WALK DIRECTIONS: From Golden Swan pub (OS ref SU143611),
follow Alton/Devizes sign up village street to Kennet & Avon
canal bridge (141613). Turn left along towpath for 2¾ miles to
Honeystreet (104615). Cross canal, heading north into Alton
Barnes. First left beyond phone box to St Mary's Church
(107620). Cobbled field path to Alton Priors Church (109621).
Bear north, left of thatched wall, to road; right for 100 yd; left by
phone box (110623 – bridleway sign) up Ridgeway. Left at road
(112629); in 200 yd, right up track (footpath sign) across Pewsey
Downs Nature Reserve.

At crossing of tracks under Adam's Grave (112635), track to
White Horse on left; Ridgeway bears right down to stile near
road (115637). Keep parallel to road on your right. After 2nd
stile, bear left (bridleway sign), keeping left of trees, up to stile
on skyline, and on to pass through earth bank, over stile on
left (107646) and on west along Wansdyke. In ½ mile, cross
bridleway (100646); in another mile, Wansdyke bends right; in
⅓ mile, signed bridleway joins from right (083651). Just beyond,
bear left off Wansdyke, keeping fence and then trig pillar
(082647) on right, due south into valley with Rybury Camp
(083639) above on left. Follow spur to cross road at Cannings
Cross Farm (078631).

Through gate to right of house; SW across field by telegraph
poles to cross canal bridge (073625). Follow road through All
Cannings (King's Arms PH on right at 070618) to village green
(church, rectory and pond – on private land – beyond). Left
beside green to cross road (074615); on ESE along farm track
for ¾ mile to end; then continue, keeping beside hedge on left.
Through rusty little gate, over stream, through more gates to
bear right by Mill Farm (089607) up drive round left bend. In
50 yd, right; in 80 yd (091606), go left on farm track for 1 mile
to road (106604). Right; in 300 yd, take *second* footpath sign on
left, through gate by Dutch barn (107601) to cross footbridge in
centre of hedge opposite.

Continue through back fields of Woodborough to lane; pass church (113601) to road. Left; in 200 yd (116598) ahead on field track with hedge on left for ¾ mile to road (127601). Ahead; in 300 yd, at entrance to Cocklebury Farm, left over stile. Diagonally across field to lane (137605); right to Wilcot Church (140608); right to Golden Swan.

LENGTH: 16 miles – allow 8 hours.

NB: for a shorter walk of 8½ miles, start at the Barge Inn at Honeystreet, returning there from All Cannings via canal towpath.

REFRESHMENTS: Barge Inn, Honeystreet (01672-851705; www. the-barge-inn.com); King's Arms, All Cannings (01380-860328; www.kingsarmallcannings.co.uk); Golden Swan, Wilcot (01682-562289; *www.thegoldenswan.co.uk*)

Stockbridge, Houghton and the River Test, Hampshire

A stroll along the most famous trout stream in England

'TROUT,' MURMURED GEORGE. 'God, they're beauties ...' Leaning over the rail in Stockbridge's wide High Street, he pointed down into the quick rush of the chalk stream. 'See the rainbow? And there's a beautiful spotted one, just by those weeds.'

Always a sharp-eyed person, my son; always the first in our family to spot the flint arrowhead or the lost coin. Now he could see every detail of each trout, from the crimson stripes of the rainbows to the brown trout's indigo specks, while my fogged eyes were still trying to pierce the shimmer and dazzle of the fast-running River Test on a sunny spring morning.

Growing up in a village on the banks of the River Stour in rural Suffolk, George had been an ardent fisherman. Now 23, it was a year or two since he had flogged water in earnest. But the prospect of a stroll along the Test, Hampshire's paramount trout river of clear water and gravel bed, had awoken the old Adam in him.

The Test is the most famous trout river in England, and Stockbridge is one of the most charming villages along its shallow valley. This morning the Barbours and cavalry twills were out in force along the single broad street of Georgian houses and shops, contemplating trays of flies in the shadowy recesses of Robjent's Country Clothing, Shooting & Fishing Accessories.

Stockbridge looks the picture of staid respectability these days, but it has enjoyed a lusty past. Stockbridge Races were wild enough affairs in Victorian times, when anyone from a gypsy huckster to the Prince of Wales might drop or pick up a fortune at the downland track above the village. In the previous century Stockbridge had been a celebrated rotten borough. The playwright Richard Steele, trying for Parliament here, offered an apple stuffed with golden guineas to the parents of the first child to be born after his election. The Stockbridge voters gave Steele and his bribe the thumbs-down, and the promise lay unfulfilled.

George and I idled a few minutes more in the village street, watching the trout sinuating in the stream. Then we struck out southward down the old 'Sprat & Winkle', the long-derelict Southampton to Andover railway line which Hampshire County Council has transformed into the Test Way footpath.

Old railway paths can be a bore to walk, especially those that cut a straight path through low-lying country. But the Test Way has been subtly landscaped, so that it winds attractively like a naturally-established footpath in a tunnel of foliage. Bud was just breaking on twisted old coppice trees along the track, and clumps of primroses lay like sulphur-yellow cushions on carpets of moss.

High above the track stood Marsh Court, a handsome white house that looked as old as the hills and sprouted giant triple chimneys like an Elizabethan mansion. But the veneer of age is a clever sham – Marsh Court was actually built on its eminence in the early 1900s, one of Sir Edward Lutyen's more extravagant commissions, ordered by a rich stockjobber who wanted to dominate the delectable Test.

The river wound away across the meadows as we followed the railway line. Peeling off westward along another of Hampshire's recently-established footpaths, the Clarendon Way, we found it rushing in spring spate under a series of pretty rustic bridges.

The Test is a quarrelsome river, forever splitting up with itself and sulking off into individual channels, then reuniting before the next inevitable separation. Hereabouts there are three main courses of the river, each with its bridge. George and I leaned over the railings and contemplated dimpling, rippling water full of trout and grayling, entirely absorbed in the mysteries of fish, weed and water.

'Better look out,' called a woman, wobbling precariously past us on a hired bicycle, 'I'm dangerous ...' Soon we caught up with her, dismounted and flirting with a young hedger whose Puritan beard framed a Greek god profile. 'You meet such *interesting* people around here,' she twinkled, laying a hand on his sleeve.

The low-lying meadows south of Stockbridge are ancient grazing land, enriched by regular flooding. Early settlers found the valley floor impassable in winter, and established themselves along the sides in long, thin villages. Houghton is one of these, a drawn-out string of half-timbered and thatched cottages.

We came to Houghton at lunchtime, hungry enough. The Boot Inn looked a good bet, with its long garden sloping down to the river. 'Masses of baby trout,' murmured George, staring into the river like an angular heron. 'Those ripples out in the stream – fish feeding … can you see 'em?'

I could not. But I spied a man up to his armpits in waders, standing hip-high in the Test as he raked a gravel ridge. Over the Boot's fireplace hung a glass case containing an enormous brown Test trout, caught on a mayfly in 1996 by Mr R. Affleck. The talk at the bar was of reels and lines, knots and lures. Everything seemed good and fishy, down along the Test Valley on this glorious spring day.

Up on the valley side stood All Saints Church, flint built under a wood-shingled spire. Inside, the round pillars were scored with dozens of little crosses, some elaborate, some no more than two crude slashes. They were gouged into the stonework by medieval pilgrims taking a rest before tackling the final stage of their trek to the tomb of St Swithun at Winchester Cathedral.

George and I sat in the shady church for five minutes, then faced out again into the mild afternoon sunshine. The path gained height gradually above Houghton, turning its back on the gentle declivity of the Test Valley and rising through big cornfields.

Over the shaggy green corn shoots, skylarks were pouring out song. A hare sat up on his hind legs to assess us, then dashed away with his dark ears flattened. Flints clinked in the pale chalky furrows as George stirred them with his boot, in hopes of spotting a Neolithic arrowhead. We moved on at snail's pace, quite happy to take it easy in the spring sun and wind.

Turning north beyond lonely Eveley Farm, we found an old trackway sunk between the fields. Hedged with old overshot yew and big twisted beeches, loud with wren song, shady and wide verged, it curled across the cultivated chalk downs, part of the land but distinct from it.

Drovers in the old days would have known this ancient road. They used the high old tracks in the 18th and 19th centuries, when they brought their animals out of Wales on epic foot journeys to the great rural sheep fairs of the downland counties.

Down in Stockbridge at the end of our walk we found the former Drover's House where the men would put up on their way through.

Painted across the brick frontage of the old inn, an advertisement – still legible – told the itinerant Welshmen what they could expect for themselves and their beasts: '*Gwair Tymherus Porfa Flasus Cwrw Da-a-Gwal Cysurus* – Seasoned Hay, Toothsome Pastures, Good Beer, Comfortable Beds.'

Back in the High Street, George and I stopped to look over the bridge rails. The trout still waved among the weeds, noses to the flow, as if they had never moved since we set out.

STEPPING OUT – *Walk 15*

MAP: OS 1:25,000 Explorer 131; 1:50,000 Landranger 185

TRAVEL: Stockbridge is on the A30, between Salisbury (14 miles) and Winchester (9 miles).

WALK DIRECTIONS: By roundabout at east (Winchester) end of village (OS ref SU359351), turn right down Trafalgar Way ('Test Way' sign) along old railway path. In 2 miles, right (350315 – 'Clarendon Way') to cross 3 channels of River Test. Right at road (341319) on pavement through Houghton.

Opposite Boot Inn (343325), left up hill. Opposite All Saints Church, left (341326 – footpath sign) down fenced path. In 150 yd right beside wire fence. Through hedge at top of field, bear right, then dogleg round field edge to join farm road and continue west. At entrance to Eveley Farm drive (327330) continue for 75 yards, then bear left down hedge for 1 field to turn right along rutted track (326330). In ⅓ mile, right at T-junction of tracks (322331); follow old track between hedges for 1 mile to meet road (322343).

Right here along hedged track ('Byway' sign) for 1 mile to A30 (337353). Right (grass verge: *take care!*) for 100 yd; A30 curves off left, but continue straight ahead on old hedged road which becomes track down Meon Hill into Stockbridge.

LENGTH OF WALK: 8 miles – allow 3 hours.

REFRESHMENTS: Several places in Stockbridge; Boot Inn, Houghton (01794-388310).

Nelson's Portsmouth, Hampshire

Through the Royal Navy's 'Pompey' on the trail of England's greatest fighting sailor

'YOU MUST POP INTO THE NUT – the Keppel's Head, really, but that's what the Navy called it – when you're in Pompey,' my father had told me. 'On The Hard, you can't miss it. High jinks for sailors, that's what we all knew The Nut for.'

Whatever the height of jinks at the Keppel's Head when Dad was a midshipman in the Royal Navy of the 1930s, they looked to have dipped a little low on this scudding grey summer's morning. The old hotel possessed the air of a good time that had been had by half the lower deck, rather a long time ago. For Dad's sake I called into The Nut for a cup of coffee; and inspecting the naval prints on the walls I got the ghost of a hint of how this pub, and a hundred more like it in downtown dockside Portsmouth, might have rollicked and roared when the great wartime fleets of the past had sailed into their home port for a little R&R.

Pompey and the Navy – you can't separate the two, and if you tried you'd probably get a black eye. The attention of the world was on the old Hampshire sea port in 2005, Trafalgar Bicentenary year, because of its indissoluble connection with Admiral Lord Horatio Nelson. And what strikes one forcibly on a walk through Portsmouth is the continuity and strength of that bond between the Senior Service and its favourite city. From the newly established Nelson Trail to the ancient seafront redoubts, the salty flavour of the pub names and the sight of today's greyhounds of the sea slipping in and out of their berths, Pompey and the Navy seem bound up in each other as fundamentally as a pair of twins.

The Nelson Trail traces the route that the 'Little Admiral' followed through the streets of Portsmouth on the morning of 14 September, 1805, as he went down to the water's edge to embark in his flagship HMS *Victory* on his way to triumph and death at the Battle of Trafalgar. Nelson had bidden farewell to his mistress Emma Hamilton and their beloved 4-year-old daughter Horatia at Merton the previous evening, and he had endured an all-night journey by jolting post-chaise so as to arrive in Portsmouth at dawn.

The Landport Gate through which Nelson entered the city, an arch of creamy Portland stone seeded with shellfish fossils, stands much as the Admiral knew it. And the High Street down which he rattled retains many of the handsome old houses he would have passed. It's tempting to view Portsmouth entirely through Nelson-tinted spectacles; but here in the High Street I crossed the hawse of another, less celebrated local hero, a contemporary of Horatio Nelson's. The nonconformist shoemaker John Pounds acted as saviour of hundreds of the city's poverty-stricken children in Georgian times. Behind the Unitarian chapel I found a replica of the tiny cobbler's shop where Pounds made it his business to feed, clothe and educate the poorest of the poor.

Wartime bombs destroyed the original chapel, though they left intact Portsmouth's architecturally jumbled but strangely beautiful cathedral just along the High Street. The bombing also demolished the George Inn where Nelson ate his last breakfast ashore. A plaque marks the site of the inn's archway, through which the Admiral slipped in order to avoid the dense and excited crowds that were gathering to witness their favourite David setting out to administer another drubbing to Mounseer Goliath.

Local legend says that Nelson scratched his name on a window pane in the nearby Dolphin Inn. It wasn't yet nine o'clock in the morning when I tapped on the door, but the nice barmaid halted her squeegee long enough to let me in. On the famous pane I made out the signatures of Mabel and Hickie, of Flo Thomson, Judy and Marget, of Si Hung and 'Honist Mum', all scored in the glass with diamond rings down the years. But try as I might, I couldn't spy that celebrated 'Nelson & Bronte'.

Now I left the Nelson Trail and struck out across the wide green acres of Southsea Common. The statue of Lord Nelson that stands looking seaward on the edge of the common is a very good likeness of the Little Admiral, if contemporary portraits caught him truly – the deeply grooved cheeks, the sensuous mouth and deepset eyes, and the defiant stance of a physically slight but enormously brave man. 'Our hero,' said a woman, quite unselfconsciously, in passing, 'a

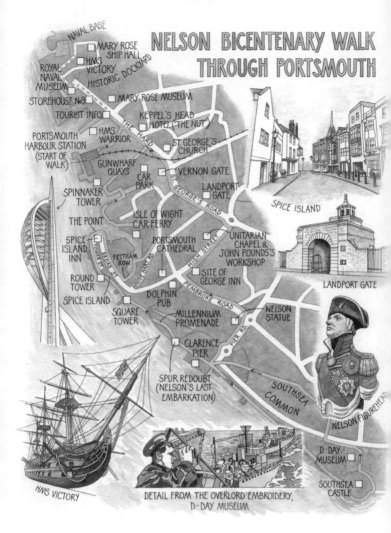

NELSON BICENTENARY WALK
THROUGH PORTSMOUTH

NAVAL BASE

MARY ROSE SHIP HALL

HMS VICTORY

HISTORIC DOCKYARD

ROYAL NAVAL MUSEUM

STOREHOUSE No.9

MARY ROSE MUSEUM

TOURIST INFO!

KEPPEL'S HEAD HOTEL ('THE NUT')

PORTSMOUTH HARBOUR STATION (START OF WALK)

HMS WARRIOR

THE HARD

ST. GEORGE'S CHURCH

GUNWHARF QUAYS

VERNON GATE

CAR PARK

ST. GEORGE'S ROAD

LANDPORT GATE

SPINNAKER TOWER

ISLE OF WIGHT CAR FERRY

THE POINT

SPICE ISLAND

SPICE ISLAND INN

TOWER ST

FELTHAM ROW

WHITE HART RD

PORTSMOUTH CATHEDRAL

HIGH STREET

UNITARIAN CHAPEL & JOHN POUNDS'S WORKSHOP

LANDPORT GATE

ROUND TOWER

BROAD ST

SITE OF GEORGE INN

PEMBROKE ROAD

SPICE ISLAND

DOLPHIN PUB

SQUARE TOWER

MILLENNIUM PROMENADE

NELSON STATUE

PIER RD

CLARENCE PIER

SPUR REDOUBT (NELSON'S LAST EMBARKATION)

SOUTHSEA COMMON

NELSON FIGUREHEAD

D-DAY MUSEUM

SOUTHSEA CASTLE

HMS VICTORY

DETAIL FROM THE OVERLORD EMBROIDERY, D-DAY MUSEUM

really wonderful man,' and she glanced up at the Admiral in obvious admiration.

On that last morning in 1805 the adoring crowds were thick upon Southsea Common. The sheer press of people had prevented Nelson's barge picking him up, as was the custom, from the city waterfront; so he walked down to the beach beside the Spur Redoubt and scrambled into the boat there. Several well-wishers tried to shake his hand; dozens knelt; many wept. 'As the barge in which he embarked pushed away from the shore, the people gave three cheers to which his Lordship returned by waving his hat.' In the boat on the way out to *Victory*, Nelson confided to his friend Captain Hardy, with a flash of prideful insight, 'I had their huzzas before; I have their hearts now.'

Portsmouth was the Little Admiral's that day, and for two centuries to follow. But there's far more to the old town than its Nelson connection alone. Down at the turn of the esplanade I learned how the squat stone fortress of Southsea Castle was built to frighten off the French and the Spaniards 300 years before Trafalgar. And in the D-Day Museum behind the castle I spent the best part of the morning inching my way along the Overlord Embroidery, a remarkable 20th-century work of art taking its inspiration from the Bayeux Tapestry, recording in meticulous stitching and appliqué that extraordinary reverse enactment of the Norman invasion of Britain – the D-Day landings of the Allies on the Normandy beaches.

Returning along the esplanade, I found myself following a linked chain motif set into the paving stones, the symbol of Portsmouth's Millennium Promenade trail. It carried me along the solid stone fortifications of the harbour, and swept me through the cramped old streets of Spice Island, a slender peninsula outside the city walls which became famous among Nelson's sailors for its punch-up pubs and seedy brothels.

Soon the delights and distractions of modern-day Portsmouth came crowding – the shops and bars of Gunwharf Quays, the giant new Spinnaker Tower on the waterfront. All fine and dandy, but where was the Nelson spirit? It lay beyond, wrapped around three magnificent, venerable ships in the Historic Dockyard – the clangorous Victorian ironclad battleship *Warrior*, the Gallipoli veteran gunboat *Monitor*, and their ancestor the mighty old warhorse *Victory*. And Nelson's tradition was at work in the background, too, where the Royal Navy's frigate 'F85' in her workaday grey paint was quietly and purposefully making ready to go to sea.

STEPPING OUT – *Walk 16*

MAP: Official 'Accessible City' map of Portsmouth, available from TIC

TRAVEL: *Rail* – Portsmouth Harbour (*www.thetrainline.co.uk*)
Road – M27, M275 to central Portsmouth; follow brown 'Gunwharf Quays' signs to Gunwharf Quay car park

WALK DIRECTIONS: From station, left to Tourist Information Centre to pick up map; then return along The Hard. From Central Square car park at Gunwharf Quay, go under railway; bear left past station to TIC, then return.

Keep to right-hand pavement. Follow The Hard past St George's Church, under railway. Don't turn left! – keep ahead past Vernon Gate along St George's Road, passing opposite Landport Gate. Right along High Street, passing Unitarian chapel. Opposite cathedral, left along Pembroke Road for ⅓ mile to Nelson statue on Southsea Common; right down Pier Road to Clarence Pier funfair. Left along seafront to Southsea Castle and D-Day Museum.

Return across Southsea Common to Clarence Pier. Continue along seafront towards Portsmouth. At Spur Redoubt join Millennium Promenade; follow its chain motif paving-stone trail past Square and Round Towers, along Tower Street and West Street to The Point. Bear right around Spice Island Inn to return along Broad Street. Follow Millennium Promenade, turning left along Feltham Row to bear left at end along White Hart Road. Left past Isle of Wight ferry terminal until opposite Spinnaker Tower. Right to Gunwharf Quays, Central Square car park and railway station.

LENGTH: 5 miles approx. – allow 3 hours, or a whole day if visiting Portsmouth Historic Dockyard.

REFRESHMENTS: Plenty available – try the smoke-free Spice Island Inn (02392-870543) at The Point, or Storehouse No. 9 in the Historic Dockyard.

PORTSMOUTH HISTORIC DOCKYARD: (02392-839766; *www. historicdockyard.co.uk*)

NELSON TRAIL, MILLENNIUM PROMENADE: For details, contact Tourist Information Centre, Historic Dockyard Gate (02392-826722; *www.visitportsmouth.co.uk*)

Overton, Harrington and Watership Down, Hampshire

Across the roof of Hampshire with the rabbits of Watership Down

THERE WAS SOMETHING about swaggering along that North Hampshire country lane, hogging the crown of the road because I hadn't yet seen a single car, that made me feel extremely good. 'Reclaim the lanes!' I exhorted the primroses in the verges.

This is what every walker dreams of in early spring: a winding lane between hedges in their first green flush, a blue sky with larks overhead, pale sunshine with a whisper of warmth, and no motors to push you into the ditch. Today was to be a dusting-the-cobwebs day, a fifteen miler, up onto the roof of Hampshire where the downs plunge over into Berkshire and there would be enough of a breeze to blow away the stuffiness of winter.

The lane wriggled forward, its tarmac giving way to clay and flint. I found myself striding field edges and woodland paths, pounding along like a man on a mission – the sheer exhilaration of stretching limbs that had been cramped up in chairs and under tables for too long. In North Oakley I pulled up to admire the woodwork in the Manor Farm's thatched barn, a hammerbeam roof of rough craftsmanship that lent the practical old building a church-like grace. There was consummate artistry to admire in All Saints Church in Hannington, just along the lane: two gorgeous windows engraved by Lawrence Whistler. Between the 'cathedral of the harvest' and the parish church I drank a pint outside the Vine, just to celebrate the day and the moment.

Now the downs billowed all round me, their chalky backs combed by seed drills into long green lines of corn tuffets. The larks went on singing overhead, climbing their aerial staircases into invisibility in the blue. I came to the breaking wave of the great escarpment and rode its green crest for a mile or two westward, to the slender beech hanger of Cannon Avenue on Watership Down. The hanger looks out across a 20-mile view towards the distant Thames and the Berkshire downs. From the very edge of Watership Down I could just make out the ridge of the roofs of Nuthanger Farm, three hundred feet below, a thin red line beyond bare trees.

Landscapes fire imaginations, and this magnificent prospect inspired Richard Adams to write his lapine masterpiece, *Watership Down*. The novel grew organically out of stories made up to pacify the Adams children on long car journeys. It wasn't easy for Adams to launch his book about 'real rabbits that talk'. Seven publishers turned the tale down before Rex Collings brought it out in 1972. Nowadays the children of the world know of Hazel, Fiver, Bigwig and the other rabbits, whose Honeycomb burrow was sited by Adams here among the roots of the beech hanger on the down.

The settings for their early adventures lay spread out before me – the woods and fields through which they made their perilous escape from the doomed Sandleford Warren; Nuthanger Farm, scene of foolhardy raids by the rabbits, with its predatory cat and the dog who features so bloodily in the book's fantastically exciting dénouement. Watership Down has become a place of pilgrimage for fans of the book. The beech tree into whose trunk someone cut 'BIG WIG' was destroyed in a recent storm, but I found splintered fragments of bark carrying rhymes and loving messages still decipherable in pen-knife calligraphy.

Turning my back at last on that uplifting view, I let the wind push me gently southward on a good hedgerow path. There were no rabbits to be seen; perhaps they were busy digging in the spinneys. Soon a long green barrier came into sight, lying across my line of march – the tremendous ribbon of woodland known as Caesar's Belt. Within its narrow strip I found a raised earthwork, resembling the trackbed of a long-disused railway. This was the Portway, a Roman road from Silchester to Old Sarum, so meticulously engineered that it has lasted for two thousand years in the protective girdle of its great tree belt.

On again, with the breeze swinging round a little to the east and a chill creeping into the air. The energy-rich marching of the morning had slowed to an exercise-drugged amble. Beyond Willesley Warren Farm I turned aside along a tangled tunnel of trees, like an immensely thick hedge with a hollow heart. Primrose clumps lay in clearings, and violets spattered mossy hummocks. 'Harroway,' said the map. This is the oldest road in Britain, an ancient trackway at least 6,000 years old that swings across southern England in a vast rutted arc. And here at a crossing of paths Richard Adams sited Efrafa, the barracks of a warren run with militaristic precision and savagery by that arch-enemy of Hazel and Co., the mighty dictator rabbit General Woundwort.

I felt good and tired now, with evening coming on. But I still lingered at Efrafa, reliving the part of the tale where the Honeycomb rabbits liberate Woundwort's does from under his much-scarred nose. Thrilling stuff, and genuinely funny too. It was high time to read it all again. I went on down to Overton, eager to pull *Watership Down* out of the bookcase the moment I got home. Springtime: gets you going, doesn't it?

STEPPING OUT – *Walk 17*

MAP: OS 1:25,000 Explorer 144; 1:50,000 Landranger 185

TRAVEL: Rail (www.thetrainline.co.uk) to Overton

Road: from north and west, M4 (Jct 13); A34 south to
Whitchurch; B3400 to Overton. From east and south, M3 (Jct
7); minor roads via North Waltham to Overton. Park at station.

WALK DIRECTIONS: From Overton station (OS ref SU518508),
down Station Road. Ahead at junction; in 80 yd, left (519504
– Polhampton sign). In ¼ mile at right bend (523505 – No
Through Road sign), keep ahead with pond on your right. In
¼ mile, beside cottage with 5 dormer windows (526507), left
up green lane, under railway to road (526512). Right for ¾ mile,
crossing lane (532515) to T-junction near Ashe Warren Farm
(536520). Keep ahead (Right Of Way fingerpost) for 1 mile.

Just before cottages on White Lane, turn left over stile
(551526 – footpath fingerpost) to follow Wayfarers' Walk
(WW). In 50 yd bear left among trees. Follow track with
WW arrows for ¾ mile to Freemantle Farm. Bear left through
farmyard (543537 – footpath fingerpost, WW); in 300 yd, right
(fingerpost, WW) through hedge. Aim half left across field for
thatched Manor farm barn at North Oakley (538541).

Leaving WW, turn left along road to Hannington, passing
Vine PH (540553) to bear left across village green and down
right side of church (539555). Dogleg round barn; in 20 yd
ignore stile and fingerpost, keeping ahead through wicket
gate. Follow field edge on path between hedges, to go through
hedge at top of For Down (531553) into a field. Bisect the angle
between direction shown by footpath fingerpost, and line of
electricity poles. Aim across field, a little to left of pylon seen
on skyline just to left of poles. Pass right edge of hollow in
field, to go through gap in far hedge and rejoin WW (526554 –
fingerpost, WW). Right along drive to road (525557). Left for
25 yd; right along green lane (Right Of Way fingerpost, WW)
for ¾ mile to cross B3051 (516565). Continue along WW for 1¼
miles, past northern end of Cannon Avenue beech hanger on
Watership Down (499569) – 'The Honeycomb'.

White railings and WW soon diverge to right (497568);
bear left here, following hedge on left, to go through gate (Hants

County Council Cycle Trail arrow). Keep south along rack by hedges for 1¾ miles, through Caesar's Belt woodland to road (502543). Right along road for ⅓ mile; at right bend go left (500536) on farm track for 1 mile, past Willesley Warren Farm (501528) and The Peak copse. In another ¼ mile, right (505515 – bridleway fingerpost) along Harroway trackway. Continue for ⅓ mile to pass post with yellow arrow pointing left (501511) – don't follow it, but continue along Harroway for another ¼ mile to crossing of tracks with bridleway fingerpost (498508) – 'Efrafa'.

Return to post with yellow arrow; bear right down field edge with hedge on left. Cross track and belt of trees, then railway (504503). On past water treatment plant, down lane for 200 yd to right bend (505498 – yellow arrow). Ahead here, down through trees. Left along Silk Mill Lane for ⅓ mile. Right at junction (512499), past church to cross B3051 (515499). Left along pavement; in 30 yd, right (515502 – footpath fingerpost) along gravelled path, past reservoir to road (518503). Left to Overton station.

LENGTH: 15 miles

REFRESHMENTS: Vine PH, Hannington (01635-298525; *www.thevineathannington.co.uk*)

READING: *Watership Down* by Richard Adams (Penguin)

Greywell and The Harroway, Hampshire

Celebrating the 200th Walk of the Month along Britain's oldest trackway

THE BREAKFAST CHEF at Tylney Hall had pushed out the bacon sandwich boat in proper style. It was just as well. Thirty walkers had got up around dawn this summer morning in places as far removed as Somerset and Surrey, Cambridge and the Isle of Wight, to make their way to the handsome old red brick hotel on the Berkshire/Hampshire border. Dedicated Telegraph readers all, they were intent on celebrating the 200th Walk of the Month to be contributed by your Walking Correspondent to these pages. And they were plenty hungry.

Five minutes over the crispy bacon and orange juice sufficed to thaw any reserve. After that it was a nest of chattering magpies as everyone settled in to look back to September 1990 and all the years of Walks of the Month since then. How about that lovely one on Wordsworth's Quantocks? No, I preferred the walk on the South Downs at Alfriston, the one with the girl on the horse holding up the traffic. Really? Oh no, we preferred that Northumberland beach walk between the castles. Yes, but what about the time you wrote left when you meant right, Christopher? Good Lord, you had us wandering over half of Scotland!

As for the 100th Walk back in 1998, celebrated with a so-called gentle stroll around Henley-on-Thames … David and Val Cheffy gleefully reminded me of that stormy morning of gales and lashing rain, when they'd battled up from Southampton through the most atrocious weather to join a handful of equally intrepid readers for an absolute soaker of a walk. What was that nice pub where we all dried off? The Flower Pot at Aston, that was it, with all those stuffed fish in glass cases. And great beer! We were completely drenched. Happy days, eh!

The sandwich mountain was quarried away to nothing, the coffee went cold, and still we chatted and reminisced. Blue summer sky and bright sunlight called us all outside eventually, to travel the couple of miles to Greywell and the start of our communal ramble. No worries about how 30 strangers might get on with each other; we set out under the spell of that particular sociable alchemy that operates when a bunch of people gather to go walking together.

What must the odds have been against encountering a walking party even larger than ours, exclusively composed of earnest Japanese ramblers? That's what happened before we had got fairly into our stride. We stood aside for them on the narrow towpath of the Basingstoke Canal, contemplating the clear water full of gracefully trailing plants and the dark hollow of the mouth of Greywell Tunnel. Back in the 19th century it could take a bargeman half a day to 'leg' it through the cold, damp and utterly dark brick tube of the 1,230-yard tunnel, nowadays home to several huge colonies of bats.

Two dogs accompanied our celebration walk – Harry, a supremely tolerant golden retriever from Reigate who had brought along his pets Tony and Diane Morgan, and westcountryman Bramble from Thurloxton in Somerset, a charming mutt of portmanteau breed with his humans Ann and Edwin Quick in tow. Bramble's natural chocolate colour was soon enriched by puddle mud. Harry fell into the water. They were out to have a brilliant day.

We passed a family of coot, the 'teenagers' sporting pale bumfluff on throat and breast, and stopped to admire the ruin of Odiham Castle. It was from this sturdy octagonal stronghold of flint cobbles that King John set out in 1215 for his fateful meeting with the barons at Runnymede and the signing of Magna Carta. The castle's outlines now stand so blurred by wind and weather that it looks more like a vast modern sculpture – Henry Moore circa 1960, say – than a fortress.

A field full of sedges and buttery yellow flag iris led us away from the canal and into the outskirts of Greywell. The straggly petals of ragged robin, as pink as nail polish, gleamed in the marshy ground of the Wallace Memorial Reserve, a fine stretch of wet woodland each side of the village church of St Mary. Here we called a halt for a few minutes to enjoy that rare phenomenon, a Home Counties church left unlocked for the pleasure of all comers. Around the round-arched Norman north doorway, Crusader pilgrims on their way to Palestine 800 years ago had incised crosses, some merely crude scratches, other reverently crafted.

Somebody had to act as back marker or long-stop for our 30-strong group, and it was Cambridge man Bob who volunteered. His shepherding was pretty effective, for the Telegraph walking party lost no members as we splashed on along a plank causeway through the wetlands. Beyond Greywell Mill a stretch through hay meadows and beanfields brought us to the mysterious old upland track called the Hoary Way or Harroway. Around the time of my first Walk of the Month I'd set out to walk the whole 150-mile length of the Harroway from Seaton on the Devon coast to Farnham in Surrey, where it links up with the North Downs Way. It was a magical ten days along the chalk high ground of England, tracing the rutted, forgotten track through ancient groves of yew and holly and along the deepest of sunken byways.

I'd forgotten the powerful atmosphere of the Harroway, the oldest road in Britain. It undulated under its elder and beech trees in a sunken groove deeply scored into the chalk and flint face of the land by three millennia of wheeled traffic and twice or three times as many of hoof prints and human footfalls. A chiffchaff sent out its duotonous call from the shelter of a field maple's crown, and larks exulted in the blue heavens as we reached Five Lanes End.

Here in a high place with far views in all directions the old tin-trading route of the Harroway crosses another ancient trackway, White Lane, under a canopy of gnarled old beeches. We left this resonant place, site of countless forgotten rendezvous, with regret. But a pint in the sunny garden of the Fox & Goose in Greywell and a slap-up lunch at Tylney Hall were calling with voices yet more seductive.

What a great walk, and what a splendid day. Thank you, Joan and Drostan, Harry and Marilyn, Dawn, 'Back Man' Bob and Brenda, Derek, Phil and Sue, Steve, Tony, Cynthia and Michael, Barbara, Jennifer, Ann and Edwin (and Bramble), John, Sarah, Mo, Zenah, Lindsaye, Tony and Diane (and Harry), Christi, Vanessa, and the intrepid David and Val, for turning my 200th Daily Telegraph Walk of the Month into such a brilliant celebration. Here's to the next ... and the one after that!

STEPPING OUT – *Walk 18*

MAP: OS 1:25,000 Explorer 144; 1:50,000 Landranger 186

TRAVEL: Rail (*www.thetrainline.co.uk*) to Hook station
   Road: M3 to Jct 5; A287 towards Farnham; turn immediately
   right to Greywell. Park at Fox & Goose (please ask permission
   first, and please give the pub your custom too!)

WALK DIRECTIONS: From Fox & Goose (OC ref SU718514)
   turn left along road; immediately right down Deptford Lane;
   in 20 yards, left up path to cross Basingstoke Canal (719514).
   Right along towpath to pass Odiham Castle on left (725519).
   Continue to cross canal by swing bridge (728517); return down
   opposite bank for 150 yards; left over stile (727517); up hedge to
   top of sedgy field. Left (725515) along grass path, bearing right
   to reach road (723513). Right for 150 yards; left through gate
   onto Greywell Moors nature reserve (sign). Follow left hedge for
   250 yards; right past memorial stone (721511) through Wallace
   Memorial Reserve. Cross footbridge and stile, then bear left
   across stile to reach St Mary's Church, Greywell (719510).

   Follow path through graveyard; bear right along fen
   duckboard trail to Greywell Mill (717506). Right up drive for 20
   yards; left (footpath fingerpost) over stile, and along 3 fields with
   hedge on left to reach Harroway ancient trackway at corner of
   Bidden Road (711498). Right along Harroway for 600 yards to
   cross road at Four Lanes End (705499); continue for ¾ mile to
   Five Lanes End (696502).

   Sharp right along White Lane (1st track on right) for 1 mile
   to Nateley Road (712509); forward into Greywell. Opposite
   Manor Farm, left up lane (716510 – 'Greywell Hill'); in 20 yards,
   bear right beside gate up short incline; through gate into field.
   Right along hedge. 150 yards past a left/right dogleg, turn right
   (717513 – waymark arrow) to village street; left to Fox & Goose.

LENGTH: 5½ miles

CONDITIONS: Field paths and tracks. Can be wet/boggy after rain.

REFRESHMENTS: Fox & Goose, Greywell (01256-702062) – very
   friendly and characterful pub

Walk 19

Chilgrove, Stoughton and the Mardens, West Sussex

Farmlands, wood and uplands of the Sussex Downs

THE WHITE HORSE INN in the West Sussex village of Chilgrove was a cheerful place when Jane and I last stayed there, an exceptionally friendly, picture-perfect old pub by the village green. It had tickled the owners Charles and Carin Burton no end to discover that one of Jane's ancestors in mid-Victorian times had combined the rôles of Chilgrove's village blacksmith and publican. 'Well, you're sort of family – what a nice thought!' Charles had beamed. 'Better toast it!'

It came as a shock, a few months later, to discover that the White Horse had fallen into new hands and reinvented itself as 'The Fish House', a place to 'redefine culinary excellence'. However tiptop the new manifestation, we couldn't help but mourn the crankiness and comfort of the old ...

The October day we set out from the White Horse couldn't have been more glorious if it had been auditioning for Autumn Morning of the Year. Up in the beechwoods that overhung the village the trees were on the turn, a fretwork of old gold against the blue sky. Spiders' webs sagged between sprigs of old man's beard, heavy with diamonds of sunlit dew. Yews stood in the shade of beech and oak, with thick veins of ivy twisted round their limbs. 'I just love the smell of the woods at this time of year,' Jane murmured, 'that rich damp savour they've got after a bit of rain in the night. And the fungi, Good Lord, look at them ...'

From the dank mulch of sodden mossy sticks and black leaf-mould on the woodland floor rose the multiform shapes of fungi, exuding their faintly sexual, faintly sinister smell. Now, what are these white ones like old-fashioned darning mushrooms? False death caps? These coolie hats with purple points growing out of this rotten log – trooping crumble cap, d'you reckon, or are they more like milking bonnet? And ooh missus, get a load of this bulbous ellipsoid at the edge of the wood, swelling at the top of its stalk like a schoolboy's graffito. It could be an ink-cap; it's sure as eggs a humdinger. Frankie Howerd would have loved it. Don't take your maiden auntie for a walk in these woods, dear, not unless she's got her smelling salts with her …

Goldcrests were *see-see-see*-ing in the tops of the conifers around Blackbush House, a brick and flint hideaway deep in the woods. There was a sudden snap and crackle of twigs as three roe deer started away under the oaks, dark shadows that flickered in and out of shafts of sunlight. Stock doves burbled overhead and pheasants scuttered in the dry leaves at the edge of the trees as we emerged to a stupendous view broadening to the west, between rosehip hedges down a secret valley in a shallow fold of the downs and away over wooded chalk ridges. 'Sussex,' said Jane, 'that catches it exactly.'

Pungent farm smells of hay bales and a fruity silage clamp followed us down into Stoughton, where a cat sat on picket duty at Old Bartons to watch us go by. We stopped for a pint in the sunshine outside the Hare and Hounds, and a peep into the thousand-year-old St Mary's Church with its windows high in the walls in Saxon style and its north door tall enough to let a mounted man ride through. Then it was on and up through Inholmes Wood, following a flinty lane where we counted ten tree species in a hundred-yard stretch, a rough rule of thumb that made the deep-sunk holloway as old as St Mary's, and maybe a lot older.

A broad swell of flinty ploughland brought us into Blinkard Copse. Under the trees something half-grunted, half-snarled loudly enough to make us jump. If that wasn't a lion, it was certainly the father of all wild boars. I hadn't hefted a pig-sticking spear since the Kadir Cup Meet at Meerut in '27, so we tiptoed by, all a-quake, and made it unscathed into the hamlet of Up Marden.

Beyond a slate-roofed well house stood the 13th-century Church of St Michael. No electricity sullies the timeless air of this downland chapel, whose doorways were incised with crosses by medieval pilgrims on their way between Winchester and the shrine of St Richard at Chichester Cathedral. Summer evensong services at St Michael's are lit by late sunlight through the tall lancet windows. A faded wall painting shows an extravagantly bearded St Christopher carrying the Christ child across a torrent on one brawny shoulder. Among the few

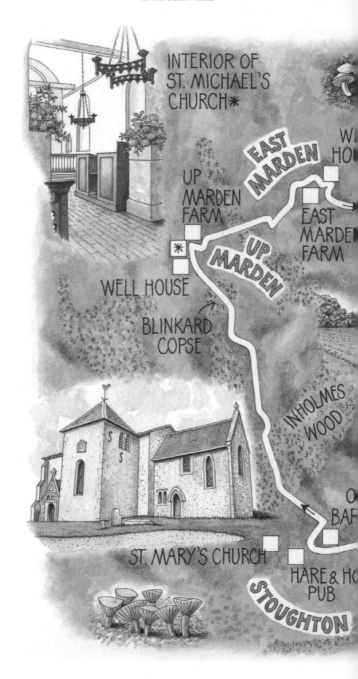

INTERIOR OF
ST. MICHAEL'S
CHURCH*

EAST
MARDEN

W
HO

UP
MARDEN
FARM

EAST
MARDEN
FARM

UP
MARDEN

*

WELL HOUSE

BLINKARD
COPSE

INHOLMES
WOOD

O
BAR

S
S

ST. MARY'S CHURCH

HARE & HO
PUB

STOUGHTON

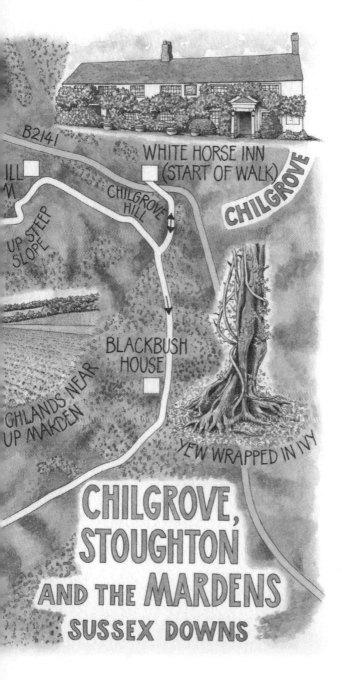

B2141

ILL
M

WHITE HORSE INN
(START OF WALK)

CHILGROVE
HILL

CHILGROVE

UP STEEP
SLOPE

BLACKBUSH
HOUSE

GHLANDS NEAR
UP MARDEN

YEW WRAPPED IN IVY

CHILGROVE, STOUGHTON
AND THE MARDENS
SUSSEX DOWNS

upright pews on the simple brick floor there's a sense of peace, catching you gently by the hand.

Imperceptibly, late afternoon stole in. We shook ourselves free of the spell of St Michael's and went slowly on. In the field by East Marden farm a bull was sniffing the hindquarters of his harem like a sleepy old colonel comparing the Fonseca Bin 27 with the Cockburn Special Reserve. He didn't harrumph at us.

Now came the last haul up the steep green breast of a slope, with far downland views to east and west as a reward from Hillbarn at the top. We followed the long grassy ridge of Chilgrove Hill, the sun in the south flooding trees, hedges, copses and the meadows in the valley with pale lemon light. Then it was down the flint-cobbled lane through the trees and back to Chilgrove, with rooks cawing in the beeches and the evening shadows stretching out to capture the ploughed fields and village green below.

STEPPING OUT – *Walk 19*

MAP: OS 1:50,000 Landranger 197; OS 1:25,000 Explorer 120

TRAVEL: By rail (*www.thetrainline.com*) – nearest station is
  Chichester (6 miles); then taxi
  By road – M3, M27, A27 to Chichester, A286 Midhurst road,
  B2141 to Chilgrove.

WALK DIRECTIONS: From The Fish House (OS ref SU828145)
  cross road (please take care!). Left for 50 yards; right up rising
  lane. In 400 yards, ignore faint track on left. At fork in track
  at top of rise (828139 – stile with blue arrow on right), bear
  left to pass West Dean Estate notice on gate. Pass Kingley Vale
  NNR noticeboard, then Blackbush House (828127). In 30 yards,
  through gate (3-finger post). Ahead to curve left; pass post (blue
  arrow); in 50 yards, right (828125 – 4-finger post, 'Monarch's
  Way' – MW – waymark). At edge of trees, over path crossing
  (824121 – 3-finger post, MW) and on into valley for 1⅓ miles to
  reach road by Old Bartons house (805115).

  Turn left into Stoughton if you want to visit Hare& Hounds
PH and St Mary's Church; otherwise, right along road for 250
yards; left (806117 – fingerpost) up sunken lane. Keep ahead
over path crossings, following yellow arrows through Inholmes
Wood. On far side (801125) follow fingerposts across 2 big fields,
keeping same direction. At far side of second field (800133
– blue arrow), left along green lane for 200 yards, opposite
house, right (yellow arrow) across field to right corner of wood
(799136). Fingerpost points way through Blinkard Copse. Leave
wood over stile (797138); diagonally across paddock to cross lane
(796139 – fingerpost). Cross field and pass well house to reach St
Michael's Church, Up Marden (795141).

  Right along gravel path beyond to road; left for 100 yards;
opposite Up Marden Farm (797142 – fingerpost), right down
lane. In 50 yards follow green arrow with hedge on right. In 200
yards, steeply down through wood. Over path crossing (800143
– fingerpost); on down out of trees. Up field edge, hedge on
right. Over stile (802143 – yellow arrow); right for 70 yards;
left, with fence on left, for 400 yards; diagonally right (805146
– fingerpost) across field to stile into road in East Marden.
Right to well house (807146); left along road for 100 yards;

opposite letterbox, right (fingerpost) along lane. In 100 yards, left (fingerpost) over stile by barns and on along lane for 2 fields, crossing a stile (yellow arrow) to reach another in valley bottom (814142). Through trees, over stile, up steep hill, cross stile at top (816142 – fingerpost). Along fenced path to barn conversion house. Left (fingerpost) to pass neighbouring house. In another 100 yards, right (817144 – fingerpost, yellow arrow) up lane. Left over stile at top (yellow arrow); through gate to skirt Bow Hill Farm and cross stile. Ahead (fingerpost, blue arrow) along concrete drive; through gate (822144 – blue arrow) and on along ridge of Chilgrove Hill, following fence past copse for ½ mile to go through gate into woodland (828139). Left down track to Chilgrove.

LENGTH: 8½ miles.

REFRESHMENTS: Hare & Hounds, Stoughton (02392-631433; *www.hareandhoundspub.co.uk*)

INFORMATION: *www.visitchichester.org*

West Wittering and West Itchenor, West Sussex

Along the shores of Chichester Harbour and through the cornfields of Selsey

IN THE EARLY MORNING sunshine the two horses, the bay and the white, went cantering through the shallows of West Wittering beach like a clip from a shampoo advertisement. Spray flew in diamond showers, the eight hooves drummed the wet sand, and a little cheeky terrier twisted joyfully in mid-leap, barking madly as he chased the fleeing shadows of the horses.

Jane stooped to furl up her trouser legs, then ran ahead, splashing along the edge of the outgoing tide as she had done countless times in a Sussex childhood spent on and around this beach. Our daughter Mary – five days shy of her 14th birthday, and already taller than her mother – stalked after her like a long-legged heron. It was going to be one of those hot blue summer days so characteristic of the Sussex coast, perfect for a stroll by beach and field paths along the byways of Chichester Harbour and the Selsey peninsula.

Selsey remains a land apart, a broad flat arrow-head of farming country pointing south from Chichester towards the rounded neb of Selsey Bill. This is a landscape entirely different in appearance and character from the classic rolling downs of West Sussex. The two Witterings, East and West, lie on the coast in the south-western corner of the peninsula – East Wittering a cheerful holiday place, West Wittering a pretty little village that stretches a broad sandy toe towards the Isle of Wight and juts a marshy elbow into the wide waters of Chichester Harbour.

We rounded the great tide-exposed sand flats off West Wittering and turned north along the dunes that make up the club-shaped spit called East Head. Shaggy with marram grass and spattered with the yellow flowers of lady's bedstraw, these sand dunes – a National Trust

Nature reserve – are constantly shifting under the subtle but unceasing pressure of wind and tide.

The outer edge of East Head faces Chichester Harbour and forms a beautiful sandy beach. The sheltered inner face of the spit, in contrast, is all dun-coloured marsh and curling creeks. Oystercatchers and curlews were probing and feeding here, raising their piping cries to compete with the reeling, sky-filling song of larks high over the dunes.

'Hey, have you seen these?' exclaimed Mary, bending low over what looked like a pale ribbon laid along the tideline. It was composed of countless thousands of dead crabs, dry and weightless under the sun. 'Yes, we get a lot of people reporting those, thinking it's some kind of dreadful epidemic,' said the reserve's warden, Daniel Delaney, stopping his Land Rover on the beach for a chat. 'What's happening is that the shore crabs are moulting, and those are the external skeletons they've discarded. My dog loves eating them – but, my God, does it make him smell awful!'

The temperature was rising all the time, moving well into the 80s and putting a brassy sheen on the sun that told of a change in the weather not too far down the line. We soaked our faces and T-shirts under the tap in the beach car park and went on up the footpath that skirts the eastern rim of Chichester Harbour. This sea inlet is shaped like a hand, with the four crooked fingers of Chichester, Bosham, Thorney and Emsworth Channels poking inland.

Bracken, bramble and overarching trees made sun-dappled tunnels of shade to walk in. On one side stretched the flat fields and dark green woods of the peninsula; on the other the mirror-blue water of the harbour dotted with boat sails, tiny triangles of scarlet, brown and sulphur-yellow. A handful of houses lay sprinkled along this shore, their gardens and paintwork of a trimness that spoke of sailorly hands at the domestic helm.

Beyond Ella Nore's hooked shingle spit we passed below the balcony of a house where an upright man in shorts was dipping a Union Jack on his flagpole. 'Just saluting that boat,' he told us, indicating a smart blue ketch passing the point of the spit. 'Do you know her?' I asked. 'I should do,' he replied with a hint of pride, 'she's mine.'

Up at West Itchenor a faint breeze was slapping halyards against masts in the boatyard. Along the village street the red-brick and white-washed houses in their neat flower gardens invoked every archetype of English summer sleepiness. Too hot for walking, decided Mary and Jane. Why don't we just stay here outside The Ship and dawdle over a salad while you go and get the car, Dad? Yes, I agreed, eyeing the other loungers and their nice cool pints of bitter – why don't I?

The afternoon was as sultry and hot as a French summer's day, but in the east window of St Nicholas's Church there were wintry sleets and rainstorms blowing and blustering about. How Sir Andrew Caldecott (1884–1951) must have loved rough winds and the sting of the English seasons, for his memorial window is a celebration of vigorous weather. Skaters slide on frosty ponds, a man bends under a stormy blast, a gumbooted girl watches her bonfire smoke swirling in an autumn gale. Walking out of the church into the still heat of summer felt strange, as if a shiver of rude weather somehow clung to the day.

A gardener was filling his watering can at the tap outside West Itchenor Memorial Hall, but he stood courteously back while I gulped the cold water. Out in the fields the ripening corn was a dull gold carpet smoothly unrolled under the sun. Insects hummed sleepily in the black shadows under the trees, backed by the thick, throaty cooing of wood pigeons. From the high gable of Redlands Farm house a Union Jack and a Canadian maple flag fluttered in a breath of air – flown in tandem for reasons personal to the owner, no doubt.

I stumbled on dreamily through the gently rustling cornfields, lulled half to sleep by the soporific chorus of the pigeons. A sparrowhawk fluttering above the corn was the only lively being in all the Selsey peninsula. It wasn't until I had got back down to the beach in East Wittering, where the shouts of bathers and the salty tang of the incoming tide pierced through the veil of the hot afternoon, that I woke up and began to look forward to that nice cool pint.

STEPPING OUT – *Walk 20*

MAP: OS 1:25,000 Explorer 120; 1:50,000 Landranger 197

TRAVEL: By rail to Chichester (*www.thetrainline.co.uk*)

Bus: 52, 53 Chichester-Witterings (*www.stagecoachbus.com/south*)
Road: A27, A286, B2198 to East Wittering. Village car park in
Marine Drive, right off Shore Road.

WALK DIRECTIONS: From car park (794971) turn left to Shore
Road, right to the beach (794968). Bear right for 2¼ miles
to southern neck of East Head (765985). Follow duckboard
trails clockwise around East Head; then follow shore path for
3½ miles up east side of Chichester Harbour to West Itchenor
(800014). Walk down village street, (Ship Inn is on your right),
and continue to sharp left bend (799007 – St Nicholas's Church
is another 150 yards on your left).

At bend, go through Itchenor Park House Farm entrance
gate, and immediately left (footpath fingerpost in hedge)
along field edge path. From here the field paths are very well
waymarked with fingerposts. Bear right around end of second
field, then left (795004 – fingerpost) over farm track, across
centre of field and on down left side of next field. In ¼ mile
you reach a flinty track among trees on a sharp bend (793998).
Bear left and keep ahead in tunnel of trees. In ¼ mile a
footpath (marked 'FP No. 7' – 796996) runs off left over plank
footbridge; but turn *right* here (fingerpost), heading south. Soon
you dogleg right, then left past a caravan park; continue to B2179
(795993). Turn right here along road round a long right-hand
bend (*NB Please take care! Walk in single file and use the verges!*).

After ¼ mile turn left off road on footpath (791991 –
fingerpost), walking south for ½ mile to Elm Lane (791984).
Turn right along tarmac for 50 yards, then left by a yard
(fingerpost) along footpath. Emerging from bushes bear left
(791980 – fingerpost) around left edge of field (*NB OS Explorer
map shows path going across middle of this field*). Cross B2179
road (792973) and go down Jolliffe Road to beach (790970); left
to return to East Wittering.

LENGTH OF WALK: 11 miles

CONDITIONS: Sand or shingle and well-marked field paths. Some
gorse and thorn bushes: long trousers and walking shoes advised.

REFRESHMENTS: Ice-cream van often at West Wittering beach car
park; Ship Inn, West Itchenor (01243-512284; *www.theshipinn.biz*)

Walk 21

Amberley, Bignor and Sutton, West Sussex

River valley, Roman mosaics and an ancient road over the downs

SPARKS SPURTED UP as the blacksmith clanged iron on anvil. Beyond the forge a steam locomotive puffed and clanked, and a group of schoolchildren squealed as they showered each other with water from an old-fashioned pump. A breezy morning at Amberley Working Museum, with a stiff westerly wind scattering train smoke and flying drops of water.

I lingered idly, watching the iron bar beaten into a glowing curve, relishing the heat of the forge fire. It was going to be a brisk day up on the crest of the Sussex Downs. Big white and silver clouds were massing behind the smooth curve of Bury Hill, and there was a nip to the wind that said summer might not be going to last too long.

The River Arun looked salt-thick and silty brown this morning, its tidal water eddying through the arches of Houghton Bridge and snaking on inland. The whalebacks of the downs rose in a flotilla around the green river plain. As always, their billowing shapes put me in mind of great sails anchored to the earth and blown taut by an upward gale. Whales and sails, billows and gales: strange how aptly these bracing seadog images fit the high, dry downs.

At Bury Wharf the parish council had placed a noticeboard with old photographs and some notes about the ferry that used to cross the Arun here – a penny for parishioners, tuppence for strangers. Bob Dudden had been the last ferryman, working until the 1950s; it was he who taught the village children to swim in the Ferry Hole.

Back then, the Bury churchwardens might have thought it very strange to keep the church door locked. I had done my reading, and had been looking forward to seeing the medieval mural and screen, the carved capitals, the frieze of grapes and wheat. But there was no notice of keyholders in the porch, and no luck at the various doors I tried with a knock.

In a tree-choked coombe beyond Bury, a blackbird's agitated clatter warned me of something afoot. I peered into the shadows in time to see a lean fox trotting off under the beeches, bouncing athletically from stride to stride as if on springs.

West Burton looked as pretty as a picture with its thatched cottages bedded in their flowery gardens. On the outskirts stood a half-timbered farmhouse framed by a weeping willow, so harmoniously set against a shoulder of cornfield and the green wooded brow of the down that it might have been placed there solely for some landscape painter's delight.

Out in the fields the corn looked overdue for cutting. The stumpy stalks stood knee-high, each head loaded with fifty fat ears. The Roman landowner who farmed these fields would have gasped to see such fruitfulness, such succulent crops in a flowing pale gold sheet entirely free of bugs and diseases – and of wild flowers, too.

When George Tupper's plough became snagged on a large stone on 18 July 1811, Bignor's magnificent Roman villa and farmyard, its hypocaust heating system and bathing chambers, its thousands of household treasures and its splendid mosaic floors had all lain forgotten under the fields for 1500 years. These days the Tupper family open the excavated villa to the public in a pleasantly low-key style.

I wandered through the thatched buildings, absorbed by the beauty and the craftmanship of the mosaics. A graceful Ganymede rose from Mount Ida in the clutch of an eagle; diaphanously draped nymphs cavorted; a black dolphin with red beak and fins plunged through white chalk seas. Winged cupids dressed as gladiators fought under the cool gaze of a large-eyed Venus.

Most striking of all was Winter, a pinched old woman with shrivelled cheeks, cowled in a heavy cloak and clutching a bare branch. Warm air wafting under the villa's floors would have kept the landowner and his family snug enough, but for the peasants beyond the farmyard walls winter on the Sussex downs must have been bitter indeed.

The houses of Bignor were tucked away behind hedges and walls, but the half-timbered Old Shop stood proud at a junction of lanes, its panels rammed solid over five centuries with a higgledy-piggledy selection of bricks, stones, flints and cob. The Church of the Holy Cross proved to be unlocked; inside I found a rough Norman tub font and a simple wooden chancel screen, the medieval village carpenter's chisel and plane marks still clearly seen. Beyond the screen, calm pre-Raphaelite faces glowed from the chancel windows.

A mile of muddy woodland paths, and I was drinking a pint of Rain Dance bitter in the White Horse at Sutton. Not an omen, I hoped, as I climbed through beechwoods behind the village with rain-drops spattering among the leaves overhead. But up on the nape of Farm Hill all was blue and blowy. The dark clouds tramped away east, and full white ones marched in from the west. Sunlight and shadow raced across rape fields flooded with scarlet poppies. Enormous views opened to the north-east, so that I half-fancied I could see all the way into Kent, thirty miles off.

High on the crest of Bignor Hill the white trackway of chalk and flint was crossed by a wide raised embankment, a grassy old road that forged south-west as straight as a die. This was Stane Street, the highway built by the Romans between Londinium and the port of Noviomagus Regnensium – now called Chichester. From his front door the Bignor villa owner could watch the wagons bringing wine and spices up from the coast, and others going down to the ships with Sussex corn and Wealden iron.

My way back to Amberley lay east along the much more ancient trackway of the South Downs Way. But before embarking on those final miles I walked a piece of Stane Street, until at the edge of the escarpment I could look out over the trees and see the spire of Chichester Cathedral, dead ahead in the coastal plain below.

STEPPING OUT – *Walk 21*

MAP: OS 1:25,000 Explorer 121; 1:50,000 Landranger 197

TRAVEL: Rail to Amberley (www.thetrainline.co.uk)

Road: From north – A29. From south – A27/A29 (from
Chichester), A27/A284 (from Brighton). At Whiteways Lodge
roundabout, B2139 for 2 miles to Amberley station and Working
Museum entrance (large car park).

WALK DIRECTIONS: From station entrance (OS ref TQ026118),
left to cross Houghton Bridge. Right along river. In 1¼ miles,
left (017130) past Bury Church, up lane; right at crossroads.
Opposite Black Dog and Duck pub (012134), left past Kesters
House along footpath (beware of ankle-turning holes!). Cross
A29 (010135); dog-leg round left end of flint cottage, and on
(fingerpost) for 1 mile, following yellow arrows and fingerposts
into and out of wooded valley, to road in West Burton
(000140). Right; in 30 yd, left (Roman Villa sign); in 200 yd,
left down tree-tunnel lane. Right at bottom (998138) along field
paths for 1 mile to road at Bignor (986144).

NB *To visit Bignor Roman Villa* – right for 100 yd, then
left up drive to villa. Returning, go right halfway down drive
(986146) on grassy track to Old Shop.

Out of villa's opening hours – left along road, then 1st right to
Old Shop.

From Old Shop (984144) continue up lane to church
(982147). Left down lane by Ivy Cottage. Past Charmans, right
(fingerpost) through gate; boggy path through woods, then
fields for ½ mile to White Horse at Sutton (978152). Up bank to
right of pub (fingerpost), through house garden and field. Left
(975155 – blue arrow) along broad bridleway; cross road (970154
– yellow arrow); up field and into wood (967154 – stile). Steeply
up to meet track. *Cross this track* (fingerpost); continue steeply
up hill on faint path among fallen trees for 300 yd to meet a
sunken track (964152). Right for 300 yd to wood edge and
4-way fingerpost (963152). Go left, following bridleway signs
over Farm Hill for 1 mile to meet sunken bridleway (962140).
Bear right, then immediately left on broad trackway for 1 mile
to cross Stane Street (971129) and meet South Downs Way at
Bignor Hill car park (973129). Follow SDW for 4 miles back to
Amberley station.

LENGTH OF WALK: 12 miles – allow 6 hours.

CONDITIONS: Holes in track just past Bury; boggy mud in woods between Bignor and Sutton.

REFRESHMENTS: Bridge Inn, Houghton Bridge (01798-831619); White Horse, Sutton (01798-869221; *www.whitehorse-sutton. co.uk*); tea rooms at Bignor Roman Villa and Houghton Bridge.

AMBERLEY WORKING MUSEUM: 01798-831370; *www. amberleymuseum.co.uk*

BIGNOR ROMAN VILLA: 01798-869259; *www.bignorromanvilla. co.uk*

Walk 22

Alfriston, Jevington and the South Downs, East Sussex

Smugglers and saints, giants and dragons in the back-country downs

I T WAS ONE OF THOSE CLEAR, cold winter mornings of wall-to-wall blue sky that call you to spend the few hours of daylight somewhere out wide and up high. The red roof tiles and brick pavements, the white paintwork and black flint cobbles of Alfriston's houses glowed in the low sunlight.

I paused to look at the oddball carvings on the beams of the Star Inn, one of several old smugglers' pubs in the village. Alfriston lies in a gap in the East Sussex downs, only four miles upriver of the discreet landing place of Cuckmere Haven, and 18th-century excise men had their work cut out to combat the 'free-traders' of the village and their contraband business. Stanton Collins ran one of England's most notorious smuggling gangs from his headquarters in Alfriston's Market Cross House, and locals still insist that a secret smugglers' tunnel connects the Star Inn to Cuckmere Haven.

I gave the scarlet lion figurehead outside the inn door a pat on the nose for good luck, then turned east across the Cuckmere River and up along downland paths. The beet fields were sticky underfoot after yesterday's downpour, and in the clear rain-washed air the voices of children floated up from Alfriston's school playground, a shrill gabble like wild geese. A wonderful view opened across the village, lying centred round the jester's cap spire of its church, and away over the green whaleback of the downs beyond.

The deeply rutted, flint-studded chalk track of the South Downs Way carried me up the shoulder of Windover Hill. A man was coming downhill with a beautiful slender model aeroplane in his hands. 'A Stork,' he said, beaming with pride. 'Very high specifica-tion, it'll fly even in calm air. I've been gliding thirty years, happy every moment I can be on the downs.' Other happy souls were up on Windover, sailing Star Wars wings of green and blue on the draughts rushing skywards from the dry valley of Ewe Dean.

The view north can't have been less than 40 miles out across the Wealden plain, over distant ridges and woodlands to the pale-line of the North Downs on the edge of sight. The Long Man of Wilmington contemplated it blankly from his steep hillside, clutching his two enormous staves and turning his feet eastwards as if about to cross Kent in a few enormous strides. No-one knows the age of the Long Man, nor who first outlined his 226-ft figure in the chalk of Wilmington Hill. He has certainly changed shape in the three centuries since people began to sketch and make notes about him; gone now is the martial helmet he wore, along with the features of the face that once stared out from beneath it.

In midwinter the Long Man never sees the sun. Shadows lie cold across these northern slopes, where at this time of year the plump scarlet hawthorn berries are beginning to wrinkle and turn brown. Down in Holt woods I found the track smothered with ochre and black leaves of beech and sycamore. Bloated, rain-sodden remains of last autumn's fungi drooped out of rotting boughs. My boots made soft kissing noises in the slippy clay. The woods exhaled a damp breath, rich with the decay that was already nurturing next spring's life in suspension.

St Peter's Church at Folkington stood dappled in sunlight among its trees. In the churchyard I found the grave of Elizabeth David, marked by an elaborately carved black slate headstone. She was one of the pioneer celebrity chefs, enticing the post-war English to spice up their act in the kitchen. Garlic, pepper, aubergine, artichoke, lemon and olives were among the fruits of the earth etched on her memorial stone around a big, homely marmite – symbols of a culinary culture the staid and stodgy Brits would soon learn to embrace.

On the rising track to Jevington, between hedges frothing with old man's beard and tangled with strings of bryony, a ball of naked enthusiasm in the body of a spaniel came hurtling at me. 'Don't jump up! No, don't!' commanded his mistress ineffectually from her seat on horseback, while the spaniel danced on his hind legs and planted both muddy forefeet on my knees. 'Oh, God! Sorr-*eeee!*' I carried his furry paw-prints in pale grey clay on my trousers for the rest of the day.

A chilly wind began to pile clouds into the sky from behind the

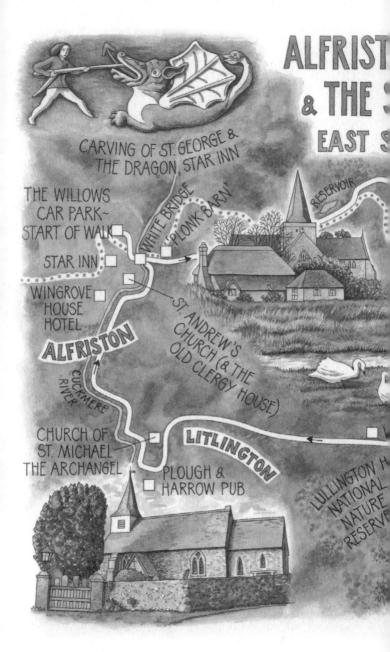

ALFRIST

& THE S

EAST S

CARVING OF ST. GEORGE &
THE DRAGON, STAR INN

THE WILLOWS
CAR PARK~
START OF WALK

WHITE BRIDGE

PLONK BARN

RESERVOIR

STAR INN

WINGROVE
HOUSE
HOTEL

ALFRISTON

ST. ANDREW'S
CHURCH (& THE
OLD CLERGY HOUSE)

CUCKMERE
RIVER

CHURCH OF
ST. MICHAEL
THE ARCHANGEL

LITLINGTON

PLOUGH &
HARROW PUB

LULLINGTON H
NATIONAL
NATURE
RESERV

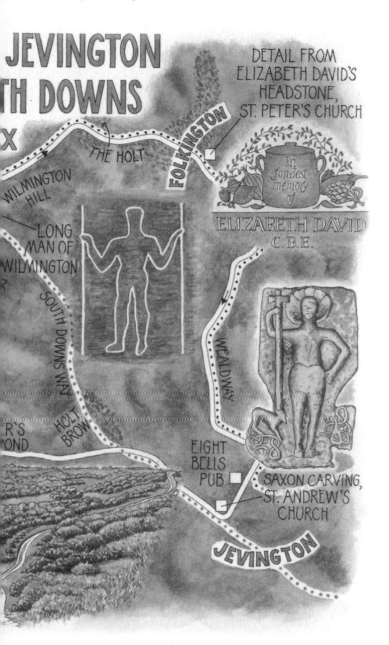

JEVINGTON
TH DOWNS
X

THE HOLT

WILMINGTON
HILL

LONG
MAN OF
WILMINGTON

SOUTH DOWNS WAY

R'S
OND

HOLT
BROW

FOLKINGTON

DETAIL FROM
ELIZABETH DAVID'S
HEADSTONE,
ST. PETER'S CHURCH

In
fondest
memory
of

ELIZABETH DAVID
C.B.E.

WEALDWAY

EIGHT
BELLS
PUB

SAXON CARVING,
ST. ANDREW'S
CHURCH

JEVINGTON

line of the downs. The church of St Andrew in Jevington looked a likely place to sit out the oncoming shower. The men who built the tower of St Andrew's some 1100 years ago made it stout and strong, sturdy enough to resist attack by Viking landing parties. On a south-facing wall inside the church I found the Christ figure that they carved – a conquering hero, lancing to death a loathly beast of evil that more closely resembled a meek little lamb than a ramping dragon. I sat admiring this Dark Ages testament to fear and faith until the rain stopped pattering on the church windows, then went crunching up a flinty track to the roof of the hills where the green sea lay in view in the dips of the downs.

The path switch-backed west across the bushy slopes of Lullington Heath nature reserve – a wide chalk heathland, sombre coloured and seemingly barren at this stage of the year, but in spring and summer bursting with flowering plants, with butterflies and songbirds. Winchester's Pond, an old dewpond where dragonflies would breed in their hundreds in summer, lay dark and lifeless in its collar of decaying bulrushes. I hurried on, disinclined to linger, content to feel the miles crunch by and watch the clouds scud up from the sea.

Down at Litlington the Cuckmere River crept seaward in sluggish coils. I turned north along its muddy flood bank towards the spire of St Andrew's Church at Alfriston. When the 14th-century founders of St Andrew's started building in a nearby meadow, says legend, the stones kept mysteriously shifting overnight to the Tye, the site beside the river where the church now stands. Each morning the builders would return the foundation stones to the meadow they'd chosen; every night God put them back in the place that He'd selected.

Eventually, exasperated by this virtual tug-of-war, God caused four oxen to be discovered on the Tye, lying rump to rump in the form of a cross. Light dawned on the builders at last. They built a cruciform church on the Tye, and it turned out a masterpiece. Moral of the story: don't mess with the Man Upstairs.

STEPPING OUT – *Walk 22*

MAP: OS 1:25,000 Explorer 123; 1:50,000 Landranger 199

TRAVEL: Rail to Eastbourne (*www.thetrainline.co.uk*); then bus
service 126.

Road: A27 east from Brighton; nearing Eastbourne, right on
minor road (signposted) to Alfriston. Park in The Willows car
park.

WALK DIRECTIONS: From The Willows car park (TQ521033),
follow footpath by wall on right of coach park. Cross stile; right
to cross another; right along river bank; left across White Bridge
(522031) to road. Cross road; take footpath on right of house
(named 'Plonk Barn' on Explorer map). In 20 yards up steps;
on up hedged path. In 100 yards, left through hedge (525031 –
South Downs Way/SDW marker post); diagonally right on path
across field; through hedge; across next field to cross stile onto
SDW (532033).

Right to cross road; follow SDW uphill past Windover
Reservoir to go through gate into Access Land (538035). SDW
continues ahead, but turn left along fence over ridge; in 30 yards,
right along track, through gate and on for a mile, passing Long
Man of Wilmington (542034) where you join the Wealdway
path. At The Holt, through gate into wood (551040); right along
track for ½ mile to St Peter's Church, Folkington (559038). Bear
right (as you approach church) along Wealdway for just over a
mile to T-junction of track; left (561021 – 'Wealdway' arrow) to
road; right through Jevington, passing Eight Bells pub (563017).

Continue for 100 yards to left bend; take path on right
of road to St Andrew's Church (562015). On up SDW for ⅔
mile to Holt Brow (553019). SDW turns right here, but keep
ahead for 1¼ miles through Lullington Heath NNR, passing
Winchester's Pond (540020), to fork (533020). 'Lullington
Court' sign points right, but keep ahead ('Litlington'), down to
road (523021). Left past Litlington church. Just before Plough
& Harrow pub, right (523017 – 'Vanguard Way') to Cuckmere
River; right along bank for 1 mile to Alfriston.

LENGTH: 8½ miles

REFRESHMENTS: Eight Bells, Jevington (01323-484442); Plough
& Harrow, Litlington (01323-870632); Litlington tea gardens
(01323-870222 – NB closed winter).

Winchelsea, Fairlight Downs and Hastings, East Sussex

Pre-Raphaelite landscapes of the East Sussex coast

THE SHEEP seemed terribly near the cliff edge. I certainly wouldn't have let them hang around just there, and I don't suppose any self-respecting Sussex shepherd would really have exposed his flock to such danger. But in fact it was William Holman Hunt who'd placed them in a jostling bunch at the lip of the Fairlight cliffs, and painters have to be allowed their artistic licence, don't they?

Not that Holman Hunt or the other young artists who came to paint the coasts of East Sussex in the 1850s wanted to claim such licence for themselves. On the contrary: Hunt, John Everett Millais, Edward Lear and their fellow members and supporters of the Pre-Raphaelite Brotherhood were painting out in the open air to catch what they actually saw, to record one scene at one moment in time as precisely and exactly as they could. Their champion John Ruskin had laid down as gospel that truth depends on facts but simultaneously transcends them – a transcendence I'd always thought had touched the free-and-easy Impressionists rather than the nigglingly precise Pre-Raphaelites, until I had a proper look at their Sussex coast paintings in a magnificent exhibition of Pre-Raphaelite landscapes in Tate Britain.

Once I'd seen the brilliant colours of these pictures brought out by modern lighting, and discovered the realism of their details through a magnifying glass with my nose almost touching the paint, I realised that they weren't at all as chocolate-boxily sentimental as I'd imagined. In Holman Hunt's *Our English Coasts* the late afternoon sun glowed blood-red through the delicate ear membrane of one of those cliff-bound sheep, while a pair of red admiral butterflies on tufty sprigs of hemp agrimony were fixed in perfection between one wing-beat and the next. In *Fairlight Downs* Hunt showed a sea between two curves of cliff, flooded with mirrored light of such dazzling intensity it hurt to look at it; while in *The Blind Girl* the hill town of Winchelsea was depicted by J.E. Millais stunningly lit from the east against a wonderful slate-grey English rainstorm sky slashed across by a blurry double rainbow.

Having tasted by proxy all this richness of colour and light, I just had to go out and sample the real thing. And that particular stretch of easternmost Sussex, I found to my delight, has changed extraordinarily little in the century and a half since Hunt and Millais came down from London to take up lodgings and paint what they found.

There's a rare – in fact, a rarefied – air about Winchelsea, a tiny, perfect early medieval lay-out of gridded streets guarded by three ancient gatehouses. Perched on a crag overlooking the dead flat marshes of Pett Level, the town centres round a fragment of a glorious 14th-century church. In *The Blind Girl* Millais used the eastern aspect of Winchelsea as a backdrop to his figures of the blind girl and her younger sister sheltering from the rain under the older girl's cloak. I found the spot where he sat to paint on the banks of the Royal Military Canal, and was amused to see that the artist had transcended facts to the point of bringing Winchelsea's church forward a couple of hundred yards to get its picturesquely ivied east windows into his composition.

The level marshes, dotted with sheep, stretched away seaward in the low early morning light. Napoleon Bonaparte would have invaded England across these flatlands if he could; the Royal Military Canal that rims the marshes was dug to keep him at bay. I followed the watercourse until it trickled to an unemphatic end near the sea wall, then turned southwest through the aptly named Cliff End to climb the first of the great yellow cliff ramparts of the east Sussex coast.

It was a ferocious storm in 1287 that wrecked the prosperous port of Old Winchelsea, causing the town to be rebuilt further inland on its knoll. Storms, waves and weathers have continued to bite at this coast. Cliff falls are commonplace, the ground tumbling away to the shore or forming ledges that soon become green wooded undercliffs and secret, unstable hanging valleys. In between the cliff peaks lie the glens, deep clefts with a stream apiece that run down to the sea. From Fairlight Cove all the way to Hastings – the stretch where Holman Hunt and his friend Edward Lear made so many painting and sketching expeditions from their farmhouse lodging – cliffs and glens form a secluded run of lonely walking country, all managed nowadays under the title of Hastings Country Park.

This March day was turning out one of muted, steamy light, so the sea gleamed like freshly cut lead rather than the highly polished silver that Hunt recorded in *Fairlight Downs*. But the individual components of his vision seemed unchanged: the lines of wind-stunted trees, the wandering sheep, red grasses and yellow horizons, cloud-shadowed sails out at sea.

Lover's Seat, the old beauty spot from which Hunt painted *Our English Coasts*, has long since toppled into the sea. But from high on the saddle between Warren Glen and Fairlight Glen I could make out the overhung brow of the cliff, the slope of the upper fields bathed in sunlight (the smoky light of March rather than Hunt's buttery autumnal gold), and the skirts of fallen rock slanting away to the sea. There were even sheep in view, though not as suicidally close to the edge as Hunt's had been.

I walked down into Hastings among brightly coloured old houses and the gaunt black net shops where fishermen store their equipment. In the chippie the woman laid my portion of battered plaice on a mound of chips. Then she paused, frowned judicially, repositioned the fish slightly, and gave a little nod of satisfaction. They're all artists in Hastings.

STEPPING OUT – *Walk 23*

MAP: OS 1:25,000 Explorer 124; 1:50,000 Landranger 189, 199

TRAVEL: Rail to Winchelsea (*www.thetrainline.com*). Return from Hastings, trains hourly

Road: M25 (Jct 5), A21 towards Hastings, B2089 towards Rye. 1 mile before Rye, turn right down Dumb Woman's Lane ('Narrow Road' sign) past Winchelsea station to Winchelsea.

WALK DIRECTIONS: From Winchelsea station (OS ref TQ900184), right down Station Road to A259 (903178); uphill into Winchelsea; left at top through Pipewell Gate; first right to church. Coming out of church, right across churchyard to museum; downhill past The Little Shop and through Strand Gate (907174) to bottom of hill. Right along A259 past Strand House and Bridge Inn. At following left bend, bear right ('Winchelsea Beach' sign); in 50 yd, right (909175 – 'Pett Level' fingerpost) along east bank of Royal Military Canal.

Follow canal for 3 miles around Pett Level till it ends at road in Cliff End (889133). Right along road; in 100 yd, by 'Pett Village' sign, left up lane; immediately join footpath on right (yellow arrow) and climb over down for ⅔ mile, descending to Fairlight Cove. At bottom of cliff path bear right round field edge; in 100 yd, left (882124), following white arrow on post and *not* public footpath fingerposts. In 10 yd meet 3-way junction of lanes; follow middle lane (rising, then levelling) between houses. After ⅓ mile pass Broad Way on right; in 250 yd road forks (876118). For The Cove pub, right up slope to road, and right for 100 yd to pub (875120).

To continue walk from fork, left along Smugglers Way to Bramble Way; right to T-junction; left to cliff (875115). Right along Channel Way and on along cliff path into Hastings Country Park. Path immediately forks (870113); follow upper path west for 1 mile to radar scanner (861112); turn inland up lane to Visitor Centre (860116) to collect a Country Park footpath map.

Return to path and continue west for 2½ miles, keeping sea close on your left. Path is marked by numbered wooden bollards – Nos. 13, 11, 10, 8, 4a, 4 and 2 lead you steeply in and out of Warren Glen (857109), Fairlight Glen (852107) and Ecclesbourne Glen (837100). Descend to seafront in Hastings (827095); turn right for ⅓ mile, then right (817093) to railway station (814097)

LENGTH: 11 miles – allow 7 hours

CONDITIONS: Steep steps in and out of coastal glens. Take sunglasses and/or hat with peak against afternoon sun from west.

REFRESHMENTS: New Inn (01797-226252; *www.thenewinnwinchelsea.co.uk*) or Bridge Inn (01797-226453; *www.bridgeinnwinchelsea.co.uk*), Winchelsea; Smuggler Inn, Cliff End (01424-813491; *www.thesmugglerpettlevel.com*); The Cove, Fairlight Cove (01424-812110).

WINCHELSEA COURT HALL MUSEUM: (01797-226382; *www.winchelseacourthallmuseum.co.uk*

HASTINGS COUNTRY PARK VISITOR CENTRE: 01424-451338

VIEWING LOCATIONS: *The Blind Girl* (J.E. Millais, 1854–6) from 909173; *Our English Coasts* (W. Holman Hunt, 1852) from Lovers' Seat, 854108.

Hollingbourne, Thurnham and the North Downs Way, Kent

A work of art, a high old track and a mighty man of willow and leather

A SHARP WIND streamed from a blue winter sky across the break-ing wave of the North Downs. Clouds of steamy breath carried the greetings of early dog-walkers. I watched the light of the rising sun hit the crest of the hills and slowly run a seam of gold down their green slope. It was going to be a beautiful day in north Kent.

Hollingbourne has a nucleus of venerable houses, and wears the air of a place passed over by the outside world. But the village had its moment of tabloid-style fame – four centuries ago, admittedly – through the prodigious appetite of one of its residents. Nicholas Wood was an obsessive trencherman. He once entered a wager to eat at one sitting as much black pudding as would stretch across the River Thames between London and Richmond. But Wood's eating compulsion went far beyond such stunts. It was reported that he would 'devour at one meal what was provided for twenty men, eat a whole hog at a sitting, and at another time thirty dozen of pigeons'. The poor man was suffer-ing from a rampaging eating disorder, probably bulimia. Contempo-rary medical men named it *caninus appetitus*, 'Hound's Hunger'. Wood died a pauper in 1630, having spent all he possessed on food.

In All Saints Church I wandered among grand monuments to the Colepeper family of Hollingbourne Manor. In the north chapel lay the cold white marble effigy of Lady Elizabeth Colepeper, her feet resting on a snub-nosed and snarling animal with a dog's head, leop-ard's spots, a cow's tail and cloven hooves – a 'thoye', one of heraldry's most improbable beasts. On the north chancel wall was a plaque to Sir John Colepeper, a brave Royalist who fought alongside King Charles I at the battles of Naseby and Keinton, and went into exile with the king-in-waiting, Charles II.

While Sir John was in exile his four daughters created the Colepeper Cloth – maybe as an altar cloth, maybe as a pall for a coffin. It took the young women twelve years and cost one of them her eyesight, ruined through so many hours of close work by candle-light. The Cloth is not available for public show, but I had arranged in advance to see this wonderful work, a rectangle of purple velvet six feet long, surrounded by a broad border of Kentish fruits worked in natural coloured dyes and gold thread – acorns, cobnuts, pears and plums, pomegranates with star-like flowers, mulberries and quinces, peaches and grapes. All these were embroidered by the Colepeper girls onto coarse linen, then stitched to the work with gold thread. A border of angels separates the inner rectangle of velvet from the frame of fruit, and another angel border follows the outer edge of the piece. It's a remarkable and moving work of art and of daughterly devotion

I climbed the slope of the North Downs at a good lick, pushing against the cold wind and rubbing water from my eyes to bring the stupendous view into focus. High over Hollingbourne I was master of fifty miles of country, from the great curved rampart of the downs to the thick woods and neat farmlands of the Kentish Weald. The blue line of the South Downs ran wavering along the southern horizon. I turned north-east along the North Downs Way and tramped for four miles in high and heavenly surroundings.

For the drovers, merchants, warriors and others who travelled the North Downs 5,000 years ago it was a matter of life and death to keep the open country in view. Their high trackway ran just below the crest of the downs on the southward side, a course that gave shelter from the weather, a grandstand lookout, and concealment from the eyes of potential enemies.

Medieval penitents used the old road to travel to the shrine of St Thomas à Becket at Canterbury. The ancient trackway sprouted side-shoots, detours down to the villages at the feet of the downs where the pilgrims could expect to find food, fire and a bed for the night. The Pilgrims' Way is a shadowy route these days – in places a clear hill track, in other parts vanished under crops or woodland in the valleys. It intertwines with the North Downs Way National Trail, which keeps to the high ground and is much the better track for walkers.

The sharp slap of the wind against my face pushed me off the ridge in the end, down into the drowsy warmth of the Black Horse at Thurnham. A pie and a pint, and I walked out with cheeks on fire.

The frosty air soon cooled me off, as I went to pay my respects to a famous old Kentish cricketer.

The Mighty Mynn rests under a yew tree in Thurnham churchyard. Alfred Mynn (1807–1861), the 'Lion of Kent', was a 17-stone round-arm fast bowler and ferocious batsman. With the ball he could 'maintain a terrific pace for hours without fatigue'. With the bat he was a whirlwind. In 1836 he made four consecutive scores of 283 – two of these not out.

The Mighty Mynn was a popular figure. Four hundred of his friends subscribed to erect his memorial stone, which praises his 'kindness of heart and generosity of disposition'. Walking back along the valley to Hollingbourne as cold blue shadows crept out from the downs across the wide arable fields, I pictured the kindly giant in action – a proper hero, a man of action with open hands and a heart as big as his body.

STEPPING OUT – *Walk 24*

MAPS: OS 1:25,000 Explorer 148; 1:50,000 Landranger 188
TRAVEL: Rail to Hollingbourne (www.thetrainline.co.uk)
Road – M25, M20 (Jct 8), A20 towards Lenham for ½ mile, left to Hollingbourne.
WALK DIRECTIONS: From Hollingbourne Station (OS ref TQ834551), up station approach; left under railway. In 150 yards, left to All Saints Church (843551). Through lychgate; left along road past Hollingbourne Manor. Ahead over crossroads by Dirty Habit PH; in 50 yards, left (845554 – North Downs Way/'NDW' fingerpost) up steps along field edges to kissing gate. NDW yellow-arrow-with-acorn waymark points uphill to post with yellow arrow (847557). Turn left to follow North Downs Way National Trail for 3½ miles.

Tracks diverge from NDW here and there, so look out for its waymarks. At 836581, cross a lane. In another mile, where NDW descends southward out of trees and around Cat's Mount, watch out for NDW arrow on post on left of track; turn right over stile here (825577). At 818578 cross another lane. In 50 yards ignore FP fingerpost on left, and keep ahead on NDW. At a road (868580) leave NDW and turn left downhill into Thurnham. Pass Black Horse PH (806579); in 300 yards, right along path ('St Mary's Church' fingerpost) to church.

From church return up road. In 150 yards, right (805577 – footpath fingerpost) to pass Thurnham Keep Farm (811574). Follow yellow arrows over stile and ahead to road (815572) at Cobham Manor. Right for 50 yards; just past weather-boarded oast house, left (footpath fingerpost half-smothered in hedge) through gate and across house courtyard; then across 3 stiles in quick succession. Through gate, then up steps in bank, over stile (816572 – yellow arrow) and on along fence. Over stile and down slope Bear slightly left to cross stile; through gate in belt of trees (yellow arrow). Ahead along hedge to cross another stile (820570 – yellow arrow). Ahead across scrubby ground for 20 yards; cross stile; along fenced path to Whitehall; through two wicket gates to road (821570 – bridleway fingerpost).

Turn right through left/right dogleg; in 150 yards, left at 'Riddle Manor' sign (821567 – yellow arrow on post). Up field edge, then left side of wood. At wood end (826563 – yellow arrow) aim diagonally right for lone oak tree, then to left corner of wood beyond (827561 – yellow arrow on post). From this wood corner aim for right corner of short strip of trees, then left to bottom right corner of wood ahead (829560 – yellow arrow on post: toppled at time of writing). From here, diagonally right across field; once over ridge, make for short yellow-topped post seen ahead (831557). Right here along wood edge, then down right side of wood beyond. Keep ahead (831555 – post with yellow arrow) to bottom left corner of field (832552 – yellow arrow). Left over footbridge; up field edge. In 100 yards, right to cross railway. Left along hedge; in 150 yards, left over stile to Hollingbourne Station.

LENGTH OF WALK: 8 miles

REFRESHMENTS: The Dirty Habit PH, Hollingbourne (01622-880800); Black Horse PH, Thurnham (01622-737185; *www. wellieboot.net*)

Walk 25

Ashdown Forest, East Sussex

Woodland, heath, wetland and water – the subtle magic of Ashdown Forest

'FLY AGARIC, YES,' mused Hew Prendergast, contemplating the glossy redcaps with their white spots in the lemon-yellow leaf litter under the birch saplings. 'One of my favourite sights in the Forest at this time of year. The shamen of the Kamchatka peninsula use them for spirit flights, generally by drinking the urine of someone who's ingested one. Useful things – and beautiful. Absolutely deadly, too, of course.'

The Clerk to the Conservators of Ashdown Forest is a man who wears his learning lightly. The Conservators are charged with the duty of looking after the delicate, irreplaceable mosaic of heath, scrub and woodland, of wetland, bogs and streams that lies along the High Weald of Sussex. Staving off the encroachments of developers and bypass builders, mitigating the effects of litter-strewers and fag-end chuckers while at the same time keeping the Forest open and welcoming to all comers is one hell of a job; but Hew brings a cool capability and an understated humour to his coordinating role.

Fallow deer had been feeding on the dewy lawns of Ashdown Park Hotel since dawn. Fifteen of us gathered at the hotel – local walkers and painters, people with a love for the Forest, ramblers who had never ventured to this particular corner of their countryside. Chatting and introducing ourselves, we set off into the kind of autumn morning of blue sky and warm sunshine that you don't even dare to hope for. As we went down the slope under the trees that fringed Broadstone Warren, sunlight came filtering over us through the sweet chestnut and silver birch leaves in brilliant scarlet and acid yellows that a stained-glass maker could only sigh after.

Great beeches gripped the earthen wall of Broadstone Warren's boundary bank. 'Built at the end of the 17th century when land in

Ashdown Forest was starting to be bought up for private ownership and agriculture – privatised, you could say,' Hew told us. 'The bank was put there to mark off what was private land, the wood, from the open common land where we're standing. The whole Forest could easily have been turned into farms and estates. The fact that it wasn't, is really largely thanks to the Board of Conservators. They were set up in 1885 to do exactly that, to conserve what was left and to make sure that the place was run and looked after properly.'

Britain is one of the most poorly wooded countries in Europe, and one of the most urbanised – a state of affairs that has obscured our concept of what a forest actually is. Familiarity with the Forestry Commission's corduroy armies of sombre conifers has conditioned most modern Britons to picture a forest as a dense mass of trees. In fact, said Hew, forests as introduced to this country by the Normans were exclusion zones, enormous stretches of country whose prime purpose was to raise deer for hunting.

The deer needed open land for grazing as much as they needed trees for shelter, so the forests were patchwork places rather than solid belts of trees. Many were set aside for the King and his courtiers to hunt in, and there were fantastically savage penalties of blinding, hand-chopping and death for anyone caught chasing and killing the deer. But in an era where most people were poor, and depended on getting their subsistence-level living from the land, it simply wasn't practical to bar everyone permanently from the forests. So locals became Commoners, with rights of grazing and fuel-gathering – rights they jealously guarded and preserved.

Down at the bottom of the long slope we crossed a couple of starveling brooks, their meagre trickles stained orange with iron leached out of the Forest floor. Then we turned our back on the trees and patches of sphagnum bog to climb an open hillside spread with rusty bracken and ochre-coloured birch scrub. The views opened out over shallow ridges like blue waves, crested with a dark foam of trees – wooded views, the trees dominant in the gently rolling landscape. Yet until halfway through the 20th century this had been a bald forest, a place of bare slopes whose only tree cover was a handful of conifer clumps introduced by landowners to relieve the monotony of the views.

Ashdown Forest is rich in iron, the foundation of a medieval industry that grew to huge prosperity. Time and again the Forest was stripped of trees to make charcoal for the furnaces. Other open parts

ASHDOWN FOREST

EAST SUSSEX

MIRY GHYLL

BEAR UPHILL
AWAY FROM TREES

RED DEER

BROADSTONE
WARREN

ASHDOWN FOREST
CENTRE
(START & FINISH
OF WALK)

BILBERRY

ASHDOWN
PARK HOTEL

SWEET
CHESTNUT

HATCH
INN

BOWLING
GREEN

TURN RIGHT
AT JUNCTION
OF TRACKS

NEWBRIDGE

FURNACE
FARM

STREAM VALLEY

CROSS
STREAM

were grazed back as the Ashdown Commoners exercised their privileges of Pasture and Herbage. 'They made use of various exotically-named rights,' Hew said. 'Brakes and Litter allowed them to collect heather for animal bedding, Estover let them cut trees for firewood and bits of repair work. But all that faded out after the Second World War.'

We were standing in clear sunshine between a rustic cricket pitch and a neat little bowling green, gazing out across dense woodland that to the untrained eye looked as if it might have been growing since Domesday. 'I play cricket here, and one of the other cricketers tells me that as a boy he can remember looking out from this ground and seeing just one clump of trees. All these –' indicating birch clumps thirty feet high, sturdy conifers, sycamores, oaks – 'they've all grown in the past 30 years.'

Now the Board of Conservators has reintroduced grazing to control the encroaching scrub and restore diversity to this ancient and unique landscape. As a direct result songbirds, fallow deer, dragonflies, butterflies, rare plants and many other forms of wildlife thrive here in a way they don't in the surrounding intensively farmed or built-up areas.

Down in the hollow we walked the banks of a beautifully boggy stream valley, trickling with water and full of mosses, lichens and ferns. At the edge of the wood we parted company with Hew. The Clerk to the Conservators was bound for his house in the Forest, while we walkers were already setting course for Ashdown Park, a cup of tea and a plate of sandwiches on the terrace in the last of this unbelievable October sunshine.

STEPPING OUT – *Walk 25*

MAP: OS 1:25,000 Explorer 135; 1:50,000 Landranger 198

TRAVEL: Rail to East Grinstead (5 miles): *www.thetrainline.co.uk*
Road – M25 to Jct 6; A22 through East Grinstead. At Wych
Cross, 2 miles south of Forest Row, left at traffic lights; Ashdown
Forest Centre is 1 mile on left, opposite Ashdown Park Hotel.

WALK DIRECTIONS: From Ashdown Forest Centre car park (OS
ref TQ433323), down slope on left side of open grassy area,
on path under trees on edge of Broadstone Warren, keeping
boundary bank on left. In 200 yards, red waymark triangle
points right; but continue downhill, keeping woodland
boundary bank just on your left all the way. Half a mile from
Forest Centre, join rutted track, cross 2 footbridges, then
(438330) up hillside away from trees. At top of slope (443329),
follow path with trees on right and open slope on left. Ignore
first side path on right (red triangle waymark on left of track);
ignore next 2, and the one after ('Ashdown Forest' horse's head
symbol). Continue for 250 yards to T-junction of tracks; right
(448332) to road (449331).

*For Hatch Inn (452334), left along road for 400 yards. NB
Road can be dangerous because of fast traffic and bends – please
take great care!*

Cross road (please take care); ignore left-hand driveway ('The
Ridge') and take right ('Spinningdale', 'White Platt'). In 250
yards, beside bowling green on right (448329), left off driveway
down firebreak on right side of cricket pitch. Slope down for
500 yards/metres to T-junction (452325) with faint path ahead
and clearer track crossing. Right along track, descending to cross
footbridge over stream (452324). 20 yards up far bank, sharp
right along path on left (south) bank of stream.

Keep stream gully and fence close on right for ⅔ miles (1
km) to meet track (443323); right over stream gully. In 170
yards leave trees; left on wide grassy ride along their outer edge.
In 300 yards cross driveway (440322) onto grass path, curving
right and then left along outskirts of trees. In 250 yards cross
another driveway; ahead along grass path, curving right to
road (437324). Cross (please take care!); left through car park,
along grass ride marked 'Forest Centre', parallel with road, to
Ashdown Forest Centre.

LENGTH: 3½ miles.
CONDITIONS: boggy in valleys – waterproof footwear essential!
REFRESHMENTS: Hatch Inn, Coleman's Hatch; or picnic
ASHDOWN FOREST CENTRE: (01342-823583; *www.ashdownforest. org*): Information Centre (info, displays, shop) open weekends and BH 11–5, weekdays (1 April-30 Sept) 2–5. When Centre closed, maps and leaflets available from office next door (open Mon-Fri, 9–1 and 2–5)

Henley-on-Thames and Hambleden Mill, Oxfordshire/Berkshire border

The 100th Walk of the Month – a Thames-side outing for intrepid readers

THE TV WEATHER CHART on Friday evening did not make pretty viewing. It looked as if some mischievous child had stuck a large black liquorice whirl on the map, just to the west of Ireland. 'The Met Office has issued a severe weather warning,' intoned the weatherman solemnly. 'Saturday is going to be *very* wet, and *very* windy ... persistent, driving rain ... red alerts on several rivers in the south, and the likelihood of extensive flooding ...'

Under my breath – and not only under my breath – I cursed bitterly. The walk I had planned for tomorrow, five miles through the autumnal river country around Henley-on-Thames, was not supposed to be just any old ramble. It would be my 100th Walk of the Month for the Daily Telegraph, and I had issued an open invitation to readers to join me. Two hundred were expected to come along, wearing special identifying badges, to help celebrate the centenary. Fat chance, I thought gloomily, hearing the first heavy raindrops beat against my window.

In the morning, swishing up the M4 through dense sheets of lorry spray, I couldn't imagine one solitary rambler braving such a dirty day. But I had hardly entered Henley when I spied the first '100' badge, adhering to the coat of Penelope Tay from south London. 'Should have brought some waterproof trousers,' she grinned from under her umbrella, and disappeared behind the rain curtain like a cheerful water nymph.

The Thames looked agitated, a coffee brown torrent surging powerfully through the low arches of Henley Bridge. I leaned on the parapet, watching sticks and leaves rushing by below. Henley is a handsome town, crowned by the flint tower of its parish church.

Along the river stand immaculately groomed houses with trim white balconies and close-shaven lawns. Skiffs and dinghies tugged at their moorings, made restless by the energy of the rain-engorged Thames.

On a fine weekend in early July at Henley, the sun sparkles on a flat calm river and reddens the already pink cheeks of blazered and boatered champers-swillers at Henley Royal Regatta. It is not all well-heeled hobsnobbery, though; serious rowing goes on, too. Downstream of the bridge is the red brick club house of Leander, Henley's famous old rowing club, while upstream squats the bulky headquarters of the Regatta itself. All along the river are scattered the spectators' grandstands, skeletal and empty this rainy autumn day, but crammed with onlookers and fluttering with bunting each Henley Week.

Out beyond the town the Thames rushed north, a muddy tide risen to within a couple of feet of the bank's top. Grebes, coots and Canada geese sailed the wavelets. On the towpath, umbrellas bobbed and bowed – more hardy walkers, gleaming with rain and sporting the blue '100' badges.

Ted and Stella Casson had come over from Marlow, Elizabeth Wells from Aldbury, Diana Young from Berkhamsted, Steve and Pam Turner from Farnborough. Brave souls; and braver still were Val and David Cheffy, up from Southampton, and Martin and Jane Longbottom who had endured a nasty couple of hours on their motorway journey from Bristol.

Hadn't they been put off by the weatherman's dire predictions? 'Oh no,' said Jane Longbottom, 'we weren't going to let a little wind and rain spoil our fun. We really *enjoy* walking, you see.'

A mile and a half below Henley Bridge, the Thames divided around tree-covered Temple Island. Birches and poplars hissed, willows and alders swung and shook their leaves around a white-painted Georgian folly at the water's edge. James Wyatt designed the bow front and the dainty little cupola, tacking them bizarrely but to great effect on to a simple cottage to form a 'temple of pleasure' on the islet.

Another umbrella bowling along the towpath; under it, Maureen Silver from Hampstead. 'I almost turned back when I found I couldn't see through the spray on the road,' she told me. 'But I'm so glad I pressed on. It's beautiful here, isn't it? – the island, and all these colours on the trees.'

More Londoners now, ploughing up through the rain – my sister

Louisa, determined walker in any and every weather, and her two walking companions Geraldine and Susan. This was beginning to be a party, albeit a wet and windy one. 'See you in the pub,' was the password.

Below Temple Island the river swung from north to south round a wide bend, passing the neat green lawns of Hambleden Lock. Everyone on the river in Georgian times knew the lock-keeper here, tough old Caleb Gould, who lived to the age of 92 on a diet of fresh air, hard work and a daily dish of onion porridge.

Beyond the lock the swollen Thames went belching in yellow foam through a line of sluices. I lingered on the walkway above the cataracts, mesmerised by the hypnotic sight and sound of water made furious under enormous pressure. By contrast, weatherboarded Hambleden Mill under its turret and weather vane was the picture of rustic calm and quiet.

What is it about centuries-old working buildings, watermills and barns in particular, that lends them that look of blending so perfectly with their surroundings? The outer curve of the Thames here is lined with the riverbank residences of the rich – notably the Italianate wedding-cake pile of Greenlands, built for Victorian stationery magnate W.H.Smith – but none fits in so harmoniously as the old mill by the sluices.

Three counties meet hereabouts – Oxfordshire and Buckinghamshire rubbing shoulders among the beechwood hills of the north bank, Berkshire lying flat in broad green meadows south of the river. I crossed the meadows and came to Aston, last of the gang to make it to the pub. The hallway of the Flower Pot Hotel was hung with damp raingear and piled with soaked boots. From the buzz of conversation in the bar, it sounded as though everyone had got well acquainted.

Steam rose from stockinged feet and drying fleeces. Baked spuds and Brakspear bitter were the order of the day. Talk was loudish, laughter frequent. Stuffed pike gaped down at us from glass cases on the wood-panelled walls. The friendly and unpretentious old Flower Pot is just perfect for this sort of gathering.

David Bounds and Dave Ramm, long known to me as compilers of admirable Berkshire walking guides, had turned up. I discovered I had a surname in common with a family who were drying off in the other bar – Ros and Neil Somerville, out for the day with their children Richard and Emily. 'Great wet walk,' they wrote in smeary pencil in my notebook. My big sister Julia appeared with partner

Jeremy, heroically prepared to outface the elements on the trek between car park and pub door.

Sitting among friends as rain splashed down outside, I thought back to my glum forebodings of a complete washout. Telegraph walkers, praise the Lord, are made of stern stuff. Thank you to every one of the intrepid people who turned out in the teeth of vile weather to make my day – a proper celebration of the first hundred Walks of the Month.

STEPPING OUT – *Walk 26*

MAP: OS 1:25,000 Explorer 171; 1:50,000 Landranger 175

TRAVEL: Rail to Henley (www.thetrainline.co.uk)

Road – M40 Jct 8/9; A404 towards Maidenhead; A4130 to Henley. Park at station or by river south of Henley Bridge (free)

WALK DIRECTIONS: From Henley railway station (OS ref SU764823) walk down Station Road towards river. Bear left into Thames-side, which leads to Henley Bridge (764826). Cross Thames from Oxfordshire into Berkshire. Turn left (green footpath sign), and follow riverside footpath for 2 miles to Hambleden Lock (782851). Cross river and weirs by walkways to view Hambleden Mill (784850); then return to lock. In 200 yd, track on right leads to Aston. Left at road, to Flower Pot Hotel (785842).

From hotel, walk up road. In 200 yd, beyond Highway Cottage, right (784840 – footpath sign) up slope and on along field track for ½ mile to road (773840). Left; in 300 yd, right by big oak (773837 – footpath sign), diagonally across field into Remenham Woods (770835). Through trees to leave wood over stile (768832 – white arrow). Cross hillside; bear left through grove of trees, descending to stile, footpath sign and plaque to dog Minty (768829). Aim diagonally left to stile in field corner, then to next stile. Cross road (766827); continue towards river for 50 yd; left beside Leander Club to reach road by Henley Bridge.

LENGTH OF WALK: 5½ miles – allow 2 hours.

REFRESHMENTS: Flower Pot Hotel, Ferry Lane, Aston, Henley-on-Thames, Oxfordshire RG9 3DG (01491-574721).

Windsor Great Park, Berkshire

From Royal Windsor through the wide spaces of the Royal Family's 'back garden'

S EVEN O'CLOCK on a sullen Bank Holiday morning in the soaking summer of 2002. The weather was set dreich and drizzly over Berkshire. I cared neither a jot nor a tittle, not with 5,000 acres of the best-kept royal parkland in Britain to explore. There was really only one choice for a walk to celebrate the Queen's Golden Jubilee. Ancient woodland, splendid avenues of trees, historic buildings, herds of deer, vast open spaces, more royal associations than you can shake a sceptre at – Windsor Great Park has it all.

The high grey stone walls of Windsor Castle loom over the curving High Street of the town. Windsor Royal, the railway station built especially for Queen Victoria, is a stylish shopping concourse these days. A gleaming vintage Royal Train locomotive stands beautifully polished opposite the ticket office of the more prosaic (and still functional) Windsor Central. Windsor can't get away from its royal connections – not that it would want to. Millions of visitors come to the little town on the Thames each year to see the castle established by King William the Conqueror, and to stroll in the great park laid out by his successors.

Of all the famous features of the park, the Long Walk is the most visually striking. It unrolled before me as I started off from the castle, 2½ miles of dead straight track arrowing off south towards the distant ridge of Snow Hill. Over to the left, peeping through the trees around Frogmore House, was the green roof of the Royal Mausoleum where Queen Victoria and Prince Albert lie buried.

King Charles II laid out the Long Walk to make a grandly impressive link between the castle and the Great Park. Nearly 100 yards wide, the roadway is flanked by a double line of trees, horse chestnuts forming the inner rank, London planes the outer. These days it is joggers, dog walkers and trainer-shod strollers who use the great avenue where monarchs rode to their hunting.

I passed through the ancient barrier of Park Pale and looked around. This early in the morning there was no-one else about. A young red deer stag with velvety antlers lay on the grass twenty feet away. Two jackdaws perched nonchalantly on his back, picking titbits out of the shaggy rain-darkened fur. He rose as I tiptoed past and kept pace with me, glancing warily every now and then in my direction, before trotting quietly off across the park grassland with a graceful springy motion.

Up on Snow Hill I stood in the shadow of the Copper Horse statue and looked back along the Great Walk where one or two walkers and riders were beginning to show. Freckling drizzle and low cloud were rolling in from north of the Thames. Rain dripped off the cheeks and plump jowls of King George III, who stolidly sat a daintily stepping horse twenty feet above my head.

It cost his son King George IV some £29,000 to erect this tribute to the 'Best of Fathers'. The Duke of Wellington authorized the issue of 25 tons of superannuated brass cannons to be melted for use in the making of the Copper Horse (actually bronze). When the statue arrived on site in October 1831, sixteen men celebrated by getting inside it to eat bread-and-cheese and sing 'God Save The King'. As soon as it was put up on its tall stone plinth at the summit of Snow Hill it was as if it had always been there, a piece of skyline drama that formed the perfect full stop for the Long Walk.

A grassy ride led me on, a hedged green thoroughfare that passed pink-faced Royal Lodge and snaked through the rolling farmland of the park. Round spinneys and blocks of woodland were reeling with bird song – blackcaps, chaffinches, warblers, thrushes – as the rain cleared away towards Surrey. Everything looked as neat as ninepence. Many of the people responsible for keeping the royal estate at Windsor in such immaculate fettle live in the Great Park's sole settlement, The Village. I was due to have a chat and a bit of a wander with Village resident Bill Cathcart, the estate's Superintendent of Parks.

'We'll take a walk through Cranbourne,' Bill decided as we sat over mugs of tea in his front room. 'Have a look at some really nice old trees, and tell you what we're trying to do to keep things healthy.'

The eastern area of Cranbourne Chase, on the edge of Windsor Great Park, was added to the park in the 1790s. Cranbourne, remnant of an ancient forest, had always been an object of interest for the castle. Around the time of the Spanish Armada, Queen Elizabeth I's favourite advisor Lord Burghley planted oaks there as part of a nationwide plan to ensure a supply of timber for building the Navy of the future. A few still survive, forest patriarchs more than 400 years old.

The oldest oak that Bill Cathcart showed me was at least twice the age of the Armada trees, a hollow giant of a thousand years' growth standing by the roadside at Forest Gate. Its massive contorted limbs, apparently lifeless, were supported on wooden props. Yet their extremities had put on six inches of new green growth in this Jubilee spring, as they had each year since well before the upstart William of Normandy built his wooden castle by the Thames.

We inspected the oaks planted for the Golden and the Diamond Jubilees of Queen Victoria, and the one planted in 1902 to mark the coronation of Victoria's son Edward VII. Beyond stood more gnarly ancient trees, each one a high-rise dwelling for a complex community of beetles, spiders, birds, fungi and lichens. 'We must have several hundred trees that are up to 400 years old,' Bill said, running his fingers over the deeply trenched bark of another thick-bodied monster. 'Fungi break down the rotten heartwood, eventually, and they make this fantastic store of rich food that helps shoots from the old tree to develop into the next generation. It's like this little miracle that keeps repeating itself.'

It is a delicate balancing act, maintaining the old while encouraging the new. In Cranbourne Park, in the shadow of the medieval royal hunting lodge of Cranbourne Tower, they were clearing away some scrubby, recently-developed woodland to create open glades for the benefit of flowers and butterflies. Along Queen Anne's Ride, where I said goodbye to Bill Cathcart and struck off north towards Windsor Castle, splendid ancient oaks had been felled because they were too decrepit, unsightly and dangerous. But new trees were already unfurling their canopies along the avenue. It's a cycle, endlessly renewed, endlessly repetitive: something our British monarchy knows all about.

STEPPING OUT – *Walk 27*

MAP: OS 1:25,000 Explorer 160; 1:50,000 Landranger 176, 175

TRAVEL: Train to Windsor Riverside or Central (*www.thetrainline. co.uk*)

Road – M4 to Jct 6; A332; follow 'Castle; Town Centre' signs. Park in Romney Lock Road car park beyond Riverside Station.

WALK DIRECTIONS: Leaving Windsor Riverside station (OS ref SU969773), turn right; in 30 yards, left up High Street, following castle walls. Where High Street bends right and becomes Sheet Street, keep ahead along Park Street and through gates (970766) into Windsor Great Park. Turn right along Long Walk for 2½ miles to reach Copper Horse Statue (967727) on Snow Hill.

Continue down far side of Snow Hill, through deer gate; on along grassy ride between hedges, past Ox Pond on right (965719). In another 200 yards, right along tarmac road (967717) to The Village. Pass the green and the post office (954724). In 100 yards, right at T-junction; in 250 yards, left (952727 – 'Cranbourne Gate: No Through Road' sign) to reach A332 at Cranbourne Gate (947727).

(NB To see 1,000-year-old oak, turn left along verge of A332 for 350 yards to find tree near Forest Gate lodge.)

From Cranbourne Gate, cross A332 and continue along tarmac road to Cranbourne Tower (943731). Return to a point halfway between tower and A332; left on sandy track through woods ('Horse Riders – Do Not Deviate From Track' notice). At north edge of wood reach tarmac road (950737 – Flemish Farm's white gates on your left); turn right here to recross A332 at Ranger's Lodge pedestrian traffic lights (954734). Go through gate; immediately take gravel path that climbs from tarmac track into trees, to reach Queen Ann's Ride (959730). Left along ride for 1⅓ miles to meet A332 at Queen Anne's Gate (965750). Right through chain-link stile by gate ('Cycles Prohibited' notice); along grass path to lodge at gates on Long Walk (969747); left to castle and station.

LENGTH OF WALK: 10 miles

REFRESHMENTS: Royal Oak PH by Riverside station (01753-865179; *www.windsorpubco.co.uk*)

INFORMATION: *www.royalresidences.com*

EAST

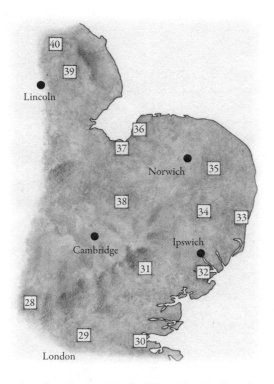

Aldbury, Ashridge and Ivinghoe Beacon, Hertfordshire-Buckinghamshire border

Dawn chorus: time to dawdle in the Chiltern beechwoods

AN ORANGE CRESCENT OF MOON hung low over the Chiltern escarpment, and down in silent Aldbury not a light showed. I was lacing my boots in the village square outside the Greyhound Inn when the church clock struck four. That seemed to be the sign that the blackbirds had been waiting for, as first one solo singer and then an impressive chorus burst sweetly into song in the village gardens.

Up in the beechwoods on the Ashridge slopes above Aldbury, a softly fluting thrush was chief herald of a dawn that had hardly broken yet. I had yawned my way out of bed at two o'clock to enjoy this moment, so often read about, so seldom experienced, when the first birds crack the silence of night before traffic roar intrudes to spoil things.

The Chiltern Hills, less than an hour away from London, are a favourite target for city escapers. And the Ashridge Estate – 4,000 acres of National Trust woodland thickly tangled with footpaths – is a mecca for walkers in its own right. To have the whole ridge entirely to myself, to be able to walk the chalk tracks through the trees without seeing another soul, was a pleasure so intoxicating that I found myself striding along through the half light more like a race walker than a man with time to dawdle and linger.

I turned off the path and sat down on a fallen tree to luxuriate in this unaccustomed sense of time in hand. Light was beginning to touch the beech trunks and leaves, and there was a pearly pink look to the sky in the east. Drifts of mist curled between the trees, and the air in the woods was cold enough to nip my fingers white.

In the treetops the dawn chorus was in full swing. Blackbirds, thrushes, chaffinches; a chiff-chaff repeating its name over and over again; a blackcap bubble-and-squeaking; wrens reeling out chattering streams of notes. From overhead came the *chak-chak* of rooks passing, and under everything lay a soft foundation of wood pigeons' throaty cooing. A glorious din; it had me spellbound for half an hour as the daylight slowly broadened.

Getting up stiffly at last, I went on up the hollow trackway with chips of flint clinking like glass fragmented under my boots. In a grassy clearing a tall stone column rose into the mist. The inscription carved into the plinth – 'In honour of Francis, Third Duke of Bridgewater, Father of Inland Navigation' – told only half the story.

The Duke was indeed a pioneer of canal building in 18th-century Britain. He left enough money from his transport and coal-mining interests to enable his heirs to build the splendid Gothic mansion of Ashridge House in the valley below the escarpment. But the peppery aristocrat would have achieved little without his right-hand-man James Brindley, a rough-and-ready engineering genius. Brindley never learned to read and write properly, but he had vision and energy to burn.

The spiral staircase ascending the monument would not be open until the afternoon, but I could remember from a previous visit the stunning view unleashed at the top: twenty miles of woodland, chalk ridge and plain. As I walked on northwards the mist began to thin as the yet unseen sun's rays penetrated the trees. Tantalising glimpses opened up through the foliage – woods saddling the backs of rolling downs, a red-roofed farmhouse tucked into a valley between a buttercup pasture and a beet field.

Somewhere among the trees ahead a tremendous bark sounded, a single grating roar repeated at regular intervals. It sounded like the mother of all Dobermans loose in the woods, and my heart was briefly in my mouth. Then a scuffling broke out in a sunken hollow, and out trotted a stocky, dark-coated muntjac deer no bigger than a sheep. He roared again, fixing me sternly with a sideways glare, then moved on deeper into the wood, chin up, the picture of dignity affronted.

The upper rim of the sun was glinting on the eastern hills as I came out of the trees and joined the wide rutted track of the Ridgeway. The ancient trackway had come ninety miles from its starting place above the great stone circle at Avebury in Wiltshire, and now brought me easily up to its culminating point, the 755-ft brow of Ivinghoe Beacon. Here the Ridgeway takes on a new name, Icknield Way, and forges on in characteristic fashion along the chalk and clay ridges for another 100 miles into East Anglia.

At this high meeting place I sat down, but not in contemplation of the eye-goggling view that should have been on offer. The sun, now a giant ball floating free of the horizon, had not yet angled down into the great plain where Buckinghamshire, Bedfordshire and Hertford-shire join hands. The beacon and its attendant green shoulders of downland were islanded in a rolling, gently swirling white sea of mist.

It was a good enough spot to read Edward Thomas, anyway. I pulled a travel-stained copy of the poet's travelogue *The Icknield Way* out of my rucksack and looked to see what it had to say about the place. Thomas had come exploring the ancient trackway in the spring and early summer of 1911, three years before his friend the American poet Robert Frost suggested that he should try his hand at verses.

In 1911 Thomas had been a hack writer with a young family to support, churning out travel books and biographies for soon-spent £50 advances. He was not capable of writing a bad or trite book, but he had not yet developed into the composer of transcendent poetry he soon became. He had arrived in this region 'stumping along on a shoeful of blisters', having just walked 80 miles in three days.

It was a murky early summer's morning when the footsore Thomas came by on 'a hot day slowly and certainly preparing in mist and silence... I saw Ivinghoe Church tower and the silly spire, short and sharp, on top of it, the misty woods behind, the Pitstone Church tower and an elm throned on a rise together, and the broad wooded valley beyond. Larks sang...'

Yawning prodigiously, I trudged southwards along the Ridgeway towards breakfast at the Greyhound in Aldbury. Church towers, silly spires and wooded valleys lay blanketed out of sight. But the larks still sang loudly over the misty cornfields, as they had done for Edward Thomas.

MAP: OS 1:25,000 Explorer 181; 1:50,000 Landranger 165

TRAVEL: Rail to Tring (www.thetrainline.com)

Road – M25 to Jct 20; A41 to Tring.

WALK DIRECTIONS: From Tring railway station (OS ref SP951122), right along road. In 150 yd pass left turning ('Pitstone; Ivinghoe'); another 100 yd, left up Westland Farm drive (953124 – Ridgeway sign). Keep ahead on left bend to cross stile. Keep ahead (Ridgeway leads off to left), following blue bridleway arrows, for ¼ mile. Right over stile (958127 – footpath fingerpost), aiming for Aldbury church tower. Beside Church Farm barn, left over stile (962125) and left of big ash tree to cross stile into school playing field. Stile in bottom right hand corner leads to Greyhound Inn at Aldbury (965125).

From Greyhound, left up road; in 150 yd, right opposite Applegarth up gravelled track (bridleway sign) into trees. Blue arrow points right; climb to turn left on sunken trackway (969125). Continue to Bridgewater Monument (970131). Just past monument, path forks; ignore No Through Road to left and keep ahead on a clear track for 2 miles to cattle grid and gate marked 'Ivinghoe Hills Nature Reserve' (962154). Bear left here on bridleway for ¼ mile to turn right along Ridgeway Path (961157). In ¼ mile keep straight ahead (following bridleway sign) where track swings right. Cross road (960163); continue to Ivinghoe Beacon (960168).

Return along well waymarked Ridgeway (acorn symbols) through woods on Pitstone Hill. Near south end of hill descend a few wooden steps, cross open area with portions fenced off, turn right down flight of steps, pass fingerpost at bottom. In 15 yd (951131) Ridgeway is signed to right. To return to Tring, follow Ridgeway here.

To return to Aldbury, turn left (footpath fingerpost) to cross golf course. Cross bridleway on far side (958127) and continue into Aldbury.

LENGTH OF WALK: 8 miles – allow 4 hours.

CONDITIONS: Chalk tracks; can be slippery and sticky after rain.

REFRESHMENTS: Greyhound Inn (01442-851228; *www. greyhoundaldbury.co.uk*) or Valiant Trooper, Aldbury (01442-851203; *www.valianttrooper.co.uk*)

READING: *The Icknield Way* by Edward Thomas (out of print)

BRIDGEWATER MONUMENT: Open at weekends

Millennium Walk of the Month
through London

Along the Thames from the London Eye to the Millennium Dome

THIS COLD MORNING on the cusp of the third millennium,
London was drifting in the soft focus of a wintry haze roofing
the city. One south bank shape rose up stark and sharp: the immense
spoked bicycle wheel of the London Eye, just installed to overhang
the River Thames in front of County Hall. How the scoffers mocked
when the Eye became stuck at a half-way angle during its erection.
Now it stood 450 ft tall, ready to unfurl a 50-mile view across London
and a good slice of the Home Counties.

The river itself, and its river life, seemed hardly changed in the
ten years since I had last walked it. Cruise boats slid up and down.
A rusty barge with 'Dordrecht' painted amidships lay moored to a
slimy landing stage. Plastic cups and mats of sodden twigs heaved
under the bridges. Black-headed gulls with scarlet beaks and legs
hopped up and down the tide-line, choosing the right instant to grab
scraps from the momentarily uncovered pebbles of the shore.

Passing the shallow scarlet and white arches of Blackfriars Bridge,
into the south bank district of Bankside, I got out my binoculars
and saw that the bridge's buttress piers rested on the shoulders of art
nouveau pelicans. The great dome of St Paul's Cathedral rose across the
river, gilded with weak winter sunlight: the glasses showed me minuscule figures lining the parapet of the Golden Gallery 350 ft in the air.

Tradition says that Sir Christopher Wren lodged on Bankside
while he was supervising the building of St Paul's in the 1670s and
80s. If so, Wren chose quite a spicy area to base himself, since Bankside then was London's most celebrated red-light district, a hive of
bear and bull baiting pits, cheap taverns, gambling hells and theatres.

Wild days on Bankside … William Shakespeare knew them when

he was tossing out plays for the Globe Theatre that he co-owned here. Now the "wooden O" stood again, beautifully rebuilt in timber and thatch for a modern pit crowd to catch the magic of open-air performance. The old power station itself, a vast hanger of sullen brick that had stood empty for years, was due to re-open in the spring of 2000, gloriously refurbished, as the modern art offshoot of the Tate Gallery. Visitors would be able to reach Tate Modern and Bankside on foot from St Paul's in ten minutes, crossing the river by way of the slender silver bow of the Millennium Bridge. So the rackety old warren of the south bank was transforming itself.

Great changes, too, along the north bank of the river. I crossed beneath the high aerial walkway of Tower Bridge, and turned down steps past David Wynne's strikingly beautiful sculpture of a naked girl and a dolphin ecstatically cavorting. From here on eastward the Thames's north bank is chopped and squared into dock basins, the work of two centuries as commercial interests tried to solve the problems of ships loading and unloading on a narrow tidal river.

In ten years St Katherine's Dock near Tower Bridge, Shadwell Basin, Limehouse Basin had been transformed. Refurbished wharf warehouses lined the river: Millers Wharf, Hermitage Wharf, Gun Wharf, Pelican Wharf. I walked through their shadowy canyons down the long snaking thoroughfare of Wapping High Street, cut by a cold east wind snapping in off the river.

Time for a pie, a pint and a warm-up. I chose the dark little Town of Ramsgate pub, squeezed tight between warehouses at the corner of Wapping Old Stairs, and found myself in a most historic spot. Bloody Judge Jeffreys was cornered here by a furious crowd in 1688 while in process of escaping to the continent, rigged out as a collier crewman. 'The dress was that of a common sailor from Newcastle,' runs a contemporary account, 'and was black with coal-dust; but there was no mistaking the savage eye and mouth of Jeffreys.' The hanging judge was rescued from the lynch mob and driven off in a coach to the Tower.

The Wapping mob lined this same waterfront thirteen years later to see the famous pirate Captain Kidd swing for his crimes at Execution Dock. The doomed brigand, taking a last look around from the gallows, felt hurt when he spotted a hard-hearted girlfriend eagerly awaiting the spectacle among the crowd. 'I have lain with that bitch three times,' he was heard to growl, 'and now she has come to see me hanged!'

Change has come most traumatically, of course, to the Isle of Dogs peninsula a couple of miles downriver. The transformation of the old West India Docks, the terraced dockers' houses of Millwall, the abandoned ropewalks and ship repairers into the towering plutopolis of tinted glass and girder features that is the Docklands development takes away the breath of all but the most blasé of river walkers.

The pyramid-headed tower of Canary Wharf reared monstrously high over all as I followed the Thames Path between the gritty highway of West Ferry Road and short stretches of Waterfront. Here beside Burrells Wharf I found the site where Isambard Kingdom Brunel broke his heart trying to launch his third and greatest steamship, the vast 680 ft *Great Eastern*, in 1856–7. The hydraulic presses used to inch the leviathan sideways down her ramp into the river were not up to the job, the press were cockahoop at the prospect of the great engineer coming unstuck, and Brunel's financial partner dropped him in the mire. The tension and overwork broke Brunel's health, and killed him shortly afterwards.

I followed the road down to Island Gardens at the toe of the peninsula, and paused on the river wall to gaze across the Thames. The hull of the famous old tea and wool clipper *Cutty Sark* was a dark shape blending with others, but her raked masts and yards stood printed blackly on a silky green evening sky. Further east, the pale stone bulk of the Royal Naval College (designed as a grand palace for King Charles II, and completed as a splendid hospital for sailors) opened its two arms to the river, backed by the tree-dotted hump of Greenwich Park. A vee of barnacle geese came honking upriver, and turned inland over my head with a sawing of wings.

Through the echoing white-tiled Greenwich Foot Tunnel, out by *Cutty Sark*, and left along the river promenade past the RNC. On now into the dusk, on a walkway that curved and jutted past wharf walls, junkyards, barge moorings and slimy tidal beaches, under pipework, gantries and cranes – a mile of the Thames in the guise of a still-working river, of industrial smells, loud clampings and blue oxy-acetylene sparkings. Take away the technology and here at last was the dark old working Thames of Sherlock Holmes and Oliver Twist, of Bill Sikes and Jack The Ripper. Walking now in pitch dark, I caught myself looking over my shoulder and trying to lighten each footfall.

Out to the roar and crash of lorries thundering into the Blackwall Tunnel. A final stretch of dusty half-made road, and ahead beside the river rose the futuristic porcupine shape of the dimly lit Millennium Dome, the tips of its roof spine glowing red like phosphorescent matches. 'Can't go in there,' said the gate guard. 'Not yet, mate. They say it's fantastic though. Have to wait till New Year's Day, won't we...?'

STEPPING OUT – *Walk 29*

MAPS: 1:25,000 Explorer 173, 162. *The Thames Path National Trail Guide* by David Sharp (Aurum Press) contains excellent maps at 1:16,000

TRAVEL: Start Westminster tube station (District, Circle, Jubilee). Finish at North Greenwich (Dome) tube station (Jubilee line); or return from Dome's Millennium Pier to Waterloo Bridge by City Cruises boat (45 min – *www.citycruises.com*)

WALK DIRECTIONS: From Westminster tube station cross Westminster Bridge; turn left (east) along south bank of Thames for 2 miles ('Thames Path' signs) to reach and cross Tower Bridge. Turn right (east) along north bank for 4 miles ('Thames Path' signs) past St Katharine Dock, Wapping High Street, Prospect of Whitby PH, Shadwell Basin, The Highway, Narrow Street and down shore of the Isle of Dogs.

By Island Gardens DLR station, turn right through Greenwich Foot Tunnel (always open) to Greenwich on south bank. By *Cutty Sark*, left (east) along south bank for 1½ mile ('Thames Path' signs) past Royal Naval College and on to Millennium Dome and North Greenwich tube station.

LENGTH OF WALK: 11 miles – allow 5 hours (a whole day if you want to visit attractions, galleries, museums etc).

REFRESHMENTS: Many and various. Characterful pubs include The Anchor, Bankside; Town of Ramsgate, Wapping High Street; Prospect of Whitby, Wapping Wall; Trafalgar Tavern, Greenwich riverside.

Canvey Island, Essex

Round the sea walls of Canvey in the footsteps of Dr. Feelgood

'GOING FOR A WALK, mate?' enquired the whey-faced man with the mobile phone, eyeing my boots and backpack as the 8 o'clock train drew into Benfleet station. 'Yes,' I said, 'round Canvey Island.' The commuter blinked incredulously, as if I'd mentioned a walk round the mountains of the moon. '*Canvey Island*? What do you want to do that for?' and he shook his head in genuine amazement.

Most travellers, commuters or otherwise, rush along the road and railway corridors of the Thames Estuary's Essex shore with never a glance out of the window. If they do spare a glance towards Canvey Island, it is only to have their prejudices confirmed: housing estates, storage silos, oil refineries, pylons marching across a flat tableland. The fact that the refineries and the pylons are not on Canvey at all, and that much of the island is a peaceful green birdwatcher's paradise, is known only to those who strike out on foot along the 14 miles of uninterrupted seawall footpath that encircles Canvey.

But Canvey Island has another dimension, too, an iconic significance, to head-over-heels Dr Feelgood fans across the world. When 'the best local band in the world' came roaring out of Canvey and into the charts in the 1970s with their spiky R&B music, they boasted a masterful songwriter in Wilko Johnson. The guitarist's short, sharp cameos presented his native island as 'Oil City', a mean place in a moody landscape where hard men and dangerous women drank, did shady deals and cheated on one another against the fume-laden, fiery backdrop of the Canvey Delta.

Dr Feelgood singer Lee Brilleaux growled out Johnson's mini-epics like a man possessed. Backing them up on bass and drums were Sparko and The Big Figure – wonderful names, and a grittily romantic image irresistible to a nice well-brought-up boy from rural Gloucestershire like me.

A lot of water has flowed under the jetty since those days. Brilleaux died of cancer in 1994, and other band members have come and gone. The two members of the Feelgood camp waiting for me at the station today, band manager Chris Fenwick and bass player turned record producer Dave Bronze, looked unlikely candidates for rock animal status in their sensible walking boots and warm fleeces. It had been a long time since either had prowled the sea walls of Canvey, and they were looking forward to getting a lungful of fresh estuary air.

We set out along the embankment of the old sea wall, with the grumble of the A130 slowly fading behind us. This western end of the island is all freshwater marshes, wide green flatlands where semi-wild palomino horses graze. Walking here, you get a good idea of what Canvey must have looked like a hundred years ago, before day trippers from the East End of London began to build themselves little dream homes beside the estuary.

'Skylarks,' murmured Dave, halting on the wall to listen. 'The sound of childhood summers to me.' The larks were singing their heads off this morning, rising and falling in the cool air over the marshes. Down on East Haven Creek the tide had drained out to low ebb, exposing shelves of gleaming mud where curlew and black-headed gulls were delicately stepping. The rural tranquillity of the low-lying scene seemed somehow enhanced by the giant geometry that loomed beyond the creek – angular chimneys and cylinders, storage silos and burning flare towers of the Shell Haven oil refinery.

From the Canvey shore the black spiderwork of an oil jetty ran far out into the Thames like a nightmarish seaside pier. '"Down By The Jetty" – remember Wilko's song?' said Chris Fenwick. 'This was his inspiration. They built the jetty to bring crude oil ashore to a huge refinery they were planning on these marshes. Thank God it never happened.'

The Lobster Smack existed as a hostelry on this south-west corner of Canvey long before refineries, jetties or the modern sea wall were built. In the 1860s Charles Dickens knew the old smugglers' pub as the loneliest inn on the Thames marshes, and sent Pip and the fugitive Magwitch in *Great Expectations* to hide out here while waiting for the continental steamer. We were too early this morning for a pint, but a cup of coffee and a bit of a sit-down put us in fettle for the next section of the sea wall.

Ranks of caravans in the shadow of aviation fuel silos; more caravans in drifts around the improbably yellow sands of Thorney Bay.
'We'd swim here as kids,' said Chris, 'when the Thames was far dirtier
than it is now.' Then the Monico nitespot, and Parkin's seafront
amusements. We walked on above the greasy Thames towards the
eastern point of the island. 'Canvey Island' was lettered along the
balcony of the cylindrical art deco Labworth Café on the river wall,
a siren lure for Thames trippers of forty years ago.

Canvey was always popular with East Enders, always a place with
its own strong flavour. Len the Hat, Lucky and Handbag Al, Ron the
Kite and Dennis the Dog; bar-room names for local characters in
the Feelgood yarns spun by Dave and Chris as we sauntered along.
'See that little Club Astairs on top of Parkin's Palace? That used to
be Cloud Nine where we started out in the early 70s, playing to a
hundred people for the door money and a few pints. But Dr Feelgood really fired up when we got on the London pub rock scene.
Then – whoosh! It took off like a rocket.'

The Feelgood image was electrifying back in those days, when
rock music had gone all self-indulgent and flabby. 'Shorter-than-
average hair,' notes Will Birch, then drummer with another gang of
local heroes The Kursaal Flyers, in his history of pub rock *No Sleep
Till Canvey Island*, 'the street clothes of an out-of-work bank clerk,
and most importantly, a menacing on-stage presence.' The tough boys
from Canvey rose like an uppercut into the soft underbelly of the
music business, which reeled and fell into the unforgiving arms of
punk. So Dr Feelgood saved the world.

A curry-and-baked-spud snack in the Windjammer pub, and then
on past the flounder fishermen on Canvey Point and round the wall
to the northern shore of the island. The tide was on the make now,
sliding up Smallgains Creek and setting the mud-bound boats of the
Island Yacht Club bobbing. Oystercatchers flew up from the flooding channels. Long tufts of saltmarsh on the mud flats of Hadleigh
Bay separated and became islets as the water crept between them.

The gradual rise of the tide looked gentle today. But the height
and sturdy construction of the sea wall bore witness to the banked-up
power of the North Sea. On the night of 31 January 1953 a north-
east gale and a high tide sent devastating floods sweeping across the
east coast of England. Canvey Island, lying below sea level behind its
inadequate walls, was the worst-hit place. When the sea broke in it
filled the island and drowned 58 people.

The sea wall was strengthened and raised after the disaster. Canvey Islanders built 'upside-down houses', whose top-floor sitting rooms allowed a view over the new wall across the marshes and creeks. Chris Fenwick and Lee Brilleaux lived near each other in upside-down houses, long before Dr Feelgood was a twinkle in rock music's bleary eye.

'Long Horse Island,' said Chris, pointing out across the saltmarsh. 'Lee and I would row over to our camp out there and be pirates for the day. That complete freedom, a pair of kids running wild – it was a wonderful start in life. Kept us sane, more or less, through all the rock'n'roll madness.'

STEPPING OUT – *Walk 30*

MAP: OS 1:25,000 Explorer 175; 1:50,000 Landranger 178

TRAVEL: Rail to Benfleet (www.thetrainline.com)

    Road – M25 to Jct 29; A127 east (Southend-on-Sea direction) for 13 miles; A130 south onto Canvey Island; at first roundabout, left to Benfleet station (¾ mile).

WALK DIRECTIONS: From Benfleet station (OS ref TQ777859), bear left along pavement. Cross bridge onto Canvey Island; in 200 yd, right onto sea wall path (779853 – footpath fingerpost). Then just keep going, anticlockwise round the island on the sea wall footpath.

LENGTH OF WALK: 14 miles – allow 6–7 hours.

CONDITIONS: Easy underfoot all the way. Waterproof footwear recommended.

REFRESHMENTS: Lobster Smack (01268-660021), Windjammer (01268-695389), Labworth Café (01268-683209).

DR FEELGOOD: All details of recordings, gigs, band history etc. on *www.drfeelgood.org*; ditto for Wilko Johnson news and activity Will Birch's definitive history of pub rock is *No Sleep Till Canvey Island* (Virgin paperback).

Walk 31

Bulmer and Belchamp Walter, Essex

Wall paintings, cornfields, bricks and tiles: a stroll through North Essex

THE SNUB-NOSED GREEN MAN stared out from the bowl of the font in Bulmer Church as if he were the presiding genius of the place. Vine stems thick with leaves and grapes came bursting from the corners of his mouth and eyes. I could make a guess at what the medieval mason might have been thinking when he carved such a pagan-looking figure for a village church sunk deep in the fields and woods of north Essex. The bunch of freshly picked hedgerow flowers that someone had already laid before the Green Man this summer morning seemed to say that this fruitful old greenwood spirit had not lost his power to enchant.

Anyone who thinks that Essex is all flashy shopping malls and London satellite towns should take a deep breath and dive into the rolling farming landscapes where the much-maligned county borders its northerly neighbour, Suffolk. And walkers under the impression that every Essex footpath ends with a chain-link fence and a snarling pit-bull ought to do themselves a favour and set off, as I did early in the day, through the cornfields that dip gently into the valley of the Belchamp Brook.

Larks poured out song like silver made audible as they ascended their invisible flights of steps into the cloudy sky. Ripe cornfields laid a cloth of gold to horizons dominated not by skyscrapers or industrial chimneys, but by church towers and solitary oaks. I crossed Belchamp Brook and made for the tower and steeply gabled roof of St Mary's at Belchamp Walter, rising from a frothy green surf of trees.

North Essex holds some of East Anglia's finest parish churches, and St Mary's with its flint cobble walls and the chequerboard flushwork that tops and tails its tower is a good example of what rich medieval woolmasters did with their money to ensure themselves a

ST. MARY'S
CHURCH

BELCHAMP
WALTER

VILLAGE
POND

BELCHAMP WALTER
HALL

BELCHAMP BROOK

HILL
FARM

WOODLAN

BULMER &
BELCHAMP WALTER
NORTH ESSEX

BULMER B
TILE C
BRICKWO

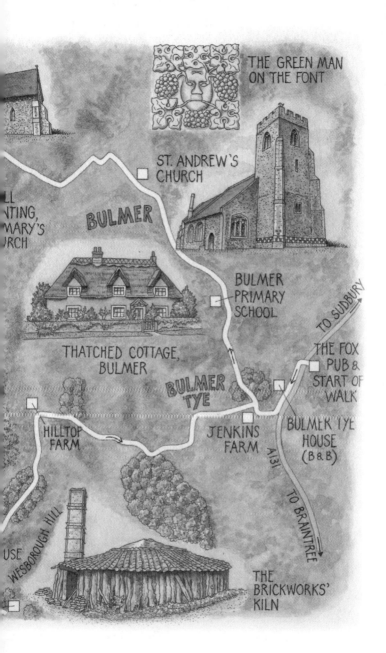

THE GREEN MAN ON THE FONT

ST. ANDREW'S CHURCH

BULMER

LL NTING, ARY'S RCH

BULMER PRIMARY SCHOOL

THATCHED COTTAGE, BULMER

TO SUDBURY

THE FOX PUB & START OF WALK

BULMER TYE

JENKINS FARM

BULMER TYE HOUSE (B&B)

HILLTOP FARM

A131

TO BRAINTREE

USE WESBOROUGH HILL

THE BRICKWORKS' KILN

snug berth in the next world and plenty of kudos in this. With the church notes in hand I was able to decipher a weather-eroded memorial tablet full of black rural humour:

> *'Snug by this wall lies old Sam Cook*
> *Who with his Spade, his Bell and Book*
> *Serv'd Sexton Three Score Years and Three,*
> *Until his Master grim Death cry'd*
> *Enough – your Tools now lay aside*
> *And let a brother bury Thee.*
> *Died 6 May 1800*
> *Aged 89 Years.'*

Inside St Mary's there are some remarkable 14th-century wall paintings. In one the Virgin Mary is depicted as a beautiful, modest young woman with curly hair flowing down like a stream. The artist shows her in the act of suckling Jesus, a moment of vulnerability and intimacy in which the onlooker is subtly invited to share. Other murals show a lively Last Supper crowded with animated figures, a shadowy Entry into Jerusalem, and a martyr – probably St Edmund, a local hero saint – being shot to death by hooded archers deploying an arsenal of fearsomely tipped arrows.

From these scenes of medieval imaginings both savage and tender I stepped into the tree-shaded lanes of Belchamp Walter. The hedges were thick with cow parsley. Horse chestnuts and weeping willows overhung ponds and neatly trimmed lawns. As I passed a cottage garden I got a cheery wave from a pneumatic lady as she bounced on a trampoline to the beat of 'Blame It On The Boogie'.

'Well,' remarked the elderly woman I chatted to as I petted her golden retriever, 'Essex is a county that's wonderful for walking, whether you're in the lanes or in the fields.' She took a long look around, savouring the green prospect. 'But not too many people know that yet, thank goodness.'

I passed the village pond where a flotilla of young moorhens was sailing out of the reeds, and dropped back down the cornfield hedges towards the Belchamp Brook. A magnificent red bull with a dewlap stretched like a spritsail under his jaw lifted his head from his willow-trunk scratching post like a ponderous old clubman, blinking his little pink eyes as he watched me go by.

From the brook a skein of field paths led me up onto the roof of

Essex, a thickly hedged and wooded countryside under a great rolling sky. Walking a flinty track beside a bean field, I almost put my boot on a crouching hare. He galloped away along the furrows, white scut bobbing and black-ear tips pricking against the bean leaves, a distillation of energy and grace flicking in and out of shade and light.

The Bulmer Brick and Tile Company's extraordinary ramshackle premises lay smoking and clanking under the trees in its shallow valley. If a committee of hobbits drew up plans for a brickworks they would come up with something like this – diminutive trestles of raw bricks drying in the wind, whistling workers barrowing clay around, a squat circular kiln with barkboard walls and a coolie's hat roof sending tendrils of smoke curling among the overhanging trees.

Essex and Suffolk are full of gorgeous old manor houses, mansions and yeomen's halls in varying states of repair. When a gale whips off the curly-edged roof tiles, or a 300-year-old strip of mortar crumbles to topple a piece of roll-edged coping or a section of chimney with a particular barley sugar twist, it's the Minter family's specialist brickworks that the householders turn to.

'We're a traditional industry', said Tony Minter, emerging from his office in gumboots and clay-streaked combat trousers, 'and that means our brick deliveries can be delayed by weather, by accident, by the clay being too wet or dry. It's not like B&Q, you know! But it does get into the blood, so to speak. I love this business, it's as simple as that.'

On the upland track above Bulmer I turned to look back. Kiln, chimney, brick stacks and clay heaps lay hidden under the trees once more, with only the seethe of white smoke among the leaves to show where the woodland brickworks carried on its timeless work. The cycle of weather and happenstance, the concealment, the ancient process of productivity in the greenwood – somehow, I thought, the Green Man would approve.

STEPPING OUT – *Walk 31*

MAP: OS 1:25,000 Explorer 196; 1:50,000 Landranger 155

TRAVEL: Rail to Sudbury (3 miles) – www.thetrainline.com
Road: M25 (Jct 27), M11 (Jct 8), A120 to Braintree, A131
towards Sudbury. Park at The Fox pub on A131 at Bulmer Tye
(OS ref TL849389).

NB Please ask in the pub if you may use their car park.

WALK DIRECTIONS: From The Fox cross A131 (take great care!).
Left along pavement to village green and monument, right here
past Jenkins Farm entrance (846388); on along track to road at
Bulmer Primary School (846394). Left into Bulmer. In ⅓ mile,
left down Chard Meadow (844400 – 'Village Hall' sign); fork
right and through churchyard to St Andrew's Church. Down
lime avenue to cross road (843403). Left for 30 yd; right by old
petrol pump (footpath fingerpost); left along field edge, and
follow yellow arrows through 2 doglegs. Near Belchamp Brook
bear left along field edge; in 200 yd right down steps to cross
brook (831406), then gate into meadow. At far side of field
(829407) bear left up lane to St Mary's Church in Belchamp
Walter (827407).

From church continue up lane, bearing left (826409 –
'Belchamp Walter, Gestingthorpe' sign) for ⅓ mile to village
pond (819405). Left here ('Gestingthorpe, Halstead' sign)
along road. Ignore first footpath fingerpost on left. 100 yds past
last house on left, bear left on right bend (819401 – concrete
footpath sign). Keep on left of ditch (yellow arrow) to cross
brook in valley bottom (820396). Cross next field to turn
left along road. In 175 yd, right up steps (823395 – footpath
fingerpost) and up field edge with hedge on your left to concrete
track (825390), with Hill Farm among trees to the right. Left for
250 yards to T-junction of paths; right, then immediately left
(827389 – waymark post in hedge), keeping hedge on your left
and aiming for house on Wesborough Hill ahead. Just before
house bear right (832384 – orange arrow) down field edge, then
lane to Bulmer Brickworks (832381).

Return up lane and field edge past Wesborough Hill. Keep
ahead NE for ½ mile – path becomes hedged lane through
woodland. Opposite Hilltop Farm on left, bear right (836390

– bridleway fingerpost) on good clear track along field edges for
¾ mile, through Jenkins Farm yard, to turn right (846388) along
lane to A131. Left to Fox PH.

LENGTH OF WALK: 7 miles

REFRESHMENTS: The Fox PH, Bulmer Tye (01787-312277 or
377505; *www.thebulmerfox.com*)

BULMER BRICK & TILE COMPANY: Visitors welcome; please ring
beforehand (01787-269232).

Mistley to Harwich, Essex

A spring walk in lonely and haunting river country

A COLD MORNING in spring, with a strong north wind blowing. The hidden sun laid a smear of pearl behind clouds marching briskly across the pointy-nosed peninsula that forms the north-east tip of Essex. 'Going far?' enquired a blue-capped miller in the yard of Edme Maltings in Mistley. 'Down along the river? Wish I was coming with you, mate!' I told him he was welcome, but he just crinkled up his nose in a laugh and turned back inside the maltings, whistling.

Mistley is a handsome small town on the south shore of the estuary of John Constable's River Stour, where Essex looks across to Suffolk. In the 1760s local MP Richard Rigby – a bit of a rogue, a bit of a fixer – tried to turn the muddy little river port into a fashionable resort. His schemes never amounted to anything. But his pavilion and fine Georgian buildings are still there, along with a pair of striking neo-classical towers designed by Robert Adam for a great riverside church, now vanished.

Mistley is still a working port, by the skin of its teeth. I mooched for an hour or so around the town and along the quays heaped with boxes, bales and stacks of Portuguese timber. Then I picked up signs for the Essex Way, and set off into countryside deeper, greener and more rural than anyone blinded by the old clichés about 'Ugly Essex' could possibly imagine.

It's a shame John Constable seldom brought a sketching pad this far downriver of his Dedham and Flatford stamping grounds. He'd have found plenty to inspire him in the huge bird-haunted skies and lonely red brick farms of the lower Stour estuary. The river made a brush-stroke of dull silver on my left as I walked the path through the woods of Mistley Heath. Under the fresh green of scarcely sprung oak and chestnut buds the coppice floor was thick with the many-rayed white stars of stitchwort, just struggling out. Sheaves of rushy green leaves shooting from the earth were blurred with a hint of blue, harbinger of sheets of bluebells that would soon be bright enough to cause spontaneous combustion on a painter's palette.

In a clearing a giant old oak spread its lightning-blasted limbs. I was admiring it when Mutley, an Irish wolfhound the size of a small-ish pony, took exception to the smell – or maybe the cut – of my trousers. 'Sorry, sorry,' fluted his lady-in-waiting as Mutley hackled up and bared his very impressive teeth. Soon my oppressor turned his attention to spraying the trees, and I was free to go.

Beyond the woods the path ran through fields green with the promise of oilseed rape and the buttery smell of the sulphur-yellow flowers of summer. Skimming low over the crop went bands of swallows, the first of the year, newly returned from Africa for the mating season. In the potato fields the pale Essex clay had been deeply furrowed by spring ploughing. Larks were crouching there, so perfectly camouflaged among the brown clods that I couldn't spot them until they rose skywards one by one, singing ecstatically.

On the far side of Bradfield I dropped down the slope of the fields to the edge of the Stour. Across the wind-ruffled estuary the Suffolk shore lay low. The old man at Ragmarsh farm was feeding his chickens under a chill light filtering through the cloud ceiling. I shivered. All of a sudden, spring seemed to have been elbowed out of the reckoning again. The wintry effect was enhanced by the sight of a great flock of brent geese, sailing on one of the inlets of Jacques Bay at a season of the year when they should by rights have been back in their breeding grounds beyond the Arctic circle.

It was up to blackcaps, whitethroats and blackbirds to reaffirm the supremacy of spring, singing their hearts out in the impenetrable scrub bushes of Wrabness Nature Reserve – an old MoD site once slated for development, but rescued for the benefit of wildlife by the persistence of local nature enthusiasts who wouldn't take no for an answer. A low, honeyed song came dancing from the bushes, a voice incomparably richer than any rival. Almost impossible for it to be a nightingale, this early in spring – but what else could match the throaty beauty of that song? I couldn't make up my mind, and whoever was making such celestial music was hidden too cleverly for my binoculars to pick out.

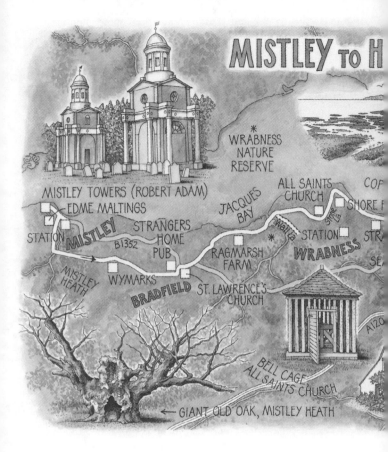

Up the bank to All Saints Church at Wrabness, where the single church bell – 'Crescent Foundry, London 1854' – hung in the churchyard in a cage of venerable worm-pitted timbers. Then it was back to the shore for a last long mile beside the Stour, listening to the needly shrieking of terns and the rich bubbling call of curlews all round the long curve of Copperas Bay.

I made inland by way of Copperas Wood, aiming for the bold cross shape of the sails on Ramsey's old post windmill. The swallows were beginning to make their mud nests in the interstices of the sails, confident that the great disused arms would not be turning.

Down on the marshy south shore of the peninsula I turned north for the last few miles into the breezy, salty old port of Harwich.

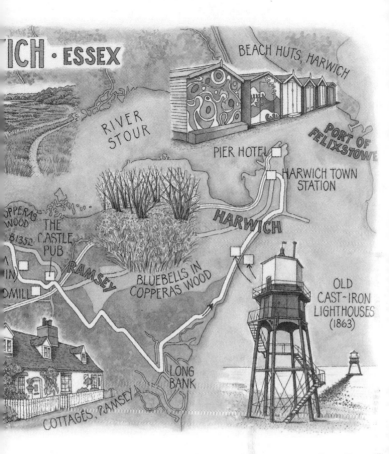

Animated shapes ran and cavorted across the grazing marshes all around my path – mad hares, great pungent kings of the emergent spring.

STEPPING OUT – *Walk 32*

MAP: OS 1:25,000 Explorer 184; 1:50,000 Landranger 169

TRAVEL: Rail to Harwich Town (*www.thetrainline.com*)

> Road – A12 to Colchester; A120 to Harwich. From Harwich, by rail to Mistley

WALK DIRECTIONS: From Mistley Station (OS ref TM119317), left to view Mistley Towers and quays. Return along High Street. 50 yd past post office, right (Essex Way – 'EW' – sign) through Edme maltings yard, following yellow 'tramlines'. At bottom of premises, right along fence; in 20 yd, left (EW) under railway (117317). Cross field and lane, then another field to stile (116312). Don't cross, but turn left (EW) across stream and stile. Continue to left of holly thicket; in 100 yd through kissing gate into wood (118311). In 15 yd (EW) keep straight ahead up slope to follow wide grassy path past rugby field. At far side veer right to meet another path; left here along wood edge and on for ⅔ mile to road on S-bend (128310). Right along road for 30 yd (take care!); then left down second of 2 turnings (EW) over stile beside Wymarks house. On across 2 fields; at far side of 2nd field, left (136307) for 20 yd, right through hedge (EW) across third field to road (140307). Ahead into Bradfield.

Left along village street past church; right by Strangers Home pub (144308) along B1352 ('Wrabness, Harwich') for 300 yd (take care!). Left (146309 – EW) through kissing gate, over fields, under railway (151313) to River Stour shore. Right past Ragmarsh Farm (157314). In 220 yd right, then left (EW) on tarmac path through Wrabness Nature Reserve. In 400 yd, left (163317 – EW) down steps; left (EW arrow on fence post) on path past gate. Forward and up steps (EW); right along bank to foot of Wall Lane (164319). Ahead through squeeze; follow hedged path for ½ mile to bear left along road (172319 – EW) past Wrabness church (174319). In 150 yd left down Stone Lane (EW) to shore (178323). Right for one and a third miles (EW signs), passing Shore Farm and Strandlands. Path leads through Copperas Wood to cross railway (199316); follow left-hand path to B1352 (200313). Left along road for 400 yd (take care!); right (203312 – EW) on field track past ruined Seagar's Farm. Continue past left end of hedge to far side of field; left (205305) to reach windmill (209304). Dogleg left and right to road in Ramsey (211303).

Left past The Castle pub, bearing right to reach roundabout on A120 (214303). Go clockwise to cross A120, then B1352. Continue towards Ramsey Hill Garage; in 5 yards, left up field edge and right edge of wood. Where wood edge turns left, keep ahead (214301) to trees on skyline; keep ahead with hedge on your right for 500 yd, through cross-hedge (EW) to reach EW marker post (220296). Left to B1414. Left for 100 yd, then right through kissing gate (222299 – EW). Follow track for 500 yd to EW post (226295); left for 130 yd, then right (EW) for ¾ mile to edge of marsh at Long Bank (235287 – EW). Left for 3½ miles into Harwich.

LENGTH: 13 miles (or return to Mistley from Wrabness station – 6 miles)

REFRESHMENTS: Strangers Home, Bradfield (01255-870304); The Castle PH, Ramsey (01255-880203)

Dunwich and Minsmere, Suffolk

*By moody coast and heath to visit the town that was eaten by the sea
and a famous bird reserve*

I T WAS ONE OF THOSE PALE, mild November days of hazy sunshine
and sketchy cloud – melancholy weather, perfect for the douce
pleasures of the Suffolk coast. Between Aldeburgh and Southwold
runs some of the loneliest country in East Anglia, a dozen miles of
heathland, freshwater marsh grazing and tattered forest fringed by a
shore of crumbling cliffs, vast shingle banks and long empty stretches
of low-tide sand. If you're looking for a stretch of moody landscape to
frame a long day's contemplative winter walking, this is it.

The Eel's Foot Inn at Eastbridge is a quiet pub in a quiet village.
The swinging sign shows an eel hopping across a reedy marsh river,
the tip of its tail encased in a huge black boot. I pulled on my own bee-
tlecrushers in the Eel's Foot car park, and dropped the pair of binoculars into the backpack. There were bound to be birds a-go-go on this
landfall coast on a winter's day, and I was planning on a bit of peeping
tommery in the RSPB's Minsmere reserve on the return leg of the
walk – a dusk-hour treat at this time of year, with ducks and geese by
the hundred thousand arriving to spend the winter in East Anglia.

The path ran straight as a die from Eastbridge, east through fields
of beet and marsh grazing towards the sea. Under the cool hand of
the cloud the land seemed to be whispering secretively – silver willow
leaves flicking and ruffling together, poplar groves shivering, reeds
murmuring into their soft mauve beards along the ditches. In the flat
grass fields swans were grazing in flocks of a dozen or so, in among the
marsh sheep and cream-coloured cattle. A cold, still light had fallen
over the land, thick above the fields, sharper in the east where the sea
bank lay sombrely on the horizon.

Busby, a livewire black Aberdeen terrier, came bouncing up and enthusiastically tried to chew off my hand with his tiny, needle-sharp teeth. 'Only 16 weeks old,' confided his lady companion, 'and he's managed to lose his collar already. But he's as sweet as pie, aren't you, you rascal?' The pie-sweet Busby gave my ankle a wee nip, and gazed up in butter-wouldn't-melt innocence.

Over the conifers to the south floated the giant white dome of Sizewell nuclear power station's reactor. Enormous, outlandish – it seemed a creature from another part of the wood entirely. I turned my back on the monster when I got to the sea wall, and spent a wonderful hour crunching north up the shingle bank and under crumbly cliffs to reach the lonely little coast hamlet of Dunwich.

There are a few monastic remains scattered along these cliff tops, but it is what has been taken by the rapacious sea that intrigues and fascinates visitors to Dunwich. The scale model in the excellent small Dunwich Museum lays it out graphically. By the 12th century Dunwich, the ancient capital of East Anglia, was a powerful and wealthy sea town trading up and down the British coast and across the North Sea. Wine, spices and silk came in; stone, tin, salt and timber went out. In its pomp Dunwich could boast a Dominican and a Franciscan monastery, a leper hospital, a busy market place, a mint, and no fewer than nine glorious churches, all seemingly well guarded by a stone wall and secured with gates of brass.

But pride came before a scarcely imaginable fall. The cliffs that underlay the town were of shaky sand and clay. Inexorably the sea came on, destroying the great hunting forest of Eastwood that stretched protectively seaward of Dunwich, eating great holes in the city itself, snatching monastery buildings, towers and churches as the centuries passed. By 1680 the market place was melting into the sea. In 1830 J.M.W. Turner painted ghostly pale ruins on the cliff top, poignant shades of better times. In 1919 the tower of All Saints, the last of the great Dunwich churches, fell from the cliff edge.

Today Dunwich is a peaceful place, a single strip of modest brick cottages and a pub on a road going nowhere. 'Have a look for Jacob Forster on the cliff,' advised the dryly humorous and knowledgeable curator of the Dunwich Museum, 'You'll find him in the bushes.' He was waiting for me there, a few yards back from the cliff edge. The proprietor of the very last named grave of All Saints Church lies under a curly-topped grave slab ('departed this life March 12th 1796 aged 38'), waiting for the storm that will mingle his dust with the beach pebbles one night not far in the future.

From Jacob Forster's grave the path cut inland through the precincts of 13th-century Greyfriars Abbey, passing the refectory ruins and the two fine gateways that still face the road. I followed the track across Dunwich Heath, a wild tract of sandy soil thickly coated with heather, gorse, bracken and loose scrub of stunted oaks, silver birch and pine trees. Heaths like this, grazed by sheep, goats and cattle, were widespread up the Suffolk coast until intensive modern agriculture and clearance for building development put paid to most of them. Now their value as wildlife havens is beginning to be appreciated. The National Trust manages 250 acres of heath along the cliffs between Dunwich and Minsmere – beautiful, lonely country.

The short winter day began to dim as evening closed in. Clouds of wigeon, teal and pochard went swirling against a smoky orange sunset. At Minsmere RSPB reserve I roosted on a bench in West Hide, binoculars to eyes, and watched the evening flights of brent geese and swans. The best moment of all, though – one that made everyone in the hide, amateur and expert alike, gasp out loud – was when a gigantic swarm of starlings came flickering across the scrapes and reedbeds. There might have been five thousand. They balled, towered, elongated, swirled, corkscrewed – a chattering, exuberant army on the wing, moving to a communal impulse we cloddish earthbound watchers could only marvel at.

STEPPING OUT – *Walk 33*

MAPS: OS 1:25,000 Explorers 212, 231; 1:50,000 Landranger 156

TRAVEL: Road – From south: A1 to Saxmundham, B1119 towards Leiston, B1122 towards Theberton.

From north: A12 to Yoxford, B1122 to Theberton. Eastbridge is signed from B1122.

WALK DIRECTIONS: From Eel's Foot Inn, Eastbridge (OS ref TM452662), turn left up road. In 200 yd, left by Rose Cottage (452660 – 'Public Footpath, Minsmere Sluice 1½' fingerpost) on path across fields and past chapel ruins (473660) to reach sea wall at sluice (477661). Turn left and walk along sea wall, marsh paths and shore to Dunwich. Left inland through car park past Flora Tea Rooms (479707). Ship PH and Dunwich Museum are in the single village street.

Returning past the Ship, turn right uphill. In 100 yd take footpath on left ('Suffolk Coast and Heath Path' waymark). Path keeps parallel with road, running through bushes beside cliff edge. Cliffs are crumbly and dangerous – take care! Path passes Jacob Forster headstone, and in 50 yd (479704) bends right through Greyfriars abbey ruins to road. Left for ⅓ mile to sharp right bend (473700); in 50 yd left ('footpath' fingerpost) down private drive (walkers permitted). Walk through woods and past houses. At bottom of drive, by caravans and bungalows (474695), follow wire fence to the right to cross a road (473693). Continue (bridleway fingerpost) on heathland path. In ¼ mile keep ahead (470690 – bridleway fingerpost) across footpath marked 'Suffolk Coast and Heaths Path', and continue for ¾ mile through Scottshall Coverts to road (460676).

To return to Eastbridge turn right; left in ½ mile (454669); left again in 300 yd (452667). Alternatively, to visit Minsmere RSPB Nature Reserve turn left; follow 'Minsmere Nature Reserve' signs for 1 mile to Reserve's Visitor Centre (474671). A path bisects reserve NW–SE, passing West and South Hides, to reach Minsmere Sluice (477661); right here on marsh path to Eastbridge.

LENGTH OF WALK: 10½ miles

CONDITIONS: Easy underfoot. Bring binoculars for birdwatching.

REFRESHMENTS: Eel's Foot Inn, Eastbridge (01728-830154; *www.*

theeelsfootinn.co.uk); Flora Tea Rooms (01728-648433) and Ship Inn (01728-648219; *www.shipatdunwich.co.uk*), Dunwich; National Trust tearoom, Dunwich Heath.

DUNWICH HEATH: (National Trust – 01728-648501): footpaths, beach, shop and tearoom etc.

MINSMERE NATURE RESERVE: (RSPB – 01728-648281; www. rspb.org.uk): Reserve open 9am–dusk (closed Tuesdays). RSPB members free.

DUNWICH MUSEUM, ST JAMES STREET, DUNWICH: 01728-648796. Open April-October. A classic small museum covering the extraordinary history of Dunwich and its losing battle with the sea.

Walk 34

Eye and Hoxne, North Suffolk

*Through rolling Suffolk farmlands to the site of St Edmund's
martyrdom by the Danes*

S PRING HAD SPRUNG all over the Suffolk market town of Eye as I
set off in early sunshine from the fabulously florid Town Hall on
a sharp windy morning. Schoolchildren were pushing each other off
the pavements, a couple of old boys were leaning on their bicycles
holding up the traffic as they chatted in Church Street, and someone
blonde and brisk came popping out of the butcher's so hastily she
gave me a high-heeled stab in the shin. '*Awfully* sorry, *frightfully*
rushed!' came floating back down the street.

Down at the turn of Church Street the half-timbered Guildhall
and the soaring flushwork tower of the Church of St Peter & St Paul
leaned their striped heads together like a pair of old acquaintances. In
the church people were getting ready for morning service, but I had
time to admire the delicate gestures and graceful posture of the saints
painted on the medieval rood screen panels. There was St Ursula,
shielding dozens of tiny fellow-martyrs in her capacious cloak, and
beside her a youthful and smiling St Edmund holding one of the
arrows with which Danish marauders slew him. I left the church and
climbed the nearby castle mound to get a view from the battlements
over the gentle, rolling green farmlands I was planning to walk, in
search of the site of that East Anglian King's cruel martyrdom in
870AD.

Wide clay fields green with spring corn, quiet lanes winding
through shallow stream valleys, ancient timber-framed hall farmhouses tucked away down green lanes on moated sites – north Suffolk
stands for every walker's dream of England's deepest agricultural back
country in springtime. The mallards that clattered skyward from the
ditches were already paired, yellow lambs'-tail catkins streamed and

shook from leafless hazel twigs, and the hedge roots around Flim-worth Hall were yellow with primroses. Larks sang over the big open fields, and chaffinches blurted out their explosive little runs of song. A morning to be sniffed and savoured and lingered over. That's why I only beat closing time at the Swan at Hoxne by the shortest of heads.

In a field down the road from the pub, the granite Saint Edmund memorial cross stood in a dark sea of beet leaves. When the great oak tree that occupied the spot mysteriously burst apart in 1843, they found an iron arrow point embedded in its heart. The tree had amassed a thousand years' worth of seasonal growth rings. Was it the one to which the captive King Edmund was dragged at the orders of Ivarr the Boneless? 'Then those wicked men bound Edmund and shamefully abused him and beat him with bludgeons,' recorded the chronicler sorrowfully, 'and after that they led the faithful king to an earth-fast tree and tied him to it with hard bonds.'

There is in fact very little evidence, apart from a rich crop of legends and a few medieval mentions of local chapels dedicated to St Edmund, to connect the East Anglian King and martyr with Hoxne. But other Suffolk and Norfolk places that claim to be the martyrdom site have even less going for them. All one can say with certainty is that local belief is still strong, as it has been through more than eleven centuries, that the Hoxne oak was the tree against which the Danish archers shot Edmund so full of arrows that 'he bristled with them like a porcupine or a thistle', before decapitating him and throwing his head into a bramble patch. There his distraught followers found it three days later, cradled between the paws of a great she-wolf.

Hoxne is a fine place to while away an afternoon – a pretty village of thatched and red-tiled cottages climbing the street on either side of a triangular green. In the wall of the village hall a medallion shows a scene from the martyrdom: Edmund hiding under the nearby Gold-brook Bridge, while above him a bride and groom come merrily from Hoxne church on their marriage day. The story says it was the glint of the king's golden spurs in the moonlight that gave away his hiding place to the wedding party; but why they then betrayed him to the invaders in the midst of their own wedding joy remains a mystery.

The shards of the venerable martyrdom tree were gathered up in 1843, and a new screen for the village church was crafted from the wood. I found it fragmented in the church, hidden under dust sheets with its carved oak leaves and acorns, wolf and crossed arrows, all awaiting restoration at some future date.

Labels on map:
HOXNE
SILVER TIGRESS FROM HOXNE ROMAN HOARD
CHURCH OF ST. PETER & ST. PAUL
SWAN INN
WHITE BRIDGE
GOLDBROOK BRIDGE
VILLAGE HALL
ST. EDMUND'S MONUMENT
ABBEY FARM
SWAN INN, HOXNE
CAPON'S FARM
PECK'S FARMHOUSE
NUTTEN VALE
OME HALL FARM
RIVER DOVE
GOLDBROOK BRIDGE
REDHOUSE FARM
ST. EDMUND'S MONUMENT
SOUTH GREEN
NIFER TAGE
STARDPOT HALL
CHURCH STREET, EYE
B1117
ANCIENT PLOUGH
BOLSER BRIDGE
EYE
CHURCH OF ST. PETER & ST. PAUL
CROWN CORNER
EYE HALL FARM
FLIMWORTH HALL FARM
HURCH ST.
GUILDHALL
ABBEY BRIDGE
CHURCH FARM
WN HALL (ART OF WALK)
CASTLE MOUND
EYE CASTLE & GUILDHALL
EYE & HOXNE NORTH SUFFOLK

Walking back through the fields in late afternoon sunshine I
kicked over the clods and flints around Capon's Farm and Mustardpot Hall, thinking of an old Suffolk boy I'd read about, a horse-age
man who ploughed pipe in mouth and could draw a furrow from
one side of a field to the other with less than half an inch devia-
tion. I watched a young farmer cutting six furrows at a time with his

multiple plough, and pictured the moment in 1992 when a local man looking for lost farm tools hereabouts unearthed a fabulous hoard of Roman silver.

In one of the newly gleaming furrows cut by the tractor plough lay a treasure of a different kind, a crudely edged flint scraper dropped here by some nameless Suffolk farmer five or six thousand years ago and hidden in the earth until this moment. Against this great solid continuity of skill and hard work, countless lives dedicated in obscurity to bringing the crops out of the clay, the hoary and gory old legend of St Edmund seemed as airy as gossamer, no more than a whisper in the walker's innermost ear.

STEPPING OUT – *Walk 34*

MAP: OS 1:25,000 Explorer 230; 1:50,000 Landranger 156

TRAVEL: Rail to Diss (4 miles) – *www.thetrainline.com*

Road: from south – M11 (Jct 9), A11, A14 to Bury St Edmunds, A143 to Scole; A140, B1077 to Eye. From north – A17 to King's Lynn, A134 to Thetford, A1066 to Diss and Scole, A140, B1077. Park near Eye Town Hall.

WALK DIRECTIONS: From Eye Town Hall (OS ref TM145739), left along Church Street past church (149738) to B1117 Hoxne Road. Right, then right again up Castle Hill to climb castle mound for view. Return and turn left along B1117 past church. Cross Abbey Bridge (151738); right down Church Farm drive. In 150 yards, left (footpath fingerpost) along ditch; cross paddock by gates and stiles, then between pheasant pens to lane (156739).

Right for 20 yards; left (footpath fingerpost in right hedge) through Eye Hall farm yard and on through fields by stiles (yellow arrows) for ⅓ mile to road (162738). Right for 400 yards, then left by grass triangle (161735 – footpath fingerpost) across field, keeping left of copse. Through gap in far field corner; across next field, following hedge on your right through a dogleg, over end of a ditch, to join field track (166734 – footpath fingerpost). Follow track on right side of hedge, past end of lane to Flimworth Hall (172734), to road (179732) at Crown Corner.

Left to B1117, left for ⅓ mile to left bend. Ahead here (177739) on old road; then forward (footpath fingerpost) along field edge. Cross through hedge to keep it on your right; in 150 yd bear left and continue along field edges for ½ mile to Redhouse Farm. Right (173750 – yellow arrow) past farm house and sheds to lane (175750). Left (footpath fingerpost); in 150 yds right (174751 – footpath fingerpost) over fields by stiles to road (173756). Right, and right again down Nuttery Vale road. In ½ mile, left (179762 – footpath fingerpost) up field and through hedge; right to road (182763); left into Hoxne past Abbey Farm. Steps on right lead to St Edmund's Monument (183767). Back on road, in 20 yd, right along track (footpath fingerpost) to Swan Inn (180772).

Up street to church, then return past Swan and on along

road. In 600 yards, right through kissing gate (176768 – fingerpost and 'Mid Suffolk Footpath' – 'MSF' – waymark). Follow hedge down to turn left along River Dove. Cross White Bridge (174770), follow 'MSF' for ⅔ mile to road (163771). Left for ½ mile; then left (157766) down drive to Pecks Farmhouse and Brome Hall Farm. Follow footpath fingerpost and 'MSF' along drive for 1⅓ miles. Opposite Conifer Cottage, left (146752 – footpath fingerpost on right) past Mustardpot Hall into fields. Follow right-hand set of parallel power lines down to turn left along green lane (150747). Left (151743 – 'MSF') to cross Bolser Bridge; continue to B1117 (152739); right into Eye.

LENGTH: 11 miles

CONDITIONS: Field paths can be muddy.

REFRESHMENTS: Swan Inn, Hoxne (01379-668275; *www. hoxneswan.co.uk*)

Norwich, Norfolk

A springtime stroll through the lovely 'City of Churches'

SPRINGTIME IN NORWICH, and everybody seemed to be at it. On the gravelled path beside the River Wensum two lovers were braving the nipping grey morning, literally in each other's pockets as they strolled beneath the willows.

Birds canoodled in the branches. A pair of mallard went skimming flat-out up the river, the yellow beak of the testosterone-crazed drake almost touching the tail feathers of his indifferent darling. The sound of her quacks, like derisive laughter, floated to me as I stood watching the reflection of the ancient cathedral watergate at Pull's Ferry break and reform in the wind-ruffled Wensum.

Norwich's wonderful heritage of medieval architecture was scarcely appreciated until this century. As late as the 1930s the corporation was prepared to demolish the narrow 3-arched Bishop Bridge, just upriver of Pull's Ferry. This is the oldest bridge in the city, brick-built in 1340, a beautiful and harmonious little gem; but only a last-minute intervention by conservationists – oddballs, they were reckoned then – saved it.

Upstream of the bridge, the ruined stump of Cow Tower stood on a crooked elbow of the river. For centuries it had sheltered cattle. But when it was built for the city's defence in 1399, it was a formidable stronghold.

That was an anxious year in East Anglia, when Henry Bolingbroke landed on the Lincolnshire coast to claim the throne. Norwich expected to be attacked. The tower's brick and flint walls were pierced for both archery and artillery. This spring morning, however, the crossbow slits and cannon embrasures held nothing more deadly than a dozen pairs of murmurously cooing pigeons.

An equally dreamy sound was sifting through the nave of Norwich

Cathedral – the soft chuckle of the organ under expert hands. It suited the muted sandy-grey interior light of the building, whose outside walls – normally glinting with the hard white light of Caen limestone – looked muted and pearly today.

This great Norman cathedral is rich in intimate detail and the human touch. I enjoyed the striking modern Stations of the Cross, inlaid in polished wood. Hidden under the choir stall seats was a riotous clutch of medieval misericords; they included a man riding a savage boar, two woodwoses clubbing each other, various demonic beasts and a fine Green Man.

Soon I had my binoculars focused on the carved and painted 15th-century bosses in the nave roof. Mr and Mrs Noah and family peeped out of the Ark's portholes, accompanied by a cheerfully smiling unicorn. A swaddled Moses was laid tenderly in a golden basket to float down a bevelled blue Nile. Pharaoh gasped in horror as the Red Sea swallowed him, his chariot and his soldiers. Adam and Eve, shapely in their nakedness, prepared to eat the golden fruit of the Tree of Knowledge.

The greatest of all the cathedral's treasures, a wonderfully painted reredos, stood behind the altar in St Luke's Chapel at the east end. It was given to the cathedral by Bishop Despenser in 1387, and was only saved from destruction at the hands of Puritan zealots three centuries later by being used as a table, with its Crucifixion and Resurrection scenes hidden face down.

This rare survivor of 14th-century English religious painting depicts the brutish satisfaction of the soldiers scourging Christ, a proud princeling riding behind the stumbling Saviour on the road to Calvary, a pale Virgin Mary fainting into the arms of St John at the foot of the cross, and a Resurrection scene in which Christ steps with calm dignity out of his coffin while his prostrate guards look up with coarse, fear-stiffened faces.

Outside the Cathedral Close, an effigy of Sir Thomas Erpingham kneels in full armour at the apex of an ornate gateway. Erpingham directed the English archers at the Battle of Agincourt in 1415, and had the gate built in thanksgiving for the victory. In *Henry V* Shakespeare has King Henry apostrophising him on the morning of the battle:

'*Good morrow, old Sir Thomas Erpingham: A good soft pillow for that good white head*
Were better than the churlish turf of France.'

The king's solicitude for old bones sleeping rough does not last long; Shakespeare has him relieving the elderly Norfolk knight of his nice warm cloak before the scene is done.

If Norwich's vigilant conservationists of the 1920s had not intervened, the all-but-perfect medieval street of Elm Hill – cobbled, quiet, full of colour-washed gables and overhanging upper storeys – would have been demolished in the name of slum clearance and road improvements. But no reformer, thank the Lord, has succeeded in sweeping away the city's central market, which has been held for almost a thousand years.

The brightly striped awnings of the jam-packed stalls on the market place sheltered every saleable item known to man, from knicker elastic to silk thread, from apples to cheap watches. I havered, hummed and hawed – then bought a fistful of dates from Gareth Butcher's stall in the centre of the maelstrom, and chewed them on my way to look into the Church of St Peter Mancroft that closes the south side of the square.

Truly Norwich is the 'City of Churches'. There are 32 of them within the old medieval walls, none more striking than St Peter Mancroft with its glorious carved angel roof and 15th-century east window – a vivid stained glass depiction of the Nativity, Crucifixion and Resurrection. But the most intriguing of all Norwich's church treats I found hidden away in an alley off King's Street towards the end of the walk.

In the tiny flint Church of St Julian candles burned before the shrine of the anchoress Mother Julian, author of *Revelations of Divine Love*, who opted to spend forty-three years immured in a cell here after receiving in 1373 a series of mysterious visions.

Anchoresses, though sealed off from outside contact, were not incommunicado. Nor were they necessarily humourless misanthropes. The 'window on the world' through which they received food could also act as a conduit for gossip, advice and news. That was certainly the case with the witty 'recluse atte Norwyche', who kept in touch via her two servants, Sara and Alice.

During her Revelations, Mother Julian saw drops of Christ's blood as round as herring scales, his crucified body as dry and shrivelled as a cold wind, a lily-white child gliding up to heaven out of a bloated body, and the devil with 'a young man's face, long and lean, the colour of a tilestone newly fired, and a foul and nauseating stench.'

What did it all mean? 'As I see it,' wrote Mother Julian, 'his words are the greatest that can be uttered, for they embrace ... I cannot tell! All I know is that the joy I saw surpasses all the heart could wish for, or the soul desire.'

I left the little chapel full of high thoughts. But they soon turned more earthy, down on the River Wensum where Norwich's lunchtime lovers were holding hands as if springtime and a young man's fancy had just been invented.

STEPPING OUT – *Walk 35*

MAP: City maps are available from the Tourist Information Centre (01603-727927; *www.visitnorwich.co.uk*)

TRAVEL: Rail to Norwich (*www.thetrainline.com*)

Road – A47/A11/A140 to Norwich: car park on Riverside, 50 yd south of railway station.

WALK DIRECTIONS: Turn right along Riverside, over traffic lights, and on for ½ mile beside river to 3-arched Bishop Bridge. Left across bridge; continue beside river past Cow Tower. In 400 yd, left beside flint wall towards cathedral. Pass Adam & Eve pub; left along Bishopgate. In 200 yd, right through gates into cathedral close.

From west door of Norwich Cathedral, through Erpingham Gate. Right down Wensum Street; in 150 yd left up Elm Hill. Left by Briton's Arms; right down Princes Street. Cross St Andrew Plain; left up Bridewell Alley; cross Bedford Street into Swan Lane. Right at top along London Street to Guildhall, market place and St Peter Mancroft.

Through Royal Arcade at bottom of market place. Right at top below Norwich Castle; bear left round castle mound by Farmers Avenue and Cattle Market Street. Right down King Street. In ⅓ mile on right, St Julian's Alley leads to St Julian's Church and shrine of Mother Julian. Continue along King Street for ¼ mile, left across Carrow Bridge, left along Riverside path back to station.

LENGTH OF WALK: Allow 4 hours.

GEAR: Take binoculars for Norwich Cathedral roof bosses and stained glass.

REFRESHMENTS: Adam and Eve, Bishopgate (01603-667423; *www.adamandevenorwich.co.uk*) – many other cafés, pubs, shops along route.

READING: *Revelations of Divine Love* by St Julian of Norwich (Penguin Classics).

Walk 36

Snettisham and The Wash, Norfolk

From Pevsner's 'fabulous' church to the bird-thronged shores of The Wash

THE PINK AND YELLOW ROSES outside the window of Snettisham's Rose & Crown glowed in early sunshine with the vividness of stained glass. After breakfast I stepped out of the dark-beamed old inn to be dazzled by a proper North Norfolk summer's morning – the iron-rich carstone of the village houses as dark as treacle, the trees so thickly green they looked almost blue, the sky so blue it made my eyes water.

On the eastern edge of Snettisham the spire of St Mary's Church lanced nearly 200 feet into an enamelled sky. 'Fabulous,' enthused Pevsner, 'perhaps the most exciting Dec parish church in Norfolk.' As with so many Norfolk villages, it was Snettisham's wool wealth during the Middle Ages that built and beautified St Mary's. The tapering spear of the 14th-century spire makes a landmark and a summons for mile around.

As for the great west window, the macabre writer L.P. Hartley based an entire short story, *The Shrimp and The Anemone*, around this supreme example of the medieval stonemason's art: 'It was as though the tapering side columns had been lit and two people, standing one on either side, had blown the flames together. Curving, straining, interlocked, they flung themselves against the retaining arch in an ecstasy of petrifaction.'

Though binoculars I admired the west window's Victorian glass – Old Testament trials and tribulations in the desert. Then I set out into the sharp bright day. Car windscreens flashed as drivers howled along the village bypass, but on the far side all was quiet on a wood-land path under sweet chestnuts and sycamores.

A salty breeze hissed across a million crinkled beet leaves as I came out from the trees. Looking west, I sensed the sea rather than saw it.

The horizon had foreshortened to the long flat bar of the sea wall, all that keeps the greedy tides out of these coastal fields.

It was a strange sensation to be standing on an East Anglian sea wall and looking west, rather than east, over the sea. But the Snettisham coast is where Norfolk stares at Lincolnshire across the square-mouthed estuary of the Wash, that mighty mud larder that feeds countless millions of wildfowl. For a birdwatcher – or for any walker with a pair of binoculars and a pair of eyes to glue them to – this place is a kind of windblown heaven.

Through my binoculars the Lincolnshire shore 15 miles away looked as strange as could be, a shimmering skyline of minute black verticals that might have been trees, church towers or coasting ships. The tide was on the make, washing in over gleaming mud banks. I could see a confused line of birds out there along the incoming edge of the water, agitated and jumpy as they were forced nearer and nearer to land. They were the vanguard of the Wash's annual autumn and winter glut of geese and ducks, refugees from General Winter's iron rule over the Arctic Circle.

With tide tables and calendar I had cherry-picked the date of today's walk, so as to be able to enjoy the first of the autumn birds at the same time as the last of the summer flowers. Some remarkably hardy plants flourish in the arid, salt-steeped and wind-battered shingle banks of the Wash coast. Large, brightly coloured flowers beckon the insects; thick fleshy leaves store rainwater. The yellow-horned poppies and royal blue viper's bugloss looked gaudy and indestructible, showy survivors as tough as old boots. This was the peak time to see them. Within a month, their fresh petals would be shrivelled by sun and salt.

A couple of miles south along the shore I took up a perch at an open window of the Rotary Hide. The RSPB's Snettisham reserve safeguards these precious few miles of bird-haunted coast, and the double-sided hide gives superb views west over the Wash and east across flooded lagoons.

There must have been 5,000 dunlin on the pebbly shore immediately below the hide – brown-speckled birds with short stubby beaks who had travelled thousands of miles from their Arctic breeding grounds to fetch up in north-west Norfolk. They stood in a solid brown wedge, all heads to wind at the same angle, all feathers ruffling.

As the tide chased them further up the beach, they began to take off in numbers; at first fifty or so, then five hundred at a time, to circle a couple of times over the water before settling once more. Finally some unfathomable balance of tide height, beach consistency or neighbour proximity prompted a communal decision, and the entire five thousand rose into the air with a pattering roar of wings.

The dunlin moved as one creature, building a tall tower of birds that collapsed into a low elongated wave, then balled into a circle. As if a telepathic command had passed instantaneously between those thousands of tiny brains, they tacked round all at the same instant, the sun flashing their dark underparts into silver. It was a truly astonishing sight, one of those moments you hope for and will never forget.

There were plenty of other birds to admire: ringed plover with their dark dog-collars, tiny purplish turnstones, common terns hanging in the wind on slender bent wings, black-headed gulls swearing at each other like fishwives as they jostled for a place on the little islands in the inland lagoons. But it was the insouciant grace of the swerving, skimming dunlin that took my breath away.

I watched them until my eyes ached. The tide had begun to ebb and the sun had climbed high before I had had enough and came stumbling out of the dark hide into the blindingly bright summer's day. Huge Norfolk cornfields filled the flat country behind the sea wall. I made my way inland, guided by the tall spire of St Mary's three miles away at Snettisham.

The Queen's family holiday house at Sandringham stands only a couple of miles south of here. Royal personages and guests would alight at the Wolferton station of the Lynn & Hunstanton Railway, before that lovely branch line was closed in 1969. Now a permissive footpath threads the disused railway, thanks to the public-spiritedness of the landowner. I followed the flowery old track slowly back from Dersingham to Snettisham, with clouds of dunlin flashing like silver across my inner eye.

STEPPING OUT – *Walk 36*

MAP: OS 1:25,000 Explorer 250; 1:50,000 Landranger 132

TRAVEL: Road – King's Lynn via A17 (east from Newark and A1); A47 (east from Peterborough, west from Norwich); or A10 (north from Cambridge). From King's Lynn, A149 north towards Hunstanton; Snettisham signed to right in 10 miles. Park near Rose & Crown PH.

WALK DIRECTIONS: From Rose & Crown (OS ref TF687343) to church, then return past Rose & Crown to main road. Right; immediately left down Alma Road to A149 bypass (680341). Cross to traffic island, then far side (*take great care!*). Right on verge for 70 yd; left (fingerpost) onto woodland track. Follow for ¾ mile to west side of woods. Path doglegs left, then right to leave wood near Lodge Hill Farm (668341). Across field to gravel track; this doglegs right, then left to cross rough track (663344 – fingerpost). Continue with wood on left; just before end of track, right over stile by gate (660345 – fingerpost). Left round field edge to fingerpost in opposite hedge. Cross field, aiming for orange streak of path on sea bank ahead, to fingerpost in far fence. Diagonally left to fingerpost and kissing gate by field gate below sea bank (654347). Climb bank, cross gully beyond; climb far bank to bird hide (652347).

Left for 1 mile to Shepherd's Port (648335).

Follow RSPB Reserve signs, skirting chalet park, to Rotary Hide 1 mile beyond on sea bank (649313). From here retrace steps for 50 yd; cross lagoon on causeway. Bear right on landward side. In 300 yd path passes through scrub. Don't continue between wooden posts (650310), but turn left over flood bank. Keep ahead, inland, on grassy track that soon becomes concrete. Follow for 2¼ miles through fields to A149 (679309).

Cross (*great care!*). Left opposite redundant Dersingham Station, along disused railway for 1¼ miles. At Ingoldisthorpe, 'No Pedestrian Access' bars track (682326). Right along road past Crossing Cottage; in 10 yd left over stile; on between gardens to path through fields to road (681335). Right to main village road; left into Snettisham.

LENGTH: 9½ miles – allow 4 hours, plus birdwatching.

SNETTISHAM RSPB RESERVE: 01485-542689; *www.rspb.org.uk*

REFRESHMENTS: Rose & Crown, Snettisham (01485-541382; *www.roseandcrownsnettisham.co.uk*).

Walk 37

East Light to King's Lynn, The Wash, Norfolk

The Peter Scott Walk around the rim of East Anglia's giant estuary

THE EARLY MORNING 505 service to Sutton Bridge was late getting under way – 'Again!' grumbled the ladies shivering in the shelter at King's Lynn bus station. 'They just run when they feel like it, I reckon.' Eventually the driver winkled himself out of his warm roost. I couldn't really blame him – it was a bitter blue stinger of a winter's morning, with a sharp frost over the fields of north-west Norfolk.

We chugged off through Clenchwarton, Terrington St Clement and Walpole Cross Keys. Tractors were ploughing in the last of the autumn stubble and fetching up showers of pale root vegetables, each big green or yellow machine followed by a long screaming train of seagulls. The dark Fenland soil, Grade One silt reclaimed from the bed of the sea, is some of the richest and most fertile in the world. The local farmers plough and sow right up to the garden fences of the brick-built houses, aiming to tax the dead level land of every last drop of profit.

Jolting in the bus and staring out of the mud-smeared windows, I thought of the two men whose adventures among the wildfowl of the Terrington and Gedney marshes sparked my own lifelong fascination with this ruler-flat country where Norfolk and Lincolnshire meet on the shores of the great Wash estuary. As a boy I'd read about Mackenzie Thorpe, 'Kenzie the Wild-Goose Man', a famous poacher, wildfowler, pugilist and general Jack-the-Lad raised in Sutton Bridge, who had gradually turned from shooting the pinkfooted geese, the wigeon and pochard of the marshes to photographing, recording and painting them.

A similar conversion befell the second of my heroes, pioneer conservationist Sir Peter Scott. Son of the most famous British Antarctic explorer of all, Scott was an enthusiastic wildfowler when he came to live near Sutton Bridge as a young man in 1933. But an incident in which he witnessed the long-drawn-out death agonies of a goose he'd shot but couldn't retrieve persuaded him to swap his fowling piece and punt-gun for a camera and a paintbrush.

Scott became one of the finest wildlife artists in Britain, and he founded several wildfowl trust reserves – including Slimbridge on the River Severn in Gloucestershire, a regular winter trip from my childhood home nearby. Occasionally I would see the great man, binoculars round neck, smiling benevolently behind enormous glasses as he strolled the Slimbridge bird pens. Admiration for Peter Scott and Kenzie the Wild-Goose Man soon led me out onto the marshes with my own binoculars at the ready.

At Sutton Bridge this morning I took my customary glance along the glutinous banks of the River Nene, hoping to catch a flash of gold or the wink of ruby. Not that there's much chance of a reappearance of the treasure that King John lost in 1216 when his baggage train failed to beat the incoming tide here. Plate, jewels, silks and furbe-lows – all must now lie many feet deep beneath the centuries of silt. No harm looking, though.

Along the straightened course of the Nene the quayside at Port Sutton Bridge was stacked with pinkish baulks of timber. Their res-inous smell came faintly across the river. Cranes were swinging them out of a Russian freighter, *Ladoga 104* of St Petersburg, a dash of the exotic in this edge-of-the-land place.

'Keep the sea on your left and you should make it round to Lynn,' deadpanned the taxi driver as he put me out by the East Light. 'And another piece of advice,' he added, 'don't bother shouting if you get lost, 'cause no-one'll hear you.'

The East Light is certainly a remote spot. From 1933 until the Second World War Peter Scott made his home in this ornamental lighthouse, which stands opposite its twin West Light at the mouth of the River Nene. From the East Light the Peter Scott Walk runs all the way round the south-eastern corner of the Wash, 11 miles of seawall walking through one of the loneliest landscapes in Britain, with the bird-haunted saltmarshes that Scott loved stretching seaward to meet immensities of mud and sand flats.

Setting off scarfed and gloved against the harsh north wind, I stared out across the marshes. The square-sided Wash is the largest

EAST LIGHT TO KING'S

THE WASH

DISUSED RESERVOIR

WEST LIGHT

EAST LIGHT (START OF WALK)

SEA WALL & DITCH

RIVER NENE

LINCS. / NORFOLK

SEA WALL &

SEA WALL &

PORT SUTTON BRIDGE

WALK OR BY TAXI

FIELDS RECLAIMED FROM THE SEA

SUTTON BRIDGE

WALPOLE CROSS KEYS

PINK-FOOTED GEESE

estuary in Britain, a giant tidal basin enclosing more than 100 square miles of saltmarsh, sand shoals and mud banks. Common seals breed here; waders haunt the marsh creeks; geese and ducks to the tune of many hundred thousand winter on the muds and sands. Horizons are pancake flat – northward to the sea which can be three miles or more from land at low tide, landward across rich farmlands reclaimed from

the sea. It's quite a stunning contrast between the untouched marsh and mud landscape to the north and the highly drilled, expertly exploited farmlands on the southern side of the seawall.

Not that the birds care about who owns what. As I put my head above the seawall a thousand pinkfooted geese rose in a jabbering mass from the ploughed furrows with a roar of wings. They straggled away in a flickering crowd across the marshes to safer stance out on the mud. I'd hardly lowered the binoculars before they were up at my eyes again, focusing on a bunch of eighty or ninety dark-bellied brent geese barking and yapping their way eastward a few feet above the saltmarsh.

The bank I was walking ran seaward of all others in this sector of the Wash. But there were other banks I could see cutting inland, squaring off different sections of agricultural land. A glance at the dates on my maps unravelled the story. The fields to my right had been tidal marsh until 1974, when the present seawall was built. The next bank inland dated from 1953, the one south of that from 1917. Another bank was dated 1775. Reclamation of the marshes had evidently been going forward through the centuries as and when the necessary money and political will were forthcoming.

What the Romans began, medieval monks continued and 17th-century Dutch engineers perfected. Millions of acres of Fenland were drained, embanked and farmed. But the relentless expansion into the Wash has finally stopped. The birds, the fish, the butterflies and the mud invertebrates have the marshes to themselves – until such time as the steadily rising sea comes back to reclaim its own once more.

I ran down the outer slope of the bank to have a closer look at the saltmarsh. A few hundred yards out into the marsh, creeks wriggled like miniature canyons, a gleam of iridescent water in their depths. Tough spearblade leaves of sea purslane – the many-rooted plant that holds the mud together – gave way to a golden forest of wheat-like grasses. Thickets of thistles shed their parachute-borne seeds along the freezing airstream of the north wind. A curlew got up and flew away, his mournful *cur-leek*! echoing back to me. The sense of isolation in these flat immensities under a huge blue sky was literally head-spinning.

Round at the mouth of the River Great Ouse I sat on the bank to munch my cheese and pickle sandwich. Then it was on south along the narrowing river, following a battered old cockling boat as she rode the now flooding tide down to the salty old port of King's Lynn.

STEPPING OUT – *Walk 37*

MAP: OS 1:25,000 Explorer 249; 1:50,000 Landrangers 131,132

TRAVEL: Rail (www.thetrainline.com) or coach (*www. nationalexpress.com*) to King's Lynn. Road – to King's Lynn: from south, M11, A10, from west, A17 or A47.

To start of walk: Norfolk Green bus 505 from King's Lynn to Sutton Bridge; walk from there, or taxi (01406-351959) to East Light lighthouse.

WALK DIRECTIONS: From Sutton Bridge, walk up the east bank of River Nene to East Light lighthouse (OS ref TF493257). From here, the Peter Scott Walk runs north up the river, soon bearing right (east) and following the sea wall path all the way to West Lynn ferry (613203).

Ferry crosses River Great Ouse to King's Lynn thrice hourly (on the hour, 20 past, 20 to), 7.00 am to 6.00 pm, Mon-Sat (not Bank Holidays).

LENGTH: From Sutton Bridge, 13½ miles; from East Light, 10½ miles.

CONDITIONS: Good, grassy seawall path all the way. Very exposed – no shelter en route, so bring warm and weatherproof clothes. Wonderful birdwatching, especially in winter – take binoculars!

REFRESHMENTS: None en route; take picnic.

INFORMATION: The Peter Scott Walk leaflet is currently out of print, but various helpful publications are available from King's Lynn TIC, The Custom House, Purfleet Quay (01553-763044; *www.visitwestnorfolk.com*)

Walk 38

Ely, Cambridgeshire

Historic Fenland cathedral town with memories of Oliver Cromwell

A BRISK GREY DAY of clouds rolling across Cambridgeshire, and a wintry light over the fens. Watercourses gleamed dully as they streaked like arrows for the horizon. I drove east towards Ely, watching straight green lines of winter wheat fan slowly by in the black peat soil of vast fields. In this landscape of extraordinary flatness, where every willow tree and telegraph pole prints itself on the sky, there was little chance of losing my way.

Before monks, adventurers and immigrant Dutchmen drained the fens for agriculture, Ely was an island in a miasmic fen swamp. The town clings to a gentle swell of raised ground. Planted square across the summit of the hill above the surrounding flatlands, the graceful bulk of Ely Cathedral draws the eye from ten miles off.

Most of Fenland's churches seem to ride their fields like ships in a level green sea. But Ely Cathedral looks more like a complete little city, compact but elaborately built, rising from trees and crowned with towers and turrets like the backdrop to some allegorical medieval painting. The famous silhouette with its two pinnacled towers dominates the countryside.

Visitors to Ely come mainly for the two Big C's – Ely Cathedral, and Oliver Cromwell. The local MP who rose to be Lord Protector of the realm – King in all but name – lived between 1636 and 1646 in a handsome black-and-white house near the cathedral. Today it serves a double purpose, as a tourist office (where I called in to pick up a Town Trail leaflet), and a museum of the great man's life and times.

I started with a stroll through the wood-panelled parlour, Cromwell's private study, and the 'Haunted Room' complete with wax figure recumbent in a low-lit four-poster. It provided an unsolemn introduction to the man – choleric, stern, passionately devoted to his wife, a violent opponent of church music who adored secular tunes, a country squire who became the greatest English general of his age. Cromwell still intrigues, a character as difficult to pin down as a fen eel.

Setting off from Oliver Cromwell's House, I peeped into St Mary's Church to see the stained glass window commemorating the Great War – St George with his spear down the throat of a properly fiery dragon. Outside, a stone tablet on the tower recorded the public hanging and communal burial of five Littleport men in 1816; they had been among a hungry crowd of jobless labourers who marched on Ely with billhooks, hayforks and a punt gun.

'The dirtyest place I ever saw: its a perfect quagmire the whole City,' wrote Celia Fiennes in her 1698 Journal. 'I had froggs and slow-worms and snailes in my roome ... it cannot but be infested with all such things being altogether moorish fenny ground which lyes low. To persons born in up and dry countryes it must destroy them like rotten sheep in consumptions and rhumes.'

Celia had just narrowly escaped drowning when her horse all but pitched her into a flooded dyke on the causeway to Ely, so she can be forgiven her jaundiced view. What any walker round the town marvels at today is the wonderful group of monastic buildings that clusters round the cathedral; not ruins, but proper houses still in use.

Ely, secure on an island surrounded by impassable fens, was always a place of refuge and resistance, a focus for trouble. Hereward the Wake and a motley band of Danes and disaffected locals held out here against the invading Normans for a defiant year in 1070–1. It was ten years later that William the Conqueror's cousin Abbot Simeon began the building of a great cathedral, round which an ecclesiastical township slowly came into being over the following centuries.

This loose congregation of mellow brick and stone buildings, dignified by age and the beauty of fine craftsmanship, charms the eye and imagination – the F-shaped Bishop's Palace, the handsome monastic gateway called Ely Porta, the monks' long barn, 14th-century Prior Crauden's Chapel. Also standing near are remnants of the monastic infirmary, alongside Powcher's Hall where the monks would be leech-bled to cool their passions, and the Black Hostelry for Benedictine visitors to Ely.

I wandered a meandering circuit of the cathedral precincts, absorbed in herringbone brick, sculpted masonry, chevroned arch-ways, tiny crooked corridors, odd angles of tiled roof. Beyond Ely

Porta the buildings gave way to a wide park where shaggy ponies put their soft muzzles over the fence to be stroked – a peaceful nugget of green countryside, sealed up in the heart of the town.

The best view of Ely, though, was waiting for me at the summit of the Octagon, the cathedral's unique central tower with its eight upstanding pinnacles. This was an astonishing feat of 14th-century engineering, its construction fraught with danger and difficulty as eight giant oak trunks were swung up into the sky to support 400 tons of stone with a 62-ft wooden lantern on top.

Somehow they did it. I had a better idea of how, after joining a tour party and climbing the spiral stairs to where painted angels and wind-eroded gargoyles kept their footing upon a web of ancient timbers like the ribs of some fantastic Heath Robinson umbrella. Out on the leads at 130ft the view was mind-boggling: at first a jackdaw's-eye view down over medieval Ely, then out for sixty miles across a vast disc of flat land encompassing Peterborough, King's Lynn, Cambridge and the Hertfordshire hills.

Seen from floor level, the cathedral's nave soars a hundred feet in perfect Romanesque harmony. The monstrous appliances of the London Warming & Ventilation Company were throwing out enough heat this morning to take the chill off the stone. I admired the lace-like masonry in the 14th-century Lady Chapel, goggled at medieval beasts and pre-Raphaelite angels in the Stained Glass Museum, and tottered out through the Sacrist's Gate, glutted with wonders.

Back in the real world, teenagers were smoking and toddlers stamping in temper. A cold fen wind cut up the streets. Hands in pockets, I hurried down the hill towards the Great Ouse where swans were bobbing for weed amongst moored narrowboats and crumb-sprinkling old gentlemen. It was a Low Countries scene: colour-washed and bare brick houses on a broad curve of water, with a bicyclist bowling downwind below the weeping willows. Stranger still, the waterside promenade was named 'Quai d'Orsay' – a friendly nod to Ely's twin town.

Returning uphill, I passed The Three Blackbirds on the corner of Broad Street, an ancient house patched and patched again with yellow, brown and orange brick. Knotty buttresses and fat chimney breasts hugged its 700-year-old walls. Only the cathedral itself and a couple of the monastic buildings predate this venerable, thickset house.

A snaking path brought me up through the park and back into the charmed world of the snug little cathedral city. In the Steeplegate Tea Rooms (founded on a beautiful vaulted medieval undercroft) I warmed up over a cup of tea. Then I went to Evensong in the cathedral, where schoolboys sang gloriously and soft light made the choir stalls glow like wax candles. There's no better way to end a winter's day in Ely.

STEPPING OUT – *Walk 38*

MAP: Map provided with Ely Town Trail leaflet guide (available from Tourist Information Office: see below).

TRAVEL: Rail to Ely (*www.thetrainline.com*)

Road – Ely is 15 miles north of Cambridge, at the junction of A10 and A142.

WALK DIRECTIONS: The leaflet guide has full instructions. In brief: from Oliver Cromwell's House (Tourist Information office), pass St Mary's Church and walk towards Ely Cathedral. Opposite west door, right down The Gallery. Left through Ely Porta; left via Prior Crauden's Chapel and Prior's House to cathedral south door (Powcher's Hall, Old Infirmary, Black Hostelry all to your right). Bear left round east end of cathedral, then right through Sacrist's Gate; right along High Street, past market; on down Fore Hill and Waterside.

Bear right beside the river; turn right by The Cutter Inn, up footpath and Jubilee Terrace to The Three Blackbirds (un-named) on the corner. Right along Broad Street; in 50 yd, left through the park to return to the cathedral and Oliver Cromwell's House.

LENGTH OF WALK: allow half a day.

REFRESHMENTS: The Lamb Hotel, 2 Lynn Road, Ely (01353-663574; *www.thelamb-ely.com*); Steeplegate Tea Rooms, 16–18 High Street (01353-664731)

ELY CATHEDRAL: (01353-660344; *www.cathedral.ely.anglican.org/ history*): Guide tours of cathedral (free)

STAINED GLASS MUSEUM: 01353-660347; *www. stainedglassmuseum.com*

ELY MUSEUM: (01353-666655; *www.elymuseum.org.uk*): The Old Gaol, Market Street

OLIVER CROMWELL'S HOUSE, 29 ST MARY'S STREET: (01353-662062; *www.ely.org.uk*): Tourist Information Centre, Oliver Cromwell Museum

Walk 39

Tetford and Somersby, Lincolnshire

Across the Lincolnshire Wolds with Alfred, Lord Tennyson

I WAS SCOURING the map of Britain for a really away-from-it-all winter walk on hilly ground. Lincolnshire slipped into view – flat coast, flat southern fens and flat northern estuarine lands. Nothing much there. Down the spine of the county, though, things looked more exciting. There in the middle rose the Lincolnshire Wolds, a tumbled sweep of chalk and greenstone hills unapproached by any motorway or railway. Just the job!

A cold blue sky was showing above shredding rainclouds as I set off from Tetford, one of a cluster of farming villages in the hills between Lincoln and Skegness. The Lincolnshire Wolds are partly chalk, partly a kind of iron-rich sandstone known as greenstone. St Mary's Church on the edge of Tetford was built of this soft stuff, its gargoyles, windows and walls all weathered and lichen-stained into a green lumpiness. Inside, high on the wall, were displayed the breast plate, backplate and peaked helmet of Captain Edward Dymoke, official Champion to King George II. The gallant Captain wore these martial garments when he threw down a gauntlet at the coronation of the King in 1727, challenging to single combat anyone who might dare to gainsay his sovereign lord.

The local moles must have been disturbed by the overnight rain; they had pushed up thousands of hills of rich iron-brown earth in the meadows. What with these, and the sticky clay-like soil of the Lincolnshire ploughlands, my boots were twice their usual size and weight by the time I had clambered to the ridge of Warden Hill. Here I idled, kicking wedges of mud into the hedge and looking down on Somersby.

The red brick barns and white houses of the farming hamlet lay sheltered by oaks and beeches, cradled in a green valley. Beyond, fold upon fold of gentle green hills rolled to the southern skyline with a wave-like motion I could almost physically feel. A scene so quintessentially English, it looked like a patriotic Brian Cook poster.

> *'Pour round mine ears the livelong bleat*
> *Of the thick-fleeced sheep from wattled folds*
> *Upon the ridged wolds,*
> *When the first matin-song hath waken'd loud*
> *Over the dark dewy earth forlorn,*
> *What time the amber morn*
> *Forth gushes from beneath a low-hung cloud.'*

They could write them like that in Victorian days, and Alfred, Lord Tennyson did – reams of romantic rustic images from the Lincolnshire countryside of his birth and childhood, underpinning the great Arthurian and classical themes of his poetry.

But childhood in Somersby Rectory was far from idyllic for the poet. His father's ill health overshadowed all – George Clayton Tennyson was epileptic and depressive, a drinker and opium-taker subject to violent rages and black fits of despair that loomed over himself, his wife and their 11 children.

Young Alfred's talent for poetry was irrepressible, however. His first book was published in 1827, when he was still a teenager. But he had to wait until the 1850 publication of *In Memoriam*, his elegy to his long-dead friend Arthur Hallam, before hitting the jackpot of fame and fortune.

From the little exhibition at the back of St Margaret's Church – another knobbly greenstone building – I learned of Tennyson's late, adulated years as peer and Poet Laureate. A bust of the poet near the chancel arch showed pouched eyes thoughtfully staring above a fine full beard, and romantically long locks streaming back from a domed bald head. In a display case lay one of his quill pens and a couple of his clay pipes – Tennyson was a formidable smoker of strong shag.

Opposite the church stood the rectory where the poet was born in 1809 – an off-white brick building under a pantiled roof, half-hidden behind neat yew topiary. From the open kitchen window came cheerful whistling and a clatter of dishes. Down the lane I sat on a brick bridge parapet, listening to the bubble and gurgle of the infant River Lymn, Tennyson's famous 'Brook':

'I chatter over stony ways,
In little sharps and trebles,
I bubble into eddying bays,
I babble on the pebbles.'

I must have been about seven years old when Mrs Tiplady at Airthrie School made us learn the whole thing by heart. What else could I remember? 'I come from haunts of coot and tern ... and something, something sally – and diddly-dum among the fern, to something down a valley.' Was that pathetic fragment all I had left in the memory banks? Mrs Tiplady would not have been amused.

Down in Bag Enderby, a mile away across the fields, I passed Ivy House Farm, a cottage of the traditional Lincolnshire 'mud, stud and thatch', its wall surfaces smoothed to a rounded, softly pleasing shape and texture. The little greenstone church among the trees shelters a great treasure: a gorgeous octagonal medieval font carved with strange sculptures – a long-muzzled deer browsing on a tree growing out of its own back, a figure seated on a cloud and playing a viol or a hurdy-gurdy, and a tender little rustic *pieta* with the dead Jesus cramped up awkwardly on his sorrowing mother's lap. The church kneelers were beautifully worked, too, a feature of the local churches hereabouts.

On the return tramp I enjoyed the pleasure of walking a country road without a single passing car to disturb me. By the time I got back to Tetford the temperature had dropped to freezing. Luckily the Cross Keys was open, and willing to serve me something hot.

Inja and Tanya, the pub dogs, sat and watched each mouthful so intently I thought their stares were burning holes in my cheeks. But it was only the cheesy pasta and the Tetleys bitter, spreading the kind of glow that's at least half the point of a good hilly walk on a cold winter's day.

STEPPING OUT – *Walk 39*

MAPS: OS 1:25,000 Explorer 273; 1:50,000 Landranger 122

TRAVEL: Bus – Service 6C: 5 a day, except Sunday, from Louth (25 min) or Horncastle (15 min). Tel CallConnect (0845-234-3344) about flexible services

Road – A1 to Newark, A46 to Lincoln, A158 to Horncastle, minor road to Tetford.

WALK DIRECTIONS: From Tetford Church (OS ref TF334748) cross stile in NE corner of churchyard, following yellow waymark arrows across fields. In ⅓ mile cross stile (340747 – yellow arrow); diagonally right across next field to cross ditch by railed footbridge. On along field edge to cross next wooden footbridge; follow left field edge path to cross Double Dike in far corner of field (344736). Through 2 kissing gates; footpath fingerpost points ahead across 2 fields to next footpath fingerpost. Continue towards Harden's Gap farm; cross ditch by railed footbridge; right (349745) to road.

Left for 150 yards; right (352743 – bridleway fingerpost) up slope with fence on left, over summit and down far side for 180 yd. Right through hedge (354737) to top corner of Fox Covert. Left down far side of wood (blue arrow on post), following track into and out of valley. At top of bank, right (351733 – blue arrow) on track past Wardenhill Farm (349733) to Somersby.

At road (344728), right for 150 yd; on right bend, left ('footpath to Bridge Road' fingerpost) along field edge to Bridge Road (342726). Right for 350 yd to bridge over 'Tennyson's Brook'/River Lymn (339727). Return past Rectory and Grange on right (343726) and St Margaret's Church on left. Ahead at road junction ('Bag Enderby, Alford' sign). In 80 yd, right (345726 – footpath fingerpost) through White House Farm yard. Through gateway; over stile (yellow arrow); down slope to cross ditch (2 stiles). Up slope to cross stile (346723); follow field edge to thatched Ivy House Farm (347721) and St Margaret's Church, Bag Enderby (349720).

Return to Ivy House Farm; left along field edge track, down through trees. Where track bends right, keep ahead to cross Tennyson's Brook (346719 – footpath fingerpost, footbridge). Ahead up left side of ditch, then down right side of plantation, following yellow arrows. Where trees end (343716) aim ahead for Stainsby House, keeping hedge on right. At Stainsby's barns, right along lane (338716) to road (334719). Right for ½ mile; left at T-junction (338728 – 'Salmonby, Tetford' signs). In ⅓ mile, round sharp left bend; in 150 yd, at end of pine copse, right (334732 – bridleway fingerpost) along field edge with hedge on left. In ⅓ mile, path swings left; in 50 yd pass 3-finger post (332739), keeping ahead along bridleway to road (329741 – Cross Keys PH is on left). Right into Tetford. Left at road; right (329745) down Mill Lane. At end of tarmac follow path to road (333744); left to return to White Hart PH.

LENGTH OF WALK: 7 ½ miles

REFRESHMENTS: White Hart (01507-533255) or Cross Keys (01507-533206; *www.thecrosskeysinn.com*), Tetford.

Nettleton and the Nettleton Beck valley, Lincolnshire

Warm country with a heart of iron

THERE IS IRON in the soul of Nettleton. This Lincolnshire farming village is built of ironstone, richly gold stuff that crumbles beneath a rub of the finger and smears with rusty streaks after rain. The ironstone has been dug over the centuries from the sides of the steep valleys that cradle Nettleton in the flanks of the Lincolnshire wolds.

It's rolling country hereabouts, with an airy upland feel, quite unlike the flat fens and coastal clays and silts that one tends to associate with Lincolnshire, England's least 'discovered' county. The Lincolnshire wolds, running north and south for thirty miles, have an enclosed beauty of hidden valleys and unexpected vistas at the turn of a corner – a sweeping view over ten or fifteen miles of farmland, perhaps, or a thousand-year-old church tower rising over a tucked-away village. Few visitors seek out these fastnesses, and the local people like it that way.

A misty summer's morning was settling over Nettleton as I wandered up the street. A tractor went clattering by, shedding wisps of hay from its laden trailer, its roar soon overlain by the crowing of cocks from the farmyards and bleating of sheep on the green hillsides that filled in the gaps between the dark gold houses.

Thistles and grasses waved high over the heads of stone seraphim kneeling in the overgrown north quarter of the graveyard. The massive tower of the church of St John the Baptist stood on a base laid down before the Norman Conquest. The tower buttresses had been nibbled and chiselled away by wind and rain over the centuries, giving the church the appearance of something quarried entire rather than built.

The Viking Way long-distance footpath winds through the village on its 112-mile journey from the River Humber to Rutland Water in Leicestershire. The horned-helmet symbols pointed me aside into the valley of the Nettleton Beck, one of those silent and sunken dingles where no other walker ever seems to be.

The last time I came this way, four or five years ago, I had seen no one; and now, too, I trod the rough track beside the beck with only myself and the rabbits for company. They were everywhere, scurrying across the newly cut hayfields, scrabbling into burrows in the loose sandy soil and bobbing in among the meadowsweet and campion along the stream.

Stands of willows grew tall in the valley floor, nourished by streamlets running down the wet, rushy slopes. Snipe burst out from under my boots, zigzagging startlingly away with a squawk and a flash of brown and white, their tiny sickle-shaped wings whirring. A sparrow hawk darted up and over the skyline from the branch where it had been sitting on watch for small birds.

The sky thickened and darkened overhead, pressing down on the valley as it swung left and right on its climb to the crest of the wolds. Nettleton Beck, narrow enough to step over, chinked and trickled in a green tunnel of foliage. The suck of a cow's hooves came clearly through the still air as it squelched down to drink at the beck two hundred yards away. Silence lay as thickly as the air haze in the lonely valley. Yet only a few decades ago this place had hummed with industry.

At the top of the slopes each side of the path the chalk showed whitely through the turf. Chalk and sand were quarried along with the ironstone for centuries here, and the scars of their diggings and delvings still pit the landscape. Chalk on top of sand; an unstable combination, which has settled and shifted over the years to form long terraces running high above the valley. In the last decades of the seventeenth century twenty-five of Nettleton's houses were smothered by sand creeping down out of the hillside. It's a landscape in motion, lumpy and undulating, in which the new conifer plantations cling like burrs in a sheep's back.

Below Nettleton Top Farm the Viking Way plunged in among the trees and lost itself in a jungle of pink-tipped rosebay willowherb. I waded through, dislodging snails with bright yellow shells, to come suddenly on the dark mouth of a tunnel that bored through an embankment built to carry a narrow-gauge railway from the ironstone mines down to the main line a few fields away.

Men from Nettleton village joined itinerant workers from further afield in the mines, driving level galleries into the hillsides or skimming off great areas of turf and chalk in sprawling opencast mines. Since the last ironstone was extracted back in 1969 the grass and trees have reclaimed the old mines, but the ground is still hummocked with their scoops and spoil mounds.

Now the valley climbed into open grassland, and I followed it up along the ever-narrowing Nettleton Beck. Under a hedge-bank the stream trickled from a spring into a tiny pool, its surface quivering with long-legged insects.

There were more hollows and humps in the field above the spring, all that was left of the medieval village of Wykeham – perhaps abandoned when the Black Death struck, perhaps emptied by a changing climate and a search for easier ground. In those days all Nettleton's land had been contained in just two enormous fields, a thousand acres each, that stretched from the village for two long miles up the valley to the source of the beck. When the land was enclosed in the 1790s the villagers saw their common land hedged about and cultivated, and their rents quadrupled.

Nettleton may have resented those enclosing hedges when they were first planted, but today they are invaluable havens for wildlife in the intensively farmed corn lands around Acre House Farm. I found the fields of Acre House shaggy-edged with luxuriant hedges and uncultivated headlands. There were thick stands of broadleaved trees, ponds and ditches around the farm.

Curious to meet the farmer responsible for this oasis of conservation in a matt yellow plateau of grain, I knocked at the door of Acre House Farm. Five minutes later I was sitting with a glass of orange juice among tables heaped with crockery (they were in the middle of painting the house) while Motley Brant and his wife Corinne explained their philosophy.

'As few chemicals as we can get away with,' said Motley, blue paintbrush in hand, 'and as many uncut verges and hedges as we can manage. We get little owls, barn owls, finches, lots of butterflies, hares, wild flowers. It saddens me to see other farms with their fields ploughed right up to the roadside and the hedges all trimmed off short. We like to see the wildlife, that's what it is.'

Out in the farmyard the Brants' son Jonathan, also a farmer, gave enthusiastic agreement to his parents' approach. Down at Nettleton Top Farm he was doing the same sort of thing. This year the Brants had left their roadside verges uncut for the first time. Spangled with blue, yellow and pink, they made a *via gloriosa* – scabious, vetch, yarrow, ragwort, mayweed, bindweed, knapweed – from which, as the murk began to clear during the two mile walk back to Nettleton, I looked out from the spine of the wolds over twenty misty miles of Lincolnshire.

STEPPING OUT – *Walk 40*

MAP: OS 1:25,000 Explorer 282; 1:50,000 Landranger Sheet 113

TRAVEL: Road – From north (Humber Bridge and A15) or west (Scunthorpe and A18) – A1084 to Caistor, A46 to Nettleton. From east (Grimsby) and south (Lincoln) – A46 to Nettleton. Park by church.

WALK DIRECTIONS: Leaving church (OS ref TF111002) walk east up village street; bear right round bend after 200 yards and continue for ¼ mile to fork in road just past Whitestone Cottage (113997). Bear left here at Viking Way horned-helmet symbol on to farm track to Grange Farm (116995). Keep left around edge of reservoir above farm and follow valley up, keeping Nettleton Beck on your right.

Cross paved road (122984) below Nettleton Top Farm and continue through plantation, through railway embankment tunnel and on up to stile above source of beck (120971). Follow line of telegraph poles up to cross kissing gate at top of valley on right, on to track which reaches road opposite Acre House Farm (114969). Turn right and walk along road back down to Nettleton.

LENGTH OF WALK: 5½ miles – 2 hours approx.

CONDITIONS: Easy walking on roads, tracks, paths. Some muddy patches.

GEAR: Good walking shoes; flower book.

REFRESHMENTS: Salutation Inn, Nettleton (01472-851228) – on A46.

READING: *The Viking Way* (Cicerone Press).

MIDLANDS

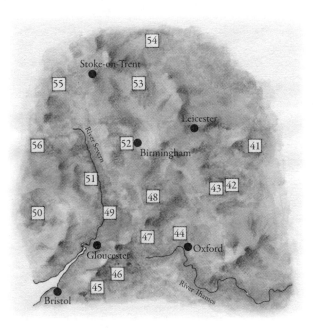

Walk 41

Oundle and the River Nene, Northamptonshire

The river valley setting where a Queen lost her head

PICTURE THE SCENE: the Northamptonshire town of Oundle more than a century ago. Dawn breaks to reveal a group of pub-lic-school masters grouped round the base of St Peter's Church, all gazing heavenwards, transfixed between fury and apprehension. Two hundred and ten feet above their heads, clinging to the apex of the gracefully tapering spire, behold young Bayley, a schoolboy who has just completed a breath-takingly brave and foolhardy climb – not his first, by some accounts – up the projecting stone crockets of the spire to reach its top.

Making my way briskly along the church footpath through crowds of present day Oundle pupils barging and banging their way to lessons, I wondered whether the current head of the school would react in a similar situation as did the headmaster when bold Bay-ley's feet finally touched the earth: first he gave his errant charge an almighty flogging – then (according to later legend, at least) he gave him a guinea for his daring.

Good stuff to grin at as I wandered round the light-flooded inte-rior of St Peter's, admiring the 500-year-old painted wooden wine-glass pulpit and the play of soft wintry sunlight on pale stone walls. Then it was out into the wind, among the stone built old houses of Oundle under their roofs of thick stone tiles darkened with moss and centuries of rainstorms.

Out in the fields to the north of the town, cows were rumi-natively grazing the half-obliterated hummocks of medieval ridge-and-furrow farming, under a sky where rain clouds were marching steadily up from the south-west. A flat landscape, with only the gen-tlest of rolls to its broad green acres; river valley country, smoothed and levelled by the River Nene and its regular, sweeping floods.

I looked back from the crest of the flood terrace to see the spire of St Peter's framed between willows; then went on along a good wide headland of grass thoughtfully left for walkers by the farmer during ploughing, into Cotterstock village.

John Dryden came to stay with his cousin Mrs Steward at Cotterstock Hall in 1698, "to unweary myself, not to drudge". The playwright found the pace of the Northamptonshire countryside so agreeable that he returned the following year and drudged away at his *Fables*. For a great man of letters, Dryden had a nice line in self-deprecation, asking his cousin in a letter: "How can you be so good to an old decrepit man – who can only be a trouble to you in all the time he stays at Cotterstock?"

A spatter of rain was pocking the waters of the millpond as I came to Cotterstock Mill. On with the anorak and waterproof trousers: then off with them again, five minutes later, as fingers of sun poked through the scurrying clouds and lit up the green meadows along the Nene.

Oundle had swung across the compass card to reappear in front of me, the spire dominating a grey scatter of houses on what I could now see was a low hillock in a flat valley – a place to keep your feet dry, a vantage point well-sited to see and be seen. St Wilfred certainly thought so: he chose Oundle as the place to found his monastery more than 1,3000 years ago.

The afternoon sun had a spring-like quality to it but the plants along the river banks told the season as faithfully as ever. Brown teazels as crisp as stubbled skin, hollow stems of hogweed and cow parsley, dark red docks that shed their empty seed cases into my palm with a feathery whisper.

I crossed over the old stone arches of Oundle Bridge that strode towards the town above the flood meadows; then under the modern bypass bridge, a graceless beast by comparison. Beyond the bridges, the high mossy roofs of Ashton Mill peeped through the willow tops. The old brick-built mill stood over its millpond reflection, closed for the winter, its doors tightly sealed.

Rooks in dozens were wheeling and cawing above the meadows, marshalling for the evening flight to their roosting woods. In a side channel of the river two brightly painted narrow-boats, *Josephine* and *Vlaardingen*, lay moored bow to stern.

I went trudging on round a great bend of the Nene under

darkening lines of trees, watching the sun go down in a diffused haze of pearly grey and thinking with increasing fondness of the love and affection I could lavish on a cup of tea. Suddenly a kingfisher shot across the river, a fast-travelling speck of brilliant silk blue that arrowed into the shadows.

Back in Oundle, the lights were on in the Talbot Inn, a comfortably aged nest of heavy dark panelling and creaky floors. I stamped the mud off my boots in the street, and went in for the long-anticipated cup that cheers. They served it to me at a table set under a big painting, and looking up at the wide-eyed expression of the lady in the centre of the composition I found myself contemplating one of the saddest moments of Northamptonshire history.

The day before this walk I had made a special pilgrimage up the Nene to the tiny riverside village of Fotheringhay, in order to climb the grassy mound where the long-vanished Fotheringhay Castle once stood. It was here that Mary Queen of Scots, seen by Queen Elizabeth I as a dangerous figurehead for treasonable Catholic plots, lay imprisoned before her execution on 8 February 1587.

Mary comported herself nobly on the day of her death. Pale and controlled, she comforted her weeping companions and absolved her executioner. Two strokes severed her head. Her lap-dog, who had been hiding under her skirts, ran to lie down between his mistress's head and body as if wishing to join them again. When the executioner held up her head to be viewed, her carefully coiffed hair under its flooring veil came treacherously free; it was a wig worn to disguise a grey crop of hair which adversity had bled of its rich colour.

Execution block and clothing were burned to make sure that there were no symbols for Catholic sympathisers to rally round, and – a final gruesome touch – Mary's blood was thoroughly scrubbed from her little dog so that he, too, could not be seized as a relic. The castle itself was demolished on the command of King James I, Mary's son, when he succeeded to the English throne in 1603; some of the stones were brought downriver to Oundle and used to build the Talbot Hotel.

At some stage during or after the demolition of Fotheringhay Castle, someone contrived to sow the castle mound with Scotch thistles. I found them there, streaming their thistledown in the wind, and wondered if dour James had ordered it himself.

That night I climbed to bed up the Talbot's handsome wooden staircase. Legend says it was the very one descended by Mary on that last sad walk. Pulling off my socks in my room among the gables, I found four big dry thistle seeds attached to the wool by cunning barbs. I unhooked them, opened the window, and let the wind float them from my palm to drift off into the rainy winter night.

STEPPING OUT – *Walk 41*

MAP: OS 1:25,000 Explorer 227; 1:50,000 Landranger Sheets 141, 142

TRAVEL: Road – A1 to Alwalton turnoff (1 mile north of A1139 Peterborough roundabout); A605 to Oundle. Park near St Peter's Church.

WALK DIRECTIONS: From the church door (OS ref TL042882), left through graveyard to road. Left along North Street and Station Road. Beyond the garage, left (043888) down New Road. In 300 yds, on left bend at St Peter's Road, go right over stile (042889 – waymark arrow); follow path across two playing fields. Through hedge, keep left with hedge on your right to cross playing-field to footbridge and waymarked path.

By willow grove (040897), bear left up bank to stile and on to road in Cotterstock (045906). Right past Cotterstock Hall and church to mill (048904); right over stile beyond (fingerpost) through meadows between Nene and mill reach. Cross guillotine lock (046902) and two weirs to Oundle Bridge (045890). Right across bridge; left over stile, under bypass and on along right bank of Nene to tubular bridge (050882) – cross to visit Ashton Mill, Ashton village and Chequered Skipper pub.

Back across bridge, continue along riverside path round long curve to go under A605 bypass (048870). In half a mile (043874) "Nene Way" arrow points across meadows to stile into Bassett Ford Road (042876). Right at top of lane, into Oundle.

LENGTH: 7½ miles – allow three hours.

CONDITIONS: Paths can be muddy.

REFRESHMENTS: Chequered Skipper PH, Ashton (01832-273494; *www.chequeredskipper.co.uk*); Talbot Hotel, New Street, Oundle (01832 273621; *www.thetalbot-oundle.com*)

Walk 42

Salcey Forest and Stoke Goldington, Northamptonshire

Peaceful woods and fields where elephants trod and bruisers battled

AND DID THOSE WRINKLY GREY FEET in ancient time walk under Salcey's trees so green? That was the local rumour – elephants abroad in wartime Northamptonshire, heaving timber with their mighty tusks, shaking the glades of ancient Salcey Forest with their trumpetings, wallowing tremendously in the woodland waterholes. The image seemed so far-fetched as to be no more than a sylvan myth. Then an elderly gentleman stepped forward to verify the story. Not only had circus elephants been pressed into forestry service; they had been ridden to work in Salcey Forest by a genuine Hollywood star, Sabu the Elephant Boy, over in England making a film with Alexander Korda.

Such exotic glamour seemed long buried on this gloriously sunny morning deep in the forest as I surveyed the waters of Elephant Pond, where only tadpoles were wriggling. Beyond the pond, though, dreams could still be spun along the swaying aerial road of Tree Top Way. The slatted walkway rose gently from the forest floor to a crow's-nest lookout 70 feet high in the pine tops. Up here in the cool morning air I got a wonderful view over the level crown of the forest towards the green surrounding countryside.

Salcey Forest, a remnant of a medieval royal hunting forest, is perfectly managed for visitors, from tiny kiddies pedalling their bikes to horse riders, naturalists, and walkers all the way up the scale from saunterers to yompers. I followed the blue-waymarked 'Woodpecker Trail' among old oaks and young birches, where warblers and wrens were reeling out their scribbly little bursts of ecstatic song, until the muted green shades of the forest suddenly intensified into a brilliant palette of open countryside – fierce yellow of oilseed rape fields, rich green of grazing meadows, pure white of may-blossom frothing in the hedges, all under a sky blue enough to make a photographer cast away his filter.

Down in the fields at Salcey Green the spire of Hanslope church rose beyond the growl of the M1. Buckinghamshire lay there, another place under other laws in 1830 when Glaswegian boxer Alexander McKay, 'The Highland Hercules', was matched against Simon Byrne of Ireland, 'The Emerald Gem', in a bare-knuckle fight for a purse of £200 each. Denied the right to fight outside the Watts Arms in Hanslope, the two bruisers and their thousands of backers decamped across the county boundary into Northamptonshire, where the magistrates were less obstructive to what was then an illegal but fanatically followed sport.

Here at Salcey Green the two men squared up. Forty-seven rounds later, McKay had been beaten unconscious. He was taken back to Hanslope, a jolting carriage ride that worsened his condition, and died of a brain haemorrhage in an upstairs room at the Watts Arms at 9 o'clock that night. When the news reached Scotland there were anti-Irish riots in Glasgow and Dundee in which seven people died. Byrne was arrested in Liverpool as he tried to flee the country, but was acquitted at his subsequent trial for murder – his well-to-do backers made sure he was represented by the best lawyers money could buy.

Three years later The Emerald Gem met the same end he had dealt to Alexander McKay; he was smashed to death by James 'The Deaf 'Un' Burke in a 99-round fight which lasted well over three hours. After these terrible events the rules of boxing were tightened up, and a measure of protection for the combatants introduced. As I walked the county boundary through the quiet sunlit landscape, the fields of Salcey Green seemed tainted by that brutal old tragedy.

Down in Stoke Goldington, Cathy Joslyn had very kindly turned out to unlock the village hall for me. Here is displayed a remarkable artefact, the Millennium Hanging, sewed and stitched by the villagers to show 115 of Stoke Goldington's houses and very much more besides. Each house is a miniature work of art in its own right, and intensely personal – I could even make out, on a tiny front lawn, the very golden retriever who had barked me into the village. Cricketers bat and bowl, tennis players leap. A minute kingfisher adds a dot of iridescent blue as he sits on a branch above the pond. The whole wonderful mosaic of life and colour is bordered by dozens of depictions of local flowers, beasts and birds.

CHURCH
PATH
OAK

TREE TOP
WAY

ATTERBURY
COPSE

SHARP LEFT
BY HORSE
CHESTNUT
TREE

ELEPHANT
POND

*

*PIDD
BLACKI
QUARTER

CAR PARK
& FOREST CAFE
(START & FINISH
OF WALK)

INFO.
POST
IO

SALCEY
LAWN
(CLEARING)

SALCEY
FOREST

NORTHAMPTONSHIR
BUCKINGHAMSHIR

FOREST FA

SALCEY
GREEN

S
TH

TREE TOP
WAY

M1

TO
HANSLOPE

FROM A
CONTEMPORARY DRAWING
OF THE McKAY v BYRNE FIGHT

DETAIL OF
MILLENNIUM
HANGING,
STOKE GOLDINGTON

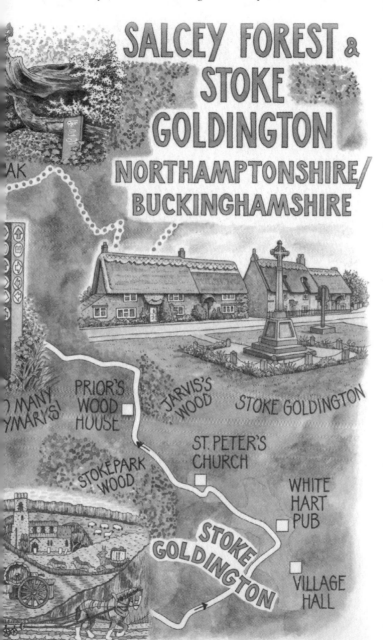

SALCEY FOREST & STOKE GOLDINGTON NORTHAMPTONSHIRE/ BUCKINGHAMSHIRE

AK

O MANY MYMARYS!

PRIOR'S WOOD HOUSE

JARVIS'S WOOD

STOKE GOLDINGTON

ST. PETER'S CHURCH

STOKEPARK WOOD

WHITE HART PUB

STOKE GOLDINGTON

VILLAGE HALL

I wandered back over the fields and through the mazy ways of Salcey Forest with a head full of marvels. Still at the back of my mind, though, nagged the hapless figures of Alexander McKay and Simon Byrne, both dead before attaining the age of thirty. The Highland Hercules lies in Hanslope churchyard under an inscription both poignant and poetic:

'Strong and athletic was my frame,
Far from my native home I came
And bravely fought with Simon Byrne,
Alas, but never to return.
Stranger, take warning from my fate
Lest you should rue your case too late: If you have ever fought before,
Determine now to fight no more.'

STEPPING OUT – *Walk 42*

MAPS: OS 1:25,000 Explorer 207; 1:50,000 Landranger 152. Map of
Salcey Forest trails from information point in car park.

TRAVEL: Road – M1 to Jct 15; A508 south towards Milton Keynes.
In 1 mile, left ('Courteenhall, Quinton'). At T-junction in
Quinton, right ('Hartwell, Quinton Green'). In 1¾ miles pass
Salcey Forest sign on left; in another ¼ mile, left at another
Salcey Forest sign into car park (794517).

WALK DIRECTIONS: From car park follow purple trail markers
('Elephant Walk') to Elephant Pond (797522) and Tree Top
Way. Return to pond; right along purple trail; right along Cycle
Trail to Church Path Oak (800524). Right along orange trail
('Church Path Walk'), bearing right over footbridge (801521) to
reach Information Post 10 (797517). Orange trail bends right,
but keep ahead on path to turn left along blue trail (797516).
Follow it for 1½ miles to south edge of forest, where it bends left
with 3 marker posts in quick succession. Between 2nd and 3rd
posts bear right (black 'bridleway' arrow on reverse of 3rd post
confirms direction), and leave forest through tall gate (804501).

Follow right-hand hedge for 3 fields; through gate (804496
– 'Circular Ride', blue arrow); left and through next gate, to turn
left on Forest Farm drive. Keep to right of farm buildings; right
along field edge (807497) with hedge on left. At field corner, by
post with 6 arrows, don't cross footbridge; turn right (811496)
along hedge, following Midshires Way (MW) and Swan's Way (SW)
arrows. At bottom of 2nd field, left across footbridge
(810489 – MW, SW); bear left again up hedge, following it
round to right. In ⅓ mile, beside telephone pole, left through
hedge, then right along field edge with hedge on right. In ½ mile
MW and SW turn off right (822485), but keep ahead through
3 cross-hedges for another ½ mile. Turn left along 4th hedge
(830480 – yellow arrow), crossing 2 stiles (arrows). Forward
along driveway with pond on left (836486) to reach road in
Stoke Goldington (837488). Right for village hall (838486); left
for White Hart (837489).

Opposite White Hart, footpath fingerpost points up lane to
church (832492). Left through gate, right around churchyard to
edge of Stokepark Wood (829492). Right over stile ('Circular

Walk' – CW) along wood edge to cross stile (CW). Ignore stile in hedge opposite; bear half left down field to cross stile in bottom left corner by pond (827495 – yellow arrows). Bear right across next field to go through gate (blue arrow), then another beside Prior's Wood House (827499). Cross Purse Lane; through two gates (blue arrows); along edge of Jarvis's Wood. Through first cross-hedge, turn left (827501 – CW) with hedge on left for ¼ mile to cross stile at corner of wood (823502 – CW). Follow oak avenue to turn right down next hedge. Cross stile (820503); follow path over rise of ground, descending to cross footplank in hedge. At bottom of following field, left (817505 – yellow and blue arrows) for ⅓ mile to enter Salcey Forest (813503 – black bridleway arrow).

In 100 yards, turn right to follow blue trail. After 1½ miles it crosses horse trail (809522 – post with white horseshoe). Don't cross here, or bear left along horse trail; instead, turn sharp left by horse chestnut tree along green path at acute angle to blue trail, with wood pasture of Blackmoor Quarter on left and woodland of Atterbury Copse on right. In ½ mile pass ruin of Piddington Oak on right (803522); keep ahead to join orange trail; follow it to car park.

LENGTH: 11 miles

REFRESHMENTS: Forest Café in car park; White Hart, Stoke Goldington (01908-551392; *www.whitehart-stokegoldington.com*)

SALCEY FOREST: 01780-444920; *www.forestry.gov.uk*

Stoke Bruerne and Grafton Regis, Northamptonshire

Best foot forward with the Gentlemen of the Ten Foot Club

IN THE END only six-tenths of the Ten Foot Club showed up on the canal wharf at Stoke Bruerne. Neat, bearded John White, cheery David Billingham and gently-spoken Stuart Knatt introduced themselves with the grins of people who are about to do something they really, really like doing.

And they do like walking, these well-seasoned ramblers. Using their ten feet to tramp the footpaths of Britain and way beyond is the great pleasure of the five long-standing members of the Ten Foot Club (20 years established and counting). The Ten Foot Club has a stirring motto: *Ite Decum Pedum*, Go Forth Ten Feet. And these men of Northamptonshire are on one particular mission above all – to raise the walking profile of their native shire.

Northants is a low-rolling and modest Midland county. Most ramblers, contemplating the map in search of a good walk, let their eyes drift briefly across Northamptonshire before deciding on the Lakes or the Peaks or somewhere with a bit more elevation and glamour. That's why the Ten Foot Club has devised a 50-mile circular walk, the Northamptonshire Round, to lure walkers into discovering some of the county's old deer parks, woods, farmlands, villages and other secrets and overlooked delights. Today the four of us were setting out to explore what John White terms 'one of the petals' – a ten-mile circuit that loops away from and then back to the main route of the Northamptonshire Round.

The murky waters of the Grand Union Canal were rippled by a buffeting autumn wind as they slapped the leaky wooden lock gates. Stoke Bruerne with its waterside cottages and old warehouses is a classic Midlands canal village. It boasts a great canal museum, housed

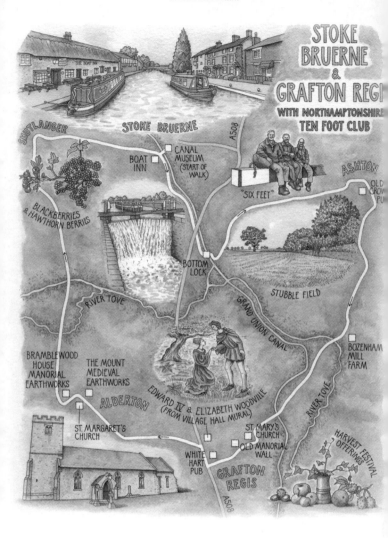

in a former grain warehouse right on the quay. Would the Six Feet mind if I whipped round it quickly? Not at all – in fact they'd come round with me.

From the museum's displays we garnered snapshot images of the tough lives of those who lived and worked on the canals – crowds of kids raised in spick-and-span narrowboat cabins, tools of cast-iron and wood, gipsy-like women in men's flat caps, bargees with forearms like legs, frosts and floods, hard work and hard drinking. Once we had struck out across the rolling stubble fields, steering with the wind in our backs to Ashton and then down the long lane to Grafton Regis, these bygone canal scenes were overlaid by others – fat black elderberries and blackberries, scarlet haws and hips and bryony berries cramming the Northamptonshire hedges.

Talk flowed, as good talk always does among walkers. 'You know how it is,' said John, chewing over the birth of the Northamptonshire Round, 'you're in the car with friends after a nice long walk and a few pints, feeling really warm and comfortable, and you find yourself saying: "I know, let's do our own footpath!" Then reality kicks in, and a whole hell of a lot of hard work ...'

It took the Ten Foot Club years of prospecting, of mapping and note-taking, of cajoling and persuading, to get their pet project nailed down and laid out on the ground. And the work didn't stop with the cutting of the inaugural ribbon. I watched Stuart clearing gates and stiles, snipping back rogue tendrils and twigs with the secateurs he'd brought along. Some of the stiles we crossed had been newly installed by Northamptonshire County Council at the behest and thanks to the politicking and pressure of John. To such modest seers and doers the rest of us owe the survival in good health of our footpath network, the best in the world.

A tiny, manic Jack Russell on springs escorted us from Bozenham Mill all the way into Grafton Regis. In this lovely village of mellow gold stone houses under thatch, a buttressed wall on the road is all that remains of the manor house where English history was made. When the 22-year-old King Edward IV – a tall golden-haired young god with the grace of a dancer and the debauched tastes of a rake-hell – came hunting at Grafton Regis, he fell like a ton of bricks for Elizabeth Woodville of Grafton Manor, a young widow. The couple were married in the village on May Day 1464. Edward continued with his womanising, while Elizabeth (in the intervals of producing ten royal children) concentrated on a programme of family social climbing, culminating in the marriage of her 20-year-old brother to the dowager Duchess of Norfolk (79 years old, but delightfully rich and well positioned).

At the White Hart the cajun tuna and the chef's own home-cooked ham proved just what the doctor ordered. Afterwards the Ten Foot Club and I had a special viewing of the murals in the village hall depicting the royal connections of Grafton Regis – Edward IV and Elizabeth Woodville flirting under an oak tree; Queen Elizabeth I sulking because the beer was bad when she visited Grafton Manor; King Henry VIII and his lover Anne Boleyn in the manor house, listening testily as Cardinal Campeggio conveyed the bad news of Pope Clement's refusal to allow Henry to divorce Catherine of Aragon in favour of the green-eyed Anne.

Under a racing sky of slate-grey and silver clouds we crunched across the stubble and vegetable fields to Alderton, talking of cabbages and kings. A knock on the door of Bramblewood House, and the owner John Kliene was courteously showing us over the lumps and bumps in his back garden where an early medieval manor house and its demesnes wait to be excavated and admired.

So much half hidden and hinted at; so many treasures beckoning from these Northamptonshire fields and hedgerows. We walked on slowly, turning over the rich soil of the day's expedition as we made across sheep pastures towards the church tower at Stoke Bruerne, with the dipping sun at our backs and our shadows lengthening before us.

STEPPING OUT – *Walk 43*

MAP: OS 1:25,000 Explorer 207; 1:50,000 Landranger 152

TRAVEL: Rail to Northampton (7 miles): *www.thetrainline.com*
Road – M1 (Jct15); A508 south towards Stony Stratford; in 3
miles, right to Stoke Bruerne. Park in village car park

WALK DIRECTIONS: Canal Museum (OS ref SP743499) is next to
car park. From museum bear left to cross lock gates; left again
to cross road at bridge. Follow right bank of canal for ¾ mile
to cross gates of bottom lock of flight (750488). In 50 yd, left
(footpath fingerpost) over stile ('Northamptonshire Round' –
NR – waymark). Over next stile and along left field edge. At end
of 2nd field, left through hedge (752493 – NR); on along field
edge. Pass brick ruin; on over open field. Cross lane (759496 –
NR); through woodland strip; bear right through 2 fields with
gates. Left (762497) past stables; through wicket gate (NR) and
next gate; right down field edge, through double gate, across
field to cross stile and reach road in Ashton (763499).

Right to T-junction by Old Crown pub; right to T-junction
(767497); right ('Bozenham Mill' sign) along lane. In ¾ mile
pass lane on left; in 100 yds, right (767483) at Bozenham Mill
Farm for 1 mile to Grafton Regis church (759469). Continue
along lane to A508; right to White Hart pub (755466).

From pub, right along A508. In 200 yd, opposite village hall,
bear left across road, then stile in hedge (754468 – footpath
fingerpost). Cross field and next stile (arrow waymark). Follow
left field edge for 500 yd; bear right by ash tree (747467 – arrow
waymark on post in hedge) across fields and over stile, aiming
for church tower, to road in Alderton (741469). Right to church
and The Mount earthworks beyond.

From The Mount, right down Church Lane, to pass
Bramblewood House (738469). Lane becomes path across
fields. In ½ mile cross brick bridge over River Tove (736477);
in another ⅓ mile, cross wooden footbridge (735483). Pass oak
in field beyond to go through gate by ash tree. Along right edge
of 3 fields for ½ mile; at end of 3rd field, right (730492 – arrow
waymark) over footbridge. Cross field to gate in far left corner
(728496); up green lane towards Shutlanger. Where lane meets
tarmac, right through kissing gate (728498 – footpath fingerpost
and NR).

Cross field to telegraph pole (NR); follow waymarks for ⅓ mile
to cross road (737498); on to reach Stoke Bruerne church and village.

LENGTH: 9½ miles.

REFRESHMENTS: Boat (01604-862428; *www.boatinn.co.uk*)
or Navigation (01604-864988), Stoke Bruerne; Old Crown,
Ashton (01604-862268); White Hart, Grafton Regis (01908-
542123; *www.pubgraftonregis.co.uk*); Plough, Shutlanger
(01604-862327)

CANAL MUSEUM: Stoke Bruerne (01604-862229; *www.
thewaterwaystrust.co.uk*)

TEN FOOT CLUB: *www.tenfootclub.org.uk*

Blenheim Park and Combe, Oxfordshire

Through frosty Oxfordshire with Dukes, Kings and jealous Queens

A ROSY DAWN and a cold blue morning, with aeroplane trails in fiery streaks across the sky and a powdering of frost on trees and fence posts. The dove-grey buildings of Woodstock glowed a rich cream in the rising sun as I passed the Glove Shop in the market place. Thin leather driving mittens in a nice cerise tan seemed to be *à la mode* for Oxfordshire ladies this winter. But I had on a pair of thermal gloves warm enough to juggle ice blocks in. It was going to be a nippy day in the landscaped dells of Blenheim Park.

The margins of the lake were skinned over with ice as brittle as glass, and the shadows thrown by the low sun blackened the great sprawl of Blenheim Palace on its rise of ground. The giant building looked hunched and formidable from this perspective, an image mirrored by the distant statue of John Churchill, 1st Duke of Marlborough, silhouetted on its column against the blue sky. Power, might and force were the impressions radiating from palace and monument – just as Queen Anne had intended them to be back in 1705, when she got Parliament to grant Churchill a staggering £240,000 towards the building of his enormous house.

Queen, Parliament and nation were all deeply indebted to the Duke for the energetic leadership and tactical nous he had displayed in thrashing the army of King Louis XIV of France at the Battle of Blenheim in August, 1704. The defeat had stymied Louis's expansionist ambitions, and Europe now rang with the name and fame of the little island off the French coast, its all-conquering general – and its queen.

Surfing along on the crest of such a euphoric wave, neither Queen Anne nor the Churchills thought to cross the t's and dot the i's over exactly who would be paying for what. By the time the giant house

DITCHLEY GATE

AKEMAN STREET ROMAN ROAD

AVENUE OF LIMES

BLENHEIM PALACE

COLUMN OF VICTORY

A44

WOODSTOC

FOOTBRIDGE

ICY RUTS AKEMAN STREET

FAIR ROSAMUND'S WELL

TRIUMPHAL ARCH

MARKE PLACE & START O WALK

GREAT BRIDGE

THE LAKE

BLENHEI PALACE

COMBE LODGE

COMBE

PARK ROAD

EAST END

COCK INN

ST. LAWRENCE'S CHURCH

BOLTON'S LANE

LANDSCAPING BY CAPABILITY BROWN

DETAIL FROM "HELL"

COMBE STATION (ALTERNATIVE START OF WALK)

BLENHEIM PARK & COMBE

OXFORDSHIRE

– more a national monument than a dwelling – was finished, and its superbly landscaped park laid out, everyone had quarrelled with everyone else. The Duke and his wife Sarah fell out with Queen Anne and were dismissed from court, Sarah and her architect John Vanbrugh became sworn enemies, and dozens of unpaid artists, craftsmen and masons cursed the name of Churchill.

Blenheim Palace and Park may have broken the hearts of their creators, but they never fail to delight the joggers, strollers and dog-walkers who take the air there today. It was beautiful in the frost-rimed miniature valleys, walking slowly north among tremendous old beeches and along the double avenue of young lime trees that leads away from Blenheim to the northern boundaries of the estate. There I turned west along a rutted old highway through stony ploughlands. The Romans built Akeman Street as straight as an arrow through the English wildwood, and I could still make out the *agger* or raised roadbed of the thoroughfare they paved with stone slabs and travelled on with such energy and confidence.

I stuck out south from Akeman Street across fields just beginning to green over with spring wheat. Under a canopy of lark song I came into Combe as a bevy of riding girls in blue velvet coats and white breeches was leaving the village. Their horses stamped and clattered, snorting jets of steam into the frosty air. Against a backdrop of church and village green, and of the Cotswold limestone cottages of Combe under their stone-tiled and thatched roofs, it all looked the absolute picture of Merrie England.

The darker side of England of the old days came vividly to life inside St Lawrence's Church, where a no-holds-barred wall painting showed 15th-century sinners exactly what they could expect – to be pitch-forked into the jaws of Hell by red-skinned, guffawing devils. But there were gentler depictions, too, in the medieval stained-glass of St Lawrence's: feathered angels with huge hands and feet, their faces full of wonder.

In the fields beyond the village, flocks of redwings and fieldfares picked over the soil side by side. I watched a cock pheasant preening himself in a blackberry clump, his scarlet cheeks blazing against the pale dry stems of the brambles. Then I plunged back into Blenheim Park among storm-shattered oaks many hundreds of years old, nodding good afternoon to more riders as they came cantering past in a fog of warm horse breath.

Half a century after the dust had settled on the Churchills and their battles, military and domestic, Capability Brown set his remarkable stamp on the landscaping of Blenheim Park. It was one of Brown's subtly curvaceous, cunningly planted valleys that brought me back to the lake by John Vanbrugh's beautiful, classical Great Bridge. And here I found Fair Rosamund's Well, its water tumbling musically into a half-frozen basin.

Long before the architects and landscapers of the 18th-century got their hands on these Oxfordshire acres, Woodstock Park had been a royal hunting ground. Fair Rosamund Clifford was installed here some time around 1165 as the mistress of King Henry II. 'A sweeter creature in this world could prince never embrace.' Legend says the besotted king made a labyrinthine lodge to keep her in, 'a house of wonderfull working, wrought like a knot in a garden, called a maze.'

There they dallied, undetected. But at last Queen Eleanor discovered Fair Rosamund's bower – some said by following a silken thread that had caught on Henry's shoe and been drawn behind him as he left his lover's bedchamber. The furious queen confronted her rival:

> ' "Cast off from thee those robes," she said,
> "That rich and costly bee,
> And drinke thee up this deadlye draught
> Which I have brought to thee."'

Did Queen Eleanor really poison Rosamund Clifford? More likely Henry simply got bored of his mistress. But the old story and its poignant allegory stayed running through my head long after the end of the walk.

STEPPING OUT – *Walk 44*

MAPS: OS 1:25,000 Explorer 180; 1:50,000 Landranger 164

TRAVEL: Rail to Combe station (*www.thetrainline.com*) – NB: only one train a day in each direction.

Road – M40 to Oxford, A44 to Woodstock.

WALK DIRECTIONS: Follow brown 'Blenheim' heritage signs in Woodstock, through market place and past church. Just before Park Street curves left to Triumphal Arch, turn right down Chaucer's Lane (OS ref SP443168). In 50 yd, ahead down steps to A44 (443169). Left for 250 yd, then left through kissing gate (441171) into Blenheim Park. Ahead towards corner of lake and Column of Victory; at lodge by lake corner (439171), ahead on tarmac road up valley for ½ mile.

With Column to your left, bear right up drive (433174) towards Ditchley Gate for ⅔ mile to second cattle grid. Left here (427183 – 'Wychwood Way' yellow arrow) along Akeman Street for ⅔ mile to descend into trees. 30 yd short of ladder-stile and wall, left (417178) along wet path. In 200 yd left over footbridge (yellow arrow) to leave trees. Bear a little to right; follow track over field to conifer plantation. Right (422175) along plantation edge to T-junction of tracks; right (421171 – yellow arrow) into another belt of trees (418168). Cross ride at bottom; climb opposite bank to bear left with high stone wall on right. In 150 yd, right (419163 – yellow arrow) over wall by ladder stile. Left for 50 yd; right (yellow arrow) up hedge to Park Road (418161). Right into Combe.

Take path across churchyard and through wall gap (414159). Right around playing field and through tree grove. Cross next field to hedge (417158). Continue along right side of wood; in 100 yards bear left, keeping trees on left. At next corner of wood (420156) bear right to reach Bolton's Lane. Right along lane if going to Combe Station (418151). Otherwise, left for 250 yd to fork; right along East End for 300 yd to Combe Lodge (427157). Left through tall kissing gate into Blenheim Park.

In 50 yd, left; follow road, which in ⅓ mile descends into valley and bends left. Bear right here (428164 – 'Slow Pheasants Crossing' sign) on grass path. In 200 yd, left over stile; follow stony track along north shore of lake. In ½ mile track rises;

200 yd beyond top of rise, bear right (435164 – 'CANADA' inscription on beech trunk), descending grassy path past Fair Rosamund's Well (437165) to reach drive at north end of Great Bridge. Turn left to face Column of Victory; take right fork and follow road for ⅓ mile to lodge (439171). Turn right to Woodstock.

LENGTH: 7½ miles (9 miles if starting at Combe Station)

GEAR: Binoculars for wall paintings in Combe Church

REFRESHMENTS: Cock Inn, Combe (01993-891288; *www. thecockatcombe.co.uk*); Blenheim Teashop, Park Street, Woodstock (01993-813814)

BLENHEIM PALACE AND PARK: *www.blenheimpalace.com*

Walk 45

Cold Ashton and St Catherine's Valley, Gloucestershire

*Through South Gloucestershire valleys with the
Director General of Ordnance Survey*

I F THE MAN IN THE CHELSEA TRACTOR had been a little more observant as he turned out of his driveway, he'd have seen the Director General of Ordnance Survey changing her trousers behind his hedge. But the A420 at Cold Ashton is a hell of a dangerous road, and he only had eyes for that. He roared off towards Bath, and a chuckling Vanessa Lawrence and I set off for our walk through the delectable valleys of the southernmost Cotswolds.

The DG of OS has to snatch whatever chances she can to get out for a walk. I'd met Vanessa briefly earlier in the year, but hadn't really thought anything would come of our parting 'be-nice-to-have-a-walk-some-day' politeness. Now here she was, taking a little down time en route from London to another West Country appointment, and looking forward mightily to getting some rain and wind in her face.

I thought a rebus was a pint-and-a-dram hard man from Edinburgh until we opened the door of Holy Trinity church. There on the wall was an elaborate stone carving of a key intertwined with a letter "I" – the rebus or pictogram of Thomas Key, Tudor-era rector of Cold Ashton, who rebuilt the church in fine style. These days the tiny ridge-top community that Rector Key once served consists of a handful of most beautiful houses in creamy grey Cotswold stone, chief among them the gabled and tall-chimneyed Tudor manor house behind its decorated stone gateway, and next to it the equally handsome and venerable Old Rectory.

Vanessa and I descended the valleys below Cold Ashton, stopping every so often to hum and haw over the wild flowers. Conversation

WHITE HART
PUB (START
OF WALK)

HOLY
TRINITY
CHURCH

THO
R

A420

COLD
ASHTON
MANOR

OLD
RECTORY

COLD
ASHTON

ST. CATHERINE'S
BROOK

OLD
MILL

COLD A

COLD A
M

ST. CATHERINE'S VA

VANESSA LAWRENCE

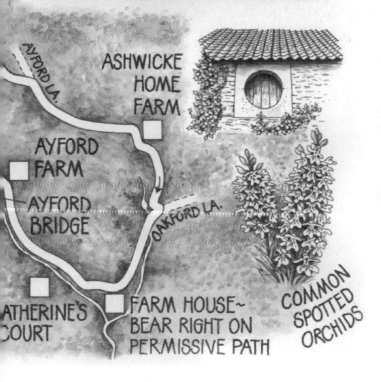

COLD ASHTON &
ST. CATHERINE'S VALLEY
SOUTH GLOUCESTERSHIRE

AYFORD LA.

ASHWICKE
HOME
FARM

AYFORD
FARM

AYFORD
BRIDGE

OAKFORD LA.

ATHERINE'S
COURT

FARM HOUSE~
BEAR RIGHT ON
PERMISSIVE PATH

COMMON
SPOTTED
ORCHIDS

bubbled along, as it does when you're out walking. A rocket-powered career trajectory saw this energetic geographer catapulted into the Director General's hot seat at Ordnance Survey eight years ago at the age of 37, the first woman to fill the post. 'They told me afterwards they'd been impressed by how quiet and calm I was at the interview, but actually I was suffering a bad bout of Cayman Island fever and feeling half dead!'

Ordnance Survey has always felt to me like a family, a friendly and supportive one. I've walked with their fabulously accurate maps all my life. I've cursed them and blessed them, torn them, lost and re-bought them. My Desert Island luxury would be a complete set of all 470 sheets of OS's incomparable 1:25,000 Explorer series of Great Britain. I'd rather have those orange-jacketed, cunningly folded, info-stuffed, fantasy-stirring masterpieces than the complete works of Shakespeare, Dickens and Wainwright combined. My Dad's old linen-backed inch-to-the-mile maps are hopelessly outdated, but I could no more bring myself to junk them than I could to throw out my children's baby photos.

I know I'm not alone in feeling this way about OS, a British institution worth its salt and anyone else's. What about Vanessa? 'Oh, it's a national treasure. I'll fight tooth and nail for Ordnance Survey. And I've made a commitment that we will go on publishing the paper maps. But we are absolutely cutting edge, too. We make 5,000 changes to our Great Britain data *every day*. What private sector organisation would commit to that, through thick and thin? We'll go on employing surveyors, too, because they get out on the ground, because they can see what lies under trees and inside holes, in a way a satellite can't. You don't know what's really there until you've actually *been* there, and our job is to record what's really there.'

From the squelchy depths of the valley we climbed with muddy boots and besmirched trousers into a network of green lanes high on the ridge, their verges thickly studded with startling blue meadow cranesbill. Slender purple rods of hedge woundwort rose among the grasses, their hairy leaves exuding a strong nettle-like stink. From here it was on down into St Catherine's Valley, rain pattering on our sleeves and collars as we slid down a hillside of bright purple pyramidal orchids and their tall pale common spotted cousins.

It felt a little odd, frankly, to be steering the Director General of Ordnance Survey through her own bailiwick, the English countryside, with her own guidance system, Explorer Sheet 155. But the talk flowed on, this way and that. I'd always thought of OS in terms of a walker's instrument, I remarked. 'Well,' said Vanessa, 'what I've learned from the job is just how much we actually underpin – keeping the mapping of Britain up to date, of course, but so many other people rely on us too: the transport network, the emergency services, the military, not to mention walkers, and drivers and ... well, basically, anybody who interacts socially with anyone else. We're there in people's lives, you could say, backing them up.'

St Catherine's valley is one of those very special places – its flowery slopes scarcely touched by modern agriculture, its woods deep and dense, its brook a winding ribbon, all presided over by the memorably graceful Tudor manor house of St Catherine's Court. Such musical luminaries as The Cure, New Order and Radiohead, captivated by its air of bucolic seclusion, have recorded seminal albums there in recent years. There were rumblings of disquiet among local residents, strange tales of goings-on, tabloid headlines. In the approaching dusk the house, now in new ownership, peeped from among its trees, exuding a dream-like tranquillity.

We threaded the silent cleft and climbed the hill towards Cold Ashton. 'Wonderful,' murmured Vanessa as we halted to stare back down the darkening curves of the valley, 'wonderful! The wild flowers, the houses, all that deep countryside hidden out of sight ... A walk I'll never forget.'

STEPPING OUT – *Walk 45*

MAPS: OS 1:25,000 Explorer 155; 1:50,000 Landranger 172

TRAVEL: Road – M4 to Jct 18; A46 ('Bath') for 3½ miles to first
roundabout; left on A420 ('Chippenham'); in ½ mile, park
at White Hart Inn on left (OS ref ST750730). NB: please ask
permission, and give the pub your custom!

WALK DIRECTIONS: Cross A420 (take care!) Follow gravelled
field track (fingerpost) to Holy Trinity Church (751727).
Through churchyard to road; left for ¼ mile; at 2nd footpath
fingerpost on right (756727), bear right off lane, descending field
to go through kissing gate under trees in lower corner (758727).
Continue down narrow cleft; by ruin at bottom, left (760726)
along valley through gates and gaps, keeping stream nearby on
right, for ¾ mile to reach metal gate ahead of you (773732).
Don't go through this, but bear right up bank to cross stile;
right (blue arrow) along Green Lane to road (769727). Left
for 100 yards; right along Halldoor Lane for ¾ mile to Ayford
Lane (778718). Right for 200 yards; on right bend, left along
green lane ('Easy Access' arrow) for ½ mile to road at Ashwicke
Home Farm (786715). Right past farm; round left bend; just
past buildings, right through kissing gate (787713 – footpath
fingerpost). Left along path above fence, then down steep slope
to Oakford Lane (787708).

Right along lane for 200 yards; right (787707 – footpath
fingerpost) to cross stream and bear left through gate (yellow
arrow). Pass lake and follow field path with fence on left for ¼
mile, to bear right just before farm house (784701 – 'permissive
path' arrow). In 200 yards, left (fingerpost) down field slope
and over stile. Fingerpost points on downhill, but bear right
on path along right (north-east) side of St Catherine's Valley,
following yellow 'Limestone Link'/LL arrows. Pass opposite
St Catherine's Court (778702) and continue up St Catherine's
Valley with St Catherine's Brook below on left for ¾ mile, to
reach lane below Ayford Farm (775710). Left for 200 yards;
round left bend, then right before Ayford Bridge, through gate
(773710 – 'LL'). Follow 'LL' through fields with brook on left
for ¾ mile to cross lane by old mill buildings (763712).

Over stile (fingerpost); half left up slope ('LL'), through gate onto road (760712). Right uphill, then immediately right down gravelly track, following field path and 'LL' along same contour, with valley and brook on right. After ¾ mile, with houses of Cold Ashton in sight on skyline to right, path descends towards valley bottom. Cross stile; in 200 yards, turn back sharply to right across valley bottom (754720). In 200 yards, left through kissing gate; follow path up valley for ¼ mile to reach post with yellow arrow under trees (752725). Bear right, steeply up bank to cross stile; up field slope to gate into lane opposite Old Rectory (751726). Right, then left through churchyard to reach White Hart.

LENGTH: 8 miles

CONDITIONS: Boggy along the valley bottom streams

REFRESHMENTS: White Hart Inn on A420 (01225-891233)

ORDNANCE SURVEY: *www.ordnancesurvey.co.uk*

Malmesbury and the Fosse Way, Wiltshire

Flying monks and marching Romans

A<small>S I CLIMBED THE STEPS</small> from the River Avon up to Malmesbury Abbey on a beautiful spring morning, a woman hurrying to work fell in step alongside. 'Visiting our town?' she cooed, in the ripest of Wiltshire accents. 'It's like going back fifty years, Malmesbury. We're a quiet little place, but there's a lot *to* us, you'll find.'

Malmesbury has plenty of time and plenty of tales on its hands, all right. Today's upstart neighbour Swindon was just a pig farm when the Normans built their magnificent abbey on the hilltop some nine hundred years ago. Only Winchester and Canterbury outdid Malmesbury in splendour and influence. Yet by the 18th century the abbey church had decayed so far that farmers were stabling their donkeys and fattening their swine within its walls.

Nowadays the church is lovingly restored and proudly displayed. The south porch in particular has wonderful Romanesque carvings of the 12 Apostles. Inside I found the tomb of King Athelstan, first king of England and a great benefactor to the town, whose burgesses turned out with sword and bow to help him beat off the marauding Danes in 930. Athelstan's tomb has lain empty since the abbey was built; the monks removed his body, perhaps to protect it from collectors of posthumous relics.

The dead king was not Malmesbury's only pre-Norman celebrity. There's a fine depiction in one of the abbey's stained glass windows of a monk holding a pair of bat-like artificial wings. Brother Eilmer enhanced the fame of the town in 1010, when he attempted to emulate the jackdaws and fly from the abbey tower. The home-made wings attached to his arms and feet carried him some six hundred yards in great style, but then the pioneer aviator attempted to flap the wings and something went wrong. Onlookers watched in horror as Eilmer crashed into a meadow, breaking both his legs.

The crippled monk was one of the sights of Malmesbury thereafter, hobbling around the lanes and expounding his theories about the mishap to anyone who would listen. I thought of brave, unlucky Eilmer and the sensation he must have caused in the superstitious Saxon community as I followed the Malmesbury Riverwalk through the meadows around the town.

The holy men of Malmesbury certainly did not lack the courage of their convictions. Daniel's Well beside the Avon was named after a Bishop Daniel, who in order to 'reduce the force of his rebellious body' would spend prayerful nights immersed up to his shoulders in the icy water. These days the spring is hidden in a damp thicket, where I struck out southward into the Wiltshire countryside under a hazy blue sky.

Bluebell shoots were beginning to thicken in the copses and hedge roots, and young lambs wriggled their tails as they butted at their mothers' udders in the fields. On Malmesbury Common – the gift of King Athelstan to the burgesses of Malmesbury, and still owned by them today – I chatted to a woman while her 4-year-old boy careered ahead with the family dogs, the personification of springtime bounce.

Here at the extreme south edge of the Cotswolds it's rich country, in many senses. Farm houses have been immaculately done up, glossy nags canter in manicured meadows, and a walker needs to keep a careful eye on the map to compensate for a distinct lack of waymarks and fingerposts. By OS Explorer and a little horse sense I steered myself to Norton and the Vine Tree Inn, where the welcome was warm and the salad nice and crunchy.

After lunch I made for the Fosse Way and gave myself up to the pleasures of walking an ancient trackway. Human determination was turning out to be the theme of this walk. The Romans who engineered the Fosse Way had no doubts about their capacity to drive a broad road for 200 miles from Exeter to Lincoln through primeval wildwood and hostile terrain. Two thousand years on, their highway still streaks like an arrow across the map of England.

Primrose clumps made cool yellow splashes in the margins of the old road, and violets studded the mossy banks under the hazels. In parts the rutted track between its tall hedges had been gravelled over, evidence of the damage done to the surface by 4-wheel-drivers.

Down in the hollow where the Fosse Way crossed the River Avon, concrete dragon's teeth defended the fragile banks of the river from selfish off-roaders who'd driven through the water. Here I lingered in the sunshine, looking under stones for the white-clawed crayfish that have recently been reintroduced to the Avon. A peaceful spot – so peaceful I could hardly spur myself on towards Malmesbury.

Back in town I went into the Abbey House Gardens for a cup of tea and a look at their famous spring display of tulips. These gardens, laid out by the 'Naked Gardeners' Ian and Barbara Pollard on the site of the old abbey gardens above the Avon, are Malmesbury's pride and joy. 'King Athelstan?' said pink-haired and pink-skinned Barbara, bounding energetically up to talk to me. 'Well, the monks took his body from the abbey and they reburied him in the abbot's garden. So he's here' – she swept her arm over knot gardens, flower beds, pathways and fountains – 'somewhere under here, resting… at peace.'

STEPPING OUT – *Walk 46*

MAP: OS 1:25,000 Explorer 168; 1:50,000 Landranger 173

TRAVEL: Road – M4 to Jct 17; A433 to Malmesbury. Park in Long Stay ('Old Station') car park

WALK DIRECTIONS: From Long Stay car park (OS ref ST933875) follow River Avon (Tetbury Branch) path by Holloway Bridge (936875) to Avon Mills, where you cross river by footbridge (935869). Bear right through Doreen Stratton memorial gate; follow riverside path to Daniel's Well (931872).

Opposite double sluice go through stone wall; left up bank between the wall and Daniel's Well thicket. At top, cross stone stile; aim across field to barn; cross 2 stiles and on with hedge on left, to stile into lane near house with tall chimneys (926869). Left, then right across stile. Cross 2 fields, going diagonally left across stiles, to cross double stile in hedge (926867). In next field cross ditch, aiming past bend of hedge ahead to reach green lane (925865). Bear left to cross gate; up field slope, to cross muddy lane (922861) by 2 gates. Keep same direction across field with hedge on left, under power lines, to cross double stiles (921860). Keep same direction across next field; bear right across stile (waymark arrow on footboard) to cross field and double stile (919859); ahead with hedge on right towards Cowage Gorse, to road (916860).

Left for 50 yd; right down drove across Malmesbury Common for 1¼ miles to road (900847). Right for 100yd; left through gate of Gorsey Leaze (899848 – the more north-westerly of the 2 Gorsey Leazes shown on the Explorer map!). This looks private, but right of way goes down right side of drive with conifer hedge on right; through gateway and on down narrow paddock; through gate at far end (896845). Cross next field and gate; bear right down track to barn, then old kissing gate on its own (893845) opposite lake at Maidford House; left here, to left side of Maidford Clump and road beyond (892840). Right into Norton; right at crossroads, then left ('Foxley, Malmesbury' signs) to Vine Tree pub (888846).

From pub return to first road fork; right here ('Easton Grey, Weston Birt' sign). In ¾ mile road bends right; in 300 yd at left bend (882858), keep ahead along Fosse Way. Follow it for 1¾ miles to pass Upper Fosse Farm (897882); in another 200 yd, right (footpath fingerpost) across field to hedge; left to road (904885). Right for 250 yd; left (906884 – bridleway sign) for ⅔ mile. Turn right (912881) along another bridleway track for ¼ mile to go through gate (913887). Bear right to Boakley Farm.

Go through farm gate to right of stables; bear left along stables (waymark) and on over stone bridge (913885).

Cross field to 5-barred fence in corner of hedge and keep ahead with this hedge on your left. Below Boakley Cliff go through 2 gates (917883); follow curve of next field with river on right to barn; ahead with hedge on right to road (922883). Right over bridge; left ('Malmesbury' sign) into Malmesbury.

Cross road junction (927878) to follow St Aldhelm's Road over crest of hill and down into town centre. Opposite Michael Thomas's butcher shop, left (931873) along Gloucester Road; in 50 yd, right between houses down narrow path to river, and car park opposite.

LENGTH: 10½ miles

REFRESHMENTS: Vine Tree PH, Norton (01666-837654; *www. thevinetree.co.uk*); Abbey House Gardens tearoom

ABBEY HOUSE GARDENS: (tel 01666-822212; *www. abbeyhousegardens.co.uk*)

Barnsley and Bibury, Gloucestershire

From Rosemary Verey's gardens through Cotswold gales and floods

'I'VE PUT A CANDLE outside,' called the girl, knocking on my bedroom door at 7.30am. 'We've got no power. Everything blew down in the night, they're saying.'

On this gale-torn morning every gutter and downpipe in Barnsley was at full gush, every tree in the village roaring. It had been a wild winter so far, with half the country now lying beneath extravagantly flooded rivers – not quite the crisp, frosty scene I'd pictured when planning this midwinter Cotswold walk back in balmy June. But at least I'd had a comfortable night in The Village Pub, as Barnsley's village pub is unequivocally named. Rupert Pendered and Tim Haigh had chiselled a friendly and cosy haven out of the rundown rural boozer they had taken over a couple of years before.

Barnsley lies in smoothly rolling country cut by gently shelving valleys through which snake shallow rivers – Leach, Coln, Churn – even-tempered streams, usually. Yesterday, after a week of almost continuous gale-driven rain, Churn had been all over the road. As I ate breakfast by the soft light of candles I wondered what I would find later that morning when I dropped into Coln's delectable valley.

Rain was still blowing about outside. I pulled on wellies and splashed off down the street to call on Rosemary Verey at Barnsley House Gardens. 'Walk in and give me a shout,' Rosemary had instructed over the telephone. 'Saves me having to come to the door.' We sat in her boudoir while Rosemary talked of her beloved 17th-century manor house and the controlled cornucopia of a garden she had been creating there for the past 40 years. (**see note in 'Stepping Out', below*)

'David and I honeymooned in this house in 1939, and we came to live here after the war. We drew up a plan for the garden, and of course we took advice and I read books old and new. Since then it's grown into a life of its own, with something beautiful and interesting for every season. We propagate our own plants, as much as possible, and they grow in soil that we make. It gives them something special – you'll see for yourself as you go round.'

I walked the narrow brick and stone paths among the herb garden's criss-cross beds, the interlaced box hedges of the knot garden, and the rich browns, greens and oranges of other winter-bound borders and beds. A Georgian temple stood over its reflection in a quiet pool where the last spits of rain plopped and died away. Colours sharpened as a ghost of pale sun stole across the garden. I could have strolled there all morning, but this gift of a break in the foul weather had to be grabbed while the chance was still there.

There were no waymarks in the grounds of Barnsley Park to the north of the village. I steered by compass and sixth sense across pasture full of handsome black-faced sheep, and crossed what the map named Cadmoor Lane. This morning it was a clay-coloured torrent eighteen inches deep. The Cotswold ploughland slopes bubbled and wept water, their rich ochre earth scoured in long streaks down to the golden oolitic limestone below. Shards of stone littered the fields, clinking to the tread of my wellingtons.

'People first built our famous walls to get the stones off the fields,' said Robin Clayton, a drystone waller I met later in the day. 'You can use pretty much any stone that's lying handy. My grandad – I learned walling from him – said to me, "Boy, if you pick up a stone, don't put'n down until you've laid'n!" It's a good occupation; I really enjoy my work, and there's plenty of it. The women don't care for wallers, though,' and he showed me his roughened, horny hands. 'They don't like to be touched with those!'

I followed the stone walls in their silvery lichen coats down into the Coln Valley among the thatched cottages of Winson. The River Coln, grossly swollen, swept between its willows at footbridge level. The water lipped the tops of my wellingtons, but I tiptoed over without getting a bootful and made tracks, squelching and slithering, up a long valley to reach the ancient Salt Way high on the downs.

In pre-refrigeration days, salt was as valuable as gold. It preserved meat, and it gave bite to a bland diet. Throughout the Middle Ages sackfuls of the precious crystals were transported by packhorse from the salt pits and wells around Droitwich, south-east along the Salt Way to the manors and monasteries of Gloucestershire.

The old ridge track, probably a prehistoric route in its origins, lay puddled and rutted. I followed it for a mile or so, head down, buffeted sideways by gusts that leaped with a shriek out of a dramatically darkening sky. Time to get off the ridge, down to more sheltered ground. I made it into St Mary's Church at Bibury just as the storm broke in earnest.

St Mary's is a good place to sit out a rainstorm. There is Saxon, Norman and Early English work to admire, and a fine display of beautifully carved stone foliage. I idled dreamily in a pew, savouring the gloomy peace of the place, until the rain ceased crashing on the windows.

Bibury gleamed as I walked its higgledy-piggledy courts and streets. The Cotswold stone houses shone in a glaze of sunlit rainwater. The River Coln sluiced viciously under the arches of the little stone footbridge that led to the crooked 17th-century weavers' cottages of Arlington Row. The green acres of Rack Isle, where the weavers once hung their wool to dry, lay drowned under four feet of water. 'No-one in the village has ever seen it like this,' said the man laying sandbags on his doorstep. 'Just have to hope for a change in the weather, won't we?'

As I climbed the trickling track of Hay Lane, thinking ahead to the fire-lit warmth of the Village Pub, the western sky was all a purple bruise. One chink of lemon yellow sun broke through, running an electric wire of gold along the upper rim of the cloud bank – a sight I would have braved a dozen rainstorms to witness.

STEPPING OUT – *Walk 47*

MAP: OS 1:25,000 OL 45; 1:50,000 Landranger 163
TRAVEL: Road – A419 (M4, Jct 15) or A429 (M4, Jct 17) to
Cirencester; B4425 to Barnsley.
WALK DIRECTIONS: From the Village Pub (OS ref SP076052)
turn left, then right through churchyard, over stile in NE corner.
Over following stile, left to cross B4425 by stone stile (078054)
into grounds of Barnsley Park. Ahead to drive; left, then bend
right round bottom of wood to cross track (080059) below
stables. Left through kissing gate opposite; right through hedge
by walled garden gates and on beside wall. Climb following
fence and cross pasture to stone stile. Cross; down slope to stile
into Cadmoor Lane (083065).

    Cross lane into field; from here, yellow arrow waymarks lead
north for ¾ mile to Fosscross Lane (084078). Cross; follow
yellow arrows north-east to road in Winson (091085). Left; in
20 yd, right down lane. Follow it round; in 50 yd, right ('Public
Footpath' stone) to cross river on footbridge (092086). Up far
bank, left between fences for 50 yd; through gate, diagonally
left up slope to wall; right and down into valley. At bottom
(096083), left up valley track for 1¼ miles to Lamborough Banks
(107096). With house on skyline ahead, left through gate and on
to road (110100). Right past house; at following right bend, keep
ahead (112098 – 'Public Path' sign) along Salt Way for 1¼ miles.
Pass New Covert Plantation; in 150 yd, through gateway; right
(123083), following stone wall and track south for 1 mile, past
Hale Barn (121079) and on down to road in Bibury (118067).

    Right to church (118065); continue to B4425; ahead for
100 yd. Left over footbridge to pass Arlington Row (115066);
up lane to B4425; left to pass Catherine Wheel PH. In 100 yd,
right opposite phone box (111067 – 'No Through Road' sign);
follow 'Ablington' sign and arrow waymarks across fields to road
(103073). Right for ¼ mile. Where 'Ablington' sign points right
(101076), turn left up Hay Lane ('RUPP' sign). Keep ahead
at road (096071); ahead again in 75 yd, along field track. In ⅓
mile track bends left; keep ahead here (092066) into woods. In
¼ mile, right along Cadmoor Lane, to stile into Barnsley Park
grounds. Retrace route to Barnsley.

LENGTH OF WALK: 11 miles

REFRESHMENTS: Village Pub, Barnsley (01285-740421; *www. thevillagepub.co.uk*); Catherine Wheel, Bibury (01285-740250; *http://catherinewheel.tablesir.com/*)

BARNSLEY HOUSE GARDENS: Barnsley House (01285-740000) is now a country house hotel, and the gardens are open to guests only.

Ford, Stanton and Stanway, Gloucestershire

A winter wander in the misty Cotswolds

THE RACEHORSES went thundering into the cold Cotswold fog, their hooves drumming on the short turf of the gallops. Jane and I, setting out after breakfast from the Plough Inn at Ford, stood staring as the young jockeys, returning from their headlong chase, pulled up their mounts and walked them round in a steaming, snorting circle.

The glossy animals, proudly high-stepping through the mist under wintry black trees, made a beautiful spectacle. Their saddle-cloths were embroidered with the letters 'JJO'. We had seen old photographs of Jonjo O'Neill on the bar walls of the Plough, holding silverware aloft with a broad grin, a champion jockey in all his glory. Here on the gallops just across the road was proof positive of his present day expertise as a trainer.

Those who go walking in the Cotswolds can hardly avoid horses. From Jonjo's fabulous thoroughbreds to pot-bellied gymkhana ponies, we must have met at least three dozen on our day-long wanderings through the north Gloucestershire woods and fields. Two fine black mares came to shadow us through their meadow at Cutsdean, and a mournful brown nag put his head out of a stable door at Carey's Farm above the infant River Windrush at Taddington to watch us go by.

It was a long time since I'd had a good day's walk with my wife, and a whole lot longer since my introduction in childhood to this gorgeous landscape of beechwoods, short steep hill slopes and hidden villages of honey-yellow limestone. My family were vale-dwellers, living down in the fens and flood meadows near the River Severn. The Cotswolds silhouetted on our skyline with their riders and pheasant-shooters, their hunt balls and sporting pubs, their golden villages and barns and field walls, were a promised land we visited for picnics and walks, especially on winter days like today with the colours of leaves, stone and sky leached to muted pastels.

Visibility was down to a hundred yards as Jane and I left the high fields and plunged down a muddy bridleway into the trees. Gundogs were yelping and shotguns popping hollowly in the depths of Oldhill Wood. Soon we met the beaters, a jolly party tramping down to the coverts in the fields below. An old man with a wrinkled, weathered face came up the track. As he passed, we noticed two pheasants slung across his back. 'I've had the good luck to find these,' he murmured, with the ghost of a rogue's wink.

The track dropped out of the mist and down to the wood's edge, then turned sharply back uphill through Lidcombe Wood, carpeted with red and gold leaves. The damp limbs of fallen trees were thick with fungi – the china white needles of 'candlesnuffers', fiery rusts, chocolate bracket fungi with frilly edges in creamy yellow. Guns were banging away in the fields around Papermill Farm. Pheasants rocketed across the valley, and the survivors came skimming and whirring in among the trees all round us.

Above the trees loomed the grassy ramparts of Shenberrow, an Iron Age hillfort commanding a superb prospect out across the patchwork fields of the Vale of Evesham. Food for the eyes and spirits on the long chilly descent down the escarpment into Stanton, where we made for the warmth of the Mount Inn and nourishment of a more practical sort.

The bacon-and-stilton baguettes were great, and so was the locally brewed Donnington's SBA; but the best thing about the Mount today was the view from the big bar window over the huddled roofs and pointed gables of Stanton's immaculate houses. A view so seductive that it drew us out into the cold once more, to wander and exclaim along the village street.

Stanton is not exactly your workaday Gloucestershire village. Almost every house is a dream of 17th-century harmony in rich gold Cotswold tones, some under thatch, some under stone roofs. The Lancashire-born architect Sir Philip Stott took on a neglected and run-down village when he bought the manor house of Stanton Court in 1906; he modernised, restored and protected Stanton with jealous care. 'Absolutely perfect – almost *too* perfect.' said Jane. 'Look, even the roses round the cottage doors are still in bloom, and it's nearly December.'

The Cotswold Way National Trail runs through Stanton, and

we followed its squelchingly muddy course southwards out of the village. The fields at the foot of the escarpment rippled with the cor-rugations of medieval ridge-and-furrow farming. Nearing Stanton's sister village of Stanway, the ground smoothed out into parkland dotted with handsome old oaks and full-grown sycamores.

The thatched pavilion on Stanway's ridged cricket field was donated to the village by J.M. Barrie, a keen cricket fan. Stories say that Barrie, while a guest at Stanway House, received inspiration for Peter Pan's fairy chum Tinkerbell when flashes of silvery moonlight, reflecting off the church's weathervane, flickered across his bedroom wall.

We passed the grand Jacobean house with its ranks of windows, the great tithe barn opposite, and the elaborate gatehouse embel-lished with carvings of foliage and scallop shells. Stanway is much smaller and less cosily grouped than Stanton, but just as charming in its golden stone houses that look as though they have grown organi-cally by the roadside.

A quick chat with Peter Gorecki, the leather-aproned blacksmith of Stanway, in his tin shed forge, and we were climbing the grassy bank of the escarpment. The Plough Inn at Ford, a cup of tea and a roaring fire lay only a mile across the fields. But when we reached the line of bare black trees along the crest of the hill, we had to stop for a moment. The view compelled us – a great backward sweep over the misty valley to Alderton Hill and Dumbleton Hill, outliers of the Cotswolds, raising their wooded backs into a wintry evening sky, lit by the last pale rays of the day.

STEPPING OUT – *Walk 48*

MAP: OS 1:25,000 Explorer OL45; 1:50,000 Landranger 150

TRAVEL: Road – M5 to Jct 9; A46 (Evesham direction); B4077 to Ford. Park at Plough Inn (OS ref SP089294).

WALK DIRECTIONS: Across B4077 from Plough Inn, 'Gloucestershire Way' sign points you up tarmac drive. In 50 yd left (yellow arrow waymark) between paddocks. In 150 yd right (088297 – footpath fingerpost) with paddock on your right. In 150 yd left across stile, then right ('Donnington Way' arrow) to top left corner of field Cross stile; then left (089300 – yellow arrow) along hedge to road in Cutsdean. Cross walled village green; continue through Manor Farm farmyard (088303 – 'Donnington Way' arrows). Cross field beyond; through far gate, left across stile, then on up Windrush valley. Cross river on footbridge (088307); follow yellow arrows up to Carey's Farm (087311); bear left to turn right along road through Taddington. In 200 yd, left (086312 – footpath fingerpost) along field hedge. Keep wall in second field on your left. Halfway along it, bear right (081313 – arrow), diagonally across field to cross road. Cross field beyond to enter wood (078317).

Bear left downhill on track for 70 yd, then right along broad bridleway. Other tracks diverge, but continue for nearly ⅔ mile on main track, steeply downhill to farm buildings at lower edge of wood (069321). Sharp right here ('Footpath/Bridleway to Snowshill, Stanton' sign) and up along edge of wood for ⅓ mile to join good forest track at gate above Papermill Farm (074323). Follow track up through woods for ½ mile until at top of rise you arrive opposite barn of Parks Farm (080329). Don't go ahead through the gate, but *bear left* here to leave trees in 200 yards. Aim ahead to cross stile in gap between trees (079332). Aim for house seen ahead. Before reaching it, left ('Cotswold Way' – CW – waymark post) down steep grassy track. By a tiny triangular green at the head of the main street, bear right to The Mount Inn (072342).

Follow CW signs for the next 3 miles (Stanton 068341 – Stanway gatehouse 061324 – B4077 at 063321 – Wood Stanway 065312 – Lower Coscombe 071307), climbing escarpment fields to Stumps Cross (076304).

Leave CW here, crossing B4077 to take lane opposite (weight restriction notice). In 300 yards, footpath fingerpost points right (078308) along left edge of quarry. At Carey's Covert follow yellow arrows on green backgrounds through the strip of trees. At far side, right along outer edge of covert. At hedge (081304), turn left down field edge to cross road (084303). Keep hedge on your left, down to road at Cutsdean sign. Left up road into Cutsdean, and follow outward route back to Ford.

LENGTH OF WALK: 10 miles

CONDITIONS: Can be very muddy in the woods.

REFRESHMENTS: Mount Inn, Stanton (01386-584316; *www. themountinn.co.uk*); Plough Inn, Ford (01386-584215; *www. theploughinnatford.co.uk*)

Tewkesbury, Deerhurst and the River Severn, Gloucestershire

After the great Flood of Tewkesbury, a walk in a boyhood landscape

PICTURE THIS as the world's media did: a quintessentially English town of mellow red brick houses and charming half-timbered cottages clustered round a stately old abbey, both church and buildings marooned in a horizon-wide sea of rust-brown water. Grim-faced women and men wading through their living rooms, holding up sodden clothes. Cars floating in the High Street. At the back of the town a racing, red-brown cataract – the River Severn, normally to be seen embracing the place like a strong, sustaining limb, now a tyrant arm squeezing in on town and townsfolk alike. That was Tewkesbury as it hit the headlines in July 2007, a victim of some of the most disastrous flooding ever seen in north-west Gloucestershire.

As one brought up on the banks of the Severn a few miles down-river, the whole scene was one of déjà vu to me. Most winters King Severn would leave his bed and march across the fields into our village. I would wake to news of the latest incursion, so thrilling to a small boy, and hare before breakfast down the lane to stand enthralled and mesmerised at the astounding sight of a world wiped out by water, of cows disconsolately lowing by barns on the hillocks we called tumps, now islands in the floods.

Later in the winter the whole mad brown sea might freeze over if we got a proper snap of cold, and then there'd be skating, sliding in gumboots, stamping to hear the ominous crack of fracturing ice, and a sudden upending of the universe as one fell through into a couple of foot of water that had come straight from the North Pole – or so my friend Andrew would assert as we ran home blue and shuddering.

Into my careless boy's head never even glanced the thought that the floods might not be quite so welcome to the grown-ups. Growing up myself, I learned to see that. And looking at the abject misery along with the stoicism that July in Tewkesbury – a town that always caught it worse than our village did, a town I saw several times in childhood swilling with floods – it felt like a sort of act of propitiation to set a walk from there.

Our family dentist had operated – the *mot juste* – in one of the oldest houses in Tewkesbury, a medieval building that still shows queer carvings among its black timbers. Other houses in the old streets have weirdly decorated beams, demonic faces to be seen peeping from the shadows. Narrow alleyways or 'courts' run crookedly down to the Mill Avon stream, and in the Abbey lurks a door plated with fragments of sword-slashed armour picked up from the Bloody Meadow outside the town, where the awful butchery of the Battle of Tewkesbury was carried out on a spring day in 1471. Such tales, such associations and oddnesses gave Tewkesbury a special appeal to me as a boy. It seemed a town both magical and sinister, where anything might suddenly happen.

How strange to find that unsettling magic still in being, as Jane and I set out from the Abbey on a blowy autumn day. Down by the tall weatherboarded water-mill where I used to step aboard the *Jolly Roger* with my sisters for cruises up the river, the half-timbered Tudor terrace of Mill Bank still ran its crookedy line along the bank. Out in the Bloody Meadow, sunshine and cloud shadow chased over the smooth grass. 'So bizarre,' Jane murmured, 'to think of that terrible horde of men struggling here, with their blood all up for slaughtering each other.'

Down by the Severn a heavy mob of geese came hissing up, waddling like bouncers with over-developed thighs. We took to the riverbank path, a lush, floodwater-enriched forest of docks, pink Himalayan balsam and great burnet whose brushy mauve heads nodded on tall stalks in the wind. A brown shading of flood-time mud dusted the plants and rose more than head high up the trunks of oaks and willows. But the river itself, slipping gently seaward far below the level of its banks, seemed a beast once more caged and contained beyond any threat.

At Deerhurst two remarkable buildings stood just back from the Severn. Odda's Chapel, for centuries in domestic use, was only recognised just over a hundred years ago for what it is – one of the most complete and beautiful Saxon chapels in Britain, with a perfect keyhole chancel arch. Just down the lane stands an even older

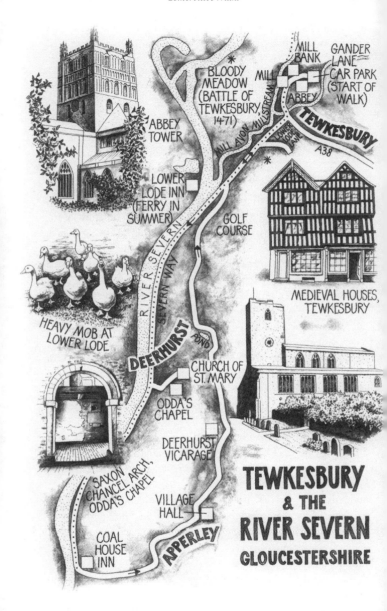

MILL
BANK

GANDER
LANE
CAR PARK
(START OF
WALK)

MILL

ABBEY

BLOODY
MEADOW
(BATTLE OF
TEWKESBURY,
1471)

MILL AVON MILLSTREAM

LOWER LODE LANE

TEWKESBURY

A38

ABBEY
TOWER

LOWER
LODE INN
(FERRY IN
SUMMER)

GOLF
COURSE

RIVER SEVERN

SEVERN WAY

MEDIEVAL HOUSES,
TEWKESBURY

HEAVY MOB AT
LOWER LODE

DEERHURST

POND

CHURCH OF
ST. MARY

ODDA'S
CHAPEL

DEERHURST
VICARAGE

SAXON
CHANCEL ARCH,
ODDA'S CHAPEL

VILLAGE
HALL

COAL
HOUSE
INN

APPERLEY

TEWKESBURY
& THE
RIVER SEVERN
GLOUCESTERSHIRE

structure, the tall Saxon minster church of St Mary with herring-bone walls and arrow-shaped internal windows. We marvelled at the carvings of snarling boar and dragon heads, a most sublime Virgin and Child welcoming incomers through the west door, and round at the east end a wonderful Byzantine angel whose broad, blank face gazes south under a horseshoe halo between two feathery wings like extravagantly raised power-shoulders.

Back beside the river we went on south through more exuberant greenery to the Coal House pub by the old coal wharf below the village of Apperley. Here we turned inland from the Severn and climbed a grassy valley, making for the homeward path through fields bristly with corn stubble and studded with mighty old oaks standing in inky pools of their own shadow. On the western skyline ran the blue humpy line of the Malvern Hills, while to the east stood up the green spine of the Cotswolds.

Six weeks before, the ancient church tower at Deerhurst had tolled the hours across the flood waters amid scenes that seemed apocalyptic in their desolation. Now the notes came to us gently across sunny fields as we sauntered back to Tewkesbury, glimpsing the broad Severn through the trees and munching the sweetest and plumpest of blackberries from hedges that might never have been inundated by those portentous waters.

STEPPING OUT – *Walk 49*

MAPS: OS 1:25,000 Explorers 190, 179; 1:50,000 Landranger 150

TRAVEL: Rail (*www.thetrainline.co.uk*) to Ashchurch for
Tewkesbury (2 miles)

Road – M5 to Jct 9; A438 to Tewkesbury; park in Gander Lane
car park (OS ref SO892324) next to Abbey.

WALK DIRECTIONS: From Tewkesbury Abbey churchyard gates
(891324) cross Church Street, go down Mill Street. Left by
mill along riverside paths; through car park; right along A38
for 100 yards; right down Lower Lode Lane (888322). In 300
yards detour left ('Battle Trail' fingerpost) to Bloody Meadow.
Back on Lower Lode Lane, follow it to picnic site at end of
road opposite Lower Lode Inn (880317); continue along Severn
Way for 1⅓ miles. Opposite Deerhurst church go through gate
(868301); in 150 yards, left by oak tree (3-way fingerpost) to
lane; left for Odda's Chapel (869299) and Church of St Mary
(870300).

Return to Severn Way; continue for 1⅓ miles to Coal
House Inn (855284). Left up lane; in 50 yards, right over cattle
(fingerpost). Aim a little right for stile (yellow arrow); on up
valley to cross stile at top; forward to road through Apperley
(862282). Left; right at phone box (863285; 'Tewkesbury,
Cheltenham'). In 400 yards, left past village hall (867285;
fingerpost) across playing field to cross right-hand of 2 stiles.
Diagonally right across field to reach top right corner (870289);
continue with hedge on right towards Deerhurst Vicarage.
Opposite Vicarage (872293) keep ahead for 100 yards; left over
stile by water tap (arrow), down left side of hedge for 100 yards,
to cross stile in right corner of dogleg (873294). Left along
hedge; in 200 yards, left over stile (arrow). Aim a little left to
cross stile into road (873298; 3-way fingerpost). Across road
are a stile (left) and a gateway (right), both with yellow arrows.
Choose stile; cross it; ahead with conifer plantation on left,
out into field. Follow hedge on right; in 100 yards cross stile
(arrows); in another 200 yards, right across footbridge (874301;
arrow, and 'Made For Walking' – MFW – waymark). Left; pass
right end of pond; cross stile. Bear left past pond, then right
(873304) up field slope with trees on left.

Continue this line along ridge, crossing stiles (arrows; MFW), keeping trees on left (NB! Watch out for badger holes!) for ⅔ mile. Just after right bend followed by 3-way fingerpost on left, bear left across stile (877312; arrow), then left down hedge with golf course on right. Continue along hedge for 350 yards; just past right bend, go left into trees (879315; yellow-topped post with arrow). In 200 yards, right over stile by gate (arrow); right along green lane to Lower Lode Lane (881317); right into Tewkesbury.

LENGTH: 8 miles

REFRESHMENTS: Tewkesbury Abbey Refectory; Coal House Inn, Gabb Lane, Apperley (01452-780211)

Dorstone and Bredwardine, Herefordshire

Around the Golden Valley in the footsteps of the curate-diarist Francis Kilvert

NINE-THIRTY, said the sundial on the village green at Dorstone. Half-past ten, contradicted my watch. After all, we were officially on BST now, though it was hard to believe it with a chill north-west wind whipping across Herefordshire from the newly snow-capped Welsh mountains.

'Did you hear?' enquired a headscarved lady in the lane, laying her gloved hand on my arm. 'We're to have Holy Communion up on Merbach Point next Sunday, Palm Sunday that is, at quarter to six in the morning! Testing our faith, he was, he said. Sounds a bit pagan to me. Going up Merbach, are you? Always cold up there, it is, but a beautiful spot, you'll find.'

They like a good chat in the Golden Valley. Up at Llan Farm the collies sniffed me over, grumbling, while the farmer took time out from bale-tossing in the barn to chew over the hard times. I climbed on, eventually, past greening hedges and the remnants of old orchards now gone wild.

Around Dorstone on Easter Sunday in times gone by they would bury a little cake and some cider in the orchards, to keep the right spirit in the place. And at the church wake, on the Sunday after the patron saint's day, there would be a mock war with crab apples instead of bullets, for much the same reason.

Up on the lumpy green crest of Merbach Hill I came to a most tremendous view. Maybe you can see a hundred miles from Merbach Point, as locals tell you; maybe more.

In the south-west rode the prows of the Black Mountains, their long hulls covered in snow, under a roof of plum-coloured cloud whose underbelly was silvered with reflected snow light. Eight hundred feet below me the River Wye ribboned back and forth down its broad valley of hedged fields, squares of green and red that glinted with standing rainwater. And out north the 2,000ft peaks of Radnor Forest and other mountains beyond shone a blurred white as snow showers marched across them.

I walked on along the north flank of Merbach Hill where lambs were bleating out thin human cries – 'Mum! Mu-u-um!' – to be answered by the gruff, phlegmy 'He-e-ere!' of the ewes in their cumbersome fleeces heavy with rain. 'Mind the daffodils!' the woman at Woolla Farm chided her trampling tot. 'We've planted tulips as well, but we never see them – a badger comes and digs them up and eats them, that's our trouble.'

Down the side of the green knoll called The Knapp I slid on red earth, in sight of the roofs of Bredwardine. Francis Kilvert was installed as vicar here in 1877, and noted with amusement what he heard about The Knapp in his diary entry for 21 January 1879: 'William Davies of Llanafan came in. The father and son were telling me of the games and sports, the fights and merriments, that went on in old times upon Bredwardine Knap. "What kind of games?" I asked. "I wouldn't suggest," said William Davies, "that they were of any spiritual good." '

Kiss chase and belly bumping: one can picture Kilvert's glee. In his happiest years of 1865–72, as curate of Clyro a few miles up the Wye, he had delighted in hinting at such rustic fun, and at his own pleasure in the idea of it. His diary for those golden years overflows with lyrical descriptions of the Clyro countryside, and with yearningly romantic, pre-Freudian raptures over the beauty and innocence of young women and girls, preferably spiced with 'sauciness'.

By the time he came to Bredwardine, however, Kilvert's health was shattered. He died in September 1879, aged only 38, just a month after marrying. On the north side of Bredwardine churchyard I came upon his grave, marked with a white marble cross, the pedestal aptly inscribed: 'He being dead yet speaketh'. Someone had arranged freshly picked daffodils in a vase in front of the grave. Inside the dark Norman church with its strange skewed chancel hung a copy of the only known photograph of Kilvert, showing a thoughtful and heavily bearded young man.

South of the church I found the tomb of George Jarvis, a remarkable man who spent his youth as a tramp around the villages of the Wye valley before going off to America and amassing a huge fortune. Jarvis died in 1793, aged 94, and left the then huge sum of £30,000 to help the youth of certain local villages, including Bredwardine, that had welcomed him in his tramping days. This started a kind of gold rush to Bredwardine by squatters hopeful of becoming local residents, thus qualifying for a share of the loot.

Kilvert wrote of the crooked old gravestones in Bredwardine churchyard, 'some taller, some shorter, some looking over the shoulders of others, and as they stood up all looking one way and facing the morning sun they looked like a crowd of men ... standing upon their feet all silent and solemn, all looking towards the East to meet the Rising of the Sun.' There are stranger stones than graveyard slabs hereabouts, however. I found them at the crest of the ridge, looking to the snowy ridges of the Black Mountains as I made my way back over to Dorstone.

The mighty 25-ton capstone of the neolithic grave known as Arthur's Stone is cracked across, and rests as a toppling roof on its bowed and bent supporting stones. 'Old Arthur' is said to have battled a king here, broken his back and buried him under the stones. Some say that cup marks in the stones are the dents made by a giant's elbows as he fell here, or maybe by Arthur's knees as he gave thanks for his victory.

There was often 'merrymaking' at Arthur's Stone in the old days, the Edwardian antiquarian Ella Mary Leather was told. Also 'much dancing'. How Francis Kilvert would have enjoyed the thought of that.

STEPPING OUT – *Walk 50*

MAP: OS 1:25,000 Explorer 201; 1:50,000 Landranger 148

TRAVEL: Road – M5 Jct 8; M50 Jct 2; A417 to Ledbury, A438 to Hereford; A465 towards Abergavenny. In 2 miles right on B4349 to Kingstone; B4348 to Dorstone.

WALK DIRECTIONS: From Pandy Inn in Dorstone (OS ref SO313416), walk down right side of green; pass phone box and church on right. Cross B4348 through kissing gate (314418 – fingerpost); stiles/arrow waymarks across recreation ground and two fields to farm lane; left to Llan Farm (313428). Yellow arrows lead through farmyard and up rising track. In field at top bear half-right to stile and lane (311433).

Cross lane and stile opposite (fingerpost); up hedge to stile into Pen-y-Moor Farm lane. Left for 50 yd; right over stile (arrow) up two fields to road (311438). Left; in 300 yd, keep ahead at Golden View house (310440). Along track for 50 yd; then keep ahead with old hedge on left for ¼ m to pass rock outcrop. In 100 yd bear half right (305443 – arrow on tree), aiming for two trees on skyline. Though gate beyond, to trig pillar on Merbach Point (303447). Descend for 100 yd to turn right along broad green track of Wye Valley Walk (WVW) following waymarks with leaping salmon logo.

Cross brackeny common to WVW waymark post at 309448. *Beware!* Yellow arrow points right, but *keep ahead* through metal gate, to see WVW on next gatepost. Continue following WVW waymarks past barn (313450) and Woolla Farm (317449), through shank of wood to cattle grid (320447). At 2nd telegraph pole in field beyond (blue arrows) bear left across field on sheep path. Pass WVW/arrow post in first hedge; bear downhill to cross next gate. Follow hedge to farm track (326446 – gate/WVW/arrow). Right to road; left down to Bredwardine. By Red Lion PH (332445), cross B4352 ('Hereford, Staunton-on-Wye' signs). In 100 yd, right to church (335445).

Returning to Red Lion, follow lane up left side of pub. Pass timbered cottage (331443). In 20 yd, 3 metal gates close together; cross middle gate; aim half-right to bisect diamond-shaped field beyond. Left over stile in top corner, steeply up slope, right along hedge (stiles, yellow arrows) to skirt to left of Finestreet

Farm (327439). At farm lane, left for 50 yd; at right bend, keep
ahead (stiles, yellow arrows) very steeply uphill past woodland
(324437) and on for ⅔ mile to road at Arthur's Stone (319431).

From Arthur's Stone cross stile in hedge (fingerpost); bear
diagonally half left downhill. Stiles/yellow arrows back down to
Dorstone.

LENGTH: 7 miles (4 hours).

REFRESHMENTS: Pandy Inn, Dorstone (01981-550273; *www.
pandyinn.co.uk*); Red Lion, Bredwardine (01981-500503; *www.
redlion-hotel.com*)

READING: *Kilvert's Diary* (Penguin paperback).

Walk 51

Malvern Link to Chase End Hill, Worcestershire

Along the spine of the Malvern Hills from end to end

D AWN CAME UP like thunder out of Worcestershire. Beyond the gauze of misty rain it looked as if some giant had carelessly spilled a vat of rhubarb and custard across the eastern horizon. But the sky was brighter as I finished breakfast at Colwall Park Hotel.

Colwall, sitting in the western shadow of the Malvern Hills about halfway along the range, seemed a good jumping-off point for a long day's hike down the central spine of the hills. 'Oh, certainly,' smiled the nice receptionist, 'if you just ring us when you get to the end we'll send someone to pick you up. No, it'll be a pleasure.' I could well see why the hotel had just won the AA's Courtesy and Care Award.

From Colwall's shabby old railway platform I boarded the nine o'clock chunter-and-chug train for Malvern Link. A spruce, choleric elderly man – beyond question an army officer retired to Malvern – sat beside me, reading titbits out of the *Telegraph* to his wife. 'Hah! Says here that Birmingham has cancelled Christmas ... Parents keep 22-stone boy on diet of chips, hmmm ... Good God, Dorothy, chicken tikka massala's being *exported* from Britain to *India*! What *are* we all coming to ...?'

They do enjoy a good fulminate, the military retirees of Malvern. And the dog walkers on Link Common like saying hello with maximum heartiness. '*Good* morning! And a fine one!' snapped a dachshund-wielding lady, chest out, cheeks ruddy. It was a fine morning, at that, with a sky of feathery clouds overhead and low winter sun splashing up against the twin humps of North Hill and the Worcestershire Beacon.

It's an eleven-mile stride from north to south of the Malvern chain, and you climb a few thousand feet while at it. The Malverns are mini-mountains, hard rock as old as any in Europe, rising steeply from the flat Severn countryside of South Worcestershire. 'Some term them the English Alps,' said Celia Fiennes in 1696, 'they are at least 2 or 3 miles up and are a Pirramidy fashion on the top.' They swoop and soar, up and down like a dragon's backbone; and it was as a dragon that I first pictured them, laid excitingly along the skyline of my Gloucestershire childhood.

Going up the slope of North Hill, 650 feet of straight-up climb, I found myself clambering between two enormous redundant quarry faces. It was Great Malvern's huge Victorian expansion as a fashionable spa town, encroaching on the open common land of the hills, that caused the Malvern Hills Conservators to come into being as a safeguarding body in 1884. It was the threat from unrestricted stone quarrying in the 1920s that saw the Conservators embark on a programme of buying up the Malvern quarries and closing them down. Nowadays the old open-face delvings, some of them flooded, are sanctuaries for birds, trees, wild flowers and water creatures.

Worcestershire Beacon's cone-shaped summit tops the Malvern range at 1,395 ft. 'The Earth is the Lord's and the Fullness Thereof' sermonises the inscription round the Victorian toposcope. Locals say you can see 15 counties from here, one-fifth of all England. I turned slowly round, absorbing a 50-mile view that hardened and melted as the skyline murk lifted and dropped: Cotswolds edging the flat Worcestershire plain in the east, the prow-like profile of the Welsh Black Mountains beyond the tumbled Herefordshire landscape out west; a blur of the Clee Hills whispering for attention up north.

Down below lay Great Malvern, a forgotten medieval priory until Dr John Wall's 1756 treatise on the benefits of Malvern spring water brought fine folk a-flocking.

> *The Malvern Water, says Doctor John Wall,*
> *Is famed for containing just nothing at all.'*

It was almost certainly the fresh air the patients gulped as they climbed to the springs, the plain country fare they ate, and an absence of stress, rather than the purity of the hill-filtered water, that effected the 'Malvern Cure'. But it made Malvern's fortune.

'Glorious, isn't it?' said a hale-looking, white-haired man who stood contemplating the view beside me. 'I come up almost every day, you know. What's really nice about the Malverns is that you can have any sort of walk you like, from rock scrambling to flat strolls. I've lived here all my life and I never tire of it at all.'

Momentarily, the sun broke through. It was a bizarre combination: hot sun on the forehead, a wintry wind freezing the cheeks, and low cloud rolling like gunsmoke on all horizons, shot through with Blakean shafts of sun that struck the plain below in intense silver pools like downward-fixed searchlights. The Malverns undulated away south, a sunlit water beast rising from a stormy grey sea.

Now I followed the steadfast southward run of the Red Earl's Dyke, a low stone and earthen bank forming the boundary between Herefordshire and Worcestershire. It stands as a relic of 13th-century strife between two proud men. The Red Earl, Gilbert de Clare, built the Dyke around 1287 after he had failed to appropriate the deer-hunting lands of the Bishop of Hereford. It was said to be so cunningly constructed that deer were able to leap eastward from the Bishop's ground into the Red Earl's, but could not jump back again.

The wind blew a premonition of winter straight from Wales. I went on south, dipping across the ancient salt track at Wyche, hurdling Perseverance and Pinnacle Hills. Up on the Bristol Camp, ramparts writhed under the turf as the Dobunni built them centuries before the Romans came to Britain. Great brown swathes of bracken clothed the slopes of Swinyard Hill, left there to provide shelter for the endangered high brown fritillary, a handsome cheetah-spotted butterfly that breeds in the Malverns.

Up Raggedstone Hill I puffed, feeling the miles now. A fornicating friar from Little Malvern Priory, sentenced to a daily penitential crawl up the hill on his knees, once cursed Raggedstone and all on whom its shadow should fall. But I came down to Bromesberrow, in the washy dark light of evening, humming contentedly to myself and thinking of Edward Elgar. The composer lived in Malvern Wells at the turn of the century, and loved the miniature mountains that so inspired him. 'If ever you are walking in the hills,' Elgar said, á propos of his cello concerto, 'and you should hear this – don't be frightened. It's only me.'

MAP: OS 1:25,000 Explorer 190; 1:50,000 Landranger 150

TRAVEL: Rail to Malvern Link (*www.thetrainline.com*)

Road: M5 to Jct 7; A4440, A449 to Malvern Link

Return: Hills Hopper bus (*http://www.malvernhillsaonb.org.uk/ pages/transport.asp*) from Hollybush

WALK DIRECTIONS: From Malvern Link station, cross railway by bridge (782425); diagonally left across Link Common, aiming for peak of North Hill, to cross road up Moorlands Road (778469). 3rd left (Link Terrace); right along Oxford Road; in 10 yd, up steps to cross A449. Left up Trinity Road. Right at top; immediately left uphill (North Hill Gardens' sign). In ¼ mile, pass clock tower on left (770470); steps behind rise to path, in 100 yd fork left up steps and then path.

Keep heading south, rising in ½ mile to saddle beside North Hill (768463). Clear path from here over Worcestershire Beacon (768452), down to cross B4218 at Wyche Cutting (769437). Continue south for 2 miles, over Perseverance and Pinnacle Hills, down to car park on B4232 (766406). Left on road for 300 yd to A449 and Malvern Hills Hotel.

Cross A449; rising path right of car park; in 30 yd, right up zig zags to top of British Camp (760400). Continue along ridge past Clutter's Cave (762394). In ¼ mile path forks; go right (stone 'The Gullet/Midsummer Hill' sign), south over Sunniford Hill and steeply down through bracken (762382) to car park beside Gullet Quarry (762381). Right (west) on woodland path for ⅓ mile to meet Worcestershire Way (756380). Left (south) for ¾ mile to A438 in Hollybush (758368). *Car park here, opposite bus stop for return journey to Malvern Link.*

To finish walk: turn left for 250 yd; right before phone box (761369), up track past Old Post Office into woods. In ¼ mile, just before right bend, go right up narrow muddy path over Ragged Stone hill; on down to road at Whiteleaved Oak (761359). Right for 200 yd; past post box, left ('No Horses' sign); over Chase End Hill, down to road (758350) at south end of Malvern Hills chain.

Retrace steps to Hollybush (758368) for return journey to Malvern Link.

LENGTH OF WALK: 11 miles

REFRESHMENTS: Malvern Hills Hotel (01684-540690; *www. malvernhillshotel.co.uk*)

Birmingham, West Midlands

Along the canals and through the heart of the 'Venice of the North'

'What mortals so happy as Birmingham Boys?
What people so flushed with the sweetest of joys?
All hearts fraught with mirth at the Wharf shall appear,
Their aspects proclaim it the Jubilee year...'

WHEN BIRMINGHAM'S LOCAL BARD John Freeth penned his *Inland Navigation: An Ode* in 1769, it was in sincere tribute to a great man's vision. That was the year that the pioneer canal engineer, James Brindley, brought his Birmingham Canal Navigation, the first of many, into the city centre from the coalfields at Wednesbury, nine miles away in the Black Country to the north-west.

The brass workers, iron-masters and toolmakers of Birmingham had become desperate for cheap coal and sick of the delays caused by horse-drawn consignments bumping slowly over bad roads. Now their hearts were fraught with mirth, as coal prices plummeted and coal came pouring in. Brindley, the semi-literate innovator, had introduced a transport system that was to catapult the city and its neighbouring Black Country district to their peak of Victorian prosperity.

The remarkable writer Elihu Burritt, US Consul in Great Britain in the mid-19th century, has left a tremendously vigorous description of the Black Country at night, taking a battlefield as his extended metaphor: 'Wolverhampton stood by her black mortars which shot their red volleys into the night. Coseley and Bilston and Wednesbury replied bomb for bomb, and set the clouds on fire above with their lighted matches. Dudley, Oldbury, Albion, and Smethwick, on the right, piled their heavy-breachers at the iron-works on the other side; while West Bromwich and distant Walsall showed that their men were standing as bravely to their guns, and that their guns were charged to the muzzle with the grape and canister of the mine. The canals twisting and crossing through the field of battle, showed by patches in the light like bleeding veins.'

Burritt and Brindley might have gasped – perhaps with horror, more likely with admiration – if they could have stood with me and stared around Gas Street Basin today. Up to 30 feet above canal level the scene looked Victorian: red-brick toll-houses and whitewashed canal-company offices, arched bridges, a stumpy factory chimney, lines of moored narrow-boats.

Behind and over these towered the architectural grandiosities of the late 20th century – smooth-faced giants of tinted glass and concrete, 10 and 15 times the height of the canal-side buildings, so monstrously out of scale that the eye discarded them as irrelevant beside the human details of lunchtime drinkers in the pubs, two men eating sandwiches, a Shetland sheepdog barking from the narrow-boat *Ash*.

'She's a butty boat,' said the woman who emerged from the narrow-boat's cabin to quieten her dog. 'See the big rudder? No motor – she'd have been towed behind another boat. Comfortable enough to live in, really, even today.'

We stood yarning in the sunshine, the kind of talk you fall into sooner or later along the Birmingham canals. 'Back in the 1960s the canals were in a terrible state. You couldn't even give a boat away in those days – no one wanted them. Different now, of course, with all the leisure interest. And I must say they've made a good job of restoring these canals, making them more pleasant.'

When James Brindley cut out the path to Birmingham, others were not slow to follow. By 1792 the Worcester & Birmingham Canal Company had begun to dig southward from Gas Street Basin to open a route to the River Severn and the Bristol Channel. The Birmingham Canal Navigation was so terrified of losing trade that it built a prophylactic barrier – the Worcester Bar, on whose bricks I stood chatting with *Ash*'s dog-owner – to prevent intercourse with its unwelcome neighbour. By the 1850s, there were 160 miles of canal in the Birmingham area. 'More canals than Venice,' boasted the locals.

The genius loci caught me a smack as I crossed Broad Street and came into the windy prairies of Centenary Square. Big – not to say brash – is beautiful in Birmingham, and here were epic expressions of the city's unbounded energy. Matthew Boulton, James Watt and William Murdoch, three entrepreneurial heroes of the Industrial

Revolution, stood in their frock coats on a plinth, gravely parcelling up the future, their capable hands full of plans.

The Municipal Bank and the Civic Centre faced each other like lordly cousins in white-faced grandeur. The megalithic Hyatt Hotel was umbilically linked by an aerial walkway to the blue glass and grey concrete curves of the International Convention Centre. Children squealed and clambered on a complicated sculpture showing massed ranks of joyful citizens striding towards the hi-tech Future from the smoke-belching factory of the Past.

Beyond the square I found the dark ribbon of the Birmingham & Fazeley Canal, and dropped immediately back into that shadowy, quiet undercurrent that flows through the hidden roots of the city. The B&FC, engineered by the Scot John Smeaton and opened in 1789, was always a bitch to operate over the 13 locks at Farmer's Bridge. The flight created round the clock traffic jams, as barge skippers jostled for entry to the locks.

Halfway down the flight I paused, remembering the years when Jane and I were raising our young family here in the 'Venice of the North'. From the Farmer's Bridge locks we would steer the children up dark steps, emerging into Newhall Street in the city's Jewellery Quarter, where Birmingham's wonderful Museum of Science and Industry occupied a giant old building of great beauty, a proper Temple of the Industrial Revolution in dignified red brick with ranks of imposing semi-elliptical windows. Inside lay behemoths of steam locomotives, wheezing pistons and greasily whirring flywheels, a rattling octopus of a bottling machine, and the great beam engine made in 1779 by James Watt to lift water up the Birmingham Canal Navigation's locks at Smethwick. This was Brummagem in essence – power, inventiveness, practicality, a pinch of the grotesque and a touch of genius.

I don't know who enjoyed it more, the children or us, but it was always one of our favourite weekend ports of call. Nowadays some of the exhibits reside at the modern Millennium Point centre in a sparkling new home with a trendily run-together name, ThinkTank. Many of the clanky, clunky things our children loved are no longer to be seen there; and as for the building, it 'awaits developments'.

Down on the canal in the present day, I heaved a sigh for non-interactive education. Then I turned round, working my way back up the locks to reach Deep Cutting Junction. Here at the hub of the city is the meeting point of the Birmingham & Fazeley and the Worcester

& Birmingham canals. Deep Cutting Junction is also the exact centre of the great figure-of-eight described by the entire canal system of England.

A man in shorts and unlaced boots leaned on the railing of a cast-iron footbridge, gazing in total absorption as *Water Lillie* – 'C & M Mann' lettered among her carefully painted castles and roses – glided past. C (or perhaps M) Mann stood proudly at the tiller in a nautical cap, admiring his red geraniums in their boxes along the narrow blue roof.

Unwilling to take the last few steps back to Gas Street Basin just yet, I leaned alongside the unlaced idler and looked with him over the treacle-black water towards Birmingham's heartland. Below the loom of the futuristic glass towers, diminutive brick arches led the eye beneath hump-backed canal bridges into reflections of the city's vigorous and practical past.

STEPPING OUT – *Walk 52*

MAP: Canal maps, walks leaflets and books from Birmingham Tourism Centre and Ticket Shop (see below), and downloadable from *http://www.waterscape.com/canals-and-rivers/bcn*

TRAVEL: Rail to Birmingham New Street (*www.thetrainline.com*) Road: M6/M5

From New Street Station, follow City Centre or International Convention Centre signs. Gas Street Basin is next to Hyatt Regency Hotel.

WALK DIRECTIONS: From Gas Street Basin, climb steps to Bridge Street; left to cross Broad Street. Diagonally right across Centenary Square; down left side of Baskerville House; cross Cambridge Street; ahead down Brindley Drive to reach canal Turn right down Farmer's Bridge lock flight. Return under Saturday Bridge; on along towpath to Deep Cutting Junction (named Old Turn Junction on three-armed signpost). Continue below Sheepcote Street Bridge; cross St Vincent Street Bridge and return on opposite towpath to Deep Cutting Junction; bear right for Gas Street Basin.

LENGTH OF WALK: Allow two hours

REFRESHMENTS: Tap & Spile, Gas Street Basin (0121-632-5602; *www.tapandspilebirmingham.co.uk*); Prince of Wales, Cambridge Street (0121-643-9460); The Malthouse, Deep Cutting Junction (0121-633-4171)

INFORMATION: Birmingham Tourism Centre and Ticket Shop, The Rotunda, 150 New Street, Birmingham (0844-888-3883; *www.beinbirmingham.com*)

ALSO WATERSCAPE: *http://www.waterscape.com/canals-and-rivers/bcn*

Dovedale, Derbyshire/Staffordshire border

Spectacular Peak District scenery along the Compleat Angler's river

SHIVERING IN A DAWN WIND on the footbridge at the entrance to Dovedale, I looked eastward to see the sky over Derbyshire a delicate pink and gold. Above Staffordshire in the west it was the pure, translucent blue you only get on a chilly winter's morning before sunrise. Below my feet the River Dove ran barging down the dale, muddy brown and roaring, as a reminder of just how violent yesterday's rainbursts over the Peak District had been.

Dovedale is the showpiece dale of the White Peak, a dramatically deep and sinuous cleft from whose depths rise naked pinnacles of rock a hundred feet tall and more. The River Dove has cut this great gorge for itself, wearing gradually down through the limestone. The Dove can be a gentle, sparkling stream, or a loud sluice of floodwater like today's river. It's always beautiful, whatever its mood. This early on a cold morning at the dead season of the year, I had the place entirely to myself. Just me and the dippers.

The stout brown birds with large white bibs were excited by the fresh food being washed out of the riverbed mud by the risen Dove. They pattered on the wet grass by the riverside, stopping every few seconds to bob down and up. One dipper jumped boldly into a backwater, and I watched it disappear under the water to walk along the riverbed in search of drowned grubs. In a few seconds it was back on the grass and had resumed its clockwork bobbing and intent scrutiny of the river.

The dippers kept me company until the path rose from the waterside to the bald knob of rock called Lover's Leap. From here I had a wonderful view over the pinnacles on the Staffordshire bank, appropriately bearded with lichens, that the tourists of the Romantic Age named the Twelve Apostles. Upriver the sharp teeth of Tissington Spires cut the skyline of the Derbyshire rim of Dovedale.

When Dean Langton of Clougher ascended Lover's Leap on horseback in 1761, he may have leaned a little too far out from the saddle to admire the Spires or the Apostles, or perhaps the bare rock was slippery with rain. Whatever the cause, the unlucky cleric and his horse skidded over the edge and fell to their deaths. His lady companion fell as well; but her long hair became entangled in the branches of a tree and brought her up short. Someone climbed the tree and rescued her, 'much alarmed but not seriously hurt'.

Further up the dale there were caves high in the rocky sides of the gorge: the forty-foot rounded arch of Reynard's Cave, the dark owl's-eye hollows of Dove Holes. The river gouged them out of the rock many millennia ago, when it flowed as a giant tide that ran halfway up the dale sides.

Up at Milldale the houses huddled picturesquely under their slate roofs near the river. There used to be two mills at Milldale: a lead mill, and an ochre mill that turned the Dove brilliant orange. Mill leats and the river are spanned by a slender old packhorse bridge, known as Viator's Bridge. 'Viator, the Wayfarer' was the name the old London ironmonger Izaak Walton gave himself in 1654 in *The Compleat Angler,* his best-selling paean to the joys of fishing. 'Piscator' was how he referred to his young friend and angling companion Charles Cotton of Beresford Hall, just up the dale.

Viator and Piscator came often to the old packhorse bridge to fish the Dove. 'The finest river that I ever saw,' declared Walton, 'and the fullest of fish.' Gentle Walton with his sincere Christianity and the spendthrift gambler and scapegrace Cotton were an unlikely pair. But when they were together beside the Dove, plying their six-yard hazel rods and their horsehair lines dyed with beer and soot to fool the trout, the old and the young angler were as one.

In the Church of St Peter up at Alstonefield above the dale, I found the big old canopied pew – dashingly carved with dragons – in which the Cotton family used to worship. Izaak Walton must have prayed there, too, while a guest at Beresford Hall. I don't know whether Alstonefield's George Inn was in business back in the 1660s and '70s, but Viator and Piscator with their taste for decent inns would certainly have enjoyed sipping a pint or two there, as I did around midday.

Last time I had entered the George, fifteen years before, it had been in drowned rat mode. Rain had soaked me to such an extent that I'd had to strip off and hang every stitch across the chair backs to dry out in front of the bar fire. All I was suffering from this time was thirst and cold fingers, and it didn't take long to fix both complaints.

My morning road to Alstonefield had been the low road of the dale bottom. The afternoon's return journey was all high plateau, a ramble by Stanshope and Damgate through green fields striped with pale drystone walls. In one field lay three dozen ewes with the blue smear of raddle on their rumps. An exhausted-looking tup stood head down and motionless among them, literally ridden to a standstill.

Back down at the dale mouth I turned aside for an hour's idling around the gorgeous little estate village of Ilam. The River Manifold rushed through the arches of Ilam bridge, as swollen and thunderous as the Dove a mile or two away. An ominous thickening of the dusk light showed that more rain was on the way. I put my back to the cold west wind, and made for the Izaak Walton Hotel and a nice hot cup of tea.

STEPPING OUT – *Walk 53*

MAP: 1:25,000 Explorer OL 24; OS 1:50,000 Landranger 119

TRAVEL: Road – A523 or A515 (N), A52 (E and W) or A515 (S)
to Ashbourne; then follow brown 'Dove Dale' signs to Izaak
Walton Hotel or Dovedale car park, both between Thorpe and
Ilam.

WALK DIRECTIONS: From terrace of Izaak Walton Hotel (OS ref
SK144508), 'Dovedale & Stepping Stones' sign points across
field and down to Dovedale car park (146509). From car park
walk along road towards Dovedale; in 100 yd cross river by
footbridge. Turn left along east bank of River Dove through
Dovedale for 3 miles, to cross packhorse bridge at Milldale
(139547). Bear right off bridge, then immediately left ('1896'
house on left) and right (by Polly's Cottage) up walled Millway
Lane to Alstonefield. Pass church (133554); continue along road
to George PH (131556).

Leaving George (and facing village green), turn right to
pass The Cottage Studio: continue past one grass triangle
to T-junction at the next triangle. Left here ('Wetton, Ilam,
Dovedale' sign); immediately left again (130555 – footpath
fingerpost) along walled lane. In 150 yds lane turns right ('Top of
Hope' sign); but keep ahead here ('Stanshope' fingerpost) with
field wall on right. At bottom of field, bear right by tree (131551);
follow wall down to road (129549). Up walled lane opposite to
Stanshope.

At T-junction by Stanshope Hall (128542), left along walled
lane ('Milldale, Dovedale' fingerpost). In 100 yds, right through
wicket gate ('Dovedale, Hall Dale' fingerpost); follow yellow
arrows, cutting corners of 3 fields. At third post (130541) arrows
point forward down Hall Dale; but go right through wicket
gate and on through following stile. Keep ahead with wall on
right to cross next stile (arrow). In 70 yd wall ends (130537);
keep ahead across field to cross ladder stile. Bear right with wall
on right to cross stone stile in tumbledown wall near Damgate
Farm. Aim diagonally left, climbing field to far corner. Cross
wall stile; follow wall up for 40 yd, past gate, to cross stile on
right (130533). Diagonally left across field to road (129531). Left
along road.

In ½ mile road dips and bends right. Left here on track
(133523 – 'Air Cottage Farm' sign). In 70 yds go through stone
gateway; right across field, aiming for left edge of trees ahead.
On far side of field cross wall stile (135518); right along wall.
Cross bumpy hillside to go through stile in wall (137517). Tracks
diverge here; left one rises over Bunster Hill spur, back to Izaak
Walton Hotel. If you want to explore Ilam, bear downhill,
keeping wall on your right, for ½ mile to road (137509). For
Ilam village, descend onto road and turn right; for Izaak Walton
Hotel, stay above road and continue on path through several
fields (stiles, yellow arrows) to reach hotel.

LENGTH OF WALK: 8½ miles

REFRESHMENTS: George PH, Alstonefield (01335-310205; *www.
thegeorgeatalstonefield.com*); National Trust teashop, Ilam
(01335-350254; www.nationaltrust.org.uk); Izaak Walton Hotel,
Dovedale (01335-350555; *www.izaakwaltonhotel.com*)

Walk 54

Hathersage and Stanage Edge, Derbyshire

Giants and madwomen, climbers and gliders of the Dark Peak

I T WAS A RED DAWN and a murky sunrise over the Midlands as I
drove north into Derbyshire. But as I swung over Bradwell Edge
and looked down into the lush farmland of the Hope Valley, the
snake of mist that traced the sinuous curves of the River Derwent
was already shredding away. By the time I got to Hathersage, the gritstone houses and road walls were beginning to sparkle under a pale
disc of sun.

On a pub sign in the village street I spotted a likeness of Little
John, Hathersage's favourite and most famous son. The fierce but
genial giant who once tumbled Robin Hood into a stream stood
depicted in tunic of untraditional blue, his nickname abbreviated to
a curt, if trendy, 'LJ'. Up in the churchyard of St Michael and All
Angels I found his grave, long enough for two ordinary mortals.
Those who opened the grave in 1784 reported finding an immense
thighbone nearly 3 feet long. Little John's mighty bow and his cap
of Lincoln green hung in St Michael's Church for hundreds of years;
his cottage near the churchyard stood until it was demolished during
the 19th century. Whatever the verifiable facts about Robin Hood's
right-hand man, Hathersage continues to bask in the reflected glory
of the Big Man of Sherwood Forest.

I pondered his provenance as I climbed the frost-whitened field
paths north of the valley, munching my breakfast – one of Hathersage bakery's delectable meat-and-potato pies. Back in the 12th
century the Hope Valley lay within the northern bounds of Sherwood Forest. Could bold Robin and brave John have crouched once
upon a time among the ancestors of these oaks and beeches, the grey
goose-feather flights pulled tight beside their ears, a fine fallow hart
in their sights?

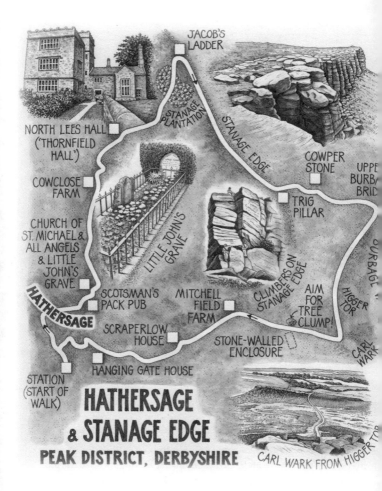

The handsome Tudor house of North Lees Hall stands close under Stanage Edge. Its tall old tower spawned a tale in the mind of a 19th-century governess, a fable which has earned an immortality to equal that of Robin and his Merrie Men. Charlotte Brontë first caught sight of the pale stone tower in 1845 when she came for a three-week stay in Hathersage with her friend Ellen Nussey, sister of the town's vicar. The local surname of Eyre caught Charlotte's inner ear, too. Soon Jane Eyre would apprehensively approach the dark tower of Thornfield Hall, lair of the saturnine Mr Rochester: 'It was three storeys high, of proportions not vast, though considerable: a gentleman's manor-house, not a nobleman's seat: battlements round the top gave it a picturesque look.'

Those battlements were to be the setting for one of the most dramatic scenes in literature, as poor mad Mrs Rochester made her final bid for freedom from a terrible fire she had herself started: 'She was on the roof, where she was standing, waving her arms above the battlements, and shouting out till they could hear her a mile off... She had long black hair: we could see it streaming against the flames as Mr Rochester ascended through the skylight; we saw him approach her; and then ma'am, she yelled and gave a spring, and the next minute she lay smashed on the pavement.'

For five minutes I stood at the gate, staring up at the sunlit tower, struck still and dumb by the power of that tremendous moment. I had walked on through the bare trees and up the ancient packhorse road to the summit of Stanage Edge before the picture faded and was overlaid by other, more immediate images – helmeted rock climbers festooned with spaghetti strings of rope, walkers filing up the rocky path of Jacob's Ladder, and soaring above all the rainbow-coloured arc of a brave (and cold-impervious) paraglider's sail.

Stanage Edge, the rocky rim of what was once a gigantic dome of millstone grit, is a climber's and boulderer's heaven. The grey adhesive rock, fractured into steps, cracks and layers, offers challenges to test the virgin tyro as well as the complete and utter expert. Famous names from that introverted, macho and phenomenally athletic world, the hardest of the 'hard man' school – Don Whillans, Nat Allen, Joe Brown and their ilk – cut their climbing teeth along these modest-looking crags. They and their successors dubbed every climbable crack and interstice with names superbly curt and clipped: Goliath's Groove, Agony Crack, The Unconquerables, The Vice, Blockhead Direct, Queersville, The Eliminator.

I strode the flat, tricky gritstone pavement along the Edge, face to the cold wind, in a kind of high-level ecstasy. Climbers crouched and sprawled in impossibly heroic poses on every crag, and beyond them a most enormous view opened to the south and west across the frosted fields and shadowy moors and edges of the Dark Peak. To the left ran cream and purple moors, the wind streaming their pale grasses so that the whole wide upland appeared to be in motion, racing north into Yorkshire.

Quitting Stanage Edge at last did not mean quitting these

wonderful heights. Higger Tor and Carl Wark lay ahead, flat-topped tors like castles. I stormed their walls in an outpouring of super-charged energy. Then, breathless and buffeted by the cold and wind, I dropped down through tumbled meadows around Mitchell Field Farm and the mock-baronial miniature fortress of Scraperlow House; down towards Hathersage, the warmth and light of the Scotsman's Pack inn, and the grey church spire that marks where Little John lies sleeping until Robin's horn wakes him for one last chase through the glades of the eternal Forest.

STEPPING OUT – *Walk 54*

MAP: OS 1:25,000 Explorer OL1; 1:50,000 Landranger 110

TRAVEL: Rail to Hathersage (*www.thetrainline.com*)

Road – M6 to Jct 17; A534 to Congleton, A54 to Buxton; A6
towards Matlock, B6049 to Tidewell, Brough and A6187 to
Hathersage.

WALK DIRECTIONS: From Hathersage station (OS ref SK233811),
up approach road; right along B6001 to village main street
(230815); right to end of village; left down School Lane.
Opposite Scotsman's Pack pub (235817), up Church Bank; left
to church (234818). Leaving church, left from lych gate for 50
yards; at left bend, right over stile (fingerpost); in 50 yards, left
(arrow) down steps to cross stile and footbridge (234820). Up
field edge with hedge on left; at top of slope bear right (233822;
arrow). Follow stiles and arrows with fence on left to Cowclose
Farm (234829). Follow track to right of buildings, through gate
and on along hillside, bending right above farm drive to road
(235831). Left for 100 yards; right (fingerpost) up drive to North
Lees Hall (235834).

Follow stony track round left bend; in 50 yards, right
(arrow) through gate; follow grassy path (fingerpost) into wood
(238835). Up stony track for 200 yards; left up steps to cross
road (239837). Follow bridleway across open ground and up
through Stanage Plantation (240839) onto crest of Stanage Edge
(240844). Right along Edge for 1 mile to trig pillar (251830).
Just before it, bear left past rock outcrop with wooden rail,
on clear moor path. Before Cowper Stone bear right (253831),
descending through boulders to follow moor path for 700 yards
to road just west of Upper Burbage Bridge (259830).

Left along road for 100 yards; right into car park, left through
gate (fingerpost). Bear right on path along west edge of Burbage
Valley, to reach top of Higger Tor (257820). Keep near left edge;
scramble down boulders at south-east end; follow path towards
Carl Wark. 50 yards before path begins to climb up Carl Wark,
right (258815) on narrow path, aiming a little left of left end of
Higger Tor, then making for bushy tree clump just to right of
stone-walled animal enclosure. At end of enclosure (253816),
bear half right past trees; descend beside wall to cross road and
stile (251816).

Bear left downhill to Mitchell Field farm. Left along stony track (248817) past farm gate; right (fingerpost), climbing to cross wall stile; half right across next wall stile; diagonally left over bracken field, through gate (244814) onto drive at Scraperlow House. Left through entrance gate; in 100 yards, on left bend, ahead (arrow) with wall on right to pass through gap with stile (242812). Descend for 30 yards; cross stile and descend sunken lane with wall on left, trees on right. Near bottom of wood 239812), left down slope and on down lane, passing Hanging Gate house to reach A6187 (234813). For Hathersage turn right. For station, left for 100 yards; right (fingerpost) through gate, down field slope, then right to lane (233813). Left to B6001, left and left again to station.

LENGTH: 7 ½ miles

REFRESHMENTS: Scotsman's Pack, School Lane, Hathersage (01433-650253; *www.scotsmanspack.com*)

GUIDEBOOKS: 'Hathersage Sunday Walk' in *Walking Weekends: Peak District* by Mark Reid (InnWay Publications, *www.innway. co.uk*).

Wem, Fenn's and Whixall Mosses, Shropshire/Clwyd border

Out among the great forgotten bogs of the north Welsh Borders

I HUDDLED MYSELF DOWN into my thrice-wound scarf, bunching gloved hands in pockets and shivering like a new-born calf. It was nippy out in the early chill with a northerly breeze blowing from the great mosses of North Shropshire, where I was headed from North-wood village this wintry morning.

What is really remarkable about the mosses or raised bogs of this low-lying region along the Welsh border is how very little known they are. Most of the mosses were cut to ribbons in the past for their peat, so slow and hot to burn on a domestic hearth, so fertile as a garden compost. All cutting ceased in 1990. Nowadays the 2,300 acres of this huge Site of Special Scientific Interest and National Nature Reserve nurture thousands of white-fronted geese in winter, along with the stiff-winged short-eared owls that hunt the flat boglands.

Here is more solitude than the most hard-pressed poet in a city could ever yearn for, and a sombre beauty of muted colours and subtle shapes, all under a vast bowl of sky. Yet you can pretty much guarantee having the squelchy peatland trails across Fenn's, Whixall, Bettisfield, Wem and Cadney Mosses to yourself, at this time of year in particular. Somehow, shielded among swathes of undramatic farming country, the North Shropshire mosses and their winter charms exist below the radar of all but a handful of admirers lucky enough to have heard of or stumbled upon them at this season.

Hurrying briskly north against the cold, I moved through a countryside of brick built farmhouses and frosty cabbage fields, low-lying and open to the elements. A flock of fieldfares, recently arrived for the winter, skittered out of a hedge where they had been stripping scarlet hawthorn berries and flew in front of me, dipping

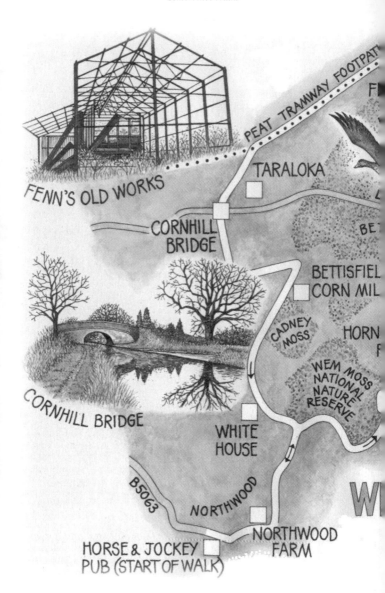

FENN'S OLD WORKS

PEAT TRAMWAY FOOTPAT

TARALOKA

CORNHILL
BRIDGE

BETTISFIEL
CORN MIL

CADNEY
MOSS

HORN

WEM MOSS
NATIONAL
NATURE
RESERVE

CORNHILL BRIDGE

WHITE
HOUSE

B5063

NORTHWOOD

W

NORTHWOOD
FARM

HORSE & JOCKEY
PUB (START OF WALK)

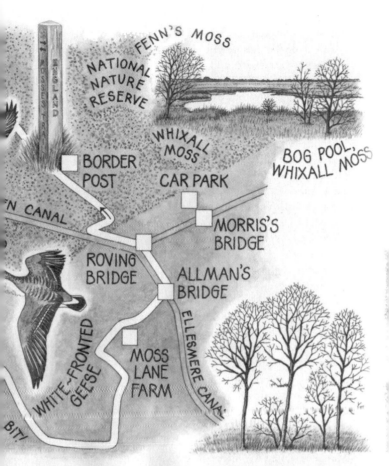

FENN'S MOSS

NATIONAL
NATURE
RESERVE

WHIXALL
MOSS

BOG POOL,
WHIXALL MOSS

BORDER
POST

CAR PARK

MORRIS'S
BRIDGE

N CANAL

ROVING
BRIDGE

ALLMAN'S
BRIDGE

ELLESMERE CANAL

WHITE-FRONTED
GEESE

MOSS
LANE
FARM

BIT!

FENN'S & WHIXALL MOSSES
IROPSHIRE/CLWYD BORDER

up and down until they swerved away like one organism across the stubbles. I walked by the side of Wem Moss, one of the few pieces of raised bog that has never been cut, a perfect mosaic of sundews, bog rosemary, cranberry and lesser butterfly orchid in their seasons. Alder, poplar and willow, water-drinking trees with a liking for shaky ground, rimmed the moss; a giant gall hung suspended like a shaggy hornet nest from a silver birch branch, with a mesh of thinly leaved wet woodland as a backdrop.

Near Hornspike Farm I entered the trees and became entangled as if in a fairy-tale thicket. No-one had walked the path for years. Elder trailers and ivy did their best to trip me up, brambles plucked at my sleeve. Out along the lanes, too, houses and barns stood silent and ghost-like in a faint mist curling from the ice-cold waters of the Llangollen Canal. The narrowboat *Bacchus*, smart in her coast of maroon, cream and black, lay stock still above her unbroken reflection, mirror-perfect and lifeless. I would not have been surprised to come upon an enchanted castle, with guards and mastiffs asleep at their posts.

As soon as I had turned off the towpath and entered the vast plain of the main area of bog, life and movement burst into the morning. A big flock of fifty white-fronted geese, which had been contentedly feeding out of sight behind the tuffets of sphagnum, took wing with a roar like a wave on a shingle bank and a gabble of voices as hoarse and emphatic as hounds on a good-going scent. They went away flying low and slow, their stiff wings rowing the big bodies along with an easily audible creaking that drifted to me through the still air over the bog.

Following the waymarked trail between Fenn's Moss and Whixall Moss as it passed the international border post – literally a post, a wooden stake with 'England' and 'Wales' lettered on opposing sides – I found myself humming 'The Geese In The Bog', and no wonder. Only an Irish tune could fit this scene: the great plain in its brown winter coat patched with russet of shrivelling ferns and pale cream of dried grasses, leafless birch and alder standing out against a white sky, the sense of time and space enormously magnified that are characteristic of walks at the back end of the year in Offaly or Longford, but which in this Welsh border setting strike a note that is both strange and seductive.

These mosses, now so prized for their ecological diversity, were thoroughly exploited for centuries. On Whixall Moss the harvesting of 'Whixall Bibles' – small, square black peats – left big pits that have flooded into dark pools. Hand-cutting of domestic fuel on Fenn's Moss produced long, low ramparts in the undulating body of the bog. And further into the moss, large-scale machine-milling in the 20th century resulted in wide areas of land being sliced open, their raw wounds now bound once more in heather, moor grass and sphagnum.

At the far edge of the moss I passed the skeletal sheds of Fenn's Old Works peat factory, its spoked flywheels and rusting presses now abandoned to wind and rain. As I took to the line of the old peat tramway and headed away, the flock of white-fronts came sawing and barking low across the bog as their forebears must have done for uncounted thousands of winters, pitching in the shelter of the pale grass to reclaim the great mosses from yet another transient intruder.

STEPPING OUT – *Walk 55*

MAPS: OS 1:25,000 Explorer 241; 1:50,000 Landranger 126
TRAVEL: Rail (www.thetrainline.com) to Wem (5 miles).
  Road – M6, M54, A5 to Shrewsbury; A49 towards Whitchurch;
  B5063 to Horse & Jockey PH, Northwood (OS ref SJ464333).
  NB Please ask permission to use car park, and please give
  pub your custom! There's another car park at Morris's Bridge,
  Whixall (493354).
WALK DIRECTIONS: Leaving Horse & Jockey PH, turn right along
  B5063. In 100 yards, left along lane ('Whixall, Prees'; brown
  'Fenn's & Whixall Mosses NNR' sign). In 300 yards, just past
  Northwood Farm, left along bridleway (469334; blue horseshoe
  fingerpost). In ½ mile, right along edge of Wem Moss NNR.
  In 400 yards, cross stile (yellow arrow/YA). Ignore next YA
  pointing right and cross stile; continue along Moss edge for 150
  yards to cross stile and footbridge in hedge on left in field corner.
  In another 300 yards, at foot of slight rise in field (477342), look
  for YA pointing left into margins of Wem Moss. After 300 very
  jungly yards through trees, right over stile into field (477343).
  Cross stile, then another by pond; ahead down Hornspike drive
  to lane (480344).

  Right down lane for ½ mile; left along road. In 100 yards, left
  again (487338; 'Whixall, Whitchurch') for ⅓ mile. Pass chapel
  on right; in 150 yards, on sharp right bend (488343), turn left
  up No Through Road. In 250 yards, opposite The Hollies, right
  (horseshoe fingerpost) to Moss Lane Farm. Dog-leg round barn
  (488347; YA), cross stile and aim half right to cross stile (YA) in
  far right corner of field. Follow ditch to cross Ellesmere Canal by
  Allman's Bridge (491349). Right along canal to cross Llangollen
  Canal by Roving Bridge (489353 – N.B. Morris's Bridge car park
  is ¼ mile to the right). Turn left along Llangollen Canal for 300
  yards, to turn right (486353; 'Mosses Trail' fingerpost), out of
  trees onto Fenn's and Whixall Moss.

  Follow Purple Trail (posts with arrows). In 100 yards bear
  right (Post 11) to go round left bend, In another 100 yards, left
  (Post No 10) and keep ahead to pass Post 18 ('England' on one
  side, 'Wales' on the other). Keep ahead for another ¾ mile, past
  Post 17 and Post 16 (ignore blue arrow here, pointing left), to

reach Fenn's Old Works peatworks (478367). Left along disused tramway for ⅔ mile. Opposite Taraloka house, left over stile (469361; YA). Aim a little right between bushy pond and solo oak tree; keep same line to cross drive over 2 stiles (467357; YA). Keep ahead to cross Llangollen Canal by Cornhill Bridge (466356). Through kissing gate; ahead to lane by Corner House Farm (467351). Left along lane to T-jct (471352); right past Bettisfield corn mill and on along green lane. Over gate at end and on with ditch on left. In 200 yards path become distinct grassy track. Aim for white house (468342); down drive to corner of Wem Moss NNR (471341); right to return to Northwood.

LENGTH: 8 miles

CONDITIONS: Moss paths can be boggy

REFRESHMENTS: Horse & Jockey, Northwood (01948-710427)

INFORMATION: *Mosses Trail leaflet guide* from dispensers at Fenn's Old Works (478367), Morris's Bridge, Roundthorn Bridge (501357) or Manor House NNR site centre (505365). Also downloadable at *www.naturalengland.org.uk*.

Clunton and Clunbury,
Clungunford and Clun, Shropshire

Through the 'quietest country under the sun' with the Shropshire Lad

'In valleys of springs of rivers,
By Ony and Teme and Clun,
The country for easy livers,
The quietest under the sun ...'

IT'S A SEDUCTIVE ENOUGH PICTURE to start with, certainly.
But then A.E. Housman gets the blues bit between his teeth as
he usually does, and he runs on about sorrows, troubles and grief-
stricken lads until you want to shake him by his quivering shoulders
and snap, 'Brace up, man!' I'm a sucker for the magic of places juxta-
posed, though, a subtle poetry of not-quite-galumphing names that
Housman shapes into his chorus irresistibly:

Clunton and Clunbury,
Clungunford and Clun
Are the quietest places
Under the sun.

The dry-as-dust Professor of Latin at University College, London,
a forbiddingly remote figure to students and colleagues alike, unexpectedly burst out in 1896 with this most romantic and nostalgic
poem, and 62 more besides, in a slim, self-published volume entitled
A Shropshire Lad. In point of fact Housman was a Worcestershire
lad, and knew little of Clunton and Clunbury, Clungunford and
Clun. The Shropshire settings of his poems welled up from his own
imagination. They were fired by unrequited love for Moses Jackson, a
golden youth who had shared his rooms at Oxford. Blue remembered

hills were sighed for, honest fellows' fists were wrung in farewell, Ludlow and Severn shore were bidden melting adieux.

No-one suspected the austere academic of harbouring a painful private life. Housman's students and colleagues were staggered to see these yearning emotions unmasked. It was as if a desiccated old cactus had suddenly shot forth an extravagant scarlet bloom. And the poet's sentiments certainly struck a chord with his readers. After a slow start *A Shropshire Lad* sold millions, especially during the Boer War and the First World War when servicemen found that the slender collection could be slipped comfortably into a tunic pocket and carried there as a poignant little slice of home.

In this hundredth anniversary year of the first publication, Jane and I set out early on a summer's morning to see if we could make a circuit of Housman's 'Famous Four' of the Clun valley in a long day's walk. There was another purpose to today's expedition, too – we wanted to check out the footpaths in OS Grid Square SO3878 and report their current state to the Ramblers' Association, our minuscule contribution to the RA's on-going 'Use Your Paths' campaign.

The evening before, we had reclined among the ruins of medieval fortifications on Clun's grassy castle mound and watched the town's bowls club pursuing their stately play on the green sward below, lit by buttery late sunshine. But this morning stretched cool and grey above the sleeping town and over the Shropshire lanes and their verges, which lay spattered with campion, dog roses and cow parsley.

Up in Sowdley Wood the birds were still singing their little heads off as church clocks chimed eight. Ferns grew in damp hollows under beech and spruce; liverworts and mosses matted every hillside trickle. It was a beautiful walk down to silent little Clunton, where a man was hustling sheep out of his paddock by flapping an ancient waterproof at them. 'Best dog I've ever had,' he grinned, 'it do scare 'em off properly, do you see?'

We found a damp green lane to take us squelching and slopping into Purslow. The war memorial of this tiny hamlet holds 14 names, the last of them from 1991 and the Gulf War – Shropshire lads laid low, as in so many of Housman's sad little verses. Across the fields in Clunbury a life-size stag of straw lay majestically on the thatched roof of Dutch Cottage. In St Swithin's Church beyond there was a holy hush and a savour of candle wax and polish. A couple of gardeners were clipping their hedges and weeding their immaculate cottage

CLUNTON & CLUNBURY,
CLUNGUNFORD & CLUN
SHROPSHIRE

A.E. HOUSMAN

CLUNTON

River Clun

BUSH FARM

CASTLE RUINS

CLUN

SOWDLEY WOOD

WOODSIDE FARM

ST. GEORGE'S CHURCH

OLD BAMFORD'S

gardens, the soft click of shears and clink of trowels only accentuating the peacefulness of the cloudy green valley.

A steep pull up the brackeny rampart of Clunbury Hill, and a long and lovely descent on the far side with a tremendous view east towards the Clee Hills across the valleys of Onny and Teme and Clun. The church clock at Clungunford sent a single dolorous note across the fields as we reached it, with the village in the valley lying as neat and quiet as its three sisters under slowly gathering rainclouds.

Grid square SO3878 turned out to have one poorly positioned waymark arrow and one 'which-side-of-the-hedge-is-it?' point of confusion. We noted them down for our 'Use Your Paths' report, and went on to Hopton Castle to view the stark old fort. Here in

1644, at the savage height of the Civil War, thirty-two helpless and hamstrung Roundhead prisoners were tied in pairs and thrown into the moat to give their Royalist captors the sadistic pleasure of watching them drown.

Forest paths led back towards Clun through a rose-tinted coniferous gloom. There was a twilight air about the trees, a sweet undertone of melancholy. If A.E. Housman's shade ever walked the Shropshire hills, it was there along the misty rides of Sowdley Wood.

STEPPING OUT – *Walk 56*

MAP: OS 1:25,000 Explorer 201; 1:50,000 Landranger 137

TRAVEL: Rail (*www.thetrainline.co.uk*) to Knighton (7 miles)
Road – From north – M6, M54 to Telford; A5 to Shrewsbury;
A49 to Craven Arms; B4368 to Clun. From south – M6 to Jct
6; A449, A443, A456 to A49, north to Craven Arms; B4368 to
Clun.

WALK DIRECTIONS: From Clun church (OS ref S0300806) along
Vicarage Road; 1st right (302806 – 'Woodside') for ½ mile to
pass Woodside Farm (310802 – 'Obley'). In 150 yd left ('Byway');
immediately left at fork. In 300 yd keep ahead at fork (313803);
in 100 yd ignore left bend and keep ahead on bridleway through
Sowdley Wood for 1½ miles to road (335810). Left into Clunton.
Returning, cross bridge (335812); left to pass Bush Farm (338811).
In 250 yd at 3 gates keep ahead along boggy green lane for ⅔ mile
to road (349805). Left past Old Cider House; in 50 yd, left over
stile (footpath fingerpost). Aim half right for big oak; follow
hedge down field to cross stile (yellow arrow), then footbridge
(353806). Half right across field, through gate (arrow); on for ½
mile to B4385 (360807). Left into Purslow.

Right along B4368. 50 yd past Hundred House PH,
right over stile (footpath fingerpost); follow arrows through
plantation, into field. In far right corner (365809), through
left-hand gate; in 150 yd right over stile (arrow); left along 2
field edges to house; gate and footbridge to road in Clunbury
opposite church (371807). Right for ⅓ mile to right bend at
Cherry Bryn (373802). Footpath fingerpost points up bank.
In 50 yd through gate; left (blue arrow), steeply up Clunbury
Hill. At top, through gate (377802 – arrow) and following one
(arrow); descend beside horse gallop. Round left bend (379799);
in 150 yd through gate; continue down to ruined house (383798).
Through gate; immediately right through another gate; aim half
left for tree clump. Pass New House (383796); half left to cross
stile (arrow) in hedge. Left along hedge to bottom right corner
(386793). Left over stile (arrow); follow right-hand hedge,
through gate (arrow); left along lane, under railway to road
(391792). Right for ⅓ mile past Abcott Manor to road in Abcott
(391786).

For Bird on the Rock tearoom and/or Clungunford, left to B4367. Otherwise, right from 391786; in 200 yd left over stile (389787 – fingerpost), through farmyard, over stile (arrow); follow hedge to right, through gate, across railway (388785). Half left to stile in far hedge; through next field to end of hedge (385784); bear right to stile, ahead to hedge (382783). Left; in 200 yd right across rail stile; up hedge to cross B4385 (378782). Aim ahead for left side of larger of 2 plantations; through gate and on; right through next gate (374780) and down to road (371778). Right through Hopton Castle. Right (364781) through churchyard and up by stiles across fields to climb track through Well Wood. At Llantop Farm (359788), right along drive to road; left for a mile to fork right past Cwm Barn (342797). In ⅓ mile, on right bend, keep ahead (340799) up rising green lane towards Sowdley Wood. In 350 yd track passes through gateway; in another 200 yd, right through gate (335801 – Forestry Authority 'Welcome' notice). Follow bridleway (blue arrows) through wood for 1⅓ miles, to leave trees and rejoin outer route (313803); return to Clun.

LENGTH: 15 miles

REFRESHMENTS: Hundred House, Purslow (01588-660541; www. hundredhouseinn.co.uk); Bird on the Rock teashop, Abcott (booking advisable, tel 01588-660631).

A SHROPSHIRE LAD BY A.E. HOUSMAN: (Dover Thrift paperback, or online at *http://www.bartleby.com/123/*

THE HOUSMAN SOCIETY: *www.housman-society.co.uk*

WALES

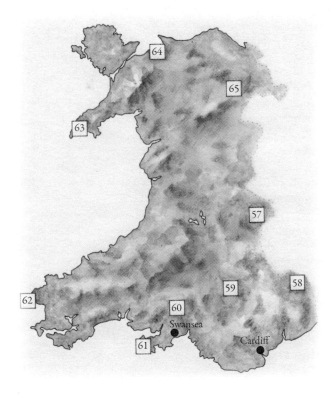

Old Radnor and Hergest Ridge, Herefordshire/Powys border

Where wicked ghosts and hell hounds haunt the Borders

T HE TORTOISESHELL CAT with the truncated tail gave me an affectionate send-off from the Harp Inn at Old Radnor. It was obviously not a mind-reader, because at that moment I was picturing the hellish black dog in whose guise wicked Black Vaughan haunts the Welsh Borders. There were legends a-plenty to spice this month's walk among the hills where Herefordshire tips over into Radnorshire.

These days Old Radnor lies as quiet and secluded as can be, tucked into the eastern hem of Wales in its folds of ground just across the border from the old market town of Kington. But judging by the magnificence of its Church of St Stephen, in medieval times this must have been much more than a sleepy border hamlet.

A richly carved rood screen writhing with vine trails runs the full width of the church. The organ casing, the oldest in Britain, was beautifully carved in linenfold panelling shortly after Henry Tudor came to the throne. In a window of the chapel hidden away behind the organ I found a 15th-century stained glass St Catherine, thoughtfully contemplating her spiked wheel of martyrdom.

The oldest item in St Stephen's is also the plainest – a massive tub font that predates the Normans by many centuries. Carved out of a single boulder, it stands on four elephantine feet near the church doorway. This mighty vessel has been baptising Old Radnor children for thirteen hundred years at least.

Out in the open air, all the wrens and finches of Herefordshire and Radnorshire seemed to be singing. They didn't give a damn for the dark clouds massing beyond the hills, and neither did I. This border country is made for walkers – rounded, green, soft with grass. The fields and roadsides are bounded with good thick hedges, exuding pungent vegetable smells as they steamed on this warm summer's day.

I walked south towards Hanter Hill, rising flat-topped and bracken coated. The high green spine of Hergest Ridge propped it from the back like a strong arm. Up on the side of the hill, a shirtless man leaned in the sun over the gate of a house ingeniously constructed out of a blue-painted caravan and a batch of four-by-two.

'I've lived here more than thirty years,' he told me. 'Well, it's a lovely spot, and a quiet one. Yes, I made the house. 'Tis not a bad house, though the rain do get in. But I use plenty of bitumen, and I think ... yes, I think I've conquered her.'

A broad grassy track curved round the flank of Hanter Hill, then on up to the crest of Hergest Ridge. This great five-mile green whaleback, rising just west of Kington, straddles the border and forms one of the oldest east-west routes between England and Wales.

Offa, 8th-century King of the Mercians and subduer of the termagant Welsh, knew that he who holds the heights controls the country. When he ordered his great defensive dyke to be built along the border, Offa had it sited to take advantage of every slope and ridge that commanded a view into Wales. Walking Offa's Dyke (a National Trail long-distance footpath) along the spine of Hergest Ridge today, I looked out across the same vast view that Offa's sentries must have known – abruptly scarped hills rolling like waves to break on the green lowlands of the border country.

Just off the path I found a great triangular slab of stone encompassed by a little moat of rainwater. 'You'll see the Whetstone up on the ridge,' the caravan man had advised me. 'That's where the old farmers would do their bargaining – years ago now, that would be.'

Is the Whetstone really the 'Wheat Stone', its name echoing a local folk-memory of the Black Death? Stories say that plague-stricken villagers in those horrific years left their money on the stone's flat top, in exchange for bushels of wheat placed there by merchants too canny to cease trading but too cautious to risk infection. Or was it in truth a whet-stone, as others insist – a gathering place where ancient warriors whetted their sword blades before moving off together towards some long-forgotten battle?

As for Black Vaughan – fact says he was a 15th-century local lordling, who lived at Hergest Court under the southern slope of Hergest Ridge, and was beheaded after ending up on the losing side at the Battle of Banbury. But border legend-spinners, of course, have a better story ...

Thirteen parsons, so they say, gathered in Presteigne church to exorcise the malevolent spirit of bloody Black Vaughan. When it materialized, twelve of the exorcists were struck senseless with terror. The lucky thirteenth, however, managed to reduce Black Vaughan's ghost to the size of a fly and trap it in a snuffbox. This was then sunk under a great stone in the pool below Hergest Court. But an unlucky accident released the evil spirit, to roam the Borders for ever more in the shape of a ghastly black dog.

'Sir Arthur Conan Doyle based *The Hound of the Baskervilles* on that legend', said the receptionist at Hergest Croft Gardens. 'He stayed here at the Croft while he was researching the story. Mind you, I know someone who saw the black hound. Saw its legs anyway, disappearing down the end of a corridor at Hergest Court.'

The 50 acres of gardens at Hergest Croft have been nurtured by three generations of the Banks family. Here I wandered in a daze of shapes and colours, from the fuchsias in the Edwardian conservatory to the Azalea Garden and its blazingly showy blooms of crimson and mauve, pale pink and orange. Enormous trees have grown in the century since the garden's creation, giant firs and beeches well over a hundred feet tall.

From the garden the path ambled back through woods of beech, sycamore and old holly, wandering west below the ridge. The complex web of birdsong among the trees was woven through with the ecstatic warbling of wrens. Last year's brown leaves crunched satisfyingly underfoot.

Back at the blue caravan house, the owner was cutting his grass. He looked up as I went by and lifted his hand in benediction, then bent again to his work in the sunshine. As I went on down the lane I could still hear the swish and chop of the sickle, the very sound of an old-fashioned rural summer afternoon.

STEPPING OUT – *Walk 57*

MAP: OS 1:25,000 Explorer 201; 1:50,000 Landranger 148

TRAVEL: Road – M5 to Jct 7; A44 west through Bromyard, Leominster and Kington. 5 miles beyond Kington, Old Radnor is signed off to left.

WALK DIRECTIONS: From Harp Inn pass church (OS ref SO250591). Left at road; in ¼ mile, at fork (249585), keep ahead right; in 10 yd, left over stile in hedge. Down to cross stile at bottom; across next field to cross footbridge, then B4594 (250582). Along cul-de-sac lane opposite. At Lower Hanter at end of lane (254577), right through gate; immediately left up steep green path; at top, left along green track around Hanter Hill. Pass white cottage, then blue caravan house (254575).

Ahead up hill on grassy track through bracken (in ¼ mile ignore faint track to left). At crossroads of tracks by fir plantation (254568) keep ahead (yellow arrow) up flank of Hergest Ridge to Offa's Dyke Path (ODP) on crest (254564 – ODP white acorn sign). Turn left (east) along it for 1½ miles, to go through gate into lane (278567). Entrance to Hergest Croft gardens is another ½ mile on right (286567).

20 yd beyond car park, cross gate on left (footpath sign), then stile; left down field edge; in 40 yd left (stile; yellow arrow) into wood. Yellow arrow waymarks on trees direct you. In ¼ mile, descend steps to cross tracks (282569); left up grassy path. In 1 mile, keep ahead at 3-fingered footpath sign (270573). In 300 yd, over stile; descend outside wood for 200 yd and pass gate below on right (269574). In 10 yd, right over stile (yellow arrow) to descend track. At bottom of trees, left through gate (267575), keeping hedge at lower edge of field on your right. Over double stile at end of field (yellow arrow). In 200 yd, where hedge bends half left, ahead through hedge over plank bridge and stile (258575). Through gate on far side of field, then along grassy embankment, over gate by blue caravan house (254575).

Retrace route to Old Radnor.

LENGTH OF WALK: 7 miles

REFRESHMENTS: Harp Inn, Old Radnor, Presteigne, Powys LD8 2RH (01544-350655; *www.harpinnradnor.co.uk*); tea room at Hergest Croft Gardens.

HERGEST CROFT GARDENS: (01544-230160; *www.hergest.co.uk*)

Grosmont, Skenfrith and White Castle, Monmouthshire

The Three Castle Walk

ONMOUTHSHIRE'S FALLOW DEER and foxes were still making their way home across the fields as I stood at dawn on top of the gap-toothed west wall of Grosmont Castle, watching a great red sun haul itself out of the mists curling along the River Monnow. The castle's protection had ensured growth and prosperity for the hilltop town of Grosmont during the Middle Ages. These days the white-washed houses sit close about their broken stronghold, half forgotten in the heart of wonderful countryside.

When the Normans came to Monmouthshire on their great push west into the lands of the Celts, they found themselves vulnerable to guerrilla attack in this broken hilly country. The three castles they built during the 12th century – Grosmont, Skenfrith and White Castle – still stand today, more or less in ruins. They form the three corners of the long triangular walk I was setting out to tackle today.

The Three Castles Walk is superbly waymarked, a great feather in the cap of Monmouthshire County Council's countryside service. All I had to do by way of route-finding was to study the booklet and follow the little yellow arrows, which kept popping faithfully up in all the right places.

Early morning sunshine flooded the steep green side of Graig Syfyrddin as I slogged up to the tree line and eased off through bluebell woods and across rounded shoulders of grassland. Buzzards sailed out from the pine trees, curling up their broad wingtips to every nuance of breeze. This was exhilarating walking, plunging down towards Skenfrith and a skyline of the Forest of Dean bristling with treetops ten miles beyond.

As at Grosmont, the church and houses of Skenfrith form a tight huddle around their protective castle. But Skenfrith is a valley set-tlement, placed on an elbow of the River Monnow to plug a gap in the barrier of hills between England and Wales. Of the three castles that make up the 'Welsh Trilateral', Skenfrith is the most ruinous, its stumpy sandstone drum towers connected by ragged curtain walls.

Skenfrith's Church of St Bridget is a typically squat and solid border church, with a fortress of a tower capped by a dovecote. Inside I admired the Skenfrith cope, a faded but still beautiful piece of 15th-century embroidery. Nearby stood the carved tomb of John Morgan, the last Governor of the Three Castles, who died in 1557. By then the Welsh Trilateral had been obsolete for centuries, and the castles' rulers – to judge by Governor Morgan's effigy – had become well-to-do merchants rather than battling commanders of soldiery.

South and west of Skenfrith the path dipped and climbed through a series of lonely stream valleys, quiet sheep-rearing country of small rounded hills and hidden farmsteads. From the old ridgeback coach-ing road near Lettravane Farm there were long views west towards the Black Mountains. Smothered in bushes at the bottom of the next valley I found the shattered roof and walls of the Traveller's Rest, an inn with a tiny smithy where coach passengers once refreshed them-selves while the horses were reshod.

Down in Llantilio Crossenny, a mile or so off the path, I passed the hospitable and ancient Hostry Inn, now a private house after 500 years of hospitality. I silently raised a phantom pint to the memory of Boris, the pub's giant and soppy wolfhound, fondly remembered from previous visits. Where was he? Gone to the great hunting ground in the sky, for sure.

A couple of miles up the road, battlemented walls and towers loomed darkly out of the landscape. White Castle is by far the most impressive of the Three Castles, fortified with massive drum towers, a gatehouse, and a crescent-shaped hornwork in its deep moat.

The atmosphere of this lonely stronghold hangs as heavy as lead. There is something gloomy and doom laden about it. Maybe that was why it was a favourite outing for the moody Rudolf Hess, Hitler's fugitive deputy, when he was being held secretly at a military hospi-tal outside Abergavenny from 1942–5. Hess, described by one of his guards as 'a wild man with the look of the animals in Bristol Zoo', would stare into the moat at White Castle while dropping bread-crumbs to the giant carp.

White Castle was one of the most formidable castles of its day.

But events bypassed it. Today it exerts its domination over a silent valley, a grim grey benchmark in Welsh border history, frowning out towards the high whaleback hill of Ysgyryd Fawr.

The path turned north now, snaking and switchbacking through the fields as a deep old hollow way, trickling with water and lush with hart's-tongue ferns. Around Newordden Farm the hedges had been recently and expertly laid. I stopped to cool my hot feet in a stream under hazels where a blackcap was singing his afternoon observations. A starling took up the theme, copying the blackcap's trills and throwing in a couple of bubbling curlew cries for good measure.

Now Graig Syfyrddin stood up ahead, a green hump crowned with conifers. The Three Castles Way had saved a sting in its tail, a sharp climb up to the crest of the mini-mountain. I put my head down and went at it, ignoring the twanging in my calves. Up at the top the view was reward enough for effort – west to the long ridges of the Black Mountains and the distinctive peaks of Blorenge and the Sugar Loaf flanking Abergavenny, east over the Wye Valley and the Forest of Dean.

A stony path trodden out by monks brought me the final couple of miles down from the hill to where Grosmont lay under cloudy evening skies, rising up its steep ridge around the church spire and tall grey castle ruins.

STEPPING OUT – *Walk 58*

MAPS: OS 1:25,000 Explorers OL13, OL14, 189; 1:50,000
Landranger 161

TRAVEL: Road – M4/M48 across Severn Bridge; A466 Chepstow-
Monmouth; B4233 to Rockfield, B4347 to Grosmont. Park in
village street near Grosmont Castle (OS ref SO405244.

WALK DIRECTIONS: Three Castles Walk (3CW) waymarking –
'Three Castles Walk' inside a yellow arrow – is excellent, and can
be followed with complete confidence.

In brief, head south-east (downhill) out of Grosmont along
B4347. At the 2nd gate on the right after Lower Tresenny
farmhouse (410240), follow 3CW waymarks up and over Graig
Syfyrddin. Bear left by a barn (421223), and continue down
to the road. Left to B4347 at White House Farm (431220);
right for 300 yd; left down Box Farm drive and follow 3CW
waymarks past Box Farm (439219) and Trevonny (444219),
along Monnow Valley to Skenfrith.

From Skenfrith Castle (457202) to B4521; right for ½ mile.
Follow 3CW waymarks parallel to the road, past the crossing
of B4347, then left over a stile (444200), past The Lade farm
(441193) to B4347 (440185). Right along the road for a long
mile to a sharp right bend near Lettravane Farm (425183);
ahead on a rough road, following 3CW waymarks into and out
of Llymon Brook valley, past Llanllwydd (416179) into and
out of the next valley, and under pylons up to a lane (408168).
Turn right. In ¼ mile leave 3CW (NB the waymark points on
along the lane), over a stile to the left (404167), heading due
south towards trees around Llantilio Crossenny. Cross Coed-
Canol farm track 3 fields east of a lane (404162); continue to
the lane under electricity post (401157). Left to B4233; right to
a crossroads (395151); left into Llantilio Crossenny, to view the
church (399149).

From the church keep forward along the village street, and
take the next lane on the right to cross B4233 (394146). In 1¼
miles, turn right at Treadam (380150) along a tarmac lane to
White Castle (379167).

Just south of White Castle, a lane leads north to B4521 at
380180. Turn right; in 75 yd, turn left, following 3CW arrows

to a road (383190). Turn right past Upper Green (387190); then left across fields by St Mary's Chapel (390193) and on north for 1½ miles to a road (395208). Turn left; in 300 yd, right; in 100 yd right over a stile (396209) and steeply up the flank of Graig Syfyrddin to join a forest track in trees (401210). Bear left and follow 3CW waymarks for 3 miles to Grosmont.

LENGTH OF WALK: 20 miles (allow 10 hours). * NB Official walk, excluding Llantilio Crossenny diversion, is 18 miles.

CONDITIONS: Very well waymarked. Some parts steep; some boggy. Very enjoyable for those in no hurry.

REFRESHMENTS: Angel Inn, Grosmont (01981-240646); Bell Inn, Skenfrith (01600-750235; *www.skenfrith.co.uk*)

READING: *The Three Castles Walk* guide booklet, available from Abergavenny TIC (01873-853254) or Monmouth TIC (01600-713899)

Walk 59

Pen y Fan and Cribyn, Brecon Beacons

A rainy climb to the roof of the Brecon Beacons

'AH, THE BEACONS, is it?' said the Radnorshire farmer we got chatting to in the windy streets of Brecon. 'Well, you'll be up and down again in half a day, I shouldn't wonder.' He looked up at the distant peaked profiles of Pen y Fan and Cribyn, dark against racing cloud. 'Good drying weather,' he observed with a mischievous twinkle, 'but I expect you'll be wet enough, now, by the time you've finished.'

The flat-topped and high-shouldered Brecon Beacons, irresistible magnets for walkers, stand sentinel over the Welsh market town of Brecon and its surrounding farmlands and hills. The four main summits – Corn Du, Cribyn, Fan y Big, and the daddy of them all, the 2,906-ft Pen y Fan – form a rollercoaster north-facing escarpment edge, three rugged promontories nosing out from black walls of cliff and great sweeping corries. Driving up to Brecon the night before, Jane and I had admired the Beacons bathed in full golden evening light. This morning, though, the mid-Wales weather gods were throwing a bit of a wobbler.

Rainproof trousers, inelegant garments at the best of times, are not Jane's favourite legwear. But we hauled them on anyway, and were glad of their protection as we forded the Nant Gwdi and swished our way through wet bracken towards the mountain path. It led under the grey rock scars of Allt Ddu – the Dark Hillside, we guessed from our sketchy store of Welsh – and climbed towards the skyline high overhead.

A little brown bird with a flash of fox-red on its breast perched on the top of a heather clump, flicking its tail and calling *whee-ch-ch!* 'Stonechat,' I hazarded, without much conviction. 'And what's this?' murmured Jane, crouching over a wayside plant with minuscule white flowers. 'Purging flax? Well, I'm certainly not going to suck it and see ... or is it heath bedstraw? Hmmm ... '

This was the first good hill walk we'd set out on together for many a long day, and Jane was enjoying it in her characteristic style – puzzling here, poking about there, generally taking her time. For me, usually the steam-ahead-at-all-costs merchant, this was entirely delightful. We sat on the mountainside and looked back over the wide spread of patchwork fields around Brecon, the intense green of meadows, the gold of cut hayfields brilliant under glints of sun, then dull the next moment as cloud shadows chased across them and rain showers came pattering up from the southwest.

Slugs in shiny black PVC coats were crawling across the path as we reached the col, wondering what view would hit us as we topped the rise. It didn't disappoint. The sharp tooth of Pen y Fan rose ahead into rolling dark cloud that came sluicing over the mountain's shoulder like sea foam across a rock. The stepped pyramid shape of Cribyn stood on our left, with tremendous horizontally striated cliffs falling from the peak a thousand feet into the sheep-dotted depths of Cwm Sere.

Jane lay flat on her back among greenish bilberries and the pale purple spots of unopened heather flowers, drinking in rain, wind, sun splashes and the unreeling song of larks. I gazed into Cwm Sere, looking down on the chocolate-brown outstretched wings of a buzzard wheeling five hundred feet below. A German couple stopped to shoot the breeze. 'Oh, we love to walk around Wales! Yes, we go to the Beacons now, tomorrow the seaside; and after, the Snowdon. Even the rain is beautiful among this happy hills!'

We followed them along a narrow ridge path. A plum-coloured murk was gathering ominously in the west, and the wind grew colder and gustier as we gained height. We just had time to fix our bearings on a couple of sighting points – the pillbox-hat tump of Corn Du, the round steel mirror of Llyn Cwm Llwch in its mountain hollow – before the peak of Pen y Fan was blotted out.

But it wasn't too bad at all, in spite of the proximity of path and cliff edge. The path had been carefully pitched with stone treads to combat erosion, and there was only one short section of scrambling before the summit cairn appeared blearily through the mist. Jane and I stood at 2,906 ft, the highest human beings south of Snowdon, masters of a twenty-yard view. 'Don't fret,' advised the Brummagem man who came up with his girl and an Alsatian out of the cloud. 'It's sunshine just down there below all this crap.'

So it was – weak but beautiful sunshine. We lowered ourselves into it as into a warm bath, then scampered on to the top of Cribyn where a giant view opened to all points of the compass. The sphinx-like summit of Pen y Fan behind us was backed by the flat table top of Corn Du. Ahead were the twisted forelock of the Sugar Loaf, the long dark ships' prows of the Black Mountains, and the gleam of Upper Neuadd reservoir in the south. Two cheery squaddies toting packs hefty enough to crush a bull gave us a loud hello. 'Oh, we've done about 20 miles,' said one in a strong Staffordshire accent, without even a flutter of heavy breathing. 'Twenty more to do, eh!'

We had to watch every step on the first bit of the descent off Cribyn, but after that it was plain sailing. The northward ridge of Bryn Teg, its short grasses streamed by the breeze, was perfect for quick, wind-assisted progress. Down near Cwmcynwyn a flock of newly shorn sheep with fresh red and green brand marks regarded us suspiciously from the bracken. Their shaven bodies were seamed with ridges of wool where each stroke of the shearer's clippers had overlain the previous one.

We followed stony lanes between high hedgebanks thick with foxgloves, harebells and honeysuckle. We picked and savoured tiny wild strawberries. 'A perfect day,' was Jane's verdict as we got back to the car. Our German friends had been right. Rain showers, cloud and sun, wind and mist, the high peaks and the flowery farm lanes – there had been beauty in all of them, among these happy hills.

STEPPING OUT – *Walk 59*

MAP: OS 1:25,000 Explorer OL12; 1:50,000 Landranger 160

TRAVEL: Road – M4 to Jct 32; A470 to Brecon. Right on B4601
towards town centre; cross river; in another 200 yd, right along
Ffrwdgrech Road under A40. In ⅔ mile, at 3-way fork (OS ref
S0028273), bear left along narrow lane for 1½ miles. ¼ mile past
Cwmgwdi, lane bends right by shed (026251); keep forward here
to car park (025249).

WALK DIRECTIONS: Forty yards up road from first tarmac area on
right, turn left over scrubby ground, down bank to cross stile in
fence, then ford stream in gully below. Climb bank on far side and
continue in same direction (east), with wall and then fence and trees
close on your left, for ⅓ mile to a 'Cwm Gwdi Car Park' fingerpost
near a gate on the left (031247). Turn right here on track through
bracken, aiming for Allt Ddu hill. Soon you see path to Pen y Fan,
slanting diagonally up to right across flank of Allt Ddu. Follow it
SW up to col (020235) under Cwar Mawr quarry. Make half-right
up to ridge path; keep ahead to summit of Pen y Fan (012216).

Continue SE down to saddle, then E up to summit of Cribyn
(024213). Follow very steep short descent NE, then along Bryn
Teg ridge for 1½ miles to meet stone wall by wire fence (036235)
above Cwmcynwyn. Cross fence, go through adjacent gate in
wall by NT 'Cwm Cynwyn' notice, and along stony lane. In
250 yd, left (038237) on tarmac lane for ½ mile to cross Pont y
Caniedydd bridge (039244). In 100 yd, left over stile by gate; up
stony track. In 100 yd, by ruin of Pant, right over stile (038245
– yellow arrow). Aim up field to cross stile (waymark). Up next
field to cross next stile (037247), then follow path with hedge
and fence on your left for 2 fields to Plas-y-gaer Farm (034248).

Go through gate; dogleg left and right round left end of barn
and house, then on along farm lane. After 2 fields, left (032249 –
'Allt Ddu' fingerpost); over stile in 20 yd, then on up green lane
to go through gate at top (031247). Turn right along hedge, back
to car park.

LENGTH OF WALK: 7 miles – allow 3–4 hours

CONDITIONS: Steady climb with short steep finish up to Pen y
Fan; short steep descent from Cribyn. Path clearly visible all the
way, but could be tricky in thick mist.

REFRESHMENTS: Take a picnic

Carreg Cennen Castle and Bethlehem, Dyfed, South Wales

Bethlehem Christmas Fair, and the castle with a secret at its heart

YOU CAN'T MISS Carreg Cennen Castle. The gaunt grey walls on their grassy limestone bluff dominate the tumbled landscape south of Llandeilo and the River Tywi. Coming to the castle in a spitting dawn after a blusterous November night, I found a countryside trickling with rainwater, each green lane a stream and every stream a bubbling torrent.

Carreg Cennen Castle was a treat to be saved for the end of the walk. This brief winter's day in south Wales had to be grabbed in short order. I turned my back on the enticements of ruined battlements and towers, and set course for Cilmaenllwyd – 'Grey Stone Corner', if my shaky Welsh was not sorely askew.

Three red kites were sailing over the abandoned farmhouse of Cilmaenllwyd, mewing to each other, their wings bent at the elbow to allow for each tremor and ripple in the upper air. Thirty years ago, with numbers decimated by shooting and poisoning, you would have been hard pushed to sight a single red kite anywhere within the borders of Wales. This damp winter's day I lost count of the kites I saw over the fields and woods – fruit of one of the 20th century's most stunning conservation victories.

Through the wet countryside I followed a quiet green lane. Down in the west the horizon was milky with advancing rain showers. Willow groves and field sedges whistled and stirred uneasily in the rising wind. I bowled along country roads and hedge paths under the bare-headed double hump of Trichrug, where I struck into a long descending holloway going purposefully north towards Carn Goch, the Red Cairn.

The great heap of stones on its ridge, raised by some forgotten

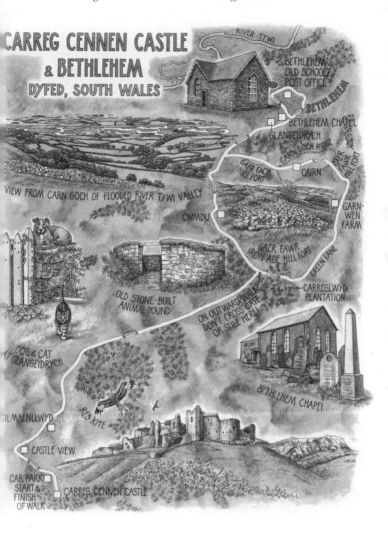

CARREG CENNEN CASTLE & BETHLEHEM
DYFED, SOUTH WALES

RIVER TYWI

BETHLEHEM OLD SCHOOL/ POST OFFICE

BETHLEHEM

BETHLEHEM CHAPEL

GLANGEIDRYCH

CARN GOCH RIDGE

CAER FACH HILL FORT

CAIRN

CAER FAWR HILL FORT

GARN WEN FARM

VIEW FROM CARN GOCH OF FLOODED RIVER TYWI VALLEY

CWMDU

CAER FAWR IRON AGE HILL FORT

GREEN LANE

DOG & CAT AT GLANGEIDRYCH

OLD STONE-BUILT ANIMAL POUND

ON OUTWARD WALK DON'T CROSS GATE OR STILE HERE

CARREGLWYD PLANTATION

BETHLEHEM CHAPEL

GILMAENLLWYD

RED KITE

CASTLE VIEW

CAR PARK START & FINISH OF WALK

CARREG CENNEN CASTLE

Bronze Age tribe to their dead leader, looks down to the snaking River Tywi over a slope whose bracken in this winter season glowed as russet red as a fox pelt. The monument stands enclosed within a mighty stone wall, built to fortify the hilltop by Iron Age people some 1500 years after the anonymous chief of the cairn was laid to rest up here. Staring out north from his burial mound I saw the Tywi valley silvered by floods, the hills beyond leached to delicate pinks and greys in the low November light.

How many miles to Bethlehem? Less than two from Carn Goch by the mountain road. I descended by way of a roofless old pound, a cylinder of stone for the retention of stray beasts. At Glangeidrych ('the piece of land on the riverbank where the waters rush'?) both dog and cat came out to sniff me over.

Bethlehem chapel loomed grey and grim in its overgrown grave-yard. Up on the ridge road the old school that houses the village post office stood closed and silent. Things would be different come early December and Bethlehem Christmas Fair, the start of the hamlet's annual fortnight of glory when thousands make a pilgrimage here to have their Christmas cards franked 'Bethlehem'.

Looking in through the blank windows I recalled the colour, loud gossip and laughter when we came to the Fair a couple of years ago. We'd bought beetroot chutney and organic mincemeat, munched on deliciously greasy pork sandwiches from Sam's Hog Roast, and got two dozen of our Christmas card envelopes stamped with the coveted 'Cyfarchion y Timor, Season's Greetings from Bethlehem'.

It was a bit of a haul back up the lane and on over the splashy fields around Cwmdu, the Dark Valley. But I made it back to Carreg Cennen before the fall of dusk, with time to spare for a cup of tea and a look around the castle.

The old pile resembles nothing so much as a rank of broken fangs – long out of service, stained and blunted, but still possessed of latent bite. Carreg Cennen is potent with the air of threat and of power so common to medieval strongholds, even in a state of ruin. There is mystery and magic buried at the heart of the castle, too.

I hired a torch from the café in the farmyard and walked up to the castle. A loopholed passage led from ancient steps deep into a pitch-black cavern. Crouching in this secret chamber it wasn't hard to picture Urien Rheged, knight of the Round Table and legendary guardian of Carreg Cennen, folded in enchanted sleep somewhere close by in the heart of the crag, waiting for King Arthur's call to rise and bring salvation to a benighted land.

STEPPING OUT – *Walk 60*

MAP: OS 1:25,000 Explorers 186, OL12; 1:50,000 Landranger 146, 159

TRAVEL: Rail to Llandeilo (5 miles) – *www.thetrainline.com*
Road – M4 to Jct 49; A483 through Ammanford towards Llandeilo. In Llandybie, right on minor road following 'Castell Carreg Cennen' signs through Trap to castle car park.

WALK DIRECTIONS: From Carreg Cennen Castle car park (OS ref SN666193) left along road to T-junction at Castle View (662195). Up red gravelled lane (Beacons Way waymark – 'BW' – and yellow waymark arrow – 'ywa') to pass Cilmaenllwyd farmhouse (665199). In 200 yards track swings left, but keep ahead here over stile (BW) and along green lane. In 250 yards right over stile (667202 – ywa); follow fence on left to cross stile (ywa) in far top corner of field. Cross and continue, with wall on left; in 200 yards cross stile (666206); continue, now with wall on right. In 150 yards, wall bears away right; left here up slope for 10 yards, then right along grass track, aiming for 'camel humps' of hill in distance, to cross ladder stile in wall (667209). From stile aim about 100 yards to left of where wall and fence on your right meet a wood. Cross stile here onto road (668211 – 'Cilmaenllwyd, Castle View' fingerpost).

Right along road for ¾ mile to crossroads (679218). Cross stile between Bethlehem and Gwynfe roads (BW, 'Carreglwyd' fingerpost). Aim across field for gate on skyline. Don't go through! Keep same direction with fence on left; cross ladder stile (683221); continue beside fence to enter Carreglwyd plantation over stile by gate (687225 – BW, ywa). On down descending track to gate at bottom of plantation (689228 – BW, ywa).

Don't cross stile in fence here! Instead, 5 yards before reaching gate, bear sharp right uphill on faint, steep path through bracken and gorse of plantation slope. In 200 yards, at BW on post, left along faint path with raised bank on left through gorse and heather for 300 yards to leave plantation over stile (BW, ywa). In 60 yards left through wall (ywa); on with fence on right. In 100 yards right through gate; cross stream; left over stile (BW, ywa – can be very boggy!); in 60 yards left (695229 – BW, ywa) through gate and down green lane, going northwards.

In 500 yards, through gate (696234); dogleg left, then right (BW, ywa) down green lane past Garn-wen farm. Over stile here (696240 – BW, ywa); on along tarmac lane. In 200 yards, left (BW on telephone pole) on path across open ground of Carn Goch. Through wall of Gaer Fawr hill fort (694244 approx – heap of stones); forward for 30 yards, then left on grassy track to big skyline cairn (690243 approx). Same direction through SW wall of fort (688242); bear right into dip, up over back of Gaer Fach hill fort, down to road (681242). Right for ¾ mile past Glangeidrych and Bethlehem chapel (687249) to T-junction (688252). Left ('Llandeilo' sign) for 200 yd; left ('Ffairfach') past Bethlehem school/post office (686253).

200 yards past school, left (footpath fingerpost) along lane. In 200 yards, left round back of farmhouse (686251); right through gate; follow right-hand hedge to return to chapel. Right along road past Glangeidrych. Climb to pass end of Gaer Fach footpath (681242), on for another ½ mile, round sharp right bend at Cwmdu. In 50 yards pass house on left; left over gate (682235 – footpath fingerpost). Through gap in hedge bank; then aim half right up slope of field to angle of stone wall. Ahead with wall on left to go through gate (683233 – ywa); half left across field to waymark post. Cross ditch (boggy!) and stile; climb field slope to top left corner; cross hedge bank here (ywa) and next field, aiming for left corner of wood (686231). Cross stile (ywa); up edge of wood, crossing 3 more waymarked stiles, to rejoin Beacons Way on edge of Carreglwyd plantation (689228). Retrace outward journey back to Carreg Cennen Castle.

LENGTH: 12 miles

REFRESHMENTS: Carreg Cennen Castle café (01558-822291; *www.caregcennencastle.com*)

BETHLEHEM CHRISTMAS FAIR: (info: Swansea TIC, 01792-468321): Usually first Saturday in December. NB. Allow 6–8 hours for round walk + Christmas Fair.

Worm's Head, Gower

Out along the spine of the old Norsemen's 'sea dragon'

THE OLD SEA RAIDERS from Denmark must have liked the Gower Peninsula. They laid some of their chiefs to rest in this lush corner of South Wales, burying them in the tombs of Sweyne's Howes on top of Rhossili Down. From that high eyrie the spirits of the departed could look out to the open sea over a magnificent beach and a promontory shaped like a westward-striking sea beast. The Vikings named it 'Wurm', or dragon.

Taking the two-mile scramble to the tip of Worm's Head and back is not as easy as it looks. You have to read your tides right – otherwise you could find yourself stranded on the rocky causeway that connects the promontory to the mainland. Currents are fierce here in the widening throat of the Bristol Channel, and many a careless venturer down the centuries has been swept away to death as the rising tides come swirling together across the causeway.

Then there are the rocks that span the gaps between the three humps of Worm's Head. These sharp-cornered slabs, bristling with barnacles, have been canted by ancient subterranean upheavals to an awkward, near-horizontal angle, and cut down by waves and winds over the millennia into the kind of unreasonable surface just made to snag a boot or bend an ankle.

Mist and drizzle cloaked Worm's Head this early summer morning. But even as I set off from Rhossili the green spine of the dragon was drifting clear of the murk. By the time I had got down to the causeway it stood cleanly cut against a speedwell-blue streak of sky. Doubts and difficulties melted from my mind. This is a magical place, whose air of isolation and mystery is only made more seductive by the little hurdles it sets in a walker's way.

The rocks of the causeway lay coated with millions of mussel shells that were themselves encrusted with a camel-brown layer of barnacles. In the rock pools blennies flicked from sunlight into the shelter of weed and anemone fringes, and hermit crabs went tip-toeing hastily from one dark crevice to the next as my shadow barred the water round them.

As the falling tide seethed back from the northern and south-ern edges of the causeway, the pattern of the rocks of Worm's Head became clear. Hundreds of close-packed parallel lines of strata lay upended in the floor of the sea, ground down flat on the margins of the shore, rising to show through the meagre turf of the Inner Head's nape like cranium skin peeking between the lines of a comb dragged through thinning hair.

I crunched on over carpets of broken mussel shells, passing a big rusted ship's anchor lying tines up, and clambered up from the cause-way on to the slope of the Inner Head. A strange name, since this 150ft-high lozenge of grass-grown rock is so obviously the body of the Norsemen's dragon. I checked my watch as I came ashore. Better be back here in a couple of hour's time ...

The turf on the far side of the causeway was beautiful; lush, wind-rippled, pearled with the early morning's mist and studded with wild flowers. I knew the nodding pink flowers of thrift, and those white ones with the bulbous base must be sea campion. But what on earth was this, with roundish leaves and tiny white flowers?

I rummaged in the backpack for my battered old Fitter, Fitter and Blamey. Hmmm ... fleshy leaves, certainly, for retaining fresh water. Hairless, too. And flowers no more than a centimetre across. Must be *cochlearia* – scurvy-grass. Was this what they gave wretched Jack Tars in the days of sail to prevent them falling ill through lack of vitamin C?

A disgusting disease, scurvy. 'The gums are loosed, swolne and exulcerate,' wrote the 16th-century herbalist Gerard, 'the mouth greevously stinking; the thighes and legs are withall verie often full of blewe spots.' Let's try a bit of *cochlearia*. Good God, it's bitter! Wonder if the Vikings knew about it. Can't see those roaring blood-letters being made to eat up their greens, somehow ...

Rounding the corner of the Inner Head a few minutes later I had my first proper sight of Low Neck and Outer Head, the two more seaward humps of the Worm. Something I had not seen from the mainland, too: the canted arch of the Devil's Bridge, cut by the sea clean through the neck of the beast.

The path to the Devil's Bridge across upstanding rock plates is a case of scramble and slither, boot toe and finger tip. With a skinned palm I made it out beyond the arch. A final clamber led to the suddenly towering nape of the Outer Head. Now I took notice of a background noise which had been steadily growing as I neared the tip of the promontory: the '*ee-wake! ee-wake!*' of kittiwakes, and the harsh chakker of black-backed gulls.

As a landfall for migrating birds, the dragon's Outer Head is notable. As a nesting place for seabirds it is even better. All the west and north faces of the 200ft cliffs were crammed with adults and young. I could hear their row, and I could see multitudes of white and dark dots flying out over Rhossili Bay. But I couldn't actually count them on the nest. Walkers who get as far as the Outer Head are asked not to climb so far round that they can be seen by the birds, for fear of disturbing the colony.

I found an unobtrusive niche, a little cliff garden of thrift and sea campion which gave me a vee-shaped eyrie over the water. Out with the bird book, then, and up with the binoculars.

As the birds came flashing through I did my best to hold them in the field of vision. Fulmars on stiff, pointed wings. Razorbills flapping in the sea, in the throes of ecstatic bathing. Guillemots like tubby little businessmen in white shirts, scurrying from one meeting to the next. A rapacious great black-backed gull harrying what looked like a solitary gannet, though I couldn't have sworn to it. Puffins in a flock, skimming importantly by.

The sun stole through the cloud, warming the perch where I lay. I thought of Dylan Thomas, wandering Worm's Head in boyhood 'with a book and a bag of food, the gulls crying mad over me.' Thomas had got himself marooned after falling asleep and missing his tide. 'I stayed on that Worm', he recalled, 'from dusk to midnight, sitting on that top grass, frightened to go further in because of the rats and because of things I am ashamed to be frightened of. Then the tips of the reef began to poke out of the water and, perilously, I climbed along them to the shore.'

If you don't want that to happen to *you*, said my tyrannical watch, you'd better start back now. Oh, come on, time, you bully ... just ten minutes more lazing in this sun-warmed cradle, OK? ... Oh, all *right*, then, I'm coming ...

STEPPING OUT – *Walk 61*

MAP: OS 1:25,000 Explorer 164; 1:50,000 Landranger 159

TRAVEL: Road – M4 to Jct 42; A483 to Swansea, A4067 towards
Mumbles (signed 'Gower'); in 3 miles, right on B4436 ('South
Gower'); through Pennard, left on A4118; in 7 miles, right in
Scurlage ('Rhossili') to Rhossili. Park in car park at end of road
opposite Worm's Head Hotel.

WALK DIRECTIONS: From car park (OS ref SS415880), walk down
track past National Trust Visitor Centre and shop; through
gate, continue along track for 1 mile to coastguard lookout hut
(403874). Right here; descend to cross causeway (see below).
Follow clear path round south side of Inner Head, across Devil's
Bridge (389877), round south side of Low Neck, and out to
Outer Head (see below). Return same way.

LENGTH OF WALK: 4½ miles, there and back. Allow at least 3
hours for full enjoyment.

CONDITIONS: Causeway is rough, jagged and wet. Scramble across
upended blades of rock between Inner Head and Low Neck is
taxing, and requires some agility. Bring strong boots with good
tread, raingear, drink.

SAFETY ON WORM'S HEAD CAUSEWAY: Causeway is accessible for
2 ½ hours each side of low water – a total of 5 hours. Tide times
are posted in National Trust Visitor Centre below Rhossili car
park (tel 01792-390707; *www.nationaltrust.org.uk*). It takes at
least 15 minutes of rough scrambling to cross the causeway.

NESTING BIRDS ON OUTER HEAD: You are requested not to
climb to the top of Outer Head between 1 March and 31 August,
to avoid disturbing nesting birds.

REFRESHMENTS: Worm's Head Hotel (01792-390512; *www.
thewormshead.co.uk*) and cafés in Rhossili.

Whitesands Bay and St David's Head, Pembrokeshire

A Sunday stroll with shearers, savers, shepherds and saints

A BLOWY SUNDAY morning in westernmost Pembrokeshire after a week of grey, horizontal weather – and boyo, were we sick for a sight of the sun. When the clouds began to shred away off the moor tops and the hint of a tint of blue to show through, Jane and I were out of our holiday cottage and down in St David's before you could say, 'Mae fy hofrenfad yn llawn o lyswennod.'

St David's is one of those neat little towns you don't want to leave in a hurry. We slipped into the Cathedral between Holy Communion and Parish Eucharist to admire the beautiful Norman pillars of purple slate, the chisel marks of the masons still plain beneath the patina of eight hundred years' smoothing by hands, backs and shoulders. I ducked into the choir to indulge my passion for medieval misericord carvings. There were some beauties, including two very fine leafy Green Men, a curly dragon, and a crafty fox in a clerical cowl preaching to some trusting inhabitants of the farmyard. The light was low and muted in the church, built deep in a hollow so that – legend says – marauding Vikings might pass by without suspecting it was there.

We caught the little Celtic Coaster bus and went rattling down the twisting, high-banked lane to St Justinian's. From the cliff we gazed across the mile-wide strip of Ramsey Sound to the twin peaks of Ramsey Island RSPB Reserve. The solitary farmhouse stood above the landing slip, a tiny gleaming cube of white. Here was a pure drop of nostalgia for me. Twenty years ago I had waited on this cliff above the cream-and-crimson corrugated tin shed of the lifeboat, looking out to the ferocious tide-rips of Ramsey Sound through which a rubber boat was bouncing and smacking its way towards me. It had

ARTHUR'S QUOIT

STONE~ WALLED ENCLOSURE

OGOF COETAN

CLAWDD-Y-MILWYR

CARN LLIDI

CARN LLIDI BYCHAN

SEA BINDWEED & BELL HEATHER

ST. DAVID'S HEAD

UPPER PORTHMAWR FARM

WHITESANDS BAY

CAR PARK (FINISH)

TO ST. DAVID'S

SITE OF CHAPEL OF ST. PATRICK

WHITESANDS BAY & CARN LLIDI

POINT ST. JOHN

CAR PARK (START)

ST. JUSTINIAN'S

TO ST. DAVID'S

LIFEBOAT STATION

RAMSEY SOUND

RAMSEY ISLAND

THE FARMHOUSE

RAMSEY ISLAND & WHITESANDS B. FROM CARN LLI

ST. DAVID'S HEAD
PEMBROKESHIRE, S.W. WALES

been a bumpy and spray-drenched old journey to the island, and a strangely enthusiastic welcome on arrival. I soon found out why – I had arrived just in time for the annual sheep shearing, and Ramsey was short-staffed.

What a hell of a weekend that turned out to be. Ramsey back then had been privately owned, under covenant of the National Trust, and its flock of sheep had been let run completely wild. Six of us, 'assisted' by a half-trained pup called Spot, set out to gather them off the hills and slippery cliffs of the two-mile-long island. The tough guys sheared them in the stuffy shed, between glugs of beer and puffs of tobacco. I was appointed tallyman/door wallah, and scored a mark in purple wax crayon on the shed wall for each bucking, tittuping beast that sprang past me naked and terrified from the hands of the shearers. By the end of the day there were 198 strokes on the shed wall. I have never been sworn and shouted at so much, laughed so hard or ended the day in such a drunken daze of exhaustion and triumph. Sheer anarchic magic.

Holidaymakers who had booked a boat trip round the island were waiting at the lifeboat shed today, staring across the white horses of Ramsey Sound and cracking nervous jokes about losing their breakfast. Jane and I, turning along the cliff path where the wind was shaking the clumps of thrift and toadflax, felt glad to be keeping to terra firma. Sea wind is a constant here on the coast of Pembrokeshire, streaming the hedges of sea buckthorn inland and sculpting the gorse sprigs into rounded yellow clubs. The sharply canted cliffs fell away to the waves in weather-smoothed flanks of green and mauve, and a solitary sparrowhawk hung in the sun and wind a few feet above our craning faces.

Looking ahead into the long curve of Whitesands Bay, we saw the sands between the rocky headlands of Point St John and St David's Head covered in short figures, most of them in suits of black, running, screaming and leaping. It looked like a painting by L.S. Lowry with added glee. Down on the beach we discovered it was Young Life-Savers Day. In spite of the barking instructors and their gung-ho exhortations, most of the wet-suited youngsters looked as though what they were out for was a good scamper and splash in the pounding surf.

Among the dunes lay a humpy green mound, all that remains of the little Chapel of St Patrick where newly landed seafarers of the Dark Ages would kneel and give thanks for deliverance from the dangers of the twin headlands. Others, outward bound, would pray before embarkation for the saint's protection amid the hazards of the sea. St Patrick was felt likely to lend a sympathetic ear, since stories said that it was from Whitesands Bay that he himself had set sail in AD 432 to bring the Word across the sea to the heathen Irish.

Did the great patron saints of Ireland and Wales, Patrick and David, ever meet each other on Ramsey Island, as other tales tell?

Certainly the rugged island had its own macho 5th-century saint in the person of Justinian, a nobly-born Breton both misogynistic and imperious, who expelled two holy women from Ramsey so that he could live there, and so infuriated his own monks that they cut his head off. Nothing daunted, Justinian marched across the Sound to his burial place on the mainland with his head under his arm. They seem to have made them tough back then.

Out on the windy extremity of St David's Head we passed through the double wall of Clawdd-y-Milwyr, the Warrior's Dyke, built 15 feet high by the Iron Age farmers who lived out here behind this formidable barrier. Who did they fear so greatly? Now their great wall lies less than man height, scattered and tumbled among blue feathery buttons of scabious and white bells of sea campion. Nearby along the cliff path loomed Arthur's Quoit, a giant stone slab propped open by a slender upright. Our ancestors raised it as the capstone of a kingly tomb nearly 6,000 years ago. Or was it mighty Arthur, hero-giant of Welsh folklore, who hurled it here from Moelfre Hill? The head urges one story, the heart another, when one walks these rocky moors and cliffs so drenched in the mythological past.

The clink of rock climbing harness recalled us to the practical present as a breath of warm sunlight stole along the coast. Climbers were inching their way down to the rocks of Ogof Coetan, the Cave of the Quoit, where the waves leaped fitfully and tongues of foam came licking up at the adventurers. Jane and I moved on along the path, threading our way through beautiful coastal heath of gorse and heather whose topmost sprigs held black-capped and russet-breasted stonechats. Time for a little climbing on our own account.

By tip of boot and finger we scrambled up the 600-ft volcanic tor of Carn Llidi. Little kids in shorts and trainers were prancing around the summit like mountain goats. Down below lay Whitesands Bay, a crescent of sand where lines of surf were creaming. Out at sea, gathering clouds hid the horizon. Here on Carn Llidi Patrick the Welsh-born shepherd once stood, gazing west to where the pale blue peaks of Wicklow pierced the skyline a hundred miles off. There was no chance of seeing them this day. But the thought of them made me smile as we picked our way back down to the sea shore once more.

STEPPING OUT – *Walk 62*

MAPS: OS 1:25,000 Explorer OL35, 1:50,000 Landranger 157

TRAVEL: Bus – Celtic Coaster bus (service 403, operates March-September) between St David's, St Justinian's and Whitesands Bay.

Road – M4, A48, A40 to Haverfordwest; A487 to St David's; minor road signposted to St Justinian's.

WALK DIRECTIONS: From St Justinian's car park (OS ref SM724252), down lane towards sea; right along Pembrokeshire Coast Path (fingerposts, acorn symbols) for 4 miles via Whitesands Bay (734272), St David's Head (722279) and Arthur's Quoit (725281) to reach a short fingerpost (736287 – acorn symbols, 'YHA') just before stone-walled enclosure. Follow 'YHA' to right; in 100 yards, left on broad grass track uphill. At saddle (739283 approx.), right along track to summit of Carn Llidi (738280). Continue across 2 crests, descending by rock scramble to lower of two concrete wartime emplacements below Carn Llidi Bychan (735279). Left down path past Upper Porthmawr farm (737276) to Whitesands Bay car park (734272).

LENGTH: 5½ miles (7½ to return to St Justinian's via coast path)

CONDITIONS: Climb to top of Carn Llydi involves a little scrambling. Wear walking trainers/boots.

REFRESHMENTS: Café and public loos at Whitesands Bay; Old Cross Hotel, St David's (01437-720394; *www.oldcrosshotel.co.uk*)

Aberdaron and St Mary's Well,
Llŷn Peninsula

On a pilgrim path to the Gate of Paradise

A NORTH WALES spring morning of blue sky from sea horizon to distant mountains, but cold enough at the outermost tip of the Llŷn Peninsula for the grasses in the steeply sloping graveyard of Aberdaron's Church of St Hywyn to be stiff with frost. Standing high above the squat old church by the sea, I looked down on a village bathed in sunlight, ladled full of early morning peace.

'I have crawled out at last,' wrote the Vicar of Aberdaron:

*'... far as I dare on to a bough
of country that is suspended
between sky and sea.*

From what was I escaping? ...'

Aberdaron remembers its best-known parson with mixed emotions. R.S. Thomas was not an easy man. He served here from 1967 until his retirement in 1978, and wrote some of the most memorable and highly-charged of the hundreds of poems that made him Wales's most celebrated poet of the late 20th century. Thomas was a man of complicated psyche, by turns frosty and fiery, a passionate Welsh nationalist and a lifelong wrestler with God. Skeins of love and dispassion were tightly woven through the poems he wrote about the village and its people, and the buttoned-up vicar with his sudden flashes of temperament both hot and cold is still a topic of vigorous debate here.

Last night in the Ship Inn I'd read my fill of R.S. Thomas. His *Collected Poems* was one of a vast number of books that Peter Hewlett of Edge of Wales Walk had dropped off at the hotel for me. Peter runs walking trips and holidays around this most delectable part of Wales, and was determined I should not go short of information on any bird, flower, legend or poem of the area. I was looking forward to our rendezvous on the cliffs a little later in the day.

Warm smells of coconut from gorse blooms newly opened by the spring sunshine drifted across the coast path beyond Aberdaron. In the narrow cove of Porth Meudwy a salt-rusted old tractor was pushing a crabbing boat into the water, its hoarse grunting underlying the musical Welsh language conversation of the two fishermen. I walked the cliff path among banks of violets and rocks seeded with crimson stonecrop, then crossed the prickly waves of coastal heath on Mynydd Bychestyn, looking seaward to the green sleeping-otter shape of Bardsey Island beyond a tide-ripped sound.

'This place was the final step on the great medieval pilgrimage to Bardsey,' said Peter Hewlett when we met on the green sward by the foundations of St Mary's Church. 'Countless thousands wanted to cross to the Island of Saints. They were hoping to die and be buried there, halfway between the world and heaven.'

At St Mary's Church those seekers and escapers received their final shriving before crossing to the 'Gate of Paradise', holy Bardsey. Ffynon Fair, St Mary's Well, in the rocks below offered a last chance of refreshment and of blessing with the water that the Virgin herself had hallowed – so said legend - when she visited the place. Peter and I inched down narrow rock-cut steps to the shore and clawed our way along a wave-washed ledge to the holy well, a triangular cleft a few feet above the sea, filled with fresh water, cold in the scooping hand, sweet in the mouth to us as to R.S. Thomas:

> *'... clear water, brackish at times,*
> *complicated by the white frosts*
> *of the sea, but thawing quickly.'*

In a country of poets it is inevitable that these outermost lands, so near to the Gate of Paradise and the 'unplumb'd, salt, estranging sea', should have many poetic voices to bear them witness. Christine Evans, mother of the present-day Bardsey boatman and for many years resident on the island, describes crossing the sound:

> *'We get to it through troughs and rainbows*

flying and falling, falling and flying
rocked in an eggshell
over drowned mountain ranges.
The island swings towards us, slowly.
We slide in on an oiled keel,
step ashore with birth-wet, wind-red faces ...'

Tomorrow I was to cross to the Island of Saints, to savour its particular, ethereal magic. Today was for the walk and more earthly delights. Peter and I climbed to the old coastguard lookout at the summit of Mynydd Mawr, the Big Mountain, to enjoy the National Trust's exhibition about the fragile and beautiful coastal heath of the peninsula. Then I strode on alone over the headlands, with Bardsey dipping behind me and an enormous view opening ahead over the whole spread of Llŷn as far as the twin horns of Mount Snowdon, 40 miles off.

Red-legged choughs tumbled and soared on the thermals, and sulphur-yellow celandines shivered in the grasses of the cliffs. Poetry in motion, literally. With the rest of the walk back to Aberdaron laid out below like a living relief model I lingered, looking down on fan-shaped waves breaking in the cove of Whistling Sands, tasting the sunlight and wind of a peerless spring day at the outer edge of Wales.

STEPPING OUT – *Walk 63*

MAPS: OS 1:25,000 Explorer 253; 1:50,000 Landranger 123

TRAVEL: Road – M6 to Jct 10a or 11; M54, A5 to Betws-y-Coed, A 470/A487 to Porthmadog; A497, A499 to Llanbedrog, B4413 to Aberdaron.

WALK DIRECTIONS: Start from Ship Inn (173264). At low tide, right along beach to Porth Simdde, up steps, left along coast path. At high tide, cross bridge, take road ahead ('Porth Oer'); in ¼ mile, left opposite Dwyros (168265 – footpath fingerpost) down lane; in 200 yards, left by National Trust 'Cwrt' sign along coast path past Porth Simdde. In 1 mile path passes Porth Cloch and diverts inland (162249 – yellow arrows) to road (158251). Left to end of tarmac; through gate (fingerpost); make for ladder stile ahead, but *don't cross it!* Instead, bear right through another gate in angle of wall (156245 – fingerpost). Ahead (west) with fence on right for ½ mile, across NT's Bychestyn heath, to meet stony lane (149249). Left to bottom of lane (147247); over gate; right along path with fence on right. Above Porth Felen cross 2 ladder stiles; right uphill (143250) with fence on right. Bear left with it (143254) – now a wall – till it turns right inland (142255). Left downhill here on right of stream with Mynydd Gwyddel on left. In 300 yards, square foundation banks of St Mary's Church are on right (140253).

To visit St Mary's Well at low tide (*NB – potentially dangerous – at your own risk!*): Continue down above right bank of stream to cleft in clifftop and steep, uneven steps down to shore rocks. Well is 30 yards to right, under overhang (138252), reached by scramble along rocks.

From St Mary's Church foundations, aim ahead (NNW) to where mountain slope meets open saddle. Follow narrow path with steep slope to sea on left. In ½ mile bear right uphill by quarry spoil tip (137257) to NT hut at summit of Mynydd Mawr (140259). Follow concrete road NE for 200 yards to right bend (141260). Bear left on path across heath here, keeping to seaward slopes of headlands, crossing stiles, keeping seaward of fences, hugging coast for one and a quarter miles to reach left corner of big field directly under Mynydd Anelog (148271). Cross stile; skirt right along top edge of field. At end, left uphill (153267) on track with fence on right. In 200 yards path forks at post (NB – *short cut* – right fork leads in ⅓ mile to Gors and lane to Aberdaron). Main walk: ahead past Craft View Cottage and continue on green track across slope of Mynydd Anelog, bearing right around Mount Pleasant (151274) and on along cliffs for another 2 miles to Whistling Sands (164298).

Right along track to beach car park; right along lane to road (168293); right for 300 yards to left bend; left (165291 – fingerpost) along farm lane. 150 yards beyond right bend, ahead (171289) through 3 successive kissing gates past Tir-bouog and across footbridge 171287). Right up field edge; in 150 yards, left across field and over stile and footbridge; up right field edge to cross ladder stile in top right corner (169285). Left over stile through Ty Fwg caravan site; down drive past Ysgubor Bach to road (166280); left to follow road for 1¼ miles back to Aberdaron.

LENGTH: 13 miles (via short cut, 10 miles)

CONDITIONS: Steep slopes, steps, unfenced drops (vertigo possibility). St Mary's Well can be dangerous to reach; visit at low tide only.

REFRESHMENTS: Take a picnic

EDGE OF WALES WALK: 01758-760652; *www.edgeofwaleswalk.co.uk*

BARDSEY ISLAND: *www.bardsey.org*

POEMS: *Collected Poems*, R.S. Thomas (Phoenix); *Selected Poems*, Christine Evans (Seren)

Walk 64

Conwy to Penmaenmawr, Snowdonia

Tremendous views from castle and town walls, and from the mountainside beyond

Y OU CAN'T PICK your walking weather in early winter; but if you could, you'd pick it just like this. A crisp cold blue sky over the turrets and battlements of Conwy Castle, the Afon Conwy a gleaming estuarine snake of silver between mud banks of icy blue and tan, a breath of winter in the north-west wind off the Menai Strait, and a dark smoke of cloud over the mountains of Snowdonia to give just a tantalising hint of the possibility of snow.

Gazing from the tower tops of the castle I pictured shivering men-at-arms in the approaches to winter, posted at the 'Who goes there?' when King Edward I first built this coastal stronghold. Conwy was a link in the Ring of Iron that 'King Longshanks' forged round the mountains of North Wales at the end of the 13th century, to chain up the Welsh and their fiery freedom leaders. From the castle I walked the miraculously surviving medieval walls of the town, and got the impression of a settlement crouched inside protective arms of stone as if expecting a blow. These must be the finest town walls in Britain, with breathtaking views from their sloping walkway over the town and its great castle, the three estuary bridges and the mountains beyond.

In Lower Gate Street I dropped my pen, notebook and camera, and gave them an inadvertent boot down the slope for good measure. 'Oh, you're kicking your pieces about, now,' an old man said, watching my possessions skitter down the lane. 'But at least you're all going downhill together!'

A tree-hung promenade curves seaward with the Conwy estuary, and I went with it against the flow of the incoming tide, listening to oystercatchers and gulls. Mendicant swans came up from a muddy creek in hope of crisps. The birds seemed all paired off, but the young

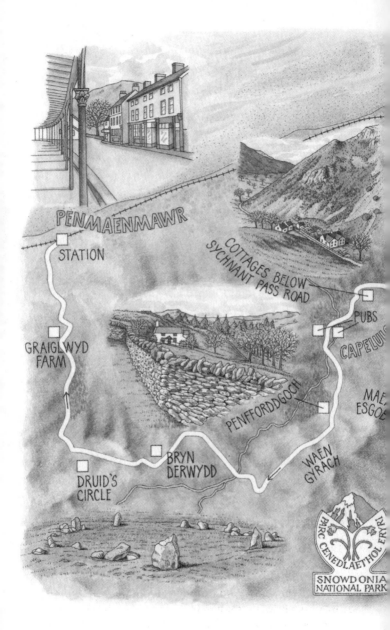

PENMAENMAWR

STATION

COTTAGES BELOW
SYCHNANT PASS ROAD

PUBS

CAPELUL

GRAIGLWYD
FARM

PENFFORDDGOCH

MAE
ESGOE

DRUID'S
CIRCLE

BRYN
DERWYDD

WAEN
GYRACH

PARC CENEDLAETHOL ERYRI

SNOWDONIA
NATIONAL PARK

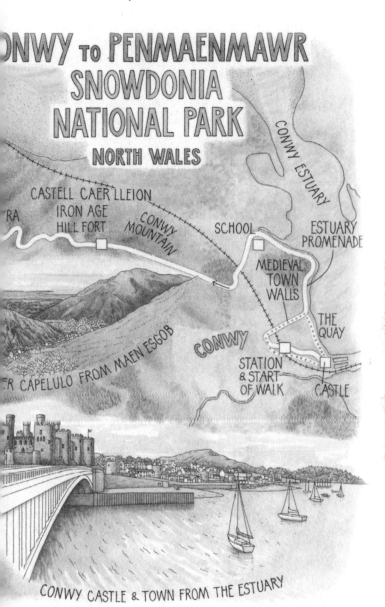

ONWY TO PENMAENMAWR
SNOWDONIA
NATIONAL PARK
NORTH WALES

CASTELL CAER LLEION
IRON AGE
HILL FORT

CONWY MOUNTAIN

SCHOOL

CONWY ESTUARY

ESTUARY
PROMENADE

MEDIEVAL
TOWN
WALLS

THE
QUAY

CONWY

...ER CAPELULO FROM MAEN ESGOB

STATION
& START
OF WALK

CASTLE

CONWY CASTLE & TOWN FROM THE ESTUARY

persons jostling from lesson to lesson around the school near Bod-londeb Woods were still negotiating love matches. 'Loz is so sexy + cute + gorgeous + lovez CRAIG', was the state of play they'd tip-pexed along the railway footbridge.

Up on the bank of Conwy Mountain the wind smacked right into my face. A few purple bell flowers still clung on among pale seed pods trembling in the heather clumps. Here were views even better than those from Conwy's walls – castle and bridges standing solid far below, the gradually filling channels of the estuary, and dark cloud castles drifting eastward as they built and dissolved on fields of blue sky over the long green hills south of the town. Out across the estuary mouth the pale promontory head of Great Orme lay in a sea cream-ing on shallows far out from the beach.

A great viewing place for a leisure walker, to whom a view from a mountain is a sensual pleasure rather than a life-or-death vantage point. It must have been quite an imperative that caused the Iron Age builders of Castell Caer Lleion to wall in the top of Conwy Moun-tain and plant their round huts and cattle pens up here in the teeth of all that the sea gales of winters two thousand years ago could throw at them. These fort-builders were no crude heapers of rubble; the gateway they made into their stronghold shows that the drystone waller's subtle art was flourishing long before the Romans came to Wales.

The village of Capelulo has a mellifluous name, like joyful singing in a chapel. I found it harder to articulate the title of the pub there. Try singing Y Dwygyfylchi through a cheese sandwich. 'The meeting of two valleys, it means,' said the woman who courteously directed me up the steep mountain path. At the top I found the farmstead of Penfforddgoch, 'the top of the red road,' and the upland moors of Maen Esgob, 'the Bishop's Stone'.

What the Bishop's Stone signified is open to conjecture. So are the druidical credentials of Y Meini Hirion, 'The Long Stones', better known to walkers of the hills above Penmaenmawr as the Druid's Circle. The stones stand beyond the lonely house of Bryn Derwydd, or Druid's Hill. It was probably the famously overheated romantic imaginations of the Victorians that made the druid connection, for this circle of standing stones seems to have been constructed around 2000 BC, well before the druidical religion reached its pomp.

Why let cold fact spoil a good tale? – especially when excavations uncovered the remains of Bronze Age children buried within the circle. Human sacrifices? It's possible. A more likely explanation is that our ancestors sensed – as the Victorians acknowledged, and as I felt today, lingering in the stone circle under a blasting wind and racing sky – the raw power and majesty of a wild moor hemmed by mountains and fringed by an unbounded sea.

STEPPING OUT – *Walk 64*

MAP: OS 1:25,000 Explorer OL17; 1:50,000 Landranger 115

TRAVEL: Rail to Conwy (*www.thetrainline.com*)

Road – A55/A547 to Conwy. Park in Rosehill Street car park (782775).

Return from Penmaenmawr station by

WALK DIRECTIONS: From station, right along Rosehill Street to visit Conwy Castle (OS ref SU783775). Return along Rosehill Street; left at station up Rosemary Lane; at top, climb to town walls (779775 – see conditions below). Follow wall walkway; descend near the Quay (781778). Descend Lower Gate Street; left along estuary promenade for ⅔ mile to road by school (775783). Left to cross A547 (775780), then railway. Continue along path, which becomes walled lane, to T-junction (775778). Right (North Wales Path sign – 'NWP'). In 100 yards, right ('NWP'); cross ladder stile; climb mountain path.

In 400 yards, at flat boulder (771778), waymark arrow points ahead; but bear right off NWP for 20 yards, then left on green track climbing spine of Conwy Mountain. In 200 yards by sloping rock face, bear right up grassy path. In 500 yards at fork, right up slope towards rocky crag. Path skirts seaward side of crag; in 150 yards bear left up to ridge. Right along ridge to hillfort at summit of Conwy Mountain (761778).

Continue on path to descend (keeping sharp crag on your left after 100 yards). In 250 yards fork right, in 100 yards, right again to descend to NWP (754776 – 'NWP'). Right; in 200 yards, left ('NWP'); in 200 yards, ahead ('NWP'); descend to cross lane to Pen-pyra farm (750773). Keep ahead to join gravelly lane with wall on left; keep forward. Just before Sychnant Pass Road bear right off NWP (749770) down steep grassy path to cottages (746769); left along road; right (746768) down Sychnant Pass Road into Capelulo.

Between pubs, left up no-through-road (744766). In 200 yards, left across footbridge. At gates, left (744764 – footpath fingerpost) up steep hillside path. Near top (745760), forward along walled green path. Pass Penfforddgoch house (745758); in 100 yards bear left away from wall to rejoin NWP. Right ('NWP') on green track with wall on right; in 200 yards, left

(744756 – 'NWP') away from wall, across Waen Gyrach moor
for ½ mile to meet wall.

Right (740750 – 'NWP'); at wall end, left ('NWP') across
stream (738751 – footbridge). Cross ladder stile; ahead on path
up field. Through gate at top (733753); left ('NWP') along stony
lane. Through gate to pass Bryn Derwydd (730750); in 100
yards, right; through gate, then left (729749 – 'NWP') with wall
on left. At wall end (726748), on across open moor. In 200 yards,
diverge left to Druid's Circle (723747).

Return to NWP and continue. In 200 yd right off NWP,
through wall kissing gate (721748 – footpath fingerpost). Cross
railed causeway, then right, steeply downhill for ⅔ mile. At
Graiglwyd Farm (719757), right through kissing gate; follow
yellow arrow to farm drive; right to road. Left; in 100 yd, right
through kissing gate (719759 – 'Llwybr Cyhoeddus' fingerpost)
across field. Through gate to left of hut, down hedged lane;
through kissing gate; follow housing estate road round to left.
At T-junction (718761), right downhill to Bron Eryri pub.
Continue down Station Road West to Penmaenmawr station
(718766).

LENGTH: 8 miles.

CONDITIONS: Hill paths, some steep, some muddy. Wear hill-
walking gear; take compass. NB *Conwy town walls walkway* –
steep slopes, uneven surface. 50 ft drops guarded only by a rail.
Watch the kids!

REFRESHMENTS: Fairy Glen (01492-623187) or Y Dwygyfylchi
pubs in Capelulo (Y Dwygyfylchi closed lunch Mon–Fri).

CONWY CASTLE: 01492-592358; *www.conwy.com*

TOURIST INFORMATION: Conwy Visitor Centre (01492-592248;
www.conwy.com)

READING: *Walks on the North Wales Coast* by David Berry
(Kittiwake Press) and *Populating The Past – Penmaenmawr's
Mysterious Beginnings* by Alwyn S. Evans (Carreg Gwalch) –
from Conwy TIC

Llangollen, Valle Crucis and World's End, Denbighshire

With George Borrow in search of a bardic tomb and a romantic love-nest

THE BLUE-PAINTED NARROWBOATS lay reflected in the copper-brown waters of the Llangollen Canal. At 8 o'clock on an early autumn morning everything was calm and still in the Vale of Llangollen, with a soft mist curling above the town and the River Dee rushing over its rocky shallows below the canal.

Setting off north along the towpath, I thought of George Borrow walking this way with his wife and step-daughter on a Monday evening in the summer of 1854. The impulsive East Anglian writer, a plodding Saxon by birth but an incandescent Celt in his head, was staying in Llangollen in order to practise his sketchy Welsh and his half-baked historical theories on the natives, and to walk prodigious distances – all of which resulted in his cranky masterpiece *Wild Wales*, one of my personal Bibles of rural writing.

Borrow would certainly have come up with some clever-clogs Bardic stanzas to edify the father and son who sat fishing in the canal just beyond the wharf. I contented myself with: 'Had any luck?' That was the right question. The boy grinned from ear to ear, and blurted out, 'I've had a grayling! And I've seen a trout in there!'

A mile north, the valley of the Eglwyseg River comes down to meet the Vale of Llangollen. This side valley winds between high, rounded green hills, their tops in this ragwort summer stained bright yellow. The Cistercian 'white monks' always had an eye for a quiet, remote and spiritually uplifting place where they could farm and pray, and at the start of the 13th century they built a magnificent abbey here.

I wandered among the abbey ruins, superbly sited under the hills, and found a viewpoint where the tall east windows stood reflected in the abbot's fishpond. Whether Iolo Goch, Owain Glyndwr's bard, really lies buried in the church is open to question. George Borrow was certain of it. Borrow did enjoy bringing his family here: he was able to show off in the ruins in front of his wife and step-daughter, by knowing more about Welsh poets and poetry than any of the locals.

The white monks named the place Valle Crucis, the Vale of the Cross, in honour of a stone cross known as the Pillar of Eliseg which they found planted in a burial mound nearby. It was put up around 850 AD to mark the grave of Eliseg, Prince of Powys. When the Roundheads came this way during the Civil War they knocked it down as a popish symbol. Local landowner Mr Lloyd of Trevor House had it re-erected in1779, after he had excavated the mound and discovered human remains sealed in a rough stone coffin. The body of Prince Eliseg? Who knows? The ancient memorial still stands near the abbey, phallic and enigmatic.

A straggling back-country road runs north into the narrowing jaws of the valley, with high green hills on one side and the dramatic grey bulges of Creigiau Eglwyseg, the Church Crags, on the other. The limestone crags form a succession of layered bluffs, billowing out like sails with a stiff wind behind them, their feet lost in great downward-spreading fans of scree. They flank a high and wild canyon, naked and grand.

At the furthest stretch of the valley I came to World's End, and climbed on a section of Offa's Dyke through conifers and out onto the face of the crags. From here there was a wonderful view down to the tall chimneys and herringbone woodwork of the Tudor manor house at World's End, tucked down behind the trees.

George Borrow did not include in *Wild Wales* the story of hotheaded Owain ap Cadwgan and beautiful Nesta, a rumbustious tragedy that belongs to this valley and maybe to the hunting lodge that preceded the present house at World's End. The story tells how Owain, 12th-century Prince of Powys, fell in love with Nesta, and took a band of men down to Cilgerran Castle in Pembrokeshire to remove her forcibly from her Norman husband Gerald of Windsor.

The baron had to escape from his burning castle by sliding down his own lavatory chute in his nightshirt, while the prince galloped with the 'Helen of Wales' back to the love-nest he had prepared in the valley of Eglwyseg. He did not enjoy his prize for long. King Henry, avenging the insult to his Constable of Pembrokeshire, laid waste the lands of Owain's father, and the old man ordered his son to return Nesta to her husband.

Revenge, the cuckolded baron found, was a dish better tasted cold. He had to wait years for his opportunity, but at last found himself in battle as an ally of Owain ap Cadwgan. The Norman contrived to get alongside the Welshman while they were on their own, and wasted no time in dispatching his love rival with his sword.

I walked on along the narrow shelf of the scree path, rounding one grey flank after another, stepping aside from time to time to let other Offa's Dyke walkers come past. 'Lovely day,' they said. 'Lovely view.'

Sunshine flooded the long south-running valley, turning the fields and slopes a brilliant green, and the mountain breeze brought fruity smells of warm rock and grass, bracken and heather, and sheep dung. A gnarled tree stump stuck out of the path, shaped uncannily like a dog's head, its cocked ears and sharp nose pointing downhill to Plas yn Eglwyseg as if listening to the farm dogs yelling at walkers on the road far below.

A couple of rising miles on a mountain road down in the valley, and I came level with the round green thousand-foot knoll of Castell Dinas Bran, topped by the jagged ruins of a 13th-century Welsh castle. At the summit, after a breathless climb, I sat among the shattered walls and window arches, gazing out towards the Berwyn Hills and the far-off mountains of Snowdonia.

George Borrow ascended Dinas Bran on his first morning after arriving in Llangollen. Crowds of impertinent urchins followed him, but he ignored them. The view pleased Borrow; but what pleased him more was when a hay-mower, hearing him speak Welsh, asked if he was indeed a native.

Readers of *Wild Wales* today can see that the haymakers were laughing at the eccentric Borrow behind his back. But the would-be Welshman paid them no heed. He was far too busy assembling his jackdaw's pickings of verse, bigotry, legend, fact and plain misunderstanding into what would turn out to be one of the most entertaining travel books ever written.

STEPPING OUT – *Walk 65*

MAP: OS 1:25,000 Explorer 256; 1:50,000 Landranger 117

TRAVEL: Road – A5 from east and west: A483 from north and south.

WALK DIRECTIONS: Cross bridge over River Dee (OS ref SJ215422). Opposite railway station, steps (brown pedestrian sign) climb to Llangollen Wharf on canal (215423). Turn left along towpath for 1 mile to Bridge 48 (207436). Ascend to road; turn right; in 50 yd, left ('Valle Crucis' sign) on field path for ½ mile. Descend steep steps on left (205443) to Valle Crucis Abbey (204442). Turn right on main road above for 250 yd; bear right (202445) to reach Pillar of Eliseg.

Return along road for 100 yd; first left down track. Pass white house, over stile and footbridge (204445); follow yellow arrow up bank to regain path. Turn left; dogleg right and left at Abbey Cottage (205447); continue for 1 mile to cross road and gate opposite (209458). Descend field slope diagonally right to cross stream by footbridge (212460); turn right and continue on left bank to road (216460). Turn left for 1¾ miles, passing World's End Farm (221475) and manor house (229479). Turn right up Offa's Dyke Path (232478 – acorn sign). Continue through pine trees and along scree of Creigiau Eglwyseg for 2 miles to fork; bear right to Rock Farm and road (218453). Bear left for 1½ miles, keeping ahead at junction (217446 – 'Panorama' sign), past Tan-y-Castell Farm (225435). In ¼ mile, turn right over cattle-grid, steeply uphill to Castell Dinas Bran ruins (222431).

Zigzag path down west face of knoll reaches tarmac path (217429); follow brown circle waymarks and yellow arrows forward, through kissing gates and down hill slopes to return to Llangollen Wharf (215423) and town.

LENGTH OF WALK: 12 miles – allow 6 hours.

CONDITIONS: Narrow bouldery path along Creigiau Eglwyseg screes. Stiff ascent to Castell Dinas Bran.

REFRESHMENTS: Abbey Grange Hotel (01978-860753; *www.abbey-grange-hotel.co.uk*) on A542 just north of Valle Crucis; otherwise, take picnic

READING: *Wild Wales* by George Borrow (pub: Bridge Books)

NORTH WEST

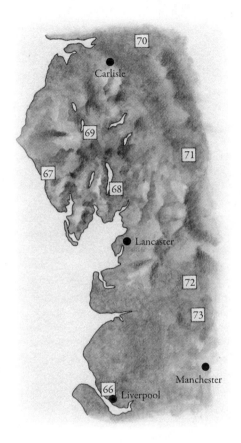

Liverpool and Birkenhead, Merseyside

Heroes old and young in the city of Merseybeat

'LIVERPOOL MUSIC? It's raw music, seamen's music – I think that's the special ingredient.' John McNally, hands in jacket pockets against the bitter spring wind off the Mersey, nodded reflectively as he walked by my side up Water Street. 'I grew up in a very working class area down by the docks, and my brother – he was a seaman – would bring back these fantastically exciting records from America. Eddie Cochrane, Gene Vincent, Hank Williams – I heard them long before you could get hold of them in record shops here. Another seaman friend of the family taught me a few chords on the guitar, and that was it. I was completely hooked.'

John McNally is a busy man these days. As a slavish fan of his band The Searchers back in the 1960s, I was as thrilled as only a true fan can be when he agreed to find time on one of his rare days at home to walk me through the Liverpool he and young guitar-slingers like him helped The Beatles to create – the Liverpool of Merseybeat.

To my mind Liverpool – designated European City of Culture in 2008 – has one significant culture above all others: its distinctive home-grown music. As a youth I adored the Searchers. 'Needles And Pins', 'Sweets For My Sweet', 'I Pretend I'm With You', 'Goodbye My Love': those harmony-rich, 12-string-driven, three-minute bursts of pop perfection had soundtracked my teenage. Who would have thought that at the age of 66 John McNally would still be touring all over the world with The Searchers, strumming out those urgent, wristy chords on his high-slung rhythm guitar?

We glanced into the windows of music shops as we strolled along Dale Street and North John Street. John shook his head in wry amusement. 'Back then we couldn't afford new strings. You'd boil up your old ones in a pan to get the crap off them, then put them back

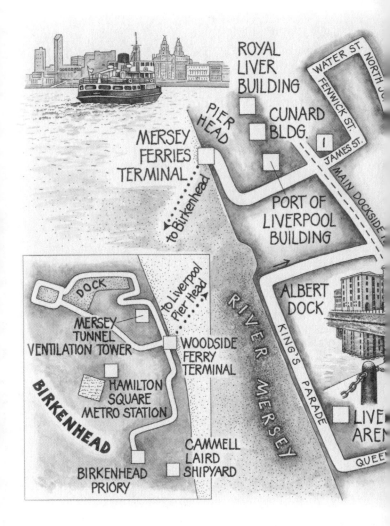

on the guitar. Our bass player Tony Jackson – a real tough feller, we called him Black Jake, and I really looked up to him – he actually made his own bass and our amps. It was all very rough and ready.'

That can-do spirit has propelled Liverpool's music ever since the 1960s. Echo and The Bunnymen, The Teardrop Explodes, The La's, The Coral, The Zutons – Merseyside has spawned more bedroom

poets and garden-shed guitarists, strumming and humming their way to glory, than any other place of comparable size. What is it with Liverpool and home-made music? The night before, I had gone to see a young local band, The Sonic Hearts, play the Carling Academy in the city. With their first LP 'Sunrise' about to come out these were exciting times for The Sonic Hearts; testing ones, too.

'A Liverpool gig is always the worst,' groaned Liverpool-born frontman and songwriter Sean Butler, a friendly chap who seemed genuinely elated to be doing so well. 'There's a lot of pressure, because of the fantastic music heritage of this city. The Beatles – they do cast a long shadow. But what a shadow to be in!'

It was a joyful, vigorous show, with Sean greeting family and friends from the stage and grinning like a man on Cloud Nine when he wasn't singing his soulful songs as if his life depended upon each successive note. 'I don't know why Liverpool has such a hugely strong musical tradition,' he mused afterwards. 'Maybe it's everyone being skint, so that's all you can afford to do. There's often a salty sort of feel to it, a shanty sound ... maybe it's to do with being so close to the river and the sea.'

Liverpool musicians all seem to know each other, a freemasonry of friends and competitors. At the gig I bumped into another of the city's famed songwriters, Ian Prowse of the band Amsterdam. Over a late-night pint of Guinness in a pub in Mathew Street – home of the Cavern Club, forever associated with the young, pre-Fabmania Beatles – Ian pointed to the Irish tradition of the city. 'In 1845, the first year of the Great Famine, you suddenly had half a million Irish on the Pierhead, emigrating to America, or settling in Liverpool. It's bound to have an effect, that tradition of making music at home. My band plays rock music, but somehow it's getting more and more Irish, more fiddle to it and a more traditional sound. Which I really love!'

Outside the Cavern, John McNally stopped to reminisce about the fledgling Beatles. 'We saw them advertised at the Cavern – "The Silver Beatles, Direct from the Star Club in Hamburg!" The Searchers always wore smart stage suits, but here were these four lads in leather jackets, smoking away, Coke bottles on the amps, looking hard and mean, with a thump-thump-thump beat and a heavy guitar sound. They'd changed, been toughened up by playing long hours to rough crowds at the Star Club. We thought: hmmm, there's something we can learn from here!'

I shook hands with John at the Whitechapel crossroads and he strode away, neat and energetic, to buy some new guitar strings. I walked on, making east along the cobbled, old-fashioned thoroughfare of Wood Street where brick-faced warehouses sprouted buddleia bushes and old boys cackled together over their fags outside the Empire pub. Pallid youth searched the boxes in Probe Records for rare vinyl. Not much change since Merseybeat days hereabouts;

nor in the majestic 'imbibing emporium' of the Philharmonic pub on Hope Street with its plasterwork friezes and elaborate stained-glass windows. There were Chinese faces beyond the dragon-festooned archway to Chinatown, Irish faces and voices in the car-breakers and furniture storage premises closer to the river. From the top of Liverpool Cathedral's tower, 300 feet in the air, I got a memorable overview of this cosmopolitan, bustling and always evolving seaport town, hunched under today's freezing white sky.

Down on the Pierhead I took a ferry across the Mersey – Gerry and The Pacemakers pounding away in my inner ear – and walked a circuit of the Birkenhead shore along cobbled and bollarded quays, with the giant yellow cranes rumbling in the distance beyond the high walls of Cammell Laird's ship-repairing yard. Here was a working river front, un-airbrushed and gritty, with an incomparable view back across the Mersey to the iconic buildings of the Liverpool waterfront in whose shadow the young Merseybeaters grew up, and the towering skyscrapers more recently built there.

Lights began to twinkle through the cold dusk, smearily moving on the river. I grinned to myself as I walked and stared, cradling a notebook in which reposed a scrawled autograph I would have killed for in 1964, and which still sent a thrill of glee through an adolescent corner of my soul: 'The Searchers – John McNally.'

STEPPING OUT – *Walk 66*

MAP: OS 1:25,000 Explorer 266; 1:50,000 Landranger 108;
'Liverpool World Heritage City' map, widely available in the
city.

TRAVEL: Rail to Lime Street Station (*www.thetrainline.com*).
Merseyrail metro (*www.merseyrail.org*) to James Street.
Road – M6 to Jct 21a; M62 to city centre.

WALK DIRECTIONS: Liverpool is a great city for wandering,
but to follow CS's route: Leaving James Street station, left up
James Street, cross Castle Street, on up Lord Street, left along
North John Street. Pass Hard Day's Night Hotel; bear right
immediately right down Mathew Street past Cavern Club. Right
along Stanley Street to Whitechapel (left here to reach Walker
Art Gallery and World Museum Liverpool). Cross Whitechapel
and go down Church Street. Right to the Bluecoat Gallery; left
along School Lane to cross Hanover Street; up Wood Street to
St Luke's Church. On up Leece Street and Hardman Street to
Philharmonic pub.

Return down Hardman Street; left along Pilgrim Street to
Anglican Cathedral. Right down Duke Street; left through
Chinatown arch past Great George Square. Right along Park
Lane; left down Blundell Street to main dockside road. Cross
road; down Queen's Wharf to turn right along waterfront
promenade of King's Parade, past the Arena, round Albert
Dock to reach Pierhead. Mersey ferry to Woodside terminal,
Birkenhead. Stroll along waterfront promenades – north
around dock and gardens, south to Birkenhead Priory and view
of Cammell Laird cranes. Make inland for brick campanile of
Hamilton Square station. Hamilton Square is just beyond. NB.
The Birkenhead waterfront paths are a work-in-progress.

LENGTH: Allow half a day.

REFRESHMENTS: The Philharmonic, Hope Street
(0151-707-9424).

MUSIC: Amsterdam (*www.amsterdam-music.com*); The
Searchers (*www.the-searchers.co.uk*); The Sonic Hearts (*www.
thesonichearts.com*).

MERSEY FERRIES: 0151-330-1000 (timetable), 0151-330-1444
(tickets and booking enquiries); *www.merseyferries.co.uk*

LIVERPOOL CATHEDRAL: 0151-709-6271; *www.liverpoolcathedral.
org.uk*

WALKER ART GALLERY AND WORLD MUSEUM LIVERPOOL:
www.liverpoolmuseums.org.uk
BLUECOAT GALLERY: 0151-702-5324; *www.thebluecoat.org.uk*
CAVERN CLUB: 0151-236-1965; *www.cavernclub.org*
INFORMATION: *www.visitliverpool.com*

Ravenglass & Muncaster Castle, Cumbria

Celebrating the 150th Walk of the Month

WAKING AT SEVEN O'CLOCK in my bedroom at the Burnmoor Inn far up Eskdale, I heard a tapping on the window. I drew the curtains and looked out. After two weeks of peerless blue skies and warm spring sunshine, rain was slanting from a racing grey sky. Oh, no, I groaned to myself – only using a different form of words – not *again!*

It was the morning of my 150th Daily Telegraph Walk of the Month, a celebration walk, to be accomplished in the company of a group of invited readers. I'd chosen West Cumbria to give Northern readers a chance to join in, because the last public Walk of the Month – the 100th – had been set near London in Henley-on-Thames. And what a day *that* had turned out to be.

The Centenary Walk took place on one of southern England's worst days of gales and flooding for many years. The Thames burst its banks, trees were uprooted, lorries were blown on their backs. A dozen brave people turned up, some struggling from as far afield as Bristol and Southampton. We did the walk bent double into the wind and rain under umbrellas blown inside out, and puddled the bar of the Flower Pot at Aston with our sodden raingear at lunchtime. Tremendous fun in adversity – but I had been hoping for kinder weather this time round.

Down on the coast in Ravenglass, however, the grey clouds were already shredding away in the face of a sharp south-westerly. Over the seaward-flowing estuary, out beyond the vast Drigg sand dunes, the sky over the Irish Sea was a polished blue. It was going to be a beautiful day.

In Ravenglass village car park we convened – nearly thirty walkers of varying shapes, sizes, ages and abilities. Most of the Telegraph walkers, naturally, were Northerners or thereabouts: Mary Edgar and

Mary and Dennis Cotterell from Carlisle, Les and Joan Hood from Preston, Fred and Marion Thornton from Kendal, Edith and Stan Suggitt from Crakehall in North Yorkshire. John and Commie Baker came from West Boldon over in Tyne & Wear, Penny and Andrew Read with their dogs Emma and Hamish from nearby Broughton-in-Furness. Jenny Benson had travelled down from Cockermouth, and Chris Wright from Grange-over-Sands on the great estuaries of South Lakeland.

Some had journeyed from further afield. Swiss-born Anne-Marie Davis had come up from Wembley in northwest London, Sylvia Lukaczynski from her cottage in North Wales at the foot of the Clwydian Hills near Ruthin. And Jane and Martin Longbottom had made the long haul up from the West Country – from my home town, Bristol, in fact. It was nice to see Jane and Martin again; they had been part of the Worshipful Company of Drowned Rats on the Hundredth Walk.

Just for this once I had decided to be lazy and to do no pre-walk research. I would put myself, like the others, in the capable hands of Malcolm Guyatt, the Lake District National Park's Area Ranger, and trust him to find a walk for us, a great walk suitable for the occasion. Malcolm not only did that, and lectured and joshed us with equal humour and insight all the way round the walk; he brought along a whole clutch of other rangers and volunteers, too, each expert in some field of outdoor knowledge, to help the day go well. There was no obligation for any of them to turn out on a Sunday; they'd come along because this part of West Cumbria is somewhere they all feel passionate about.

Ravenglass is a tiny, beautifully kept village on a vast shore of sand dunes and flats through which the three rivers of Esk, Mite and Irt combine and snake to meet the Irish Sea. Though the classic and hugely popular Lakeland fells of Scafell, Bow Fell, Great End and Lingmell stand only a few miles inland, comparatively few visitors make their way down to this wide, lonely and compelling shore. The Drigg dunes and sand flats are a European Marine Site by virtue of the complexity and richness of their wildlife in the tidal zones between low water and high flood point. A wild beauty clings to the shore, the woods, the rivers and hill slopes all along the coast. Yet those who do venture here have these delights mostly to themselves. On this gorgeously sunny spring Sunday our party met no more than half a dozen other walkers all day.

We set off, chattering like a treeful of starlings, across the bridge over 'La'al Ratty', the narrow-gauge Ravenglass & Eskdale Railway. A couple of mournful hoots from one of Ratty's miniature steam engines sent us on our way through the woods. I found myself walking with Chris Wright from Grange; it turned out he had written the Constable guidebook to the North Downs Way, one of my all-time favourite walking books.

That wasn't the only pleasure of the company I was keeping today. Walking talking tends to be uninhibited talking; something to do with the relaxation that the repetitive rhythm of walking sets up. I found myself talking about sea pollution with Rachel, Cape Breton fiddle tunes with Dennis, owls and voles with Betty Green, a recent foot-and-mouth cull – still raw and real in these parts – with Andrew. Bursts of other people's theorising and speculation – from rugby to starfish by way of skunk cabbage – went weaving in and out of my other ear. We must have been the widest-ranging band of walkers, conversationally speaking, in West Cumbria this day.

As for what we saw: the sun slanting through oak branches and rhododendron blooms, three estuaries in silver coils among the sand-banks, a bath house where Roman soldiers caroused and womanised, and wonderful views up Eskdale to the crumpled fells. At historic Muncaster Castle the Penningtons, owners and sharers of this eccentric and delightful building and its grounds, came out to greet us with real warmth. Malcolm told us of the influence of the sea, the creation of new paths, Victorian ladies viewing the scenery through their Claude glasses, and red squirrels in the Muncaster woods.

We finished the walk on the shore at Ravenglass, picking up whelks and mussels with sand and mud on our boots. Goodbyes were said on the daffodil-fringed village green. Readers and volunteers drifted off by ones and twos to their cars, satiated by the sights and sounds of West Cumbria. A few of us were left to sit outside the Holly House pub, sorting over the day in the blowy spring sunshine.

STEPPING OUT – *Walk 67*

MAP: OS 1:25,000 OL6; 1:50,000 Landranger 96

TRAVEL: Rail to Ravenglass (www.thetrainline.com)
Road: M6 to Jct 36; A590 to Greenodd; A5092 to Grizebeck;
A595 to Ravenglass.

WALK DIRECTIONS: From Ravenglass village car park (OS ref
SD085964) cross the railway line, and just before reaching the
road bear right (087965) for ⅔ mile, passing the Roman Bath
House (088959) to reach Newtown's white-painted house
(093956). Continue along the Cumbria Coastal Way under
Newtown Knott, descending to west bank of River Esk. Just
above river (098950), a Cumbrian Coastal Way sign has yellow
arrow pointing right; but keep ahead (white arrow) on signed
path: 'Permitted Path – Muncaster Estate'. Continue upstream
for 1½ miles, leaving the river halfway (101958) to reach A595 at
Hirst Lodge (110968).

Cross (with care!); left for 300 yd, to bear right on left bend
onto track (109971). In 200 yd, turn back on yourself before
the lodge at Chapel Wood (111971). Turn right up steps with
'Walkers Welcome' notice and climb path steeply up through
wood. At top of bank bear right on path that passes under
Monument. In ⅓ mile, at blocking logs across path, bear left
over a ladder stile (112976) and left again along the Eskdale
Trail. Follow this for ½ mile to junction with Fell Lane (106975
'Public Bridleway to Muncaster' fingerpost). Turn left for ½
mile to A595 (100968); left (take care!) for 400 yd to turn right
(103967) into grounds of Muncaster Castle.

From castle follow public footpath up through Dovecote
Wood. At top of slope, yellow arrow on post points left to
Muncaster; but keep ahead to leave trees (100961) onto open fell.
Keep same line over ridge and down to enter trees (095958) and
continue to Newtown. Retrace outward walk to Walls (089958);
left here under railway, then right along shore to Ravenglass.

LENGTH OF WALK: 7 miles

REFRESHMENTS: Holly House Hotel, Ravenglass (01229-717230;
www.thehollyhousehotel.com); Muncaster Castle (see below).

MUNCASTER CASTLE: (01229-717614; *www.muncaster.co.uk*): Free
passage on public footpath. A Walker's Ticket (inexpensive)
gives an hour's use of Castle facilities, grounds, Owl Centre.

Walk 68

Crosthwaite and Witherslack, Cumbria

Across the unfrequented fell of Whitbarrow in the south-east corner of Lakeland

I WANTED A GOOD DAY'S WALK in the Lake District, well away from the over-used routes up the famous fells. I was looking for something vigorous but not too hair-raising with good wide views all round. Something with character, something tucked away; a special walk for those in the know. A tall order, in fact.

'Try Whitbarrow,' suggested the young ranger in the National Park office. 'Very unfrequented; you'll find very few walkers know of it. Whitbarrow's my favourite place in South Lakeland.' And turning to Wainwright I found that the Master, too, had given Whitbarrow his *imprimatur* in *The Outlying Fells of Lakeland* : 'The walk is the most beautiful in this book; beautiful it is, every step of the way. All is fair to the eye on Whitbarrow.'

On a steely grey morning I set off from the Punch Bowl at Crosthwaite, sporting woolly hat and thermal gloves. Those were soon whipped off, though, as I worked up a sweat climbing out of the gentle green Winster Valley. This is not the familiar Lake District of heaped fells and lonely precipitous chasms. Down here in Lakeland's south-eastern corner the hills lie lower, their feet dipping into wide estuaries that snake out into the vast dun brown sands of Morecambe Bay.

Whitbarrow is shaped like a giant crab's shell washed up on the shore of the River Kent's estuary. A layer cake of limestone, it bares great teeth of grey stone all along its western rim. What lies on top you cannot even guess, until you have climbed from the valley up one of the escarpment's steep paths through scrubby woodland and emerged into that breezy, rocky upland world.

Blue moor grass carpets the summit of Whitbarrow. Grey outcrops of limestone tear through the coarse covering. Much of the stone is gashed into dry pavements made up of clints and grykes – upthrust blocks and down-cutting cracks. In summer this is supreme botanist's country, with rare ferns and helleborines, solomon's seal and lily of the valley thriving in the sheltered micro-climate of the warm and shadowy grykes.

Today the grykes still hoarded a scoop or two of late snow, shrunken and crystalline. I tramped along, sniffing cold air pungently scented by juniper bushes clinging to rocks and tiny patches of earth. The views were stupendous, scores of miles all round filled with the outlines of high Cumbrian country – humpy Pennine moors and fells to the east, sharper Lakeland peaks and ridges to the west and north. In the south the brilliant silver ribbon of the Kent estuary sinuated into the gunmetal grey of Morecambe Bay. A peregrine went dashing across this theatrical backdrop, a dark destroyer bent on business.

Under the western wall of Whitbarrow runs the narrow and road-less Witherslack Valley, deep, secret and romantic. Picking my way gingerly down the steep zig-zag path I looked across the valley to Witherslack Hall, its old roofs and gables half-drowned in a froth of greening larches and sycamores.

It did not pay to pick the wrong side in medieval disputes. Poor Sir Thomas Broughton of Witherslack Hall, who had ill-advisedly backed the hapless Lambert Simnel in his doomed bid for the throne of Henry VII, was forced to hide out as a fugitive in a cave on Whit-barrow for many years, fed by faithful retainers, unable to live in his own house. Eventually he died in the woods and was buried clandes-tinely in some long-forgotten cave.

In High Park Wood at the foot of the scar a subaqueous green light filtered through the still leafless birch and ash branches. A pair of ravens asserted ownership of the air space above Whitbarrow, dive-bombing a trespassing buzzard until he side-slipped and rolled his way out of the disputed territory.

A black-and-white afternoon film was flickering on the bar TV in the Derby Arms below Witherslack village. I warmed myself for half an hour there, eating a baked potato while sleek-headed dastards in trench coats levelled close-clipped 1930s diphthongs at each other: 'Thet's just too bed, old chyep!' I couldn't wait to see who would get the girl. The afternoon light was threatening to drain out of the sky, and Wainwright had warned of the difficulty of finding the steep track up Whitbarrow's southern crags.

In the event the adumbrated 'thin path' proved well waymarked.

There were no problems on top, either, as I yomped along to Lord's Seat and down through the conifers of the hill's north slope in the dusk. It wasn't until the final mile that I lost my way among the trees.

Stumbling out of Durham Bridge Wood to the edge of a cliff, I found stars in a pitch black sky above me and the glow of farmhouse lights two hundred feet below. The heart-in-mouth scramble to get down there, the wetness of the ditch I blundered into, and the muddiness of my hands and face when I limped into the Punch Bowl Inn long after nightfall – such were the penalties for a carelessly botched map reading. It would never have happened to the Master.

STEPPING OUT – *Walk 68*

MAPS: OS 1:25,000 OL7; 1:50,000 Landranger 97

TRAVEL: Road: M6 to Jct 36; A590 towards Barrow; A5074 (right) towards Windermere; Crosthwaite signed on right. Park at Punch Bowl Inn.

WALK DIRECTIONS: From Punch Bowl (OS ref SD445912), descend past church into walled lane to road (442908). Left; in 150 yd right ('Esp Ford' sign) through farmyard (blue arrow); along track to A5074 (444904). Right; in 400 yd left (441904 – 'The High' sign) up drive. 100 yd before farm, 2 gates together in angle of wall (439902). Through right one; up slope (fence on right); stile on right into trees. Through stone stile opposite; right (439899 – wall on right) for ¾ mile to Fell Edge farm (436890). In 200 yd, path climbs left up scar.

At top, ignore wall stile opposite; diagonally right to cross next stile near angle of wall (437886). SSE across plateau to big boulder, then cairns; then path SE to forestry wall gate (441879 – 'No Cycling' notice). Cross nearby wooden stile; yellow arrow points east along wall, but keep ahead (S) on permissive path for ⅓ mile to stone stile in wall (443875). Don't cross; bear SSW on path to cairn on Lord's Seat (442871).

Careful! A path goes temptingly SSE; but bear right (SW) on cairned path till Witherslack Hall in view. Left along wall for ¼ mile to stile (440865); cross, and descend steep path. Left at bottom (439863 – fingerpost); yellow arrows around football field, to barn and road (436859). Right; in 100 yd left ('Knot Wood' sign). Right fork at Lawns House (435857). Follow blue arrows south on wood edge and cross Yewbarrow for 1½ miles to road (435836). Left past Slate Hill footpath sign; round next left bend, right ('Latterbarrow' sign) past buildings, through gate, across field, through gate into scrub area. In 200 yd, left (438831 – fingerpost), over wall and stile (yellow arrow), past Latterbarrow Farm, through gate into track to road. Right to Derby Arms PH (442829).

Return past Witherslack village sign; fork right just past Town End Post Office (441836). In ¾ mile pass Mill Side duckpond (448842); left here; fork right in 10 yd up track. In ⅓ mile, left (452844 – white arrow) up steep 'permissive path'.

Follow white arrows to cross stream (453846); in another ¼ mile, sharp left (white arrow) on steep climb. At top of scar, through two neighbouring gaps in wall (452847 – white arrows). Keep ahead among trees; in 150 yd, bear left on to open fell (white arrows). Keep conifers on right and steer N with a touch of W to cairn. In ¾ mile cross wall stile (446861); then on to Lord's Seat cairn (442871).

On to cross wall stile (443875); ahead (E) into conifers; in 200 yd bear left (444876 – no waymark!) and keep NE through wood. In ½ mile, left (448880 – post with yellow arrows); in 200 yd, through gate and on. In ½ mile, across at crossroads (451885 – yellow arrows); in 300 yd bear ahead downhill (faint path), out of wood, across fields to The Row hamlet and road (452892). Left; continue NW on this road, then woodland track, for 1 mile to wall stile above The High farm (440899). Retrace outward route to Crosthwaite.

LENGTH OF WALK: 14 miles (allow 7–8 hours). Shorter circular walk (7 miles): Crosthwaite to Lord's Seat, returning through woods and by The Row.

CONDITIONS: Steep, slippery in parts: longer circuit for fit and active walkers only.

REFRESHMENTS: Derby Arms, Witherslack (01539-552207; *www. derbyarms.co.uk*); Punch Bowl, Crosthwaite (01539-568237; *www.the-punchbowl.co.uk*)

GUIDEBOOK: *The Outlying Fells of Lakeland* by A. Wainwright (Frances Lincoln)

Four Beatrix Potter Walks, Cumbria

Through Miss Potter's Lake District with Benjamin Bunny, Squirrel Nutkin,
Mrs Tiggy-Winkle, Jemima Puddle-Duck and chums

MANY YEARS AGO in Keswick I bought (but never got round to using) a cheap paperback guidebook, *Lakeland Walks from Beatrix Potter* by Wynne Bartlett. Though its publishers, Frederick Warne – still the publishers of Beatrix Potter's tales, as they have been from the very beginning – have let it go out of print since then, its short walks are still excellent value and full of scenes and places familiar to anyone who has read and loved Beatrix Potter. The Lake District settings she used have changed remarkably little in the hundred years since Miss Potter wrote her books.

Wynne Bartlett's three Derwent-side walks are based around the tales of *Benjamin Bunny*, *Squirrel Nutkin* and *Mrs Tiggy-Winkle*. You can do them as three separate short strolls suitable for children, or amalgamate them into one 6-mile walk. A fourth walk based on Hill Top Farm, Beatrix Potter's home near Lake Windermere, takes in her life as a hard-working sheep farmer after she married and gave up her role as a children's author – but it, too, is steeped in the landscapes, scenes and characters of her books.

These are all low-level walks on well-defined paths, tracks and lanes. Slip on comfortable walking shoes, take a few sweeties and a Beatrix Potter or two in your bag and, like Benjamin Bunny, 'set off – with a hop, skip and a jump.'

1. The Benjamin Bunny Walk

LENGTH: ¾ mile round walk.

WALK DIRECTIONS: Disembark from ferry at Nichol End Marine (254228). Climb steps by café, bear left up stony track. Soon you cross tarmac drive to Fawe Park; continue along stony lane (wooden footpath fingerpost) with Fawe Park and Derwent Water on left and woods on right. 'Rabbit wall' with boulder decorations on left is followed by fencing and trees; then stone wall commences on left where you see a wooden pole barrier ahead. Lane dips downhill here to join Lingholm drive 30 yards ahead; but turn right in front of pole barrier (252224) between two oak trees on woodland path that rises among rhododendron bushes to ridge, ther descends to road at pair of '30 mph' signs. Keep forward in edge of wood here; right along Fawe Park drive to lodge, left to return to Nichol End.

As the Derwent Water round-the-lake ferry puttered across from Keswick to the landing stage at Nichol End, a jet fighter came screaming out of the east and rocketed a couple of hundred feet above the boat. We all ducked, then grinned sheepishly at one another. What would dear Miss Potter have made of it? In 1903, the year that the Wright Brothers got the world's first powered aeroplane off the ground, she spent the whole summer as a 37-year-old spinster on holiday with her parents at Fawe Park and made the preliminary sketches for *The Tale of Benjamin Bunny* (published 1904). Aeroplanes had yet to make an appearance in the Lake District skies. All was quiet and slow-paced back then in this delectable corner of the country that Beatrix grew to love so passionately.

I disembarked and followed the stony lane through the woods beside the boundary of Fawe Park's garden. Azaleas and rhododendrons in yellow, orange, pink and crimson made blazes of colour among the trees. The garden boundary was a succession of lengths of wall and fencing with plenty of chinks and gaps to which a child could be lifted for glimpses into the garden where Peter Rabbit and Benjamin Bunny went on their onion-scrumping expedition. Looking over and through as I passed, I got a good view of the elevated terrace and the walk along which old Mr Bunny pranced pipe in mouth and switch in hand, looking for his naughty son Benjamin. The same wall reappears later in the story, with six little rabbit heads peeping over it, watching Mr McGregor the gardener contemplating his old tam-o'-shanter on the stick scarecrow.

These days Miss Potter would never have been allowed to publish her illustration of old Mr Bunny whipping Benjamin and Peter with his little switch. Walking on from Fawe Park I remembered how as a child I used to dread the turning of the page which revealed that painful scene. But a happier recollection as I walked back to Nichol End through the woods was of the reassuring end of the story in the snug rabbit burrow that Beatrix Potter sited somewhere among these big old firs and beeches.

2. The Squirrel Nutkin Walk

LENGTH: 1 mile (return by ferry)

WALK DIRECTIONS: Begin by following Benjamin Bunny walk as far as pole barrier (252224); keep ahead along the stony lane to cross Lingholm drive. Through gate marked 'Public Footpath to Catbells', follow path through woods for ⅓ mile to emerge (250218) and cross rushy field. Path continues through more woodland to reach a drive marked 'Derwent Bay' (248214). Turn left ('The Lake; Manesty' fingerpost); in 50 yd, left ('Launch Jetty' fingerpost), down through trees to Hawes End jetty (251213) and ferry back to Nichol End/Keswick.

NB – To visit 'Owl Island' (St Herbert's Island, opposite Hawes End jetty) hire rowing or motor boat from Keswick Launch Company (01768-772263; *www.keswick-launch.co.uk*) or Nichol End Marine (01768-773082; *www.nicholendmarine.co.uk*).

Walking on from the drive to Lingholm, one enters the territory not just of Squirrel Nutkin but also of Peter Rabbit. The Potter family spent nine summers at Lingholm between 1885 and 1907, and Beatrix's sketchbooks are full of drawings and paintings of garden and woodland scenes around the house that would find their way into her first book, *The Tale of Peter Rabbit*. From the path between the grounds of Lingholm and the woods there are fine glimpses of the high grey gables and chimneys of the house.

The Tale of Squirrel Nutkin came out in 1903, the second of Beatrix's books to be published by Frederick Warne. It was the first Beatrix Potter I was read as a child; always a suspenseful tale, on account of the build-up of tension between cheeky Nutkin and the infinitely sinister owl, Old Brown, more of a malevolent woodland god than a bird as he bides his time before pouncing on his victim. There are certainly still plenty of red squirrels in the woods around Lingholm; I caught one glimpse of a fluffy red tail and a pair of tufted red ears in an oak tree.

Down by the jetty, waiting for the Keswick ferry, I looked across at the thickly wooded islet of St Herbert's Island. Here Beatrix Potter set Old Brown's lair in a hollow oak. One of the most charming illustrations in *Squirrel Nutkin* is of the squirrels paddling across the lake to Owl Island with their tails spread out for sails, but there was also a terrifying picture of Old Brown with slitted eyes and claws full of dead mice, being cheeked by the impertinent Nutkin. And what about that one of Nutkin bounding off with a little stump where his tail should be, while Old Brown glares out of his hole with the rest of the tail in his beak? Scary!

3. The Mrs Tiggy-Winkle Walk

LENGTH: 3 miles round walk.

WALK DIRECTIONS: If doing this walk as a continuation of Benjamin Bunny and Squirrel Nutkin walks, keep forward at Derwent Bay drive (248214 – 'Public Footpath Catbells' fingerpost) to reach road at hairpin bend (247212). If starting from here, you can reach this point by bus (77, 77A – 'Catbells' stop); there's a small car park.

Keep ahead up road, over cattle grid, on to Skelgill Farm (242208). Carry on past metal barrier on track above farm; follow track along lower slopes of Catbells fell. In 1 mile pass through mine spoil heaps; track swings right to reach road at Little Town (234195). Left for ¼ mile, over bridge and first left to Newlands Church (230194). Back through Little Town. Just past Little Town Farm, right ('Footpath Skelgill 1 mile') down walled lane. In 20 yd, fork left through gate. Walled lane ends at East House (238200); follow grassy track over fields to Skelgill, return to Catbells bus stop.

The weather turned thundery for my Mrs Tiggy-Winkle walk. Halfway along, black clouds came rolling up through the Newlands Valley, bringing wind and hail showers. Ten minutes after starting, I found myself huddled for shelter in the doorway of the very barn painted by Beatrix Potter, looking up at the long farmhouse of Skelgill. Beatrix called it Little Town. In her charming picture little Lucie – 'always losing her pocket-handkerchiefs!' – is talking to Tabby Kitten, who sits on a box washing her white paws. I could recognise every detail of the scene as the hail spattered across the farmyard.

The path led along the lower slopes of Catbells, the high-backed green fell where Mrs Tiggy-Winkle the hedgehog laundress lived behind a little wooden door. The door was probably one that Beatrix had seen at the entrance to one of the Yewthwaite lead mines; the spoil heaps are still there beside the path.

Down at the far end of the path I took shelter from another hail storm under a yew tree in the whitewashed farming hamlet of Little Town. Beatrix Potter borrowed its name for Skelgill Farm; she also borrowed Lucie Carr, daughter of the vicar of Newlands, as inspiration for the character of Lucie, dedicating *The Tale of Mrs Tiggy-Winkle* to 'The real little Lucie of Newlands'.

The houses of Little Town appear in that delightful picture of Lucie on the pathway up Catbells; so do the great hanging shapes of the fells that flank the Newlands Valley. You can make out the hump-back bridge below Little Town, and beyond that the faint shape of Mr Carr's little whitewashed church among its trees. I ducked in out of the rain and sat in the quiet half-light of the church, thinking of all those childhood bedtimes attended by Beatrix Potter's mischievous kittens, venturesome rabbits, cheeky squirrels and cosily domesticated hedgehogs with prickles underneath their caps.

Hill Top Walk, Near Sawrey

WALK DIRECTIONS: From Hill Top car park (OS ref SD369957), left along road. At telephone box opposite Beechmount B&B (368957) bear right up tarred lane for ¾ mile. At corner of larch plantation on your left, bear right (368967 – 'permitted path' waymark arrow on post) across open ground; through gate by Moss Eccles Tarn NT notice, and on along bank of tarn to crags at the east end. Bear right here (372967) down to bridleway; right to return to Sawrey and Hill Top.

Mr McGregor's sieve, tin watering can and wooden-handled spade stood just where I had imagined them in the garden at Hill Top. The slate porch looked entirely familiar, too; I half expected to see Tom Kitten in his blue jacket and trousers, accompanied by his sisters Mittens and Moppet in clean pinafores and tuckers, teetering on their hind legs out of the cottage into the garden, with their mother Tabitha Twitchit looking after them anxiously, toasting fork in paw. 'Hill Top is to be presented to my visitors,' Beatrix Potter instructed the National Trust in her will, 'as if I had just gone out, and they had just missed me.' The remarkable thing about looking round the house that Beatrix Potter owned from 1905 until her death in 1943 is the sheer number of childhood memories it evokes in someone who has never set foot in the place before. Here are the very red-and-blue carpeted stairs where Tabitha mewed dreadfully for her lost kitten Tom in *The Tale of Samuel Whiskers*, the clock and dresser that feature in *The Tailor of Gloucester*, the doll's house ham and lobster from *The Tale of Two Bad Mice*. Children of all ages are entranced by the hundred-and-one objects familiar from Beatrix Potter's detailed little illustrations.

On the way up the old cart track to Moss Eccles Tarn, and in the stony lane descending to Sawrey again, I found myself walking in the footsteps of Jemima Puddle-duck, and of the macabre Mr Tod and his rough acquaintance Tommy Brock the badger. On the tarn itself, where Beatrix and her husband William Heelis loved to come boating, floated lily pads of just the sort that Mr Jeremy Fisher used for his own fishing expedition. And back in the outskirts of Near Sawrey, passing the Hawkshead crossroads, it wouldn't have surprised me at all to see two plump little pigs with red handkerchief bundles and striped waistcoats setting out 'over the hills and far away.'

STEPPING OUT – *Walk 69*

Derwent Water Walks (Benjamin Bunny, Squirrel Nutkin, Mrs Tiggy-Winkle)

MAP: OS 1:25,000 Explorer OL4; 1:50,000 Landranger 90
Start of walks: Nichol End Marine, Portinscale (OS ref NY254228) – NW Derwent Water, opposite Keswick.

TRAVEL: Round-the-lake ferry (anti-clockwise) to Nichol End (information: tel: 01768-772263; www.keswick-launch.co.uk).

REFRESHMENTS: Café at Nichol End Marine (01768-773082; *www.nicholendmarine.co.uk*); Swinside Inn (01768-778253; *www.theswinsideinn.com*) on Little Town–Nichol End road at OS ref 243217.

CONDITIONS: No steep climbs or descents; some parts can be wet and muddy after rain.

Hill Top Walk, Near Sawrey

MAP: OS 1:25,000 Explorer OL7; 1:50,000 Landranger 97
Start of walk: Hill Top (NT), Near Sawrey – *Travel* from Windermere by Bowness car ferry (every 20 mins), then 1½ mile drive; bus 525.

LENGTH: 2 miles

REFRESHMENTS: Tower Bank Arms PH, Near Sawrey (01539-436334; *www.towerbankarms.co.uk*)

Potter practicalities

TRAVEL: Rail to Windermere, and to Penrith for Keswick (*www.thetrainline.com*). From Penrith, bus service X4, X5 to Keswick. Road – M6 (Jct 36) and A591 for Windermere; Jct 40 and A66 for Keswick.

Hill Top, Near Sawrey (NT): 01539-436269; *www.nationaltrust.org.uk*. *Beatrix Potter Walks* with NT wardens (3 miles) from Hill Top: tel: 01539-447997.

BEATRIX POTTER GALLERY, HAWKSHEAD: 01539-436355; *www.nationaltrust.org.uk*.

READING: All the Beatrix Potter books are published by Frederick Warne & Co Ltd.

Beatrix Potter and Hill Top by Judy Taylor (NT: £2.50);

beautifully illustrated, available from Hill Top and the NT shop in Hawkshead.

The Tale of Beatrix Potter by Margaret Lane (Frederick Warne) – an excellent biography.

Beatrix Potter's Lakeland by Hunter Davies and Cressida Pemberton-Pigott (Fredrick Warne) – Beatrix Potter and the settings that inspired her.

Castle Carrock, Brampton and the River Gelt, Cumbria

A wet walk on a blustery day in the country of the 'mad river'

A CLEAN, BRIGHT LITTLE PUB-WITH-ROOMS, modern without being tricksy, friendly without being all over you, running like clockwork but thoroughly relaxed, set in a pretty village. Ian and Gill Boyd have made it all come true at The Weary Sportsman (universally known as 'The Weary') at Castle Carrock in East Cumbria. What's more, one of the great walks of north-west England begins right outside the door.

I stepped out into one of those cool, blustery days of high winds that every Pennine rambler knows, when patches of blue sky appear like a promise, to be wiped out next moment by grey fingers of cloud and rain brushing across the hills. Out in the fields the sycamores and oaks rustled along the hedgerows, and ranks of rosebay willowherb tossed their pointed pink heads around as gracefully as dancers.

In the farmyard at Hill House the collies pranced to meet the stranger with a volley of snaps and snarls, advancing and retreating on their hind legs like Kiwi rugby players doing the *haka*. I kept them at bay by inviting them to contemplate my stick, and when the farmer came out to shut them up we had a good yarn against the wind – the problems and pleasures of working in such a landscape, where the beauty of the twenty-mile view to the Galloway hills gives some visitors the idea that everything's cushy in the farming world. 'I must admit that attitude does rattle me a bit,' he confided. 'I came into farming because I wanted to produce beef, milk, lamb and wool, not to be a park keeper, you know!'

Over the meadows in Talkin all was quiet. Flower baskets swung in the wind, and grasses rippled like pale green fur across the lumpy drumlin hillocks. Ice Age glaciers dumped the gravel that formed the

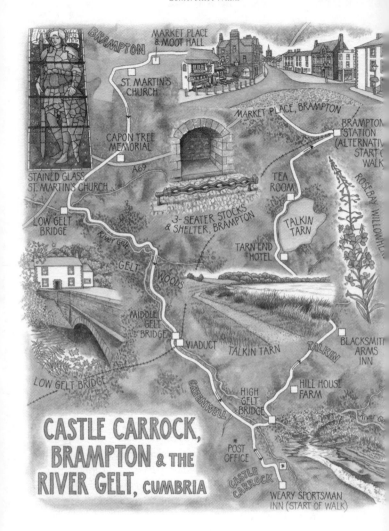

CASTLE CARROCK,
BRAMPTON & THE
RIVER GELT, CUMBRIA

drumlins 10,000 years ago, and they gouged the hollow of Talkin Tarn and filled it with meltwater. Nowadays it is underground springs that keep the lake full – a ragged circle of dull silver this morning, stippled by the breeze and pocked with raindrops. The path under the tarnside beeches was sheltered, though, and a good drying wind had chased most of the rain away eastwards over the Pennines by the time I walked into Brampton.

People were marketing with baskets and bags, stopping and greeting one another in the market square under the clock tower of the Moot Hall. Only the great bull ring sunk in the cobbles and the long iron bar of the 3-seater stocks told of wilder days in Brampton, when animals were tethered to be baited to death and drunkards and vagabonds paid for their transgressions with public humiliation. Long after the rest of England had subsided into civil obedience these regions near the Scottish border were places of violence and rough justice, largely owing to the activities of the Scots moss-troopers or cattle-thieves who dealt death and misery whenever they rode south on the rampage. They plagued Brampton until the early years of the 17th century. Then 'Belted Willie' Howard, newly married into the barony of Gilsland, confronted and drove them away, finally bringing some peace and prosperity to the little town.

Belted Willie's descendant George Howard, 9th Earl of Carlisle, was a sensitive and cultured man, very interested in the arts. It was he who commissioned the architect Philip Webb, a member of the Pre-Raphaelite Brotherhood, to build a new church in Brampton. St Martin's was consecrated in 1878, its pride and glory a set of stained glass windows designed by Edward Burne-Jones and made in William Morris's workshop.

I had meant to pop into St Martin's for a quick peek, but in the end I spent an hour there in admiration of Burne-Jones's beautiful figures – Abraham in a shell-shaped helmet, King David as a youthful harpist. Faith, Hope and Charity were three graceful women in glowing robes. In the east window angels and saints shone in a range of gorgeous translucent pinks. I savoured the contrast when I emerged into the understated light of an overcast northern afternoon, the muted greens of grass and trees and the subtle dove greys and soft purples of the far hills.

By the road to Low Gelt Bridge stood the Capon Tree monument, a tall wheel-headed stone cross, another testimony to wild days on the border. In 1745 Bonnie Prince Charlie planned the siege of Carlisle from a house in Brampton, and at the Capon Tree six of his supporters paid for the Young Pretender's hubris with their lives the following year. They were hanged from the branches of the ancient meeting-tree during the terrible outburst of retribution that followed the Battle of Culloden and the crushing of the clans and the Jacobite cause.

Immigrants from Celtic Ireland gave the River Gelt its name, 'mad river', to reflect the furious progress of the waters down their narrow gorge in times of spate. Today the Gelt flowed modestly across the sandstone plates and through the tight bends and hollows gouged by the storm waters of millennia. Ash, hazel and oak hung over the river, while up the bank the footpath wound through glades carpeted with rustling beech leaves. Grottoes of mosses and ferns lay beaded with the water trickles that had excavated them, drop by drop, through thousands of years.

I walked the gorge slowly, watching dippers bobbing and bowing on the river stones, reluctant to bring this rainy, windy and wholly delightful walk to an end. Even the prospect of one of The Weary's giant pots of tea couldn't draw me away from the mad river just yet awhile.

STEPPING OUT – *Walk 70*

MAP: OS 1:25,000 Explorer 315; 1:50,000 Landranger 86

TRAVEL: Rail to Brampton station (*www.thetrainline.com*)
 Road – south and west: M6 to Jct 43; A69 to Brampton bypass;
 right to next junction; right on B6413 to Castle Carrock. From
 Newcastle: A69 to Brampton bypass and B6413; then as from
 west.

WALK DIRECTIONS: Start from The Weary Inn in Castle Carrock,
 or from Brampton station (see below). From The Weary (OS ref
 NY543554) take Brampton road. Beyond post office, left (543557
 – 'Cowan' fingerpost) along path for 200 yards, then right along
 lane to ford and bridge over Castle Carrock Beck (540562).
 Right to B6413; left across High Gelt Bridge. In 300 yards, right
 over stile (541564 – 'Talkin' fingerpost); diagonally left across
 field, aiming just right of peaked roof on skyline. Left through
 gate (yellow arrow), up lane to Hill House farm (543566).
 Through farmyard (be bold with the collies!), following yellow
 arrows down lane into field. Aim for top left corner; through
 gate (545569), on with fence on left, through next gate (yellow
 arrow); across 2 fields; through gate onto drive (549573). Yellow
 arrow on post points forward to stone stile into Blacksmith's
 Arms yard in Talkin.

 Left to road junction; ahead ('Talkin Tarn, Brampton' sign).
 In ¾ mile, just past Tarn End Hotel, right through kissing
 gate (543584 – 'Talkin Tarn' fingerpost). Bear left around
 Talkin Tarn for ½ mile. 100 yards past tea room, left (546591 –
 'Brampton Junction' fingerpost) through trees and on to road
 (545596). Right to Brampton Station; left through kissing gate;
 cross footbridge, bear left along cinder path beside Carlisle-
 Newcastle platform. *NB: Railway travellers start walk here – if
 coming from Newcastle, cross footbridge; if from Carlisle, go under
 footbridge and hairpin back left onto cinder path*

 In ⅔ mile, path goes under A69 (542605); continue to road
 (538611). Left into Brampton via A6071. Left to Market Place
 and Moot Hall (531611); right to St Martin's Church (528610).

 Leaving church, left along Carlisle Road; first left (signed
 'Warwick Bridge'). In 200 yards, left through kissing gate
 (526608 – 'Capon Tree Road' fingerpost). Follow footpath

(yellow arrows) for just over ½ mile across fields to road (527599). Cross and go down lane opposite ('Low Gelt Bridge' fingerpost). In 150 yd pass Capon Tree Memorial on left; ahead through gate to cross A69 (please take great care!). Continue along road to Low Gelt Bridge (520591). Left ('Middle Gelt, Brampton' fingerpost) on track through woods (at fork follow 'Middle Gelt' sign) for 1¾ miles to Middle Gelt (532573). Cross bridge; take Greenwell road under viaduct. In 60 yd, left (Greenwell' fingerpost) on path beside river for ½ mile to Greenwell (537566). Ahead along road. Follow blue bridleway arrows past houses, through gates, up grassy lane, then gravel track. At ford/bridge over Castle Carrock Beck (540562), right to retrace route to Castle Carrock.

LENGTH: 10 ½ miles

REFRESHMENTS: The Weary, Castle Carrock (01228-670230; *www.theweary.com*); Blacksmiths Arms, Talkin (01697-73452; *www.blacksmithstalkin.co.uk*); Talkin Tarn tearoom (01697-741050); many places in Brampton.

Poetry Path, Kirkby Stephen, Cumbria

Seasonal poems, beautiful stone-carving: a stroll through a sheep farmer's year

EVERY WALKER WHO TRAMPS the Pennine uplands knows the Swaledales, those hardy black-faced sheep that are as much a part of these northern hills as the rocks, peat and heather. In sunshine they scatter the distant slopes with bright white dots. In mist you come on them suddenly, their dank grey fleeces dripping water as they give you their intense, mad stare from slit eyeballs. There's no more characteristic or more stunning Pennine sight than a fellside of Swaledales swirling like a single organism as a sheepdog marshals them towards a gateway at his master's call and whistle.

Thirty years ago the idea of the Pennines without their sheep would have been laughable. Today, in the atmosphere of uncertainty that's persisted in farming since the disastrous Foot & Mouth outbreak of 2001, and in the light of recent changes in subsidies to reflect the amount of land rather than the number of sheep a farmer works that prospect doesn't look quite so unlikely.

The sheep farmers of the Pennines work long, hard hours in all weather conditions, day and night, summer and winter. It's thanks to them and their skilful management of flocks, fields and fells that the uplands of northern England look as we all love them to look – sheep-nibbled turf and heather on the fells; grassy, stone-walled pastures in the valley bottoms. The Pennine hill farmers are the unsung, anonymous guardians and custodians of this delectable landscape, and lovers of walking and of upland countryside owe them a tremendous debt. But they don't often get their due. So when I heard of the Poetry Path at Kirkby Stephen, a celebration in sculpture and verse of the hill farmer's yearly round, I couldn't wait to walk it.

'Come up and stay with us for the October tup sales,' said Dorothy Metcalfe of High Greenside Farm. That's how I found myself at the

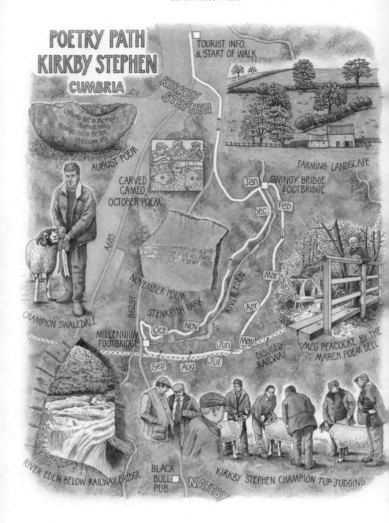

farm's kitchen table on a roaring, blustery autumn morning, learning how the sheep are gathered by Sam, Ben and Laddie, the High Greenside dogs, for dipping, shearing, tupping (mating) and lambing. We delved into the mysteries of 'hefting' (how a farm's sheep know which part of the fell is theirs), and of the progression of a female sheep from gimmer to hog to shearling to ewe – and the shorter, sadder one of most males from fully equipped tup (ram) lambs to castrated wethers.

'My husband John's a good farmer,' Dorothy observed. 'He's always on with the sheep, every day, out all hours and all weathers. I can lamb a ewe; I take my share of the work. But the only thing that makes it possible for us to carry on with the sheep is John's haulage business and my B&B. The fact is, you just can't make a decent living from sheep nowadays, even with the subsidies.'

Down at Kirkby Stephen's auction mart along the back lane, the sheds, pens and auction ring were crammed with farmers down from the hills. Flat caps and old waxed jackets, shepherding sticks and saggy trousers dark with wool grease were the order of the day. Outside against the shed wall the competitors lined up in the cold October wind, each breeder grasping the curly horns of a magnificent Swaledale yearling tup, a young ram about 18 months old. Judging was a serious business: tens of thousands of pounds were at stake. It was John Richardson of Ghyll House at Dufton whose tup was at last declared champion. Later that day the champion sold at auction for £20,000. If upland sheep breeding and farming is dead in the water, no-one has told the Pennine hill farmers.

It's not every poet who will deign to go for a walk on a filthy gale-torn day, but Meg Peacocke of North Stainmore was happy to turn out. Meg is a much-published poet, and it was an invitation she relished when she was asked by the East Cumbrian Countryside Project to provide 12 poems to be carved by a sculptor into stones which would be installed along a Poetry Path, a short circular walk in the beautiful valley of the River Eden.

'I found it very interesting and challenging,' Meg told me as we walked the muddy path on a carpet of leaves whipped from the trees by the gale. 'The poems had to be short to fit onto the stones. But more important, I wanted them to communicate themselves to anyone, non-poets really, and in particular these local farmers and farming people whom they celebrate.'

The two-mile circuit chosen to form the Poetry Path turned out to be one of Meg's favourite walks – upriver from the Swingy Bridge on the outskirts of Kirkby Stephen against the flow of the Eden, then across the river and back to town down the west bank. 'As soon as I found out where the walk was going to be, all sorts of little poems – and some longer ones – started fizzing in my head. Well, to be quite honest I was desperate to get the commission, because I couldn't bear the thought of anyone else's interpretations being set up along "my" walk! And I was able to choose the places for the poems to go, too.'

The other half of the creative process was Pip Hall, the lettering artist who smoothed suitable areas on big blocks of stone – slabs of limestone and sandstone, some quarried for the purpose, others found in yards and other places. Pip cut the lettering, much of it in dramatic, gracefully sinuating script, and embellished Meg's poems with little relief cameos. Then the blocks and slabs were set into their positions by crane, pulley and much manhandling.

The poems are subtly located – January in an angle of river bank by the Swingy Bridge, February on a pile of blocks opposite a lovely old stone barn, March in a pool below a natural spillway of tiny waterfalls. Meg was amused to see me rubbing a licked thumb over Pip Hall's carved cameos – April lambs butting milk from their mother's udder, July haymakers hefting a bale, brawny farmers inspecting sheep at an October sale – to bring out the details. 'Yes,' she smiled, 'tell 'em all – come and spit on our stones!'

With the rain-swollen river crashing majestically through the woods, and milky curtains of wind-rippled rain parting and closing on far views of the Cumbrian fells, it was a fantastically exhilarating walk. In Kirkby Stephen the local farmers would still be hanging over the pen gates at the mart, or driving the Swaledales they'd chosen in the auction ring back up to the fellside farms. Down here in the valley I ran my hand over Pip Hall's April cameo of sheep in a pen, and savoured Meg Peacocke's words:

> 'Penned in a huddle, the great tups
> are clints of panting stone. The shepherd lifts
> a sideways glance from the labour
> of dagging tails. His hands are seamed with muck
> and the sweat runs into his eyes.
> Above us, a silent plane has needled
> the clear blue. Paling behind it
> a crimped double strand of wool unravels.'

STEPPING OUT – *Walk 71*

MAP: OS 1:25,000 Landranger OL19; 1:50,000 Landranger 91
Poetry Path booklet (see below) contains a map

TRAVEL: Rail to Kirkby Stephen station (2 miles) – *www. thetrainline.com*

Road – M6 to Jct 38 (Tebay); A685 to Kirkby Stephen. Park in main street or car park (signed).

WALK DIRECTIONS: (detailed in Poetry Path booklet). From Kirkby Stephen Tourist Office walk ahead up main street to traffic lights; left ('Nateby' sign) for ⅓ mile. Left (775080 – 'footpath Stenkrith; bridleway Hartley, Nateby' fingerpost) down green lane to River Eden (777080 – January poem). Cross Swingy Bridge footbridge; right up lane past barn (February poem). Through gate; right along hedged path to cross footbridge over beck (March poem). Continue up slope past stone wall section on right (April poem) to cross disused railway bridge (May poem) and turn right (June poem). In 50 yards, right through gate and left along old railway (July poem on left, August and September on right).

At arched stone railway bridge, cross River Eden on blue-painted Millennium footbridge (773075). In 100 yards, beside kissing gate onto road, bear right ('footpath' fingerpost) through trees to river (**October** poem). Bear left along river bank through Stenkrith Park (**November** poem). Continue through fields with river on your right, passing **December** poem (777079). At Swingy Bridge turn left up lane to return to Kirkby Stephen.

LENGTH OF WALK: 2 miles

CONDITIONS: Green lanes, old railway and field paths; very boggy after rain.

REFRESHMENTS: Many pubs and cafés in Kirkby Stephen; Black Bull, Nateby (01768-371588; *www.blackbullnateby.co.uk*)

POETRY PATH: Booklet guide, £2 from Kirkby Stephen TIC (01768-371199; *www.visiteden.co.uk*)

KIRKBY STEPHEN CHAMPION TUP JUDGING AND SALES: Usually 3rd Friday in October

Pendle Hill, Lancashire

Over the hill of ill omen with visions of heaven and hell

'OH, PENDLE'S A BRILLIANT HILL,' remarked Chris – who'd got up early to cook my bacon and eggs – as he pointed out the path from the back door of the Calf's Head Hotel. He swept his hand from end to end of the great whaleback filling the eastern half of the sky. 'Never the same, always changing. We can get three completely different aspects of it in a morning. I'd say you would have to be a hell of an artist to catch Pendle on canvas.'

Birds were in full cry in the sycamores as I set out from Worston on this autumn morning. Horses were cropping the meadows around the village. A million dewdrops winked in the grass as the sun hauled itself up above the dark barrier of Pendle Hill. On the crest of the ridge, a bruise-coloured surf of night mist still brooded. Given the sombre reputation of the hill, that seemed apt.

Yesterday afternoon Pendle Hill had looked altogether beautiful, a fawn-coloured wave breaking in the eastern sky. Stone walls traced a loose geometry across its flanks, which were indented with the deep puckered clefts of gullies, as if Pendle were somehow drawing in its breath. I had sat and read of its furious mood swings, of the sudden blizzards and rainbursts to which it was subject, and of the well-documented tragedies of 1612 when ten local women and men were hanged at Lancaster for witchcraft. The persecution and bizarre confessions, the alleged murderous practices of Alizon Device, Chattox, Old Demdike, Mouldheels and other ominously named dwellers in the shadow of Pendle Hill have sullied its name with a sinister and long-lasting stain.

From the huddle of old stone farm buildings at Mearley Hall I glanced up to see the cloud beginning to scroll away from the hill. The pathless slopes looked steep enough, but enormously tempting.

The whole upper region of Pendle Hill, like so many other moorland hills of England and Wales, is now officially open to walkers, runners and climbers as Access Land under the CROW (Countryside and Rights of Way) Act of 2000.

Today I was aiming to tackle the hill with the help of Andrew Bibby's *Forest of Bowland* guidebook, one of the excellent 'Freedom To Roam' series of handy, easy-to-use little guides to walks on Access Land produced by publishers Frances Lincoln. It's a hard trick to pull off, because people don't want to be told exactly where to go on Access Land – after all, they're there to exercise their right to wander where they please. But most appreciate a little nudge in the right direction, and that's exactly what the 'Freedom To Roam' guides aim to provide.

Hmmm. Could I find the 'sheep trod through the bracken' adumbrated by Mr Bibby? I could not. Don't try climbing steeply through dew-laden bracken – it's like fighting your way through a close-packed army of pygmies brandishing wet fly whisks. Sodden and chastened, I cast about for an alternative route to the top, and soon found an old hollow way which brought me onto the crest of the ridge.

On Pendle's heights all troubles fell away. It was simply beautiful. Pennine moors rolling to the east, Lancashire hills and glimpses of sea to the west, brown shoulders of moor in the south, and to the north the long ridge of Pendle Hill itself, striped black with peat hags and glistening with gritstone flakes, beckoning me in sharp bursts of sunshine from cairn to cairn and stile to stile. There turned out to be several well-found paths – permissive routes, long in use thanks to the flexibility of local landowners. It was a two-mile step out to the trig pillar on Big End, summit of Pendle Hill at just under 2,000 ft, and up there in a shaft of sunlight I felt as if the whole world was spread below.

Between triangular reservoirs far below lay Barley village, site of Malkin Tower where the Device family were said to have brewed their occult mischief. But the crest of the hill in this remarkable incandescence of sun seemed more a place to fix one's mind on the forces of light. Forty years after the dark doings of 1612, young George Fox 'came near a very great hill, called Pendle Hill, and I was moved of the Lord to go up to the top of it; which I did with difficulty, it was so very steep and high. When I was come to the top, I saw the sea bordering upon Lancashire.'

RED ADMIRALS

WORSAW HILL

WORSAW END HOUSE

HOOKCLIFFE

A59

WORSTON

WORSTON BROOK

CALF'S HEAD HOTEL (START OF WALK)

BARKERFIELD

THE CALF'S HEAD

LITTLE MEARLEY HALL

BOUNDARY OF ACCESS LAND

SCO CAI

LANE SIDE

PENDLE

MEARLEY HALL

MEARLEY MOOR

RUINED BARN

CLAYTON-LE-MOORS HARRIERS CAIRN

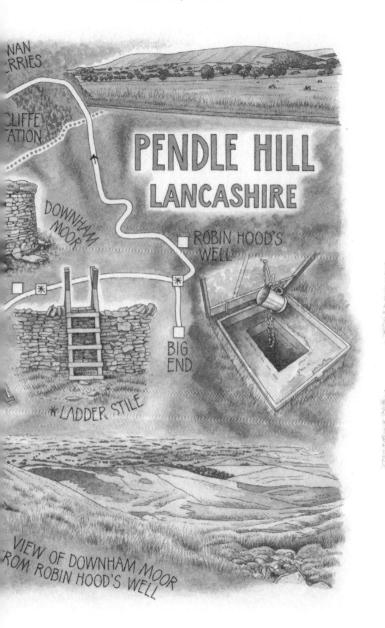

NAN
RRIES

CLIFFE
ATION

DOWNHAM
MOOR

ROBIN HOOD'S
WELL

PENDLE HILL
LANCASHIRE

BIG
END

* LADDER STILE

VIEW OF DOWNHAM MOOR
FROM ROBIN HOOD'S WELL

It was an epiphany for the young itinerant preacher, fired with spiritual energy and brimful of nonconformist zeal. Up on Pendle Hill the Lord showed George Fox where He wished him to go to gather 'a great people'. And Fox did just that, founding the Society of Friends or Quaker movement and preaching with passion all over the north of England.

On the way down from the summit, Fox recorded: 'I found a spring of water in the side of the hill, with which I refreshed myself, having eaten or drunk but little for several days before.' That spring still leaps out from under a rock in the north face of Pendle Hill. I came upon it sliding and skittering in a silver rush down a green mossy channel among the brown sedges of the slope. Just above the spring, a flat metal hatch lay closed. I prised it open, and found a silver tankard chained and ready to drop into the well of water that shivered below.

Some call this gush of water George Fox's Well. Others know it by the older name of Robin Hood's Well, maybe in homage to the man in green, maybe to the ancient teasing sprite called Robin Goodfellow. Whoever's spirit was moving in these waters today, they were stone-flavoured and icy cold. I sat a long time on the spring rock, drinking the sweet well water and gazing out north over sunlit lands from the broad brow of this most captivating hill.

STEPPING OUT – *Walk 72*

MAP: OS 1:25,000 Explorer OL41; 1:50,000 Landranger 103

TRAVEL: Rail to Clitheroe (2½ miles) – *www.thetrainline.com*
Road – M6 (Jct 29); M65 (Jct 7); A680, A671, A59; Worston
signed off A59 at Clitheroe.

WALK DIRECTIONS: Leaving Calf's Head Hotel in Worston (OS
ref SD768428), right round road bend. In 250 yards, right at
footpath fingerpost. Bear left round end of barn, cross stile; walk
towards Pendle Hill across 3 fields; right (774418) along farm
track, past Little Mearley Hall (775416) and Lane Side (770412)
to Mearley Hall (768409). Ahead over crossways and cattle grid;
in 30 yards, left before gate (yellow arrow) up fence. Over stile;
on up hillside, following wall on left to ruined barn (771403).

Next section is on Access Land – pick your own route.
Recommended: bear left up flank of Pendle Hill, climbing
old hollow way with wall a few yards to left. Halfway up,
cross through fence at gate. Keep same hollow way up hill; in
300 yards, left up grassy track to Clayton-le-Moors Harriers
cairn (782402). Follow track NE beside wall; where wall ends
(785407), continue NE to Scout cairn, visible ahead (789413).
Continue NE to stone shelter, seen ahead (793418), and cross
ladder stile ahead (795418).

From here moorland path runs E; in a few yards, next
ladder stile is in view in wall on skyline ⅔ mile away. Cross
stile (805418); bear right to trig pillar on Big End (804414).
Return over stile; right along wall for 100 yards. Where stone
stile crosses wall, left along path, descending to Robin Hood's
Well (805420). Continue on narrow path to join upper
track (802422). Keep ahead through zig-zags, descending to
Downham Moor; north on path for ½ mile to reach road just
east of Hookcliffe Plantation (798432).

Left along road; in 150 yd, left along lane to Hookcliffe. At
farm (788429), ahead along lane, bearing right past Barkerfield
(785427) to road (781429). Left for 50 yards; right (footpath
fingerpost) over cattle grid, to Worsaw Hill Farm (marked
Worsaw End House on map). Through gate in field wall above
farmhouse (779431); left along wall; in 50 yards, left through
gate and on through next gate; ahead through fields, with
Worston Brook on left, back to Worston.

LENGTH: 8½ miles – allow 4–6 hours

CONDITIONS: Boggy parts, especially along ridge path; steepish climb up Pendle Hill; narrow path on steep hillside beyond Robin Hood's Well.

REFRESHMENTS: Robin Hood's Well (water); Calf's Head, Worston (01200-441218; *www.calfshead.co.uk*)

GUIDEBOOK: *Forest of Bowland, with Pendle Hill and the West Pennine Moors* by Andrew Bibby (Frances Lincoln; *www.franceslincoln.com*)

Rossendale Annual Round-the-Hills Walk

Round the East Lancashire moors in excellent company

'Down behind the gasworks, down in Rawtenstall
(That's a little town in Lancashire) -
Last Saturday night, me and the lads,
Eh ba gum, we had some reet good cheer ... '

AT NINE O'CLOCK on Sunday morning, walking down through
Rawtenstall, I passed a pale-as-pastry man sitting groaning on
his front doorstep with his head in his hands. Saturday night's reet
good cheer was obviously still punching its way out of his cerebral
cortex.

No such whey-facedness in the hearty crowds legging it west up
Haslingden Old Road. I must have seen two hundred walkers by
the time I got to the Marl Pits recreation ground, and every cheek
seemed ruddy, every eye bright.

I hadn't expected the Rossendale Annual Round-the-Hills Walk
to start so promptly, nor with quite such a bang. By the time I signed
in (at 09.32 hrs) and collected my tag (number 320), the misty high
country north of Rawtenstall was already seething with walkers.
There's no prize for completing this 18-mile circuit of the Lancashire
hills – just a certificate signed by the Mayor of Rossendale, and a good
glow of satisfaction. Hundreds turn out in all weathers, faithfully, on
the first Sunday of each September, to pit themselves against steepish
hillsides, stony tracks, sodden peat bogs and several score stone stiles.

It's a family day out on the hills and that makes for tremendous
camaraderie. A couple of packs of knot-thighed greyhounds had
sprinted off at 9 am sharp, intent on completing the course in under
three hours. But the bulk of walkers – almost all local people from
Rawtenstall, Bacup, Haslingden and the other former textile towns

of Rossendale – were happy to take it at their own pace, a comfortable gossiping one.

Between the wars these industrial towns of east Lancashire and west Yorkshire were the cradle of the Ramblers' Association. Men and women, engaged all week in the noisy, monotonous work of the textile mills, looked to the hills for their salvation at the weekends – those high grassy ridges and heathery moors that form the Pennine roof of northern England. The tradition continues, flourishing even though the mills are silent and the towns cleaned up these days.

'First time I climbed Whernside,' chuckled Hazel, snorting with amusement, 'it snowed – and I cried. But I love this walking now.' She strode away up the boggy path towards Cribden Hill, the first proper ascent of the walk. Cribden sorted out sheep from goats. Such as Hazel reached the top in a lather of breathlessness, but were soon forging on over the sloppy skidpans of the moors. Others, self-confessed sheep, crept round the lower contours to meet the goats on less rugged ground.

Views were tremendous from here, perhaps fifteen or twenty miles across the rolling hills of the Forest of Rossendale. Tall industrial chimneys, grey stone terraces and factories with ranks of windows jammed the valley bottoms. The farmsteads crouched low, tucked hard in against their guardian slopes, houses and barns all of a piece in a style the conquering Norsemen introduced well over a thousand years ago.

I followed a young man with legs like tree trunks. 'Where are you off to?' called a white-haired onlooker from a perch on a tumbled stone wall. Tree Trunks wordlessly circled his finger – 'round-the-hills' – and the old man waved in acknowledgement, with no more explanation needed. An uproarious spaniel, wet peat from snout to stern, galloped past and stitched a spatter of muck up my trousers. The wind blew hard. This was good rugged fun.

If we hopped lightly over one stile during the course of the day, we queued at forty – V-shaped stiles, square stiles, stiles with steps, and stiles that turned out to be padlocked gates. 'What do you mean, *can I climb over a gate?*' an indignant girl broadsided her swain in Far Pasture. 'Of course I can climb over a gate! What do you take me for?' She steamed off downhill, leaving him sinking in her wake.

In the doorway of the checkpoint van parked by Clowbridge Reservoir, one of the helpers was wolfing a garlic chicken sandwich thick and solid enough to patch a stone wall. 'You seem to be enjoying that, love,' observed her colleague with heavy sarcasm.

'Aye, and when I'm done, I'll breathe it all over you.' The men were definitely getting the worst of it hereabouts.

After the ten mile mark we became more spread out. Now there was time and space to notice things: a kestrel hovering over a grass bank, lichen of intense greenness on a stone wall, a grove of ancient thorns with limbs gnarled and twisted into a vigorous silvery musculature. I fell into step with a retired engineer from Haslingden – on his third Round-The-Hills walk – and heard his story of the decline of Lancashire's textile industry, told with a mixture of humility and anger that gave grist to the thought-mill long after we had parted.

The walk route crossed the puddly track of Limersgate, an old packhorse route hollowed out by the countless hoofbeats of horses bringing sacks of lime to the acid peatlands of the moor farmers. I dropped down a wet slope into the (accurately named) hamlet of Water, and found the Commercial Inn ready and willing to serve a cool pint of Hancocks Bitter to a travel-stained walker. Then, feeling leg-weary and a bit jaded, I bought a packet of Chorley cakes from Lock's shop up the road.

Now, I don't know what it is about Chorley Cakes – they are a bit like Eccles cakes, only rather more so – but from Water onwards my feet took wing. I marched through Dean, where the Baptist choir used to sing so tunefully they were known as the Nightingales of Dean. I doubled across Grime Bridge, whose name was earned by constant contact with the coal and the colliers of the mine just up the bank. These were snippets of local history I'd learned from Tim Nuttall of Rawtenstall, for whose teapot and kitchen table I was now headed.

It was Tim who first tried out the Round-The-Hills route back in the mid-'60s, as a ten-year-old guinea pig. His approving comments persuaded the originators of the walk that it could be promoted as a family ramble. Tim's enthusiasm for the history and tradition of his native countryside are boundless. I enjoyed my cuppa in his Fern Street house, before setting my boots at the final obstacle, Cowpe Lowe.

'This walk's last bite, Cowpe Lowe,' the Haslingden engineer had told me. '1400 feet, a real rattlesnake of a hill.' Yes, Cowpe Lowe bit back hard. At the summit I felt flaked out. But I scurried on down and into Marl Pits at the end of the walk (at 5.30) to collect my hard-earned certificate, feeling as fresh as any iron-thighed hero of the hill. A strange effect. Me, I put it down to those Chorley cakes.

STEPPING OUT – *Walk 73*

MAP: OS 1:25,000 Explorer 287; 1:50,000 Landranger 103

TRAVEL: Road – M62 to Manchester; M60 northern ring road; M66 north (Bury and Burnley direction); A56 north to Rawtenstall. Walk starts from Marl Pits recreation ground on Newchurch Road (right at traffic lights on A682 Burnley road in Rawtenstall).

WALK DIRECTIONS: Full details are on instruction leaflet issued to walkers. Waymarking (circular 'Round-The-Hills' sign on yellow arrow) is good, but not perfect; following the group in front of you is the best bet. Briefly; from Marl Pits rec. (OS ref SD820230) west along Newchurch Road, cross A682, on along Old Haslingden Road past Ski Rossendale; right up exit road. Then: Cribden Hill (799240) – above Stone Fold (791260) – under signal masts on Hameldon Hill (809287) – to A682 opposite Clowbridge Reservoir (825282). Round north end of reservoir – south under power lines (837276 and 840270) – B6238 at Water (841262). East (842259) to Dean (850257); south for 3 miles to Edgeside; cross A681 at 835217. South and west to summit of Cowpe Lowe (823206); north to cross A681 at Cloughfold (823225). Up Peel Street opposite; left down Newchurch Road to Marl Pits rec.

LENGTH: 18 miles – allow up to 9 hours.

REFRESHMENTS: Bring water, picnic. Refreshments en route at Commercial Inn (01706-216043) or Locks shop, both on B6238 at Water (10 miles); also tea, etc. supplied at checkpoints.

CONDITIONS: One or two steep sections; more than enough sloppy peat bog. Bring full hill walking gear (though many walk in trainers and T-shirts).

WALK DETAILS: Walk takes place on 1st Sunday of September. Details: *www.rossendaleonline.co.uk*

YORKSHIRE

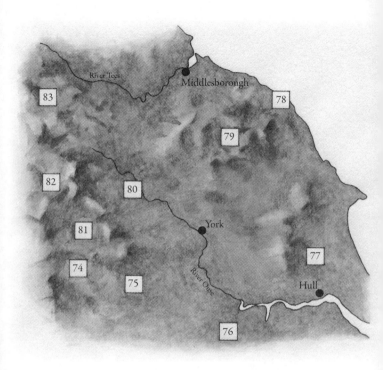

Haworth and the Brontë Moors, West Yorkshire

A stormy walk over the moors to Wuthering Heights

A COLD, STORMY WINTER'S DAY with a smudged grey sky streaking over the West Yorkshire moors on half a gale from the Irish Sea. Haworth's cobbled main street ran and chuckled with rainwater, and the dark sandstone houses of the village dripped from eaves and gutters. Up in the churchyard at the crest of the hill, ranks of grey headstones glinted under leafless black sycamores and horse chestnuts, all whistling with wind.

A right wuthering day, then, and perfect for what I had in mind: a brisk stride out into the teeth of the weather. The more blustery and blowy the better, given the reputation of my destination out there on the moors: the old ruined farmhouse of Top Withins, immortalized by Emily Brontë as Wuthering Heights, the bleak and storm-battered residence of her great anti-hero Heathcliff.

The last of the rain came hissing across Haworth, and I was glad to duck into the Parsonage museum by the church. Irish-born Patrick Brontë was appointed curate of Haworth in 1820. In these neat little rooms his three daughters, Charlotte, Emily and Anne, huddled over the dining room table with their brother Branwell, spent their childhoods of the 1820s and 30s concocting fantastic tales which they wrote in miniature hand-sewn booklets. Branwell never amounted to much – drink, opium and boredom saw to that. But the three sisters blossomed into the most remarkable literary family of the 19th century. It was a short flowering: tuberculosis claimed Anne at 29 and Emily at 30, and Charlotte was dead before she was forty. By then Charlotte had written *Jane Eyre* (1847), *Shirley* (1848) and *Villette* (1853); Anne had produced *Agnes Grey* (1847) and *The Tenant of Wildfell Hall* (1848); and Emily had published in 1847 her one

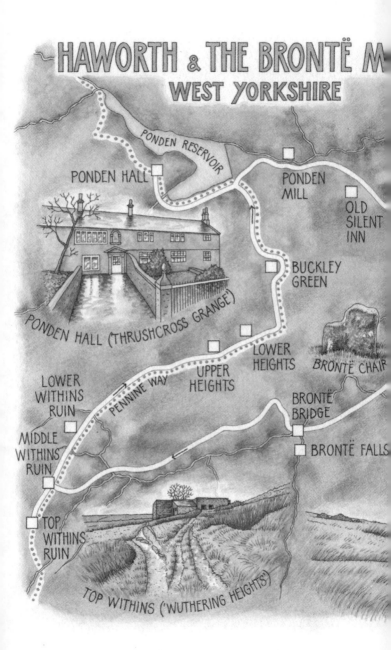

HAWORTH & THE BRONTË M
WEST YORKSHIRE

PONDEN RESERVOIR

PONDEN HALL

PONDEN MILL

OLD SILENT INN

PONDEN HALL ('THRUSHCROSS GRANGE')

BUCKLEY GREEN

LOWER HEIGHTS

BRONTË CHAIR

UPPER HEIGHTS

LOWER WITHINS RUIN

PENNINE WAY

BRONTË BRIDGE

MIDDLE WITHINS RUIN

BRONTË FALLS

TOP WITHINS RUIN

TOP WITHINS ('WUTHERING HEIGHTS')

THECARY

BLACK BULL

WUTHERING
HEIGHTS
PUB

HAWORTH

STANBURY

CHURCH

CEMETERY ROAD

BRONTË
PARSONAGE
MUSEUM
(START & FINISH
OF WALK)

LOWER LAITHE
RESERVOIR

THE PARSONAGE

VIEW OF THE MOORS FROM 'WUTHERING HEIGHTS'

towering masterpiece, the savage and tempestuous parable of *Wuthering Heights*.

Among the museum's displays of Charlotte's tiny long-sleeved dresses, Anne's collection of Scarborough pebbles and the great brass collar worn by Emily's mastiff Keeper, I found it hard to credit that dark Mr Rochester, drunken Arthur Huntingdon and demonic Heathcliff could have taken shape and force here in the hearts of three such restricted and inexperienced young women. But out on the puddled moor paths, hunching into the howling gale and looking round over wind-whipped heather and seething pale grasses, it was easy to guess the source of the power and the inspiration for Emily's brutal battering-ram of a fable.

The Brontë girls, delicate in health as they were, delighted in wandering these wild moors. Their old nurse, Tabitha Aykroyd, told them of the fairies that danced by night over Sladen Beck, the stream that tumbled down from a narrow cleft of the moors. The remote waterfalls, the rocks and the chattering beck were a favourite and a magical spot to the sisters. These days the 'Brontë Falls' attract so many visitors, native and foreign, that the footpath signposts carry Japanese translations. But on this raw winter's morning, sitting in Charlotte's special rock chair and hearing the hiss and splash of the beck, I had the moorland ravine all to myself.

I crossed the little clapper bridge and climbed up to the open moor again, where squares of blue sky and skeins of bruised purple cloud jostled for mastery. Top Withins lay in sight now, jutting dramatically from the skyline, a hard black angle of walls under a pair of skeletal winter trees. The Pennine Way runs right past the doorstep of the ruined old farm, but even on that famed hikers' highway not a solitary walker was moving today.

'One may guess the power of the north wind, blowing over the edge,' wrote Emily Brontë, 'by the excessive slant of a few stunted firs at the end of the house; and by a range of gaunt thorns all stretching their limbs one way, as if craving alms of the sun. Happily the architect had foresight to build it strong: the narrow windows are deeply set in the wall, and the corners defended with large jutting stones.'

Did Emily actually model her fortress-like 'Wuthering Heights' on Top Withins? Not as to individual details, say the Brontë experts. But the isolated farmhouse under the edge of the moor was well known to her, and in its harshly beautiful setting it makes by far the best candidate for Heathcliff's lair. I sat on the wet heather above the ruin, picturing the savage dogs, the surly servants, the cavernous hall and chill bedrooms of Wuthering Heights; the gothic horror of Cathy Linton rapping on the windows in the snowstorm, crying in vain for admittance as her blood ran down the broken pane; and arching over all, the relentless will of that passionate lover and hater, Heathcliff, the embodiment of the wild spirit of the moors.

Grouse whirred away over the heather, crying *back! back!* as I trudged down the Pennine Way from Top Withins with a fifty-mile panorama of black, tan and fox-brown moorland stretched out in front of me. The ruins of the farmhouses of Middle Withins and Lower Withins lay beside the path, their bread ovens, cupboards and windows still shaped within the tumbled stone walls. The wind shoved and knocked at my back, driving me off the moors and down a walled lane towards the slapping waves and racing whitecaps of Ponden Reservoir.

High on a bank over the reservoir stood Ponden Hall, another typical Pennine farmhouse, long and low among its shelter trees. This was Emily's 'Thrushcross Grange', home of the Linton family so sadistically and remorselessly destroyed by Heathcliff and his lover and foster-sister Catherine. But as I stood in the lane and stared at the house I was thinking of a different scene: Cathy and Heathcliff as naughty children, breaking out of Wuthering Heights by night and sneaking up to Thrushcross Grange. There the wild pair terrified the gently-bred Edgar and Isabella Linton by making faces at them through the window – a chink of light and laughter in the dark stormy sky of Emily's extraordinary imagination.

STEPPING OUT – *Walk 74*

MAP: OS 1:25,000 Explorer OL21

TRAVEL: Rail to Leeds and Keighley (www.thetrainline.com); then Keighley & Worth Valley Railway (01535-645214 or 647777 – 24 hrs; www.kwvr.co.uk), K&DT buses (01535-603284) or taxi from office next to Keighley station

Road – from south, M6 or M1; M62 to Jct 24; A629. From north, A59 or A65 to Skipton; A629.

WALK DIRECTIONS: From Brontë Parsonage (OS ref SE029372) take path ('Public Footpath to Haworth Moor' fingerpost) to West Lane (025372). Turn left; in 50 yd, left up Cemetery Road for ¾ mile to T-junction. Cross onto rough track (016365 – 'Brontë Waterfalls' fingerpost) and follow it for 1½ miles to Brontë Bridge (999358). Brontë Chair and Falls are to left of path just before bridge.

Cross bridge ('Top Withins 1¼' fingerpost); climb stepped path to fingerpost on skyline. Left here ('Top Withins 1 mile' fingerpost) on paved path. In 300 yds, in a grassy field, ignore ladder stile with yellow arrow waymark to your right, and keep ahead to cross lower ladder stile. Continue on well-marked path for ¾ mile to meet Pennine Way (PW) at multiple fingerpost; left along PW for 300 yds to Top Withins (981354).

Return down Pennine Way for 1½ miles, following PW fingerposts to pass Upper and Lower Heights. 150 yds beyond Lower Heights, Pennine Way turns left through kissing gate (998364 – National Trail acorn symbol and Millennium Way arrow), descending walled lane towards Ponden Reservoir. At track, bear right (998367 – 'PW, Brontë Way, Ponden' fingerpost) to pass Buckley Green. In 100 yds, left ('PW'), down lane; in 150 yd, right over stile ('PW, Brontë Way'), downhill to Ponden Reservoir. Left along south bank road to Ponden Hall (991371 – on right of road opposite Ponden House, just after bend).

Return along reservoir road. At dam, follow 'Ponden Mill, Stanbury' fingerpost past Ponden Mill (999372) to road. Right (take care!) for ½ mile, passing Old Silent Inn (003371), into Stanbury. At far end of Stanbury, right (013372) down Oxenhope road to cross dam of Lower Laithe Reservoir. At far end, left (016368 – 'Bridleway to Cemetery Road'); follow right-hand track to Cemetery Road, and retrace steps to Parsonage museum.

LENGTH OF WALK: 9 miles

CONDITIONS: Paths are well marked and partly paved, but are boggy in parts (footpath from 003371 to 011371 around Stanbury is a quagmire, and best avoided in favour of road). Wear hill-walking gear and walking boots.

REFRESHMENTS: Old Silent Inn (01535-647437); *www.old-silent-inn.co.uk*; The Friendly Inn (01535; 645528), Wuthering Heights (01535-643332) – all at Stanbury

BRONTË PARSONAGE MUSEUM: (01535-642323; *www.bronte.info*)

Leeds, West Yorkshire

Snowy ramble through the city that reinvented itself

A BITTER DARK DAY, the first day of spring, with snow falling softly in the streets of Leeds. Turning up my collar on the steps of the railway station I remembered my first and only other visit to the city, back in 1969 on a harsh March day like this.

Leeds had been a grimy old place in those days, a depressed post-industrial city clogged with soot and litter, its people seeming on an eternal trudge with hunched shoulders into a sleety gale. My friends and I had hitchhiked from Durham to see Donovan, our crushed velvet hero, sing at the Corn Exchange. We eked out the long trip on cigarettes and cups of tea, and took away with us lasting images of black canals, high black factory walls and the hiss of car tyres in slushy gutters.

It was strange to step out of the station and find such Gothic memories vividly stirred by the feathery touch of snow on eyelashes and the sound of car wheels swishing through snow puddles. And the Gormenghast motif was strengthened when I turned down beneath the railway line and found myself walking through the aptly named 'Dark Arches', a vaulted catacomb under the viaduct through which the River Aire rushed with an angry hiss and blast of cold river breath.

Leeds, of course, has changed a long way since the 1960s. A section of the grim arches has been turned into an arcade of smart shops, and the once shabby and neglected environs of the River Aire and the Leeds & Liverpool Canal are being appreciated at last for what they really are – a striking and historic water feature, a price-less asset in the heart of the city. These days, far from fleeing Leeds's waterfront in disgust, people are paying very good money to live and work along the old urban waterways. Before plunging in among the modern waterside developments, I took a little sidetrack along Water

Lane. The suggestions came from Leeds Civic Trust's guide booklet *Waterfront West*, one of four I'd put in my pack before setting out. With their help I was aiming to cobble together a day-long walk that would show me the cream of Leeds past and present.

Waterfront West carried me off and landed me in Marshall Street, a real old Leeds mill street with a great brick mill and warehouses hemming in the roadway in a lowering manner I well remembered. Further on down stood a genuinely eccentric building, a very early Victorian flax mill and offices built in high Egyptian style with papyrus-headed capitals to the pillars and a spread of pharaonic wings above the entrance. 'Temple Mill – modelled on the Egyptian temple at Edfu', noted the blue plaque on the wall.

Whose cultural pretensions and bulging moneybags could have realised this exotic fantasy in dour grey stone in a workaday district of Leeds? It was John Marshall, a stern and paternalistic employer. Through teaming up with Matthew Murray, an engineering genius and inspired inventor, Marshall made a fortune, a common enough chapter in the vivid, brutal story of the Industrial Revolution.

Along Water Lane another fine piece of eccentricity reared its extravagant twin head. Tower Works in Globe Road made humble pins, cards and combs for the textile industry, but the two towers that were built to grace the premises in Victorian days were lordly creations. They still dominate the skyline hereabouts – a ventilation shaft that is a faithful copy (in cruel red brick) of a 14th-century cathedral tower in Florence, and a chimney modelled on a 12th-century Romanesque tower in Verona.

Back beside the River Aire I went east beneath a succession of handsome old bridges: stone-built Victoria Bridge of 1839 with the young Queen's name in a floral wreath on the keystone, then the sturdy iron latticework of Leeds Bridge. Along the waterfront were modern office blocks, waterside apartments and light industry units, sensitively designed with red brick walls and semi-elliptical windows to harmonise with the functional but dignified architecture of the old warehouses in between.

Leeds Bridge, said a plaque, was the subject of the world's first movie film in 1888. Another plaque told of the founding of the teetotal Band of Hope here in the 1840s. Temperance movements were all the rage in those days of widespread gin shop poverty and despair. Leeds Bridge House, a few yards from the bridge, was built as a temperance hotel – an exercise in how to get a quart into a pint pot if ever there was one, for the architect of the florid Romanesque building was forced by its constricted street-corner site to design it in a remarkable wedge shape, a brick and terracotta dream ship sailing into a brave teetotal future for the working classes.

A dream not quite realised, as it turned out. Over the road from Leeds Bridge House, the Adelphi still stands as monument to the best of Victorian boozer style. Panelled woodwork, sculpted lampshades, frosted glass, tiled walls and embossed wallpaper: the Adelphi has the lot. A very handy refuge from the bite of the first day of spring, I thought. So did the 20 gossipy senior citizens settling like a flock of starlings in the front snug. 'All them used to work for Co-op,' explained the large and cheerful lady behind the bar. 'They come in for a game of bingo, y'know, love, and a cup of tay.'

After lunch, moving on along the river, I watched plumes of steam whirling and shredding from the roof vents of Tetley's Brewery. At Crown Point Bridge, a crimson and cream lattice arch, I left the river and went north into the heart of the city, following the Civic Trust's *Briggate* and *Civic Pride* trails. It was a wonderful afternoon's wander, ducking in and out of arcades and cobbled yards, moving through covered markets, giving a nod to the statuesque Black Prince (and attendant pigeon) on his pawing charger. I especially admired the colonnaded grandeur of the vast Town Hall, and the exoticism of Moorish minarets and curly doorways on St Paul's House warehouse, an exercise in overblown fantasy on an otherwise classically restrained Georgian square. Now cleaned of their centuries of soot, these grand monuments call up all the pomp and pride of Victorian Leeds and the confident industrial north.

All through the city, like a man looking for something in a dream, I had been keeping an eye out for the cylindrical bulk of the Corn Exchange where Donovan spun his fey magic back in 1969. Somehow I had missed it. But now, following the walkabout guides more attentively, I tracked it down in the shadow of a railway viaduct, as grimly grey and snow-crowned as I had always pictured it.

The tousle-haired troubadour would be hard pressed to get a hearing for his gentle songs in the Corn Exchange today. The old concert hall has become a humming nest of boutiques, cafés and sound system shops. Under the airship-shaped roof I stood lost among chattering boys and girls. They looked fully as young as I had been back then, but a good deal less starry-eyed. Then I stepped back outside, and let the curtain of snow shut it all away.

STEPPING OUT – *Walk 75*

MAP: City centre map from TIC (see below). Walk maps in Civic
Trust guide booklets (see below).

TRAVEL: Rail to Leeds City (*www.thetrainline.com*)
Road – M1 (Jct 43); or M6, M62 (Jct 27), M621 (Jct 3).

WALK DIRECTIONS: This walk amalgamates four of Leeds Civic
Trust's 'Walkabouts' – *Waterfront West, Waterfront East,
Briggate, Civic Pride Trail*. Route in brief: From Leeds City
railway station, follow signs through Dark Arches to Granary
Wharf. Left out of arches, right to canal bridge. Left across
bridge to Water Lane; right for ¼ mile; left down Marshall
Street to Temple Mill.

Return to Water Lane; right to Victoria Bridge. On along
right bank of river to Leeds Bridge, then Crown Point Bridge.
Left across bridge; aim for tower of Leeds Parish Church. From
church, left down High Court; right along The Calls. Right past
Corn Exchange to City Markets. Walk via Briggate yards and
arcades to The Headrow; left to pass Town Hall.

Left down Park Square East, across Park Square, down beside
Moorish warehouse. Left along St Paul's Street, right down King
Street past the Metropole Hotel. Left along Wellington Street to
City Square; right to station.

LENGTH: Half a day.

REFRESHMENTS: Adelphi PH by Leeds Bridge (0113-245-6377;
www.theadelphi.co.uk)

GUIDE BOOKLETS: 'Walkabout' Trails – *Waterfront West,
Waterfront East, Briggate, Civic Pride Trail*; also *Leeds Statues
Trail* and *Places of Worship Trail*, all from Leeds Civic Trust
(*www.leedscivictrust.org.uk*) or TIC (see below). Also *Leeds
Heritage Trail* (£9.95), amalgamating best of 'Walkabout' Trails.

TOURIST INFORMATION: Gateway Yorkshire, City Station (0113-
242-5242; *www.leeds.gov.uk*).

Walk 76

Thorne Moors, South Yorkshire

A landscape ruined by coal and peat extraction has come spectacularly to life

'OH, THEY'D LIKE to start coal mining again, no doubt about it,' said Darren Whitaker, assistant site manager of Natural England's Humberhead Peatlands National Nature Reserve, as he jerked his thumb towards the gaunt twin winding towers of Thorne Colliery. 'But it would ruin the whole reserve, everything we're trying to do here. The subsidence would crack the peat wide open and let all the water out.' Darren linked his cupped hands in front of him, then let them fall apart, illustrating his point. 'Like taking the plug out of a bath.'

The great spoked winding wheels inside the skeletal towers, outlined against a pale South Yorkshire sky, whirred busily round – not taking cages full of pitmen down to the coal face, but carrying the redundant mine's maintenance team to their work underground. Thorne Colliery has been closed for many years.

This flat moorland region north-east of Doncaster is rich in natural resources – coal (now deemed uneconomic), excellent soil, and a thick layer of peat. The Humberhead Peatlands reserve forms a darkly shaggy oasis of scrub, woods, grassland and water within a vast wildlife desert of intensively farmed crops. The peat of these moors has itself been harvested for the horticultural industry. But with the growth of ecological awareness and the development of viable alternatives to peat in horticulture, all that has stopped, or is about to. Darren Whitaker and his colleagues at Natural England and the Yorkshire Wildlife Trust have been left with the most wonderful opportunity and the most almighty challenge of their lives.

I had come to South Yorkshire to walk with Darren around Thorne Moor, the northern half of the Humberhead Peatlands NNR. Including Hatfield Moor to the south, the reserve contains some 7,300 acres of ground. Only 10 years ago large swathes of the moors were chocolate-coloured deserts of naked peat, exposed by commercial milling and devoid of almost all wildlife.

Much of Hatfield Moor is still in that state. But not for much longer. Natural England has recently bought all the moorland still being commercially worked, and is embarking on a tremendously ambitious programme to restore it to a state similar to the Thorne Moor reserve – a rich, diverse mosaic of landscape and habitat where people are welcome to wander.

'Look here,' said Darren Whitaker as we trod the pathways of Thorne Moor. 'The coal mine releases a small amount of saline water into the reserve, so a little patch of salt-marsh is developing. See the samphire? Just alongside,' – he pointed to cushions of bright green sphagnum moss – 'you've got the natural acid bog plants of the moors, while under our boots *here*,' – indicating the track we were following – 'we've a strip of limestone grassland, because this is the trackbed of an old peat railway and it was ballasted with chunks of limestone. Lime, salt, acid – they shouldn't be anywhere near each other in nature. This moor has such an extraordinary mix of habitats. It's wonderful for insects, birds, plants, you name it.'

Thorne Moor is bleak, harsh, open to the winds, remote – and stunningly beautiful. Earlier this morning I'd been to look at the milling fields of Hatfield Moor, a hellish flatland of sour black emptiness stretching to the horizon and beyond. It seemed incredible that this was the aspect, just a decade ago, of Thorne Moor, now an endlessly varied patchwork of bog, grassland, birch scrub, glinting fleets of water, peat banks, willow groves and open heath. How did they do it?

'Water's the key,' Darren told me, 'the control of water. Too much and nothing grows; too little, and all you get is scrub and bracken. We've blocked the old drainage ditches and put in pipes and dams. Get it right, and sphagnum and cotton grass flourish. They're ideal for forming peat, which is what we're trying to do here – to get the old workings back to the lowland raised mire that they once were.'

Considering that the peat, up to twenty feet thick, was originally laid down in South Yorkshire several thousand years ago, it seems a tall task to make more of the stuff to order. But I could see for myself the spongy, brilliant green tuffets of sphagnum, the building blocks of a raised mire, swelling and thriving where ten years before there was nothing.

We found four species of orchid as we walked; three or four types of butterfly; innumerable dragonflies. There were red and roe deer in the trees, water voles in the ditches. As for the birds – whitethroats burbled and throatily chuckled in the scrub, willow warblers let tumble their rich little waterfalls of song. A tawny owl skimmed across the path. We didn't see the hobbies or marsh harriers that hunt these moors. The nightingales and nightjars must have been saving themselves for the night. But they were certainly there, for those with the ears, eyes and good luck to spot them.

Both the Humberhead Peatlands nature reserves are Sites of Special Scientific Interest in their own right as huge tracts of acid peat bog. But it is the variety of habitat and wildlife they owe to their past industrial exploitation that makes them so special. The problem is how to maintain that delicate state of equilibrium so that one habitat does not swell up, cuckoo-style, to squash and eject another.

'It's a real balancing act,' sighed Darren. 'For example – we've got a mass of escaped rhododendrons that shouldn't be here at all, but visitors like to see them for the splashes of colour. Scrub's another thing that has to be cut back in case it takes over; but people take us to task because it harbours all kinds of songbirds, including the nightingales.

'Then there's the designations. The reserve is a SAC, a Special Area of Conservation, because it's a rare lowland raised mire. We need to raise the water table to maintain it; but if we do, we'll disturb the nightjars, who need dry heathy places to nest. And the reserve's also a SPA, a Special Protection Area, because of its nightjars – and they have to be safeguarded because they're a rare and endangered species, too!'

We came out of the green subaqueous shade of the scrub to an open aspect, looking across peaty lagoons to where swifts were hunting over flowery grassland. Darren nodded slowly as he watched them. 'It's a really fascinating, challenging place, the moor, and changing all the time. That's why I love it. I wouldn't want to work anywhere else in the world.'

STEPPING OUT – *Walk 76*

MAP: OS 1:25,000 Explorer 280, 291; 1:50,000 Landranger 111, 112
Walk route map in Natural England's *The Humberhead
Peatlands* booklet (see below).

TRAVEL: Rail to Thorne (2 miles) – www.thetrainline.com
Road – M18 Junction 6, A614 towards Goole; in ½ mile, right
('Moorends') to T-junction. Right into Moorends; left down
Grange Road and park at bottom (OS ref SE700158). Walk on
along roadway past barriers, with Thorne Colliery football club
pitch on right, to bottom of road; left by pylon to T-junction
(705161). Bear slightly right to cross road; follow track east past
north side of Thorne Colliery site to cross brick footbridge
(711161), then metal footbridge ('Thorne Moors' sign) into
Humberhead Peatlands NNR. Follow yellow route around the
reserve.

   (*If you want to see the milling fields on northern edge of
Reserve, look out for blue arrows in a few hundred yards and make
a 1-mile detour to your left along the 'blue route'. This takes you to
a viewpoint where a rough limestone road crosses the path. Please
don't cross this road – danger of deep water beyond.*)

   From metal footbridge follow yellow route along the
Rhododendron Path to the viewing platform. Then retrace
steps for 100 yards; left (yellow arrow) along grassy path. In ½
mile path makes a right angle to the right; continue to follow it
until it emerges at open fields near some tall, well-grown trees
at Woodpecker Corner. Here it turns right at right angles again
and runs up the west edge of the Reserve. At the top turn left
along the Rhododendron Path, over metal and brick bridges,
back to car park.

LENGTH OF WALK: 3–4 miles

CONDITIONS: Peat paths can be boggy and wet after rain. Wear
walking boots; bring binoculars for bird watching.

REFRESHMENTS: Belmont Hotel, Thorne (01405-812320; *www.
belmonthotel.com*)

THORNE AND HATFIELD MOORS: Guide leaflet and information
from Natural England (*www.naturalengland.org.uk*)

YORKSHIRE WILDLIFE TRUST: 01904-659570; *www.yorkshire-
wildlife-trust.org.uk*.

Beverley, East Yorkshire

*Green Men, gurning sprites, slaves and Freemen on a circuit of
Beverley and its ancient common*

THE TOWERS OF BEVERLEY MINSTER stuck nine with a clangorous carillon as I walked up Highgate, where the stone setts
lay washed and gleaming with last night's rain. A pleasing curve of
red brick houses with white facings led the eye through to the great
dun-coloured bulk of the Minster that loomed at the far end of the
street, its twin west towers pointing like spring shoots into a clearing
blue sky.

When the monks of Beverley built their great church in the mid-
13th century, they took no half measures. The stone carvers who were
called in to beautify the structure allowed their artistic and religious
sensibilities full play; their irony and their impudence, too. There's a
nice sense of mischief about their exterior work – the line of scowl-
ing and gurning Green Men who underpin the west window, the
impishly grinning sprites that carry dignified prelates on their stone
heads. As for the interior: if God can hear the music of the stones,
surely He must thrill daily to the concert of lute, harp and bagpipes,
of pipe organ, nickelharp, tambourine and viol that rises from the
carved musicians with their humorous faces in the low north wall
arcades.

Close-to, it seems impossible that Beverley Minster, so high and
dominant over the East Yorkshire town, does not boast the status of
a cathedral. In the flattish countryside of the East Riding the enormous cruciform church sails like a graceful ship of stone, its rocket
towers rising beyond pastures, commons and cornfields to beckon
pilgrims on the Wilberforce Way. This new long-distance footpath
commemorates William Wilberforce, East Yorkshire's great champion of the abolition of slavery, and runs for 60 miles between Hull,

where he was born in 1759, and York where he was declared MP for Yorkshire at the age of twenty-one. 2007 was the bicentennial year of the abolition of Britain's involvement in the transatlantic slave trade, and the Wilberforce Way, linking many sites connected with Wilberforce and with others who fought in the same cause, opened that summer as a lasting memorial to Wilberforce and his colleagues, and also as a reminder that slavery – economic, sexual and 'traditional' – continues all over the world today.

Outside the Minster in the brisk air of Eastgate, I ventured through a gate and along a slippery stone path to find what remains of the Dominican Friary established at about the same time the Minster was built – a crooked old range of buildings, now housing Beverley's youth hostel, whose walls lean outwards so precariously they look ready to plunge into their own courtyard.

Beverley has tremendous character, having somehow managed to stave off the blandness that afflicts so many old market towns. The florid red brick County Hall, straight out of the Victorian School of Civic Pride, Ye Olde Pork Shoppe traditional butchers with its window-mounted prime cuts, the fine rickety range of old pubs and premises at the heart of the vast open spaces of Saturday Market – everything speaks of a lively town with a great sense of its own style and history.

Beyond Saturday Market I came to St Mary's, a beautiful church of silvery stone that would probably be called the Cathedral of Beverley if the Minster hadn't already taken that title. Wild beast-men with pointed ears and snarling faces guarded the door. Inside, among a scattering of stars, the golden roof bosses yielded yet more Green Men and many monkeyish figures pulling fantastic faces, as well as a whole dynasty of more or less mythical English kings painted with mild, even coy smiles even as they wielded a fearsome armoury of snickersnees.

Once through the 15th-century brick arch of the North Bar gate, I was out of medieval Beverley and into the gracious Georgian parade of North Bar Without. Some of the house fronts were embellished with Arts & Crafts carvings, and one carried a bright brass plate proclaiming: 'Konsulat Rzeczypospolitej Polskiej – Consulate of the Republic of Poland'. Historically Beverley, so near the River Humber and the port of Hull, saw many Polish seafarers and merchants. These days it is electricians, plumbers and builders from Kracow and Warsaw, the East Riding's new post-Iron Curtain immigrants, who

call at the house on North Bar Without for help, advice and a bit of a chat.

At the bottom of Norfolk Street I clicked the kissing gate and walked out onto Westwood's broad acres. In an instant the whole scene and mood changed. It was as if brisk, bustling Beverley had been whipped away by a magician and I had been set down in a vast green prairie. Not that I had Beverley's great 600-acre common to myself for long – a couple of greyhounds came rascalling past, attempting to swallow each other's heads as they ran shoulder to shoulder, and as my eyes and focus adjusted to the suddenly opened distances I could see dog-walkers, kite-flyers and golf club wielders dotted about.

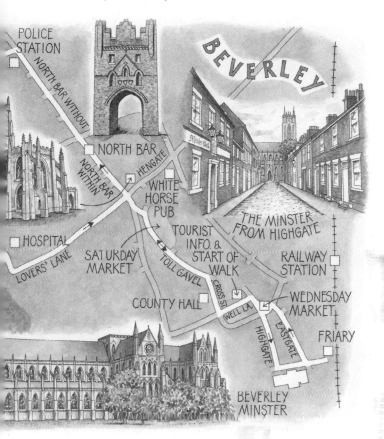

Beverley is not just lucky to have Westwood and its other, smaller commons of Swinemoor and Figham – the town works vigilantly, through its twelve annually elected Pasture Masters, to see that no developers encroach and no fly-tippers intrude on these enormous swathes of open common land. As its name suggests, Westwood was a wood pasture, a common where animals grazed under pollarded trees, when the Archbishop of York granted it to the Freemen of Beverley in 1380. The Pasture Masters, Beverley-born sons of the town's freemen, have been watching and wandering the commons since Queen Victoria came to the throne. Recently there was a bit of a panic when Beverley's freemen were found to be producing insufficient numbers of sons, but once it was agreed that daughters could also be admitted to Pasture Mastership, everyone breathed a sigh of relief.

I wandered across Beverley's white-railed racecourse and out into the wide open spaces of Westwood. Burton Bushes, a damp and boggy remnant of the medieval wood pasture, was thick with bluebells under its old oaks and hollies. Up on the heights the battlemented tower of Black Mill struck a fairytale note. I longed for a six-year-old companion, so that I could intone 'Rapunzel, Rapunzel, let down your hair' with suitable gallantry.

In a cold wind I lingered by the mill tower, listening to the ecstatic springtime singing of larks and staring east across the green plain of Westwood to where the twin stone fingers of Beverley Minster made their graceful gesture heavenwards.

STEPPING OUT – *Walk 77*

MAP: OS 1:25,000 Explorer 293, 1:50,000 Landranger 107; Beverley
Town Centre maps from Beverley TIC, 34 Butcher Row (01482-
391672; *www.realyorkshire.co.uk*)

TRAVEL: Rail to Beverley (*www.thetrainline.com*)
Road – M62 to Jct 38; B1230 to Beverley.
Railway Street leads to Wednesday Market and TIC in Butcher
Row.

WALK DIRECTIONS: Pick up town map from TIC (OS ref
TA036395). Leaving TIC, right through Wednesday Market,
along Highgate to Beverley Minster (038393). Leaving Minster
by north door, right to Eastgate. Friars Lane or Friars Walk
opposite lead to Friary. Back on Eastgate, right to Wednesday
Market. Just before TIC, left down Well Lane; right along Cross
Street past County Hall; left along Toll Gavel, through Saturday
Market to St Mary's Church (032398). Continue along left
pavement of North Bar Within; through North Bar archway;
on along North Bar Without for ¼ mile. By police station, left
down Norfolk Street onto Westwood Common (025401).

Keep ahead to cross race track by wicket gates. Head for
grandstand; just before, re-cross race track and then A1174
(019397) – please take care! Diverge at shallow angle from
road, keeping it on your right, steering for long wood of Burton
Bushes that runs south away from road. Aim half-way along line
of trees to reach stile into wood (012394). Cross wood (a muddy
quarter-mile) to far side, to reach exit stile and kissing gate to
your left (010392). Now aim for Black Mill (021390) on its hill.

From Black Mill aim for tower of St Mary's Church (to left of
twin towers of Minster). Pass through wooded dell of Newbegin
Pits to footpath on far side. Turn right with wall, then
Westwood Hospital on your left. Just past hospital, left along
Lovers Lane (027394 – kissing gate and lamp post). Follow it
past hospital and on down Wood Lane to North Bar Within
opposite St Mary's. Right to return to TIC; straight over down
Hengate for White Horse pub (033398).

LENGTH: 5 miles

GEAR: Binoculars for church roof bosses, torch for misericords.

REFRESHMENTS: White Horse, Hengate, Beverley (01482-861973;
www.nellies.co.uk)

WILBERFORCE WAY: 60 miles, Hull to York via Beverley. Guidebook by John Eckersley, available locally and from author, The Vicarage, School Lane, Heslington, York Y010 5EE (01904-410389) – all proceeds to Christian Aid.

Walk 78

Whitby and Hawsker, North Yorkshire

Smoked fish, vampires and jet miners

L INGERING IN THE EARLY MORNING COLD of Henrietta Street, I couldn't make up my mind if I should bother Barry Brown or not. I had a lot of brisk walking to fit into this short winter's day, and Mr Brown looked pretty busy going in and out of his smoking shed. On the other hand, life is short; and if you are lucky enough to find yourself in the characterful old Yorkshire fishing town of Whitby, you're a fool if you pass Fortune's Whitby-Cured Kippers without ducking in for a tasty pair and a bit of a blether.

'My mother was a Fortune,' said Mr Brown as he sold me a brace of plump kippers from the display counter of his tiny shop. 'They reckon the name came over with the Spanish Armada. We're the last real traditional curers in the town. What we do, we use North Sea herring – big ones, like yours – and smoke 'em over oak and beech shavings. There's not a flavour like it in Whitby.'

I slipped the kippers into my backpack and glanced into the dark and reeking curing shed. Firelight flickered over golden ranks of half-kippered herring hanging from tarry rods. A billow of blue vapour followed me down the street, wafting a tang of fish and salt smoke that I carried until the sea winds of the North Yorkshire coast scoured it away.

The 199 broad stone steps that climb up Whitby's East Cliff have seen many a set of feet in their day. None more fiendish, though, than the hellhound paws of Count Dracula, fleeing in the shape of a wolf from the wreck of the schooner *Demeter* as she drifted into Whitby harbour with a dead man lashed to her wheel. I had re-read that mother of all spook stories in bed last night. The crooked old steps rise to St Mary's Church in its cliff-top graveyard and to the gaunt ruins of Whitby Abbey just beyond – all grist to the Gothic

WHITBY & HAWSKER
NORTH YORKSHIRE

SALTWICK

WHITBY JET
HERITAGE
CENTRE

FORTUNE'S
KIPPER SHOP
& SMOKERY

CLEVELAND WAY
NATIONAL TRAIL

ABBEY FARM

WHITBY ABBEY

HARBOUR
BRIDGE
(START OF WALK)

CHURCH STEPS

ST. MARY'S CHURCH

WEST
CLIFF

WHITBY

EAST
CLIFF

THE
199
STEPS

RIVER ESK

A171

SCHOOL

WHITBY HARBOUR
& WEST CLIFF

LARPOOL
VIADUCT

WHITBY A

SCARBOROUGH & WHITE

WHITESTONE POINT

WHITBY LIGHTHOUSE

FOG SIGNAL STATION

HIGH WHITBY

WIDDY HEAD

DISUSED MINE WORKINGS

CROSS STREAM

FOG SIGNAL STATION

GNIPE HOWE FARM

...RIETTA STREET ...E 199 STEPS

A171

WINDMILL INN

...PATH

STAINSACRE

HAWSKER

SCARBOROUGH & WHITBY RAILWAY

...K BAY

mill that was Bram Stoker's imagination in the 1880s as he listened to the yarning of the superstitious Whitby fishermen.

St Mary's is a strange church, a lumpy-backed building of golden stone whose interior, partly constructed by Whitby shipwrights, resembles a cross between a nonconformist chapel and an admiral's cabin. A great gallery, roomy enough to accommodate several ships' companies, circumnavigates the upper regions. Columns twisted like barley-sugar guard the sanctuary, as dark and cramped as a merchantman's fo'c'sle. It's a fitting place to remember Whitby's most celebrated adoptive son, Captain James Cook, who saw out three years of apprenticeship in the town and refitted a flat-bottomed, Whitby-built collier as his famous exploration ship *Endeavour*.

After dining on the lily-white neck of Lucy Westenra, Dracula's delight was to flit around the crumbling arches and blank windows of Whitby Abbey. From the cliff beyond I looked back to admire the stately old ruin, and became aware of a pair of figures hurrying with what seemed like sinister purpose at my heels – a tall pale woman in red on the arm of a man wrapped in a loose dark waterproof that flapped behind him like the billows of a cloak. Binoculars showed me a cadaverous face and receding black hair. The fanged Count and his packed lunch! I smiled at my nonsense – but I quickened stride and glanced over my shoulder until I had put a bay or two between us.

The Cleveland Way National Trail circles for more than a hundred miles around the rim of the North York Moors National Park, ending its course with a superb run down the cliffs of the northern Yorkshire coast. On this sharp winter morning the path lay deserted. Fence wires and stiff grasses bristled with hoar crystals, and the cliffs of Saltwick Bay stood splashed with low sunlight. They cradled a beach of dull red sands and dark purple rock scars against which the sea came hissing in long, frost-white lines.

The monkey-puzzle trees that grew abundantly in these parts 150 million years were drowned, squeezed, squashed and anaerobically fossilised over millennia into the hard, light substance known as Whitby jet, a target for cliff miners and shore collectors. Whitby jet takes a polish and a readily cut shape that betters any other jet on earth for the crafting of jewellery. In Victorian times thousands of jet miners burrowed these cliffs. Other mines along the coast yielded ironstone to feed the furnaces of Teesside, and alum which was burned, leached, boiled and leavened with human urine for the tanning and dyeing trades. The miners of the Yorkshire coast lived and died hard – rough men at desperately rough and dangerous work.

Up by Whitby lighthouse, under skies increasingly cold and blue, the flat roof of the fog signal station carried a pair of immense black sound trumpets fit to blow down the walls of Jericho. 'All Rivers Flow into the Sea, yet the Sea is not Full' was the quotation from Ecclesiastes painted on the wall. Walking on along the cliffs I watched a blue and white trawler with a high storm deck hurrying north, butting the rollers aside like a little round-shouldered bull.

Beyond the gorse-grown mine workings on Widdy Head I left the Cleveland Way and made inland to Gnipe Howe farm across fields poached to sticky porridge by the hooves of cattle. Just along the farmhouse drive I found the track of the long-abandoned Scarborough & Whitby Railway, these days a beautifully maintained footpath and cycleway that led me all the way back into Whitby. I hurdled the River Esk by way of the magnificent red brick arches of Larpool Viaduct, and dropped down among the fishing boats and piled lobster pots of the quayside in the early afternoon.

The trade in Whitby jet hit its high peak around Bram Stoker's time, when the prolonged mourning of Queen Victoria made it *de rigueur* for every lady's bodice to be spangled and draped with beads of shiny black. Several workshops are still active in the town. The Whitby Jet Heritage Centre in Church Street handcrafts fine jet jewellery, and also displays a complete Victorian jetworks – grinding wheels, high stools, workmen's tools and all – discovered a few years ago in a Whitby attic.

Hal Redvers-Jones was intent on polishing a teardrop pendant, but he was happy to stop work to chat and to sell me a pair of tiny jet earrings set in delicate silver shells. In the soft light of the workshop they glowed as if lit from inside. As I turned them this way and that, admiring their beauty, a snippet of verse passed through my mind – something I'd read or heard somewhere along this memorable midwinter walk:

> 'Still, fashions change; mayhap some day
> Again the craft will thrive,
> And Yorkshire jet will ring the earth –
> Black, flashing and alive.'

STEPPING OUT – *Walk 78*

MAP: OS 1:25,000 Explorer OL27; 1:50,000 Landranger 94

TRAVEL: Rail to Whitby (*www.thetrainline.com*)

Road: A1, A66 to Middlesbrough, A171 to Whitby. Park in quayside car park.

WALK DIRECTIONS: Start at east end of harbour bridge (OS ref NZ900111). Walk forward for 100 yards, then left along Church Street. In 250 yards, right up the 199 Steps to St Mary's Church (902113) and Whitby Abbey just beyond. Continue up road on left of abbey for 150 yards; left (arrow; 'Cleveland Way' fingerpost) past Abbey Farm to turn right (905114) along Cleveland Way coast path for 3 miles. Nearing Gnipe Howe farm, descend stone steps to cross stream (934091); in another third of a mile, right over stile (936086- arrow, and 'Hawsker' fingerpost). Walk inland, up left side of stone wall, over field (footpath fingerpost) to Gnipe Howe farm (934085).

Left along farm drive for ⅔ mile. Where track starts to rise to cross bridge, left over stile (928078); then right along disused railway line for 2½ miles to cross Larpool Viaduct (896097). In 250 yards, right (arrow; Esk Valley Walk 'leaping fish' fingerpost), aiming to right of school buildings; then left (arrow; 'leaping fish' fingerpost) to cross A171 (898102 – *please take care!*). Right for 100 yards; just before bridge, left (footpath fingerpost) to descend to Whitby's west quayside. Cross railway line; ahead along River Esk to return to bridge.

LENGTH: 8 miles

REFRESHMENTS: Windmill Inn, Stainsacre (01947-602671) – OS ref 913086; Elizabeth Botham's Bakery and Teashop, 35–9 Skinner Street, Whitby (01947-602823; *www.botham.co.uk*)

FORTUNE'S WHITBY-CURED KIPPERS: Henrietta Street, Whitby (01947-601659)

WHITBY JET HERITAGE CENTRE: 123b Church Street, Whitby (01947-821530; *www.whitbyjet.net*)

WHITBY ABBEY (ENGLISH HERITAGE): 01947-603568; *www. english-heritage.org.uk/whitby*

CLEVELAND WAY NATIONAL TRAIL: *www.nationaltrail.co.uk/ clevelandway*

INFORMATION: Whitby TIC, Langborne Road (01723-383637); *www.outdooryorkshire.com*

Walk 79

Rosedale, Hutton-le-Hole and Lastingham, North Yorkshire

Shadows of the past across the North York Moors

BILLOWS OF GREY CLOUD, torn by patches of intense blue sky, were swelling across the North York Moors this windy summer morning. The village of Rosedale Abbey, tucked down below its dark moorland slopes, was zebra-striped with racing bars of shadow and sunlight. On the village green a couple in walking boots sat fondling their dog, trying to decide whether to brave the high moors.

Rosedale Chimney Bank is a tough mile, a steady climb at 1 in 3. It was a daily slog for the Rosedale iron-miners a hundred years ago, up the breakneck road built by their Rosedale Mining Company masters to the iron ore mines and kilns and the mineral railway terminus at Bank Top, 700 feet above the village.

On an elbow of the road I stopped for a breather and to look back up the dale, beautiful in its morning hush, a tranquil patchwork of green fields and woodlands where the red-roofed village nestled among trees. Back then it had been a noisy, dirty, smoky little place, a clangorous industrial village packed with 3,000 miners, where the shifts were continuous and the beds never grew cold.

Rosedale Chimney was built 100 feet tall so that the smoke from the ore roasting kilns would not upset the local landowner's grouse. John Flintoft, the builder, danced upon its capstones to celebrate its completion in 1861. It formed a landmark at the top of the bank for over a century, visible for many miles around, until pulled down in 1972. The ore kilns' arches still stand beside the road up here, and acres of spoil heaps lie half-smothered in bracken at the mine sites above Hollins Farm.

The North Eastern Railway built a moorland branch line to Bank Top, to take the roasted ore away to the furnaces on Teesside.

I stopped to admire the railwaymen's terraced cottages, stark and incongruous on the rim of the dale, and then made off across Spaunton Moor, following an old track sparkling with mica that wound through the heather.

This was grand walking. Enormous thirty-mile vistas across open moorland, and nearer at hand a series of intimate glimpses into other lives – curlews skimming low over the moor and crying *cur-leek! cur-leek!* ; bees foraging over the heather flowers; grouse coveys whirring off like clockwork toys; spiders spinning threads that shimmered like silver wire, miraculously delicate.

In a dip I came across a dozen figures dressed in white space suits, manoeuvring a fleet of strange buggies festooned with hosepipes and sloshing containers. 'Didn't think you'd meet men from the moon up here, did you?' said one of the aliens, in good rich Yorkshire. 'Got to keep the bracken down. My grandfather'd cut the stuff for animal bedding: but since the baled straw came in there's no call for bracken. Very selective, this chemical is – only kills bracken and docks. It says here.'

Hutton-le-Hole, down below the moor, was a bit of a Wild West town in Victorian times, when the paid-up miners would come roaring in with full pockets and big thirsts. They raced hounds, wrestled, matched fighting cocks and rolled drunk on the village's green banks and verges. 'Boxing Tom' Proud, landlord of the Crown Inn, kept order with a few straight lefts. These days things are less rowdy but even busier. Hutton is a pretty little place, its greenery nibbled by degenerate sheep sated with Smarties and sandwich crusts.

The prize-winning Ryedale Folk Museum, a collection of carefully reconstructed local 'period' houses and small businesses, deserves its accolades. I especially enjoyed the village shop, stocked with goods that brought back my own 1950s rural childhood – Coleman's Starch, Atora Beef Suet, National Butter, Robinson's Groats ('for Nursing Mothers and Dyspeptics') – and the cottage gardens of Victorian villagers and medieval peasants, stuffed to the borders with flowers and medicinal herbs.

Sniffing at fingers scented with thyme and feverfew, I climbed a green bank on the outskirts of Hutton-le-Hole and went east through fields of barley where the farmers were reaping astride big green and red machines. In the Blacksmith's Arms at Lastingham I made short work of a pint of very lively Black Sheep bitter, and went off to look at what St Mary's Church was hiding beneath its stone-flagged nave floor.

St Cedd built a wattle-and-daub church at Lastingham during the 7th century, and from then onwards Christianity shone a faint but persistent light from these moors into the enveloping shadows of the Dark Ages. Four hundred years later, monks from Whitby Abbey started on a soon-abandoned abbey church. What remains of that building is a nave and apse above ground, and a unique vaulted crypt, complete with aisles, below.

Down in the half-light of the crypt I fingered early Norman ram's-horn capitals, Danish tombstones, ornately carved Saxon cross heads and shafts. The cold little room with its columns and arches, a store-house for historical treasure, saw some lively times during the 18th century. Cockfights were held here, and after each Sunday service a party would be hosted by the curate, Jeremiah Carter. This genial man of God rejoiced to see his far-flung parishioners dance to his fiddle-playing and drink their fill of the beer supplied by his wife, who ran the Blacksmith's Arms. The curate's official stipend was just £20 a year.

The thickly wooded valley of the River Seven curves round the eastern flank of Spaunton Moor. Thick conifer blankets and swathes of bright green bracken mask the remnants of industry along the river banks; spoil heaps of iron-mines high in the outcropping lips of the dale, and further down the excavated hollows of a long-forgotten glassworks. It was operated furtively in late Tudor times by illegal French immigrants, who burned the bracken for the potash they needed to produce their green 'forest glass'.

A pigeon clattered up out of a patch of bilberries. The plump purple berries seemed ripe enough to pick. Chewing a sharp-tasting handful, I walked on under the green and peaceful hills of Rosedale, listening to immemorial rural sounds: wind in tree-tops, curlews crying over rainy moorland, and a farmer whistling his dog on a hillside full of madly bleating sheep around Hollins Farm.

The old Yorkshire word for holly was 'hollins' – in past times a sacred tree, but also a source of winter feed before turnips and hay were widely used. The higher the leaf grew on the tree, the less prickly. The upper branches would be stripped of their leaves, and often their bark too, to feed the sheep and cattle. Such were the shifts our ancestors were put to in older and tougher times.

STEPPING OUT – *Walk 79*

MAPS: OS 1:25,000 Explorer OL26; 1:50,000 Landranger 100

TRAVEL: Rail from Grosmont to Pickering (North York
Moors Railway (*www.nymr.co.uk*); then Moorsbus (*www.
visitnorthyorkmoors.co.uk*) to Rosedale Abbey (Sundays and
Bank Holidays, April-Oct, plus additional services in summer
holidays)
Road – A169/A170 to Pickering: A170 towards Helmsley; in
2½ miles, right in Wrelton (signed Rosedale Abbey) for 7 miles
into village.

WALK DIRECTIONS: At southern edge of Rosedale Abbey (OS ref
SE725957) walk south up steep (1 in 3) Rosedale Chimney Bank
road (signed). At summit pass kilns on right; in ½ mile bear
right off road (717939 – footpath sign) on moorland track going
SW for 1 mile. Cross 2 becks; then turn left (704930 – footpath
sign painted on rock), south for 1 mile to join road (705917).
Continue south to junction (709905); right into Hutton-le-
Hole. Ryedale Folk Museum is in village street on left (705900).

After last house on left, cross beck and turn left (706896 –
footpath sign), over stile, steeply up grassy bank and E on field
paths (yellow arrow waymarks) to road below Spaunton Manor
House Farm (723898). Turn right; follow road round to left
through Spaunton. At junction (728899), left to Lastingham
(church on left, Blacksmith's Arms across road). Right opposite
pub (728905) to cross beck; left (Lastingham Grange Hotel
sign) up road for 30 yd; right (footpath sign). Do not cross gate!
Go left over stile under tree, and on between fences in leafy
avenue. From far stile (731905) follow yellow arrows across fields
for 1 mile to ford beck (740907). Climb slope to join stony track
beyond crest (743908); left for 4 miles through bracken, past
Hollins Farm (733944) back to Rosedale Abbey.

LENGTH OF WALK : 12 miles – allow 6 hrs.

CONDITIONS : Field paths, moorland tracks. Firm underfoot (last
few miles can be boggy). Some stiles; two short, steep climbs.
Take hill-walking gear and wear boots; take compass/GPS in
poor weather.

REFRESHMENTS: Plenty of tea shops and other places in Hutton-
le-Hole; Blacksmith's Arms, Lastingham (01751-417247; *www.
blacksmithslastingham.co.uk*)

RYEDALE FOLK MUSEUM: (01751-417367; *www.
ryedalefolkmuseum.co.uk*)
INFORMATION: *www.visitnorthyorkshiremoors.co.uk*

Ripon, Studley Royal and Fountains Abbey, North Yorkshire

Pies, poems and the sonorous signals of the Wakeman of Ripon

'EXCEPT YE LORD keep ye cittie, ye wakeman waketh in vain.' So runs the legend blazoned under the pediment of Ripon's Town Hall. At ten to nine on a bleak North Yorkshire winter's night, I told myself I couldn't be bothered to quit the snug and jolly bar of the Royal Oak for the windy, puddly open spaces of the market square. Yet somehow I found myself there as the hour struck. I couldn't leave the Wakeman of Ripon to wake in vain.

I'm surprised the good man didn't turn tail when he saw me alone and palely loitering by the obelisk, hands in pockets and hood pulled low. A few nights before, he'd been insulted and jostled by drunken youths as he carried out his time-hallowed ceremonial duties. But the Wakeman is made of stern stuff. No ducking duty for him. In his black tricorne and grey coat trimmed with collar and cuffs almost as scarlet as his cheeks, he stood smartly to attention at each of the corners of the obelisk and blew four mournful blasts on his beautiful curved horn.

The Wakeman of Ripon has floated his sonorous 'I'm in charge now, and all's well' signal nightly over the town ever since 886AD, the year King Alfred carved up the country with the Danes under the Treaty of Wedmore. Ripon found itself well inside the Danelaw or Danish part of Britain, and the townsfolk prudently installed a night watchman to guard them against the ravage and rapine of their new political masters. Today's Wakeman is a gentle soul, but I wouldn't be surprised if he sometimes felt like working up a proper berserker rage, quaffing wolf blood and arriving on duty in a gore-smeared bearskin, transported with fury, to wipe the cobbles with the mannerless teenage oafs that plague him.

The following day was a beauty, one of many in this crisp blue winter. Everything in sky and earth seemed to have been washed clean. The creamy stone of Ripon Minster glowed as if dispensing rather than absorbing sunlight. I spent a happy hour flipping up the choir stall seats to admire the cheeky carvings on the misericords, those simple but effective little ledges onto which the worshipping monks and clerics could subside while appearing to be standing upright. Under their venerable buttocks the medieval carvers had lodged irreverent symbols – an inverted Green Man like a chimp, a bagpiping pig, a fox slyly grinning as he preached a sermon to a wide-eyed congregation of poultry.

'Appleton's,' proclaimed the pie shop in the market square, ' – For Cooked Meats and Table Dainties.' There was nothing in the remotest bit dainty about the monster pork pie they sold me, but as a marching brunch it couldn't have been better. Only a few peppery pastry flakes were left by the time I had reached quiet Borrage Lane on the outskirts of town. Here at No. 24 Wilfred Owen lodged in the spring of 1918, scribbling the war poems that would make him immortal, while waiting to return to France for his final, and fatal, tour of duty.

Beyond the town the rivers Skell and Laver came trickling together in a wooded dell. A black and white tom was playing panther at each twitch and scutter among the frosty leaves. I followed the Skell south into a broad green pastureland, dog-walking country. A tiny border terrier leaped up, pink tongue lapping at my hand. 'Mad as a box of frogs, this one,' said his owner with fond pride.

Around Whitcliffe Hall the countryside took a dip and roll. The tall mullioned windows of the medieval farmhouse were half blanked out with stone and partly hidden by a later wing jammed awkwardly on. 'Not exactly sure about its history,' said the farmer, stopping his tractor for a chat in the lane. 'A kind of outstation for the monks at Fountains Abbey, we think. The windows? Oh, they were blocked up when glass was taxed. No sense in paying for daylight, you know!'

The path ran through the depths of a hissing wind-trap wood, then curled out into the sunlit bowl of Studley Royal Park across a series of dimity little humpback bridges. Fallow deer trotted away up the steep valley sides. A glassy lake lay crossed by a Palladian bridge of silver stone. Specimen trees stood naked, their leafless torsos superbly displayed. This landscape was expertly shaped and marshalled into parkland during the 18th century, its ordered beauty enhanced by classical temples and statues, by geometric lawns, by grottoes and pools. At the far end, hanging over their own water-reflected image as if cut from gauze, lay the magnificently sprawling ruins of Fountains Abbey, the

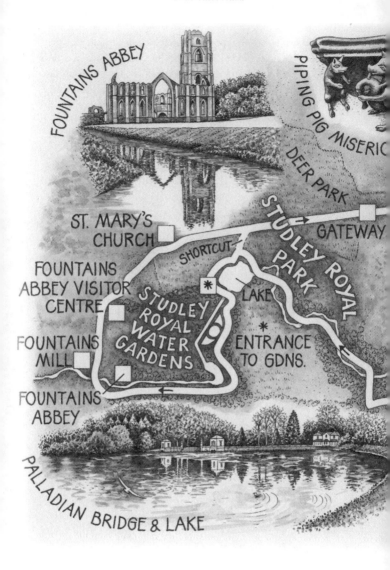

controller of vast swathes of the north of England, a mighty holy citadel of stone until Henry VIII laid it low with the stroke of a pen in 1539.

I wandered back slowly through the Deer Park as fallow deer trotted nonchalantly on either side. Two cock pheasants squared up to each other, chest to chest in a drift of chestnut leaves, locked into

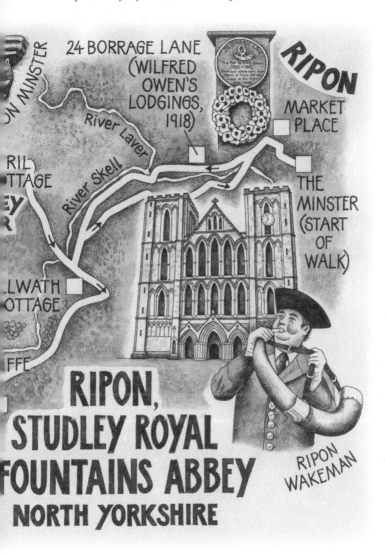

24 BORRAGE LANE
(WILFRED
OWEN'S
LODGINGS,
1918)

RIPON

N MINSTER

River Laver

RIL
TTAGE

River Skell

LWATH
OTTAGE

FFE

MARKET
PLACE

THE
MINSTER
(START
OF
WALK)

RIPON,
STUDLEY ROYAL
FOUNTAINS ABBEY
NORTH YORKSHIRE

RIPON
WAKEMAN

a staring match that suddenly exploded in a furious scuffle. Nearing
Ripon through frost-rimed fields I pulled up to watch the sun dip in
a bath of smeary orange behind the black twig net of an oakwood.
Then I set course for the Minster tower, a beacon of rose-lit stone
rising over the darkening town.

STEPPING OUT – *Walk 80*

MAP: OS 1:25,000 Explorer 298; 1:50,000 Landranger 99

TRAVEL: Road – A1 to Jct 48 or 49; A168 to Kirby Hill, B6265 to Ripon. Park in one of city centre car parks.

WALK DIRECTIONS: From west door of Minster (OS ref SE 314711), forward down Kirkgate to Market Place. Pass Wakeman's House on SW corner (312712); left down High Skelgate, over traffic lights, along Low Skelgate. In 150 yards at left bend, keep ahead (310710) along Borrage Lane for ⅓ mile. At sharp right bend (305708), left along wall to cross confluence of rivers by footbridge (305707). Right along River Skell. In 100 yards ignore steps on your left; in another 100 yards, up concrete steps ahead and on, choosing paths closest to river, for ½ mile to sharp bend. Climb bank here (300701); descend to wider track; right for 200 yards to road (300699).

Left past Hellwath Cottage; in 200 yards, right along lane (302698 – 'bridleway'). In ¾ mile pass Whitcliffe Hall farm on left; in another 100 yards, right (297688 – 'Ripon Rowel/RR' waymark) along green path with thorn trees on right for 450 yards, through gate (293687 – 'RR') into wood. In 100 yards, right along valley bottom path; in 300 yards, cross River Skell on footbridge (291689); left along river. In 300 yards, go through gate (289690) into Studley Royal Park. Forward across bridges for ½ mile to cross weir at foot of lake (282693). *NB Short cut omitting Studley Royal Water Gardens and Fountains Abbey: after crossing weir, don't turn left around lake but keep ahead up bank for 200 yards to turn right along Deer Park drive.*

Main walk: after crossing weir, left around lake to tearoom/entrance to Studley Royal Water Gardens (279691). Pick up map here and choose route to Fountains Abbey (275683), Mill (273682) and Visitor Centre (273687). Just north of Visitor Centre, follow path beside road for ⅓ mile to St Mary's Church (275693), then follow drive (*short cut joins from right in ¼ mile*) through Deer Park for almost 1 mile to pass through gateway (289699). In 200 yards, left beside lodge ('Ripon' fingerpost) into Studley Roger. In 200 yards, right by No. 10 (290702 – 'Ripon') along lane and through kissing gate by April Cottage. On between fences; in 500 yards, at crossroads of fenced paths

(295705), right between hedges for ½ mile to Hellwath Cottage. Just before cottage, left (300699) to retrace outward path beside River Skell. Keep to 'low' track, emerging in 300 yards in open space (300702). Follow its right edge, keeping forward for ⅓ mile to top of steps that descend on left to river (304706). Don't descend, but turn right between fences on path that soon curves left towards Ripon Minster. In ¼ mile, right along Borrage Green Lane opposite Skell Cottage (308708); left along road; left to cross River Skell (310710) and return to Minster.

LENGTH: 9 miles including Water Gardens and Fountains Abbey; 6½ miles short cut route.

REFRESHMENTS: Picnic pies from Appleton's, Ripon Market Place; tearooms at Studley Royal and Fountains Abbey (see below).

STUDLEY ROYAL WATER GARDENS AND FOUNTAINS ABBEY: 01765-602284; *www.fountainsabbey.org.uk*

RIPON WAKEMAN: blows nightly, 9.00 p.m., Market Square

Bolton Abbey and Appletreewick, Wharfedale, North Yorkshire

Dangers, distractions and delightful temptation along the River Wharfe

WELL ... it was bound to happen. After an almost incredible run of Walk of the Month weather luck, the day dawned – and continued – a whole-hearted drencher. The drizzle that had settled over North Yorkshire was obviously not going to shift itself. There was going to be rain in Wharfedale, and impenetrable mist on the fells. That was that.

In the shelter of Bolton Abbey's dripping walls I struggled into a full set of rain gear, not really reluctantly. I had been hoping for one of those crisp autumn days on the hills. But a walk beside the swollen River Wharfe as it raced under green and gold trees would still hold plenty of interest and excitement.

Bolton Abbey – actually a priory, built by Augustinians in 1154 – stood pale and sad in ruins over a bend in the Wharfe. The great east window of the church, empty of stone tracery, framed a wooded hillside beyond the river. The priory had been rich through wool and lead in medieval times, but after its 1539 dissolution the roof was stripped, the buildings quarried and the dignity forgotten. Only the beauty of the setting remained. It took Wordsworth and Turner to rekindle awareness of how gloriously these works of man and nature complimented each other.

A line of stepping-stones led across the river, right in front of the priory. I only saw the catch when I was out in the middle of the quickly-flowing Wharfe – one stone missing. With difficulty I turned round and teetered back to the bank, while a group of mallard quacked wheezy laughter.

The sinuous valley of Wharfedale is lined with woods, planted first by the monks of Bolton Priory and then by the Earls of Burlington and Dukes of Devonshire, incumbents of the fine house built behind the priory after the Dissolution. At the turn of the 19th century the Rector of Bolton Abbey, Rev. William Carr, laid out thirty miles of footpaths. The Bolton woodlands became a refuge for countless West Riding millhands, who flocked to Wharfedale by train and charabanc. Here under sycamore, beech and oak, beside the river in its water-sculpted bed of rock, they could escape the smoke, noise and built environment of their towns for a few precious hours.

These days the Wharfedale woods – full of lichens, mosses, fungi, birds and squirrels – are still a favourite place for strollers from the Pennine towns around. In Strid Wood I met a group of pink-cheeked and white-haired Bradford women, vigorously striding in breeches and red stockings. 'Having a good walk?' I enquired. 'Oh, aye,' said their leader, with cheerful forcefulness, 'we always do.'

The Strid itself was in full roaring form this morning. A long, narrow channel of mossy rocks, treacherously slippery, poured the Wharfe into a boiling cauldron of glass-brown water bursting with a million bubbles. The channel is a row of potholes scoured out of the millstone grit by trapped pebbles. Their communal roof collapsed, their separating walls worn away, they form a deadly passage thirty feet deep.

At the top end of the Strid the rocks rose only a few feet apart, the river sluicing furiously between them in two hissing jets. I could see how tempting it would be to try the jump; also how deceptive, for the landing place, polished smooth by spray, slopes backwards towards the rapids.

Over the years many have tried the leap. No one who fails has ever tried a second time. Local stories say that those who fall are seen later, rising from the water in the shape of a ghostly white horse.

A mile above the Strid I came to hump-backed medieval Barden Bridge, and turned up the road to find the broken walls and blank stone-mullioned windows of Barden Tower. A stark ruin with a romantic history: for this 15th-century hunting lodge was once the home of the 'Shepherd Lord', Henry Clifford.

Clifford was born in 1453 in the family home of Skipton Castle. The Wars of the Roses were being fought with massive savagery at that time, and when Henry was eight years old his father, a supporter of the House of Lancaster, was killed by an arrow in the throat at the Battle of Towton. Fearful for the safety of her son, Lady Clifford had the boy taken deep into the hills of Cumbria, where he was brought up *incognito* among the shepherds.

After Henry Tudor won the crown for Lancaster at Bosworth in 1485, Clifford was free to come back and take up residence again at Skipton Castle. But the reclusive and studious Shepherd Lord preferred to live more humbly in his hunting lodge at Barden. Here he spent his time studying astronomy, and sharing his discoveries with a couple of like-minded Blackfriar brothers from Bolton Priory just down the dale.

From Barden Bridge the Wharfe flows in more open country. The valley widens into a green landscape of stone-walled fields and clumps of trees that shelter grey stone farmhouses and barns with high arched doorways. There were herons and diving ducks along the river, careless of the rain; and I, too, hardly gave it a thought until I stamped into the warm, dry hallway of the New Inn at Appletreewick and realised that I was literally soaked through to the skin.

I hung my sodden things to steam dry, and asked about a bite to eat. They had stopped serving lunches, but obligingly found me a cheese sandwich and a pint of beer. The sandwich was great, and as for the beer ... If I had wanted to stay in out of the rain and sample specialist ales till wheeled home in a handcart, the New Inn would have been the place to do it.

Just looking at the pub's beer menu made my head reel. There were Belgian fruit beers made with peaches and cherries, Trappist ales from the Low Countries with 'subtle chocolate tones', smoked beers with the savour of moist beechwood logs. Also Samichlaus, brewed only on 6 December, the strongest beer in the world, 'only appreciated by very seasoned palates'.

I took my seasoned palate away, before temptation could capture it. Back down on the Wharfe I walked the east bank for a change, high in the golden woods on a path knotted with beech roots. Nearing Bolton Abbey, I looked down through the leaves to see a trout fisherman thigh-deep in the rising water, gracefully casting, as oblivious of the rain as any Wharfedale heron or riverbank rambler.

STEPPING OUT – *Walk 81*

MAPS: 1:25,000 Explorer OL2; OS 1:50,000 Explorer 104;

TRAVEL: Rail to Skipton or Ilkley (*www.thetrainline.com*); then buses (service 884 from Skipton, 884/874 from Ilkley; *http://getdown.org.uk/bus*) from the stations to Bolton Abbey. Road – M6 to Jct 29; M65, A56, A59 to Burnley, Colne, Skipton; A59/B6160 to Bolton Abbey. Car park at Bolton Abbey (small payment for parking and access to all paths)

WALK DIRECTIONS: From car park (OS ref SE071539) follow Priory signs through 'hole in the wall' down to River Wharfe and priory ruins (074542). Ascend steps and go through kissing gates to B6160. Right for ¼ mile to memorial fountain (075545); right down steps to riverside path; left for ⅔ mile to Cavendish Pavilion beside footbridge (076552). Continue into Strid Wood, following Green Trail (green arrows) up to the Strid (064564 – 150 yards past big notice board). *NB – Please take great care on the slippery rocks here.*

Follow Green Trail arrow ('Strid car park/Barden' sign) along high level path, passing one stone bridge to reach Barden Bridge (051574). Left up road for 250 yards to see Barden Tower (051572). Return to cross Barden Bridge; continue up east bank of Wharfe. Opposite Drebley (059592), leave river; walk between farm buildings to road; left to cross stream; left (Appletreewick sign). Follow footpath sign to rejoin riverside path; continue to Appletreewick. Reach village by one of 2 paths to right – 1st one has 20p honesty box on gate. Opposite is New Inn.

As you walk out of New Inn, turn left up village street. In ½ mile, right (Bolton Abbey sign) to reach river opposite Drebley. Return to Barden Bridge, and follow east bank path (signed) back to Bolton Abbey.

LENGTH OF WALK: 11 miles (allow 5 hours, plus lunch stop)

CONDITIONS: Easy riverside paths, but great care needed on rocks around The Strid.

REFRESHMENTS: Cavendish Pavilion (01756-710245; *www.cavendishpavilion.co.uk*); New Inn, Appletreewick (01756-720252); Craven Arms, Appletreewick (01756-720270; *www.craven-cruckbarn.co.uk*)

INFORMATION: Yorkshire Dales National Park Information Centre, Grassington, Skipton (01756-751690; *www.yorkshiredales.org.uk*)

Walk 82

Kettlewell and Conistone Moor, North Yorkshire

A ramble in Upper Wharfedale with a remarkable survivor

'I WAS VERY, VERY SICK,' said Marc Woods, 'and very, very lost in that adult ward.' He stared hard at his pint of Guinness, thinking back across fifteen years. 'I felt as if I was the only teenager in the world ever to have had cancer. No-one in the hospital treated me badly, but they just couldn't empathise with how I felt.'

Marc had come to join me for a hill walk in the Yorkshire Dales as a pleasant way of getting in some training for his forthcoming fundraising treks in Ecuador and Nepal. It would be hard to imagine anyone more positive and less self-pitying than the 32-year-old sitting beside me in the Blue Bell Inn at Kettlewell. This man is a mountain hiker, an inspirational lecturer, and a swimmer exceptional enough to win medals at the Seoul, Barcelona, Atlanta and Sydney Olympics – three of those medals gold. Yet at the age of 17, informed that he had developed osteosarcoma in the cuboid bone of his left foot and would have to have that leg amputated, Marc had endured a bitter dark night of the soul.

'The thing about being a teenager cancer sufferer is that you're in a strange, quickly changing physical and emotional state anyway; then you're hit with powerful drugs that make you look and feel terrible, a part of your body's removed, and there's no-one in the hospital that you can talk to who'll really understand what you're going through. You're too old for a children's ward, and too young for an adult ward – in a no-man's-land.'

Glancing out of the Blue Bell's window, we saw the rain curtaining away towards Grassington. Time to make a move. Foot-and-Mouth disease had hit Britain hard this summer, and precautions were still holding most of the Yorkshire Dales footpaths tantalisingly closed, but from the map we had puzzled out an 8-mile circuit along the boundary line where Wharfedale's limestone terraces rise to meet the dour gritstones and bogs of Conistone Moor. The weather forecast man had foreseen a miserable morning and a better afternoon. Full marks for the first half of the prediction, anyway.

We ducked into St Mary's Church to see the stained glass windows to the memory of the Holdsworth boys from Scargill House, killed on active service during the Second World War – beautiful memorials that would be moving in any setting, but particularly in this little Dales village under the moors. Then we struck up a bridlepath that climbed the shoulder of the limestone scar, passing through stone walls intricately and expertly built.

'Swimming's great for the upper body', said Mark, forging uphill over slippery rocks and sedgy bog, 'but I've got to build up these legs of mine for the treks later this autumn.' This mighty achiever was aiming for the high peaks of Ecuador and Nepal to raise money for the Teenage Cancer Trust, a charity set up to ensure that future teenage cancer sufferers are spared some of the indignities he had to face.

'What the TCT wants to do is establish special cancer units dedicated to teenagers and young adults in hospitals in every major city in the UK. Informally dressed staff, internet and e-mail connections, sound systems, sophisticated art materials – what you'd find in the average teenager's bedroom, really. A positive environment makes such a huge difference. The TCT has designed and built 6 already; two in London, and one each in Manchester, Birmingham, Newcastle and Leeds. We're aiming for a lot more – 20 units eventually. But they cost about £500,000 each, so you can see how much fundraising is involved.'

During the 18th and 19th centuries Wharfedale became prosperous through lead mining. Kettlewell, so pretty and well-mannered these days, was then a rough, tough miners' town, thriving on the trade generated by thousands of thirsty men determined to drink away the hardship of the moorland mines, the vile weather and the creeping lead poisoning that gave them blue skins and stripped lung linings. Marc and I found their spoil heaps and stone-clad level shafts as we gained the wall along Conistone Moor and turned south in drifting mist.

Here were the perfect conditions – wet, slippery and treacherous – for Marc to test out his new boots and the play in his replacement leg. Prosthetic limbs have come a long way since Douglas Bader's clanking tin monstrosities; but lateral ankle movement, that automatic moment-to-moment adjustment over rough ground that is taken for granted by able-bodied walkers, is still hard to come by for leg amputees. Marc, however, hopped and scampered over the mud slides and rain-swollen torrents like a mountain goat.

We passed the Seven Stacks – conical stone cairns that dominate their high skyline – and followed the moor wall south. Whoever had built this wall had done a good job. Sagging, leaning and full of holes, it continued to defy wind, weather and time, and made a reliable, if silent, guide over the couple of miles to Capplestone Gate.

As we reached this famed viewpoint over dozens of miles of Yorkshire Dales scenery, the mist lifted as if drawn upwards on wires of sunshine. Fabulous views unfolded to all parts of the compass. We looked across Wharfedale and on over the peaks and shoulders of hills above Littondale, Ribblesdale and Deepdale, all bathed in a pearly wash of weak autumn sun.

We went on down out of the gritstone moors, across the high pastures of Wharfedale where stone walls sliced southwest across the grain of limestone cliffs and bluffs. Soon we were in among wobbly plates of limestone pavement, scoured into cracks by the retreating Ice Age glaciers, then worked on by millennia of water flow. The natural pavement blocks are known as clints, the deep fissures between them as grykes. In summer this scarred landscape supports a rare, delicate flora. Today it bubbled with rainwater. It was an eerie, impressive scene, with twisted hawthorn trees jutting against a stormy, silvered late afternoon sky.

Along the grassy track of the Dales Way long-distance footpath stood Conistone Pie, an isolated limestone outcrop exactly the shape of a pork pie with a domed crust. We passed above limestone cliffs on our way back to Kettlewell in a glowing evening light. 'I really enjoy visiting teenage cancer sufferers,' Marc said. 'What I can tell them is very straightforward: it's vital to see light at the end of the tunnel, and the light can be as bright as you want it to be.'

STEPPING OUT – *Walk 82*

MAPS: OS 1:25,000 Explorers OL2, OL30; 1:50,000 Landranger 98

TRAVEL: Road – M6 to Jct 29; M65 to Colne; A56, A59 to Skipton; B6265 to Threshfield; B6160 to Kettlewell.

WALK DIRECTIONS: From Blue Bell Inn at Kettlewell (OS ref SD969723), cross bridge. Turn left ('Scargill House' sign). In 200 yd, left by maypole. At King's Head PH keep straight ahead up lane. In 400 yd lane bends to left to cross bridge. 20 yd before bridge, keep ahead (974724 – 'BW Whernside Pasture' fingerpost) up hillside on tarmac track. In 100 yd pass through gate, following 'Bridlepath' fingerposts for ½ mile through gates to enter a walled lane (983723). In 200 yd, left ('Bridleway' fingerpost) through wall by spring, on track NE across moor. Cross stile over next wall (988725), and follow posts across moor with cairns to right on skyline. Cross next ladder stile and bear right (992726 – 'Capplestone Gate' footpath fingerpost), keeping wall on your right and walking south, for 2 miles.

At Capplestone Gate (002700 – footpath fingerpost) cross wall by ladder stile. You'll see an OS triangulation pillar a few yards away. Aim SSW across pasture to cross through wall beside rock cliffs (000696); then diagonally down to next wall (track marked 'Conistone Turf Road' on map). Follow wall down below the left-hand of 2 conifer plantations. At bottom, over stile, in 10 yd, left (996690) to go through gate (995686 – 'FP to Conistone' fingerpost) and turn right down Bycliffe Road walled lane. Pass through gap in limestone pavement cliff; immediately bear right (992683 – footpath fingerpost) along Dales Way. At Conistone Pie outcrop, cross wall by ladder stile (989687); keep ahead above Swineber Scar for 1¼ miles through 4 stone walls. At 5th, cross stile (982706 – 'FP Kettlewell' fingerpost); down track through conifer plantation, and on down slope. Just before barn and road, right over stile (978707); down beside wall to road; right to Kettlewell.

LENGTH OF WALK: 7½ miles – allow 3–4 hours

CONDITIONS: Some gentle ascents; boggy parts beside top wall. Many stiles. Walking boots essential.

REFRESHMENTS: Blue Bell Inn, Kettlewell (01756-760230; *www.bluebellinn.co.uk*)

TEENAGE CANCER TRUST: *www.teencancer.org*

Langthwaite, Booze and Arkle Town, Arkengarthdale, North Yorkshire

Pints, pubs and perambulations with the author of the Inn Way guidebooks

MARK REID'S THUNDERBOLT CONVERSION came fifteen years ago – not on the road to Damascus, but on the track across Bellerby Moor. A 16-year-old saxophone player on his way to perform in the Memorial Hall at Reeth, Mark gazed into Swaledale from on high and was instantly enslaved by its sunlit beauty. It was the start of a head-over-heels love affair with the Yorkshire Dales.

Over the ensuing years this dedicated walker has covered thousands of miles on foot, visiting every dale, every village and every pub in the Dales. He gave up a drab job in Birmingham and turned himself into a full-time writer of walking guide books, setting up his own Inn Way publishing company to get them into print. Best of all, believing that no walk is complete without a pint of good beer to round it off, he structured his walks round the most characterful country pubs he could find.

I read Mark Reid's *Inn Way to Black Sheep Pubs*, 25 walks in the Dales between pubs that serve Black Sheep bitter (Prince of Yorkshire beers – and that's saying something), and recognised a true Brother of the Boot. So I came north to try out the Black Sheep walk around remote Arkengarthdale, just north of Swaledale, in the author's company.

It was the foulest of weather forecasts, a real wintry pelt and howl in prospect. But the Dales have their own weather, as every Dalesman knows. The sunshine that Mark and I set out in was a bit watery, perhaps, but it was there, lighting up the alders and sycamores along the Arkle Beck. The beck itself charged greedily down its stony bed, swollen by days of rain, stained with peat to a rich glassy brown.

We crossed the water and turned down dale into the

tightly-huddled village of Langthwaite. 'A lead mining village, a rowdy place, once upon a time,' Mark told me. 'You'll see the scars of the lead workings all over the moors and dale sides around here.' The small stone houses, neat and trim, stood close together in a silence broken only by a barking dog. 'Hard to believe that Arkengarthdale and Swaledale produced most of Britain's lead in the 18th century,' mused Mark, leaning on the hump-back bridge. 'Hundreds of men, dozens of pubs in this dale; lots of noise, lots of flare-ups. Not a peep or a curse nowadays'.

The door of the Red Lion stood open. It was mid-morning: just time for elevenses, in fact. The Black Sheep was sharp-tasting, smooth and clear. Mrs Rowena Hutchinson, long-serving licensee, sat down with us in a cushioned nook for a good chinwag. A real little gem, the Red Lion. SLOB-OUT ('Siren Lure Of Bitter and Outdoor Unwill-ingness Taint') may not have made it into the medical dictionaries, but it's certainly an insidious condition. The following stiff pull up the lane to Booze sorted us out, though.

No pub in Booze, and for centuries no booze either. This linear settlement along the contour of the dale side was set up by sternly Methodist lead miners. John Wesley and his fellow evangelists found fertile ground to nourish the seeds of independent faith in these bleak uplands of northernmost Yorkshire, where work was grind-ingly hard, pay negligible and conditions brutal.

Some locals, though, stuck to older and more arcane beliefs. 'Every farm had its hob,' said Mark, 'a goblin who'd help out around the place for a saucer of cream. And over in Wensleydale they still burn an effigy of Owd Bartle – whoever he was, nobody knows now on the feast of St Bartholomew. I've put the rhyme in my *Inn Way* guidebook, the one they chant round the bonfire, a kind of geogra-phy of the area.'

In Penhill Crags he tore his rags,
At Hunter's Thorn he blew his horn,
At Capplebank Stee he brake his knee,
At Grisgill Beck he brake his neck,
At Wadham's End he couldn't fend,
At Grisgill End he made his end -
Shout, lads, shout!

It sounds like a chase, or maybe a man-hunt. A sinister little rhyme, I thought, looking up at Fremington Edge cutting its hard line against a sky stiff with grey and bruise-purple clouds.

We descended grassy pastures into the dale bottom, and crossed the rushing Arkle Beck to walk upstream to Arkle Town. This thin scatter of houses was once the capital of Arkengarthdale, with its own fine church. Beck floods washed out the church's foundations, and all that is left now is a handful of 18th-century gravestones in a field on the river bank. Ann Harker, Mary Coate and Thomas Alderson lie under the rain-pearled grass: good dale names all, still to be found hereabouts.

A green road led up from Arkle Town, rising southwards across the open heathery moor. Rain and wind came suddenly up over the crest and beat into our faces, so that we were gleaming like seals in our waterproofs by the time we reached the moor road among the scabs and scars of lead mining.

The grey and pink spoil heaps ride out from the hillsides like inverted ships' hulls, some lightly sprinkled with grass, others as naked and repellent of plant life as when they were formed by the miners. As for the hushes, those hill becks whose water was dammed and then released to wash away the vegetation and reveal the ore beneath, their channels remain as torn and naked as ever.

Mark and I wandered through this landscape of industrial derelic-tion, tumbled and bare, that threw into greater relief the hard beauty of the moors that cradled it. We found the black hole of a mine level, its entrance neatly framed in dressed stone, and peered down the flooded, fern-sprouting tunnel into the dark heart of the hill.

It was Charles Bathurst, the local landowner, who developed these 'C.B.' mines up here on the moors above Langthwaite in the 18th century. The C.B. Inn on the road below is named in memory of him. That was where Mark and I finished our walk, shaking the rain off and settling down to relive the day over a bacon butty and a pint of bitter. The second Black Sheep, I can report, tastes even better than the first.

STEPPING OUT – *Walk 83*

MAP: OS 1:25,000 Explorer OL30; 1:50,000 Landranger 92

TRAVEL: Road – M6 to Jct 38; A685 to Kirkby Stephen; B6270 to Reeth; left on minor road to Langthwaite (3 miles)

WALK DIRECTIONS: From CB Inn (OS ref NZ000031) turn right along dale road. In a few yards, right ('Hurst' bridleway fingerpost) down to cross Arkle Beck (002033). Climb track to left of Scar House (003034) into woods. Before white gate, bear right on track through woods, then across fields to lane above Langthwaite (005025). For Red Lion PH turn right downhill; to continue walk, keep ahead uphill on tarmac lane which becomes rough track. Follow it through Booze hamlet. Pass through Town Farm gate (015025); immediately right on flagged path through 2 gates. Follow footpath fingerposts down across fields to double fingerpost (017022) above Storthwaite Hall.

Bear right along hillside; in 100 yd left ('Fremington' fingerpost) downhill to cross Slei Gill Beck and pass Storthwaite Hall (018022). Follow walled lane, then field path to cross Arkle Beck by footbridge (022019). Continue on right bank (yellow arrow waymark). In ¼ mile, right between stone walls. At West Raw Croft farm (022016) bear right on gravelled track; in 5 yd keep ahead across grass, then through red metal gate. Continue through gaps and stiles (yellow blob waymarks), walking upstream with beck a fields away to the right, until you rejoin it at 013019. Continue for ¼ mile beside beck; pass footbridge (010021 do not cross); climb steps on left to cross old graveyard field. Through stile (009020); ahead up lane to turn left along dale road (007019).

In 150 yd, over cattle grid. Immediately right up moorland bank past blank wooden signboard. In 100 yd cross narrow green track; in another 20 yd, cross another track. 100 yd beyond, bear right on wide green track (008014) for 1 mile to road (993009). Right for 1 mile. Just before road passes between spoil heaps (997024), left on track ('footpath only' fingerpost) to Cocker House farm (997029). Continue through two gates; then right downhill to dale road beside school (000030). Left to C.B. Inn.

LENGTH: 7 miles

REFRESHMENTS: C.B. Inn (01748-884567; *www.cbinn.co.uk*) and
Red Lion Inn (01748-884218; *www.langthwaite.free-online.co.uk*), Langthwaite.

GUIDEBOOK: *The Inn Way to Black Sheep Pubs* by Mark Reid
(Innway Publications, *www.innway.co.uk*)

NORTH EAST

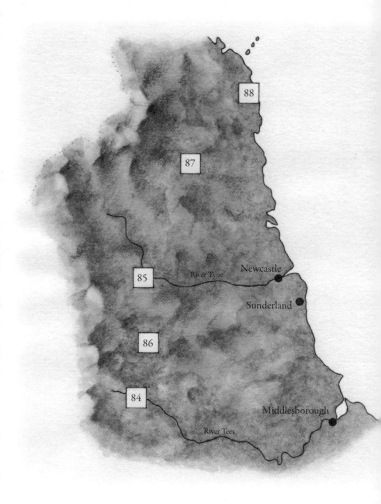

Walk 84

Upper Teesdale, County Durham

Springtime heaven: rare flowers and wild birds beside the River Tees

L APWINGS WERE FLYING above the Teesdale meadows, flapping against the stiff spring wind as they cried their name in creaking voices. Seeing the two humans approaching, they had become agitated on account of their newly hatched chicks crouching in the lee of sedge clumps. 'Holding their numbers well this year,' remarked Chris McCarty as I steadied the binoculars against the gusts. 'And listen! That's a sound you don't hear too often.' Through the incessant *pee-wit! pee-wit!* of the lapwings I made out a background whirr. 'See the snipe? He's drumming – look, just over our heads!' A small dark body was diving groundwards, long bill held out in front like an aeroplane skid. 'It's all to impress the ladies,' said Chris. 'He holds out his tail feathers, and the air drums them as it rushes by.'

It was a piece of great good fortune when Chris McCarty found his diary was flexible enough to let him spend a day walking with me through the meadows and over the fells of Upper Teesdale, a few miles above High Force waterfall. Natural England manages nearly 20,000 acres hereabouts as a National Nature Reserve, and as Site Manager there isn't much Chris doesn't know about these magnificent and beautiful uplands. 'Come in late spring, ideally,' he'd told me over the phone. 'You'll get all the ground-nesting birds in full cry, the river's generally spectacular at that time of year after the snow's melted, and then of course ... well, have you ever seen our arctic-alpine flowers in full bloom?'

Actually, I never had. I longed to set eyes on those pearls of Teesdale, rare and delicate survivals from a post-Ice Age Britain. It was John Hillaby's sublime recounting of his 1965 Land's End to John O'Groats walk in spring, *Journey Through Britain*, that first infused my imagination with the magic of this unique flora. 'No botanical

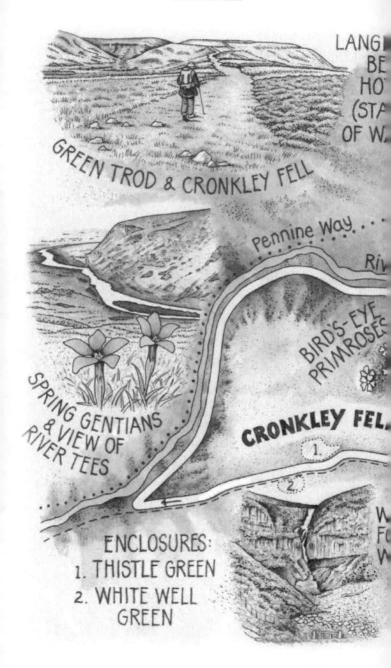

GREEN TROD & CRONKLEY FELL

LANG
BE
HO
(STA
OF W.

Pennine Way . . .

Riv

BIRD'S-EYE
PRIMROSES

SPRING GENTIANS
& VIEW OF
RIVER TEES

CRONKLEY FEL

1.

2.

W
FO
W

ENCLOSURES:
1. THISTLE GREEN
2. WHITE WELL
   GREEN

UPPER TEESDALE
COUNTY DURHAM

Langdon Beck

B6277

YOUTH HOSTEL

NEW HOUSE

DRUMMING SNIPE

HIGH HOUSE

CRONKLEY FARM

GLOBEFLOWERS

Fell Dike Sike

HIGH FORCE W'FALL

LEAD MINE RUINS

Green Trod

MOUNTAIN PANSIES

ALL

E

name-dropping,' he wrote, 'can give an adequate impression of the botanical jewels sprinkled on the ground above High Force ... In this valley a tundra has been marvellously preserved; the glint of colour, the reds, deep purples, and blues have the quality of Chartres glass.'

Last night I had been to gaze on High Force, first from the Pennine Way path beside the lip of the fall, then from the viewing place at its foot. Swollen with a winter's rain and snowmelt, the Tees crashed over its 70-foot step of gleaming black dolerite in a single mighty sluice of creamy yellow water, a furious and thunderous outrush that fell like a hammer into a basin misty with spray and brilliant with miniature rainbows. Today the rainbow colours seemed to have migrated upriver and spread themselves generously across pastures and fellsides.

Under the spell of John Hillaby's account and the observant prompting of Chris McCarty, I found myself wandering from one floral treat to the next like a kid in a sweetshop. The rain-sodden pastures beside the Tees, at first glance composed of thick grass, revealed themselves on closer inspection to be a rich salad of herbs. The leaves of great burnet and pignut, said Chris, are a good indicator of unspoiled ancient grassland. Left unblasted by chemicals and allowed to lie uncut until their flowers have set seed, the riverside fields yield pink and white milkmaids, shiny marsh marigolds, slender purple spikes of early marsh orchid, acid yellow balls of globeflower. Beautiful, one and all. But where were the arctic-alpines, the stars of the show?

Like most northern dales, Upper Teesdale lies separated into very distinct agricultural strata. The green valley-bottom pastures known as inbye land give way to rougher 'intake' land further up the dale sides. This higher land is boggy and wet, lightly grazed to prevent its cover becoming too wild and dense – ideal conditions, in fact, for wading birds such as snipe and redshank to nest and rear their young. Beyond the intake wall, darker and rougher country rises to the open heather moorland that rolls away across the fell tops.

As Chris and I crossed the racing Tees by way of the footbridge at Cronkley and began to climb towards the intake land, we started to spot the delicate arctic-alpine flowers on ledges and in crevices of the rocks among tattered juniper bushes. I got down on my knees and crawled along, transfixed by their fragile beauty. Mountain pansies, boldly coloured purple flowers with a broad lower lip of yellow striped with black; one or two tiny Teesdale violets; and then the glorious bird's-eye primroses, delicate, deep pink, with an intense yellow eye glowing at the heart of each flower. Why had they clung on here, in this particular dale? Chris McCarty, kneeling alongside, ticked off the points on his fingers.

'They're here essentially because of lack of competition. The climate in Upper Teesdale stays cold and wet till late on in spring, which most British flowers can't deal with. And the formation of the Whin Sill, the step in the River Tees down at High Force, is the other main factor. Think of it as a horizontal volcano about 300 million years ago, squeezing its lava like toothpaste between two bedding planes of carboniferous limestone. It baked the surrounding limestone into crystals full of minerals – sugar limestone, we call it, see?' He scooped up a palm full of glittering crystals like dull little diamonds. 'They've got exactly the balance of nutrients that the arctic-alpines need. A huge slice of luck, and it gave us this fabulous flora.'

We climbed the well-worn track of the Pennine Way above Cronkley Farm, then turned aside along the ancient cattle-droving road called the Green Trod. Beside the hissing jet of White Force waterfall we ate our sandwiches under the ruined gable of an old mine 'shop', a bothy where lead miners once sheltered between their shifts in the levels of White Force's mine. Then it was on up the long nape of Cronkley Fell to the fenced and walled enclosures on the broad summit. White stars of spring sandwort spattered the sugar limestone. Thousands of bird's-eye primroses trembled in the wind. Seeded in this rich pink carpet, trumpet-shaped spring gentians of a celestial royal blue vibrated as if blowing a silent paean to spring.

Down by the roaring Tees we turned back along the river bank, walking silently now. The scratchy cries of the nesting lapwings recalled the creaking of fracturing ice, and I thought of the glaciers melting away northwards 10,000 years ago, in retreat from the deep valley they had gouged, leaving behind a naked landscape ready for seeding with the ancestors of Teesdale's gentians and violets, pink primroses and gaudy pansies. John Hillaby summed it all up to perfection: 'For me Teesdale was more beautiful than I could have imagined; certainly more strange and evocative than I could have foreseen.'

STEPPING OUT – *Walk 84*

MAP: OS 1:25,000 Explorer OL31; 1:50,000 Landranger 91 or 92

TRAVEL: Road – A1 to Scotch Corner, left on A66 to Barnard Castle, B6277 to Middleton-in-Teesdale; or M6 to Junction 38, right on A685 to Brough, B6276 to Middleton-in-Teesdale. From Middleton, B6277 Alston road to Langdon Beck.

WALK DIRECTIONS: From Langdon Beck Hotel (OS ref NY853312) walk down B6277 towards Middleton-in-Teesdale. In ¾ mile pass Langdon Beck Youth Hostel and turn right (860304) down track past New House to cross cattle grid. Right to Saur Hill Bridge (855302). Don't cross, but bear left (Pennine Way/PW 'High Force' fingerpost) along bank of beck for ¾ mile to cross River Tees (862293). Left along farm track ('PW') through Cronkley Farm yard. Follow yellow arrows/National Trail acorn waymarks south, through gates and up to saddle between crags, following wall and flagged PW path into Open Access land. Pass stone marked 'PW' and 'GT' (Green Trod); PW bears left here, but you keep ahead through kissing gate to cross Fell Dike Sike beck and turn right along Green Trod path (861281).

Follow broad green track of GT up breast of Cronkley Fell and over top. Keep largest fenced enclosure (Thistle Green) on your right (844284); then follow cairns, keeping last enclosure (White Well Green) on your left (840283). Descend to River Tees (828282); bear right along river bank for 2½ miles to pass High House barn (857294). Follow 2 yellow arrows through gate; aim across wide pasture towards big wood-walled shed; then look for bridge to left of it, and aim for that (862293). Re-cross Tees; left along far bank, retracing steps to Langdon Beck.

LENGTH: 9 miles

CONDITIONS: Can be boggy underfoot; walking boots and raingear recommended.

REFRESHMENTS: None en route; take snack.

MOOR HOUSE NNR: Guided walks, volunteer days, information etc. 01833-622374; *www.ecn.ac.uk/sites/moorh.html*; *www. naturalengland.org.uk*

JOURNEY THROUGH BRITAIN BY JOHN HILLABY: (Constable 1995)

Hexham, Dipton Mill and Corbridge, Northumberland

Border country disputed down the centuries by Romans, Vikings, Scots and English

'Morning,' growled the farmer in flat cap and gumboots, as he came stumping down Hallstile Bank, 'bloody wet.'

That summed it up – Northumberland in early winter, on a mild, gauzy, oozing kind of morning. The Tyne Valley lay drowning in a freckling misty rain, and the pale stone houses of Hexham clung to their ledge above the river as if trying to get their grey slate heads above the valley murk.

No rain veils, however unwelcome, could detract from the dramatic shape of Hexham, piled up on its river terrace with the stubby tower of the 800-year-old abbey church capping the little town. Up in the market place at the top of Hallstile Bank, with the abbey on one side and the grim medieval Moot Hall gatehouse and old town gaol on the other, I caught the flavour of an ancient market town that grew up on a crossroads, sacked by Vikings and raided by Scots again and again, a place of thick stone walls and narrow slit windows developed through centuries of Border fire and sword.

Into the abbey I skulked, intending simply to wait out the rain. But I stayed an hour in fascination. The interlaced burial cross shaft of Acca, 8th-century Bishop of Hexham, is here, alongside the elaborately carved pagan memorial stone of Flavinius, a 25-year-old standard bearer with Petriana's Cavalry Regiment of the Roman Imperial Army.

In the dark, maze-like crypt I found inscribed pagan altar slabs, and ornate fragments of carved Roman stonework. Hadrian's Wall is only three miles north of Hexham. Builders of churches, houses and farms along the Tyne Valley plundered the cut and dressed stonework of the abandoned forts and villas for the best part of two millennia after the Romans left Britain.

'Bert Pagan, Builder,' read the sign on the side of a van in Beaumont Street. And there was Mr Pagan himself, chipping at a large stone block. Tradition lives long in Northumberland, it seems.

At the end of Beaumont Street, under a slowly clearing sky, I passed the striking memorial to Lt Col George Elliott Benson, who 'fell while commanding his column at the Battle of Brakenlaagie, Oct 30 1901'. The sculptor caught the handsomely moustachioed Col Benson in mid-stride, one hand on hip and the other clutching a pair of binoculars, gazing south-west towards his burial place in South Africa 6,000 miles away.

The rain had stopped, but every bare twig held a diamond drop as I headed south out of Hexham up the banks of narrow hill burns. In the woods around Wydon Burn, following a slippery path over boulders, my breath smoked in the still, water-laden air under dripping trees. High above on the crest of Plover Hill I took a last look back over the thick steamy trough of the Tyne Valley. Then I gazed forward into the rolling valley of the West Dipton Burn, from which long moor ridges rose to a bright silver southern horizon where fleets of lumpy grey clouds drifted like dream battleships.

It was well into tupping season, and most of the ewes in the high stone-walled pastures carried red blotches of raddle on their rumps. Among them the ram stalked like an emperor, wearing a leather harness and chest-pack of red raddle. He delicately sniffed the hindquarters of one of his harem, then raised his black muzzle quizzically to the sky like an oenophile pondering the provenance of a particularly subtle vintage. But it was raw sex on his mind, as he soon demonstrated with great vigour, not at all put out by this voyeur-of-passage.

Down beside the West Dipton Burn, the screeching and swearing of a jay was the loudest sound. Clear brown water gurgled under mats of ferns and ivy. A narrow secret valley, where the burn fussed in white bubbles over rapids to pass the welcoming little pub at Dipton Mill.

I didn't really need a fire on a day as mild as this, but the way the flames flickered on the dark panelling of the bar was irresistible. So was the vegetable soup, and the strong Whapweasel bitter. Stumbling out an hour later, cheeks aglow and half asleep, I was glad of the bracing effects of a chilly breeze that had stolen into the valley.

On 15 May 1464 the House of Lancaster suffered catastrophic Wars of the Roses defeat at the Battle of Hexham, fought hereabouts on the hill slopes above the meeting place of West Dipton Burn and Devil's Water. There can be no doubt of the fearful slaughter of Lancastrian supporters that took place in the peaceful valley. But legend spins a more romantic tale. Margaret of Anjou, wife of the defeated King Henry VI, was hidden in a cave beside the West Dipton Burn by a robber, so the story goes. He had intended to plunder her, but 'was charmed with the confidence she reposed in him, and vowed to abstain from all injury against the princess'.

The only sign of violence today was the distant pop of a shotgun, aimed at some unfortunate pheasant in the next valley. I followed a little rocky defile among clumps of heather and broom through the wide coniferous acres of Dipton Wood. The air, clear now in mid-afternoon, smelt of wet earth and fresh pine resin, a very Northumbrian savour.

Down at Corbridge station I checked the timetable. Just time to cross the river and view the Roman settlement of Corstopitum: low grey walls of ruined houses and forts, and a museum full of pottery, arrow heads and wonderful stone carvings. The famous Corbridge Lion, with a bearded face disarmingly like that of Sir Francis Drake, crouched threatingly over its kill, defying all comers: a symbol of Roman power and defiance, here at the northernmost limit of their empire.

STEPPING OUT – *Walk 85*

MAP: OS 1:25,000 Explorer OL43; 1:50,000 Landranger 87

TRAVEL: Rail to Hexham (*www.thetrainline.com*)

Road – A69 from east or west. Car park opposite railway station.

WALK DIRECTIONS: From Hexham railway station (OS ref NY940643) walk up to market place and abbey (935641). Along Beaumont Street to Benson statue; cross into St Wilfrid's Road. Bear right at top; in 20 yd, keep ahead along lane. Head up wooded Cowgate Burn valley, keeping burn on right. In ¼ mile cross burn on stone bridge (933635), up into playing field. Along edge of wood, then right bank of reservoir; between boulders to road (933632). Left past Wydon Burn House; up stony track to road. In 100 yd, right over stile (929627 – 'Causey Hill Road' fingerpost); follow fence on right to stile into wood. Keep Wydon Burn on right for ⅓ mile. 2 stiles and boggy field lead from trees to road (925626); left uphill to T-junction (925624). Over stile opposite ('West Dipton Burn' fingerpost).

Follow stile and gates to pass West Peterel Field farmhouse (923616). In 2nd field beyond farm, bear right through gateway; descend with fence on left, through gate into trees, down to West Dipton Burn (921611). Left for ¾ mile, with burn on right, to cross road (930610 – 'Newbiggin' sign). NB: Dipton Mill pub to right here). Continue on left bank of burn. Opposite Hole House, cross to right bank (935611); in ¼ mile, yellow arrow points right up steep bank to reach lane to left of a house (939608). Left to road at Newbiggin (944608).

Right uphill for 1 mile; on right bend go left (947595 – stile, fingerpost). Follow yellow arrow waymarks down through woods on good track; then left (951596) on path to cross Linnelswood footbridge (951597). Follow yellow arrows out of trees, along farm drive to road (959603). Right; in 100 yd, left into woods ('Corbridge' fingerpost). In 200 yd keep left at Lightwater Cottages; follow yellow arrows for 1½ miles to crossroads (976615). Ahead ('Prospect Hill' sign) for 300 yd; left (980617 – 'Corbridge' fingerpost) along field edge. Through gate beside wood; left along wood edge; then down path through wood to High Town (979628). Yellow arrow points right along field edge, then along Ladycutters Lane. By pole with black and yellow 'H' (988631), left over stile, down hedge; cross A695 (take care!) and stile opposite ('Corbridge Station' sign). Descend to Corbridge Station (989635).

For Corbridge village and church, cross bridge and keep ahead. Corbridge Roman site (982648) is ¾ mile from village centre – follow brown signs).

LENGTH OF WALK: 10 miles, station to station.

CONDITIONS: Woodland paths by Wydon and West Dipton Burns can be slippery, muddy and awkward. Wear proper hiking boots.

REFRESHMENTS: Dipton Mill PH (01434-606577; *www. diptonmill.co.uk*)

CORBRIDGE ROMAN SITE: *http://www.english-heritage.org.uk/ server/show/nav.13179*

INFORMATION AND WALKABOUT GUIDE LEAFLETS: Hexham TIC, Wentworth Car Park (01434-652220)

Walk 86

Blanchland and Rookhope, Co. Durham

Mines, moors and music of the Durham Dales

I HADN'T SEEN ANDY LYDDIATT since his return to the north-east. We'd been fellow students and aspiring musicians at Durham University in the 1960s, and now he was back living on the edge of the county's western moorlands. Old friendships are like silver spoons – all the better for a bit of polishing. It seemed the most natural thing in the world to invite myself up to Durham to visit Andy and go walking with him through the Durham Dales.

A rising wind was beginning to thrash the trees as we set off from Blanchland, an 18th-century estate village so full of charm it felt like a crime to walk away from it. Lord Crewe laid out Blanchland in its steep valley by the River Derwent in the 1750s, on the site of an early medieval monastery. The village post office is tucked into a niche in the old monastic gateway, and the Abbot's Lodging is now the ghost-ridden and crankily characterful Lord Crewe Arms Hotel.

The sky was grey and thick by the time we had breasted the hill and got out onto the open moors. But the threatened rain never actually arrived, and gleams of wintry sun broke through from time to time. They lit up slopes and shoulders of rolling brown moorland, a vast sea of heather dipping to green walled inbye land, in which we saw no other walkers all day. Though the Durham moors are crossed by a superb network of footpaths, they are still undiscovered and blissfully lonely walking country, a rare treat.

County Durham is forever associated with its huge, now defunct coal mining industry. But here in the western hills it was lead mining that dominated the life and work of the local villages. The Durham Dales – silent, deserted uplands today – were hives of industrial activity during the Victorian heyday of the lead mines. The Derwent Mining Company employed tens of thousands of local men, mining the ore from deep levels and drifts on the moors, smelting it at great smelt mills in the valleys below, and carrying the 150-lb pigs of lead by packhorse, cart and mineral railway to market in Newcastle.

Walking south across the moors, Andy and I passed the Presser Lead Mine's pumping station with its squat chimney and pyramid roof. We were steering for two tall stone-built smokestacks that lay ahead – the Sikehead Mine's pumping engine chimney, and the broken topped Jeffrey's Chimney which disgorged deadly lead vapour brought along a mile-long flue tunnel from Jeffrey's smelting mill far below. Each year some wretch would have to climb the interior of the chimney and scrape off the 'fume', the condensed lead vapour, for re-smelting. 'We get from this a great quantity of lead,' noted the Derwent Lead Company's agent, 'sufficient to remunerate for the expenses of making the tunnel.'

As we turned down the sloping track of an old industrial railway and descended Bolt's Law Incline towards Rookhope, the talk was all of Northumbrian music. I'd always marvelled at Andy's skill on the concertina, and the session of tunes we'd enjoyed at his kitchen table last night had confirmed that he'd got even better. I had been emboldened to put my melodeon across my knee and hack out a couple of tunes on my own account. 'Hmmm,' was Andy's only comment, 'I *think* you might do better to forget about that left hand until you've got the right a little bit more under control.' Old friends – they give it to you straight, eh?

The murk was beginning to clear away and the slate roofs of Rookhope stood out in a shaft of sun against the pale green bulk of Northgate Fell. We were glad enough to reach the Rookhope Inn and duck in out of the cold wind.

Back in its lead-mining heyday Rookhope played host to hundreds of miners who would sleep during the week in unsanitary, over-crowded 'lodging shops' and walk across the moors to their home villages at weekends. The Boltsburn Mine was the most productive in England, and the Rookhope smelting mill clattered and fumed by night and day.

Nowadays the little village on its curve of road is a quiet spot in a remote valley. But unlike many such back-country places, Rookhope's village life is thriving. The Rookhope Inn is run with the social welfare of the village at heart. 'Up one end there's a pool and darts room for the young lads,' said the landlord, 'but they're beginning to come down here and talk to the old boys in the bar, join in the singing. And that's really good for the life of this place.'

A nice sharp pint of bitter and we were ready for the homeward trek. It was a long, steady pull up the shoulder of Rimey Law, with black grouse bursting out of the heather screeching '*kekk-kekk-kekk*', and rabbits swerving away from under our boots. In bare patches among the heather we found tiny fluorescent green lichens, some shaped like trumpets, others like miniature frills delicately edged with scarlet. The moor wind blew hard, driving the steely waters of Burnhead Dam into black wavelets.

We dropped down a grassy slope to the old fluorspar mine of Whiteheaps, its few buildings standing forlorn, the scar of its flue still forming a long straight seam in the flank of the moor. Then it was on along the valley floor through larchwoods and pine groves, that evening's tunes already tickling at our fingers ends as we dropped back down into Blanchland.

STEPPING OUT – *Walk 86*

MAP: OS 1:25,000 Explorer 307; 1:50,000 Landranger 87

TRAVEL: Road – A1(M) to Jct 63, A693/A692 to Consett; or M6 to Jct 40, A686 to Alston, A689 to Stanhope. From Consett or Stanhope, B6278 to Edmundbyers; B6306 to Blanchland.

WALK DIRECTIONS: Leaving Lord Crewe Arms Hotel (OS ref NY966504), turn left through Blanchland village square, following B6306 across bridge and uphill. In 200 yd, right beside 'Blanchland' sign (967502); follow by-road for ⅓ mile to sharp right bend. Ahead through gate (968496) and walk south over skyline with fence on your left, and on across Buckshott Fell for a mile.

Just before a gate on the left and a fence across the track, bear diagonally right (971480) on track to road. Turn right (963477) for 300 yds, then left at the upper of 2 footpath fingerposts (962479) on track over Allenshields and Buckshott Moor, aiming for Jeffrey's Chimney (959466). When near it, bear right through gate, then left along wall of Sikehead Dam reservoir. At end, beside chimney, bear right on track, aiming for summit of Bolt's Law. In 200 yd, turn left at yellow arrow; in another 200 yd, left again (957464 – yellow arrow) to gate in fence (959463). Don't cross, but bear right on track (yellow arrow), SW across moor for ⅔ mile.

Pass lone pine tree and yellow arrow post beyond; at 2nd arrow post (952456) turn left. In ¼ mile cross fence by stile (953452) and keep ahead, to turn right (952450) along old railway track for 1¾ miles down to Rookhope and Rookhope Inn (939429).

Leaving inn, keep ahead along road to cross burn; immediately right (footpath sign) up steep track which soon bends left towards High House Farm. Pass through first wall and turn diagonally right off track (938432) to go through gate in top far corner of next field. Bear NNW across moorland for 1 mile, making for faint nick in first skyline, bump on second skyline, and on over third skyline to turn right along road (931446). In ¾ mile bear right off road (936456 – footpath fingerpost) on moorland track. Aim slightly to left of 2 chimneys ahead, keeping above Burnhead Dam; then steer for gate in wall ahead, then for Whiteheaps mine building in valley below. At Whiteheaps Dam (945465) bear right into bottom of narrow valley; turn left past old mine building (949467) and on down track to road at Ramshaw (950473).

Bear right along valley road ('Blanchland' sign) for ¾ mile. Just past pumping station (above and on right), go left off road (958482 – footpath fingerpost). In 100 yd, turn right (yellow arrow) through trees, heading north for nearly a mile to road (958497). Left downhill; just before Bay Bridge, turn right (958499 – footpath fingerpost) through trees and back to Blanchland.

LENGTH: 12 miles

CONDITIONS: Some miles of rough moorland walking. Take compass and full wet weather gear. Grouse shooting may be in progress – enquire locally.

REFRESHMENTS: Rookhope Inn, Rookhope (01388-515215; *www. rookhope.com*)

Rothbury and the Simonside Hills, Northumberland

Over the Northumbrian hills with the Border minstrels

Driving into Rothbury on a sharp morning, I let Kathryn Tickell take over the steering. Not in body, you understand, but in spirit. The hum and skirl of the Queen of the Northumbrian small-pipes pushed up from the stereo speakers and out through the open car window, floating the haunting air of 'Rothbury Hills' across the green meadows of Coquetdale. Kathryn was playing, exceptionally beautifully; but I had in my mind's eye another figure, an elderly man, bespectacled and slight, sitting on a folding chair against a farmhouse wall with the pipe bellows in the crook of one elbow, his stubby working man's fingers poised on the chanter.

Like so many other lovers of traditional music back in the 1970s, I had my initial taste of Northumberland's native instrument courtesy of 'The Border Minstrel', a hard-to-get LP that showcased the fantastically swift and exciting playing of Billy Pigg. A farmer at Wood Hall in Coquetdale, and monarch of the piping realm back in his day, Billy was a touchstone to me – not only for his liquid yet vigorous style, but also for the mystery and magic inherent in his tune titles: 'Crookit Bawbee', 'I'll Get Wedded In My Auld Claes', 'The High Level Hornpipe', and above all 'The Wild Hills of Wannies'. Where or what Wannies might be, I never found out. Yet every time I come in sight of the Simonside Hills, the shapely range that cradles the southern skyline from Rothbury on the River Coquet, I see Billy Pigg in his best suit by the wall and hear again that strange tune, as wild and mournful as a curlew's call, twining in and out of the more slow and stately 'Rothbury Hills'.

Rothbury is a real country town where you can buy bootlaces across the street from the pork pie shop. That's what I did, and then crossed

ROTHBURY & THE
SIMONSIDE HILLS
NORTHUMBERLAND

GREAT TOSSON
PELE TOWER

COQUETDALE

GREAT TOSSON

TOSSON
MILL

PELE
TOWER

LION-FACED ROCKS,
OLD STELL CRAG

SIMONSIDE RIDGE
FROM THE BEACON

SIMONSIDE

DOVE

SIMONSIDE

OLD STELL
CRAG

HILLS

QUEEN'S HEAD
(START OF WALK)

ROTHBURY
BAKERY

ROTHBURY

WHITTON
PELE
TOWER

WHITTON

COQUET

SHARPE'S
FOLLY

WHITTON BURN

WHITTONDEAN

CUP-&-RING
MARKED
ROCKS

LORDENSHAWS
HILL FORT

SESSION AT
THE QUEEN'S HEAD

THE BEACON

the Coquet and struck up the hillside by way of Whitton. In the trees around Whitton pele tower the rooks were cawing like pub singers the morning after the night before. The rookery could well have been here for centuries by the time the Lord of Harbottle built the stronghold tower in the turbulent 1380s, an era when this border region was a battleground where the English fought the Scots, the Borderers fought each other, and the reivers or roving cattle thieves picked off the goods and terminated the lives of anyone who could not defend himself. What would such fierce freebooters have made of the gentle and philanthropic astrologer Dr Thomas Sharpe, son of an 18th-century Archbishop of York, whose observatory turret (known to all as Sharpe's Folly) stands beside the lane above Whitton? Short and bloody work, probably.

Up at the crest of the rise I found the concentric rampart rings of the Iron Age hill fort of Lordenshaws, foregrounded by a massive rock whose lumpy surface lay indented with dozens of cup-and-ring marks – unfathomable ritual symbols some 5,000 years old, very characteristic of Northumberland. Their purpose may be forgotten, but the setting still inspires wonder and admiration: the noble whaleback of Simonside rising as a backdrop, a long ridge broken by a line of stepped peaks striding west towards the distant pale blue billows of the Cheviot Hills.

A brisk wind sent cloud shadows racing along the flanks of the hill as I climbed. Beetles as green and shining as emeralds went crawling over the stones of Simonside. Winged bombshells of red grouse burst cackling from the heather, and a lark sang overhead like a rook's most jealous dream. Big cat faces stared majestically west under Old Stell Crag – bluffs of rock sculpted into leonine profiles by millennia of frost, rain, drought and wind. Striding the ridge in step with Billy Pigg's tumbling tune, looking ahead to Cheviot rolling in blue undulations towards the Scottish border, then cartwheeling round to gaze back east to a steely glint of sea fifteen miles off in Druridge Bay, I felt as if I could run and race up here for ever.

At the cairn on Simonside's peak I crouched in the lee of the rocks and savoured my lunch of Rothbury-baked pork pie, with the fifty-mile view for a relish. A wild billy-goat ambled near, magnificent in a trailing rug of a coat and a pair of backswept horns that would make even a Border reiver think twice. Truffling among the rocks for heather shoots, he suddenly became aware of the trespasser on his preserves. His grunt of deep disgust and glare from a pair of devilish eyes were as good as a regal dismissal.

Down from Simonside I scrambled, dropping down through pine forest and open pasture towards Great Tosson's shattered stump of a pele tower. By the time I had reached the buttercup meadows beside the Coquet, the internal jukebox had abandoned the marching beat of 'The Wild Hills of Wannies' in favour of the dreamy flow of 'Whittingham Green Lane', a slow boat of a tune that floated me smoothly back to Rothbury bridge.

That night there was a mighty session in the Queen's Head. Lynn Tocker and Frankie McGuire from the all-stops-out band Lyra Celtica were in town, and together with their friend Dave and young check-shirted Jamie Donnelly they tore into it with a snap and panache that Billy Pigg himself might have envied. Accordions flared, whistles scurried, bodhrans thundered. They played the Barrowburn Reel, a Coquetdale tune as jaunty as a dipper on a stone. They played 'Shew's the Way to Wallington', 'Sir John Fenwick's the Flower Amang them A'', and a slow version of 'Rothbury Hills' at my request which set that whole day's walk unreeling in glorious technicolour in my private skull cinema. It all lurched to a stop some time in the wee hours, and I lurched to bed soon after, my head crammed full of wild country and wilder music.

STEPPING OUT – *Walk 87*

MAPS: OS 1:25,000 Explorer OL42; 1:50,000 Landranger 81

TRAVEL: Road – from south, A1 to Morpeth, A697 towards
Wooler, B6344 to Rothbury; from north, A1 to Alnwick, B6341
to Rothbury.

WALK DIRECTIONS: Opposite Queen's Head Hotel in Rothbury
centre, turn down Bridge Street to cross River Coquet (OS ref
NU059016). Turn right; immediately left up steep lane ('St
Oswald's Way'/SOW fingerpost). At sharp left bend (058014)
keep ahead past house gate and through kissing gate. 'Whitton'
fingerpost points up slope; ignore, and bear half right (footpath
fingerpost) across field, following yellow footpath arrows (YA)
and black SOW waymarks to road at T-junction (056011). Left
along road ('Whitton'). In 200 yards pass Hill Cottage on right;
in 20 yards, right (SOW; 'bridleway Whitton Hillhead'). Follow
this bridleway past Sharpe's Folly (058009) and on for ½ mile.
Left up farm lane (053003; SOW; 'Whittondean, Lordenshaws
Fort' fingerpost), following arrows through Whittondean
farmhouse garden. Bear right, descending to cross Whitton
Burn (053999). Follow white posts past pond to gate; bear half
left (SOW) up hillside to join green path, climbing for nearly ½
mile. At saddle (053992), bear right to prominent cup-and-ring
marked rock (053991), or left to Lordenshaws hill fort (055992);
then forward to cross road at car park (052988; SOW).

Follow clear stepped path uphill; near crest of ridge, bear
right (3 arrows on post; 'Permissive Path') on track which
follows ridge for 1¾ miles across peaks of The Beacon, Dove
Crag and Old Stell Crag to reach summit cairn on Simonside
(024987). Descend steeply to bear left along forest road. In 150
yards, right (021988; YA) on well-trodden path through heather,
down into forest, descending on rubbly path to cross forest
road (023993; YA) and on down to track at forest edge. Right
(023999; YA); in 50 yards, left through gate (YA) across 2 fields
and ladder stile to gate (023002). Follow wall on right downhill
for 300 yards; where it angles away to right (025004), bear half
right down steep field, through kissing gate and on down to stile
into lane (027006) at Great Tosson.

Right past farmhouse and pele tower ruin (029005); take left fork in lane for 500 yards to T-junction (034009). Left round bend for 200 yards; right (No Through Road; 'Tosson Mill') past mill and Weaver's Cottage and on along lane for ½ mile to cross River Coquet (042012). Bear right through kissing gate ('Rothbury' fingerpost), cross field corner and footbridge (YA) and climb bank to bear right along bridleway (046014) beside Coquet for ¾ mile back to Rothbury.

LENGTH: 8 miles

REFRESHMENTS: None en route – provision yourself at Rothbury Bakery

MUSIC: Enquire at Queen's Head (01669-620470; *www.queensheadrothbury.com*) about sessions; *www.rothbury-traditional-music.co.uk* about Rothbury Traditional Music Festival each July
Billy Pigg: The Border Minstrel CD (Leader)

Embleton, Craster and Beadnell, Northumberland

Bleak beauties of the Northumbrian coast

I t was the opening of a rare and beautiful day along the coast of north Northumberland – wall-to-wall blue sky, warm sunshine, a cool breeze from the north, and a flat calm sea shimmering and gleaming like a silk cloth laid to the horizon. In the quiet lanes of Embleton I greeted early morning dog walkers, and a party of German women who were setting forth for a day's walking with tremendous knickerbockered strides, cheeks shining and alpenstocks a-clatter.

The glorious empty sands and flowery dunes of the Northumbrian coast are justly trumpeted as a still-unspoiled national treasure. But the rolling cornfields just inland, with their lanes frothing with cow parsley and their hedgerows and bridleways full of birdsong, are fit to gladden the heart of a walker too. Beside the farm hamlet of Dunstan Square I climbed to The Heughs, a high ridge of the volcanic Whin Sill, and walked down into Craster between coconut-scented gorse bushes under a sky filled with lark song.

This shallow coast with its low cliffs holds a string of harbour villages, most of them more engaged in tourism than in fishing these days. Craster's white-washed and brown stone houses huddle round the tiny harbour like an artist's dream. There's an unmistakable whiff of fish about the village to show that here, at least, the working link with the sea is not yet broken. The smell comes from Robson's smokehouse just up the hill, where herrings are kippered and salmon smoked over oak chip fires. 'I should take these two,' advised Mr Robson, a born salesman, as he handed me a pair of Craster kippers. 'Not that there's anything between them and all the others. In fact every one of our kippers is the best of the lot!'

One feature of the coast dominates all others hereabouts – the huge shattered ruin of Dunstanburgh Castle on its volcanic knoll a mile north of Craster. The pinnacles of the great gatehouse still tower eighty feet high, yet somehow the castle looks half its actual size until you get up close. Then you gasp at the sheer scale of this 14th-century sea fortress, a stronghold of John of Gaunt in its heyday, defended on two sides by cliffs and on the third by a man-made ditch dug through the solid rock.

Leaning out from the gatehouse stair and gazing towards the blue humps of the distant Cheviot Hills, I felt the cold breath of Dunstanburgh's most poignant ghost. Sir Guy the Seeker was a homecoming crusader who took refuge from a storm in the castle. At midnight a giant woke the knight and took him to a chamber where a beautiful princess lay in an enchanted sleep. 'Choose,' roared the ogre, pointing to a sword and a horn hanging on the wall. 'Choose rightly, and you will wake the maiden and have her for your wife.'

Sir Guy blew a great blast on the horn, and instantly sank into a swoon. When he awoke it was to find himself outside the gates of Dunstanburgh, condemned for ever to tramp a circuit of the castle with an aching heart.

Slowly I shrugged off the spell of Dunstanburgh and moved along, walking sandy pathways through the sea pink clumps and rich purple bloody cranesbill patches of the dunes. Embleton Bay lay open under the blue sky, a two-mile arc of rich gold sand. I took my boots off, slung them by their laces over my shoulder, and walked barefoot on the tideline where waves as clean and cold as ice broke over my feet. Thank God for the unswimmable coldness of the Northumbrian sea. If the water were ten degrees warmer, this utterly delectable, unfrequented coast would have been developed out of all recognition long since.

The grey and white houses of Low Newton-by-the-Sea came into view in the dip of a green bay. In the cool dark bar of the Ship Inn I ordered a crab and salad stottie and received a monstrous granary wedge filled with crab and crunchy red peppers. I ate it outside, watching two fishermen in high boots and blue jerseys hauling their boat up onto the sands, a scene straight out of some Victorian snapshot album.

After lunch I went on over the buttercup-spattered headlands of Newton Point, pausing only to let a family of weasels dash across the path from the safety of one stone wall to another. One of the

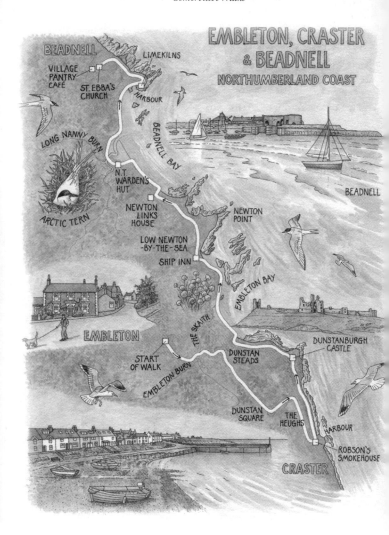

EMBLETON, CRASTER & BEADNELL
NORTHUMBERLAND COAST

BEADNELL
LIMEKILNS
VILLAGE PANTRY CAFÉ
ST. EBBA'S CHURCH
HARBOUR
LONG NANNY BURN
BEADNELL BAY
ARCTIC TERN
N.T. WARDEN'S HUT
NEWTON LINKS HOUSE
NEWTON POINT
LOW NEWTON -BY-THE-SEA
SHIP INN
EMBLETON BAY
BEADNELL
EMBLETON
THE SKAITH
DUNSTANBURGH CASTLE
START OF WALK
EMBLETON BURN
DUNSTAN STEADS
DUNSTAN SQUARE
THE HEUGHS
HARBOUR
ROBSON'S SMOKEHOUSE
CRASTER

handsome little chocolate and white beasts stood up briefly on its hind legs to inspect me with eyes as black and shiny as elderberries.

Down on Beadnell Bay – another in the succession of long curves of peerless, empty sand – it was my turn to do the staring. Volunteers at the National Trust warden's hut in the dunes were only too keen to share their knowledge of the Arctic terns that were incubating eggs among the marram grass tussocks. Arctic terns, black-capped and scarlet of beak and legs, are beautiful creatures, fantastically brave in defending their nests, and unbelievably far-ranging. It's hard to credit the journey they make each autumn, parents and youngsters both – some 11,000 miles to their winter quarters in Antarctica from this tiny patch of Northumbrian beach, to which they will unerringly return the following spring.

From the tall old limekilns on Beadnell harbour I struck inland for St Ebba's Church and the Village Pantry café. There ought to be a law against the Village Pantry's apple cake, as rich and seductive as an oil heiress. Should I, or shouldn't I? If only Sir Guy the Seeker's dilemma had been so simple. Ravenous after all that salty Northumbrian beach air, I succumbed without a murmur.

STEPPING OUT – *Walk 88*

MAPS: OS 1:25,000 Explorers 332, 340; 1:50,000 Landranger 75, 81

TRAVEL: Rail to Chathill (4 miles) – *www.thetrainline.com*

Road – A1 north past Alnwick; B6347, B1339 to Embleton. Park in Front Street near post office (OS ref NU232226).

WALK DIRECTIONS: Walk up hill to turn right along Mount Pleasant. Pass Greys Inn and Blue Bell Inn; ahead along road. In 300 yd fork left (234223 – 'Dunstan Steads' sign) for ¾ mile to Dunstan Steads, where you turn right (243223 – 'Dunstan Square' bridleway sign) for 1 mile to Dunstan Square. Left here opposite barn (250207 – 'Craster' fingerpost) down fields, then up through gap in ridge. Don't cross next stile, but turn right through gate (256210 – National Trust waymark). Ahead for ½ mile, keeping fence on your left; cross stile (256201) and on through gorse, to bear left down to Craster harbour (258200). *NB for Jolly Fisherman pub and Robson's Smokehouse, bear right up slope from harbour.*

At harbour, turn along Dunstanburgh Road and on along cliff path. Nearing Dunstanburgh Castle, go through kissing gate (258213). To visit castle, continue to right; to continue walk, coast path bears left around left side of castle. Pass through a gate ('Dunstanburgh Golf Course' sign) and bear right on track through dunes onto Embleton Beach. Follow beach for 1¾ miles to Low Newton-by-the-Sea. *(NB – halfway along, where you cross The Skaith stream (243233) you can turn inland to Embleton to finish the walk.)*

From Ship Inn at Low Newton (241245) walk up road for 70 yd; right through kissing gate ('Beadnell' fingerpost), up over slope, through wall gap near stile, and on with wall on your left to cross tarmac roadway (242251). Below crags cross a ladder stile; bear left on path through dunes for ⅔ mile, to cross car park at Newton Links House (235260). Through kissing gate, bear right through dunes; left along beach for ⅔ mile.

150 yd short of National Trust wardens' hut (229270), bear left through dunes. Follow signs to hut for information and tern nesting site viewpoint. Return to fork in dune paths; right over stile, then right to cross bridge over Long Nanny beck (227271). Right along fence for 50 yd; right through gate to resume beach

walk. From Beadnell harbour (237286) follow road inland for ⅔ mile. Take 2nd road on left (232295 – opposite post office) to St Ebba's Church and Village Pantry tearoom.

Return to Embleton on bus no. 401 (info: *www.traveline.org. uk*) – bus stop outside Village Pantry.

LENGTH: 11½ miles *(Embleton-Craster-Dunstanburgh-Embleton round walk: 7 miles)*

REFRESHMENTS: Jolly Fisherman, Craster (01665-576461; *www. silk8234.fsnet.co.uk*); Ship Inn, Low Newton-by-the-Sea (01665-576262; *www.shipinnnewton.co.uk*); Craster Arms (01665-720272) or Village Pantry teashop (01665-720220), Beadnell.

CRASTER SMOKEHOUSE: 01665-576223; *www.kipper.co.uk*

DUNSTANBURGH CASTLE: 01665-576231; *www.nationaltrust.org. uk*

GUIDEBOOK: *The Inn Way To Northumberland* by Mark Reid (Inn Way Publications, *www.innway.co.uk*)

SCOTLAND

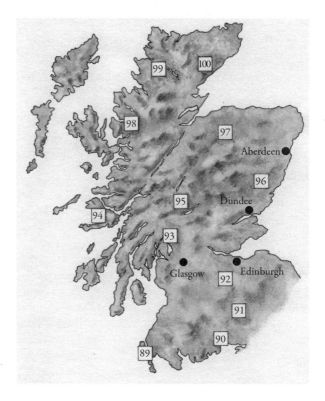

Knockinaam, Portpatrick and Port Kale, Rhinns of Galloway

Cliffs and castles of the far south-west of Scotland

'**B**OTANICAL MOMENT!' sang out Dave Richardson from the cliff path high above me. '*Equisetum telmateia*, the Giant Horsetail. On the left here – you'll see it! Sparrowhawk over the gorse, too...'

Typical of Dave to be pointing out a plant to me, and characteristic of him to be giving the Linnaean as well as the common name. Such is Dave's appetite for checking the ID and rehearsing the biographies of things that grow and things that fly, I'm sure he would have been preaching the word to the bare rocks and the four winds if I had not been there to stumble among his freshly cast pearls.

Dave and I were staying at Knockinaam Lodge down in the Rhinns of Galloway, the hammerhead peninsula that seals the tip of south-west Scotland, to yomp the cliffs and plodge the bogs for a couple of late autumn days. Knockinaam is the perfect getaway spot. Here in the heart of sporting and walking country they don't just tolerate guests returning muddy, wet and ravenous after long days out – they expect it. This was a chance for Dave to clear his head before his forthcoming mission, the 65th of his long 'other life' as a globe-travelling musician with his band The Boys of the Lough, to bring the bitter-sweet delights of acoustic Celtic music to Stateside ears and hearts.

A mild, blowy morning was spreading itself across the Rhinns. The hotel on its secluded slip of bay fell behind and out of sight as we climbed the cliff path through grass clumps and bracken fronds heavy with the night's rain. Mushrooms had sprung up large and white in the cliff-top fields, and we promised ourselves we'd pick a cartload on the way back.

Up there the view broadened as if a window had been opened:

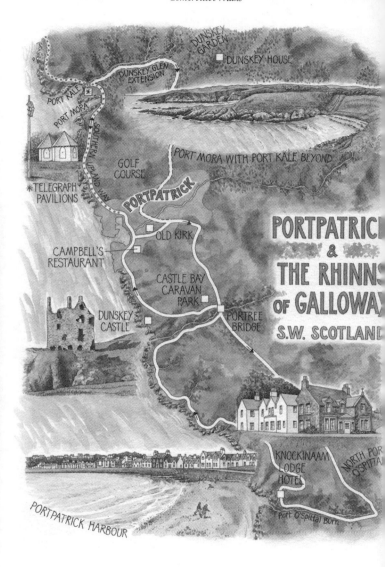

hump-backed green fields, dark rocky scoops of bays to north and south, and out on the western sea horizon a low line, a little harder and greyer than the clouds crowding down on it – the coast of County Down, twenty miles off across the water. 'Good times playing there,' said Dave, 'Northern Ireland was always full of great music. No trouble finding a party – the problem was how to get away from it and grab enough sleep.'

Black blotches on the cliff ahead resolved themselves slowly into the empty windows and doorways of a broken-down medieval stronghold. Jackdaws circled the shattered battlements of Dunskey Castle, a gloomily Gothic ruin rising from rocks as grey and lichen-stained as itself. Whatever barbarities followed the capture of this castle's precursor in 1489 by Sir Alexander McCulloch, Keeper of Falcons to King James IV, have long been forgotten. Not so the rumour of a ghost too frightful to describe more specifically than by means of its folk name – the Hairy Apparition of Dunskey.

Down in the bay beyond lay the waterfront houses and hotels of Portpatrick, drawn round their harbour like a tight and colourful collar. Before ships became too big and impatient to put up with this small haven facing west into wild Atlantic weather, Portpatrick was Scotland's most important link with Ireland. Protestant Scot settlers, known as 'planters', poured out of the little haven in the 17th and 18th centuries to take over the best land in Ulster. Countless millions of cattle made the return journey with their drovers, to travel the stony old military road to market in Dumfries. It wasn't all commerce; Portpatrick became Galloway's own Gretna Green, as Ulster lovers forbidden to wed by the laws of their land dared the stormy crossing and the tempests of family fury to plight their troth on more liberal Scottish soil.

Galloway has a hook in my own heart. It was from Leswalt, a few miles north of Portpatrick, that my distant ancestor George Somerville, Episcopalian minister, set out for Ulster on a wild night in 1690. No well-found planter vessel carried George; he was rowed across to County Down in an open boat by his son, clutching a Bible and his infant grandson, in terror of his life, fleeing from a band of Covenanters or anti-establishment non-conformists who – very late in the day for their particular sect – had threatened to burn his house, himself and his loved ones. Just fifty years before, another member of the family – William Somervil, minister of Dunsyre in the Pentland Hills – had signed the original Covenant whose provisions were now being used to force his kinsman into exile. As I stared west to Ireland, picturing the old man's desperate escape by sea, I wondered whether he had ever become aware of the irony.

Down on the harbour we steered for the ruinous Old Kirk and its round tower. The graveyard was full of memorial stones dedicated to seafarers – captains, surgeons, mates, ship's carpenters – most of them victims of sea disasters. Captain Allen Bursley of the American ship *Lion of Boston* lay buried along with seven of his ship's company, all lost in a wreck on a winter's night in 1835. William Mclean of Ballyclare in County Antrim was drowned near Carrickfergus in August 1831, 'and his body having been wafted to the Scottish coast was found near Portpatrick and here decently interred.'

The poignancy of these clipped little cameos of tragedy stayed with us as we climbed to the cliffs beyond Portpatrick. Here the humours of everyday life reasserted themselves. The steps up the cliffs had been inscribed with notes of the greatest events of history; the formation of continents, the extinction of dinosaurs, the epic struggles between sea and ice. Across all this grandeur a dog had casually trotted before the concrete had dried, stamping out whole swathes of history with his round paw prints.

From the northern corner of Portpatrick harbour the Southern Upland Way begins its 212-mile journey across the Border hills to the east coast of Scotland. We followed the Way along the cliffs, looking down into bays where the ledges of black and yellow cliffs held ranks of rock doves, necks tucked in, heads modestly lowered. 'Peregrine food,' was the succinct comment of Dave – ever the realist.

We made our way down slippery steps in the rocks to explore the neighbouring bays of Port Mora and Port Kale. Mora was a perfect little toenail of sand, its cradling rocks giving way to Kale's grey pebbly shelf of a raised beach. Twin hexagonal pavilions stood here, relics of the 1850s when Ireland's first telephone cable was laid from this tiny cove. Gazing around its silent rocks, listening to the sigh of wavelets falling on the strand, it seemed impossible to believe that such history had been made on this quietest of coasts.

STEPPING OUT – *Walk 89*

MAP: OS 1:25,000 Explorer 309; 1:50,000 Landranger 82

TRAVEL: By rail to Stranraer (*www.thetrainline.co.uk*); bus to Portpatrick.

By road: M6 to Carlisle; A77 to Portpatrick; minor road to North Port O' Spittal and Knockinaam Lodge.

WALK DIRECTIONS: Start either from Portpatrick harbour (OS ref NW999542) or Knockinaam Lodge (NX021522). From Knockinaam Lodge: 'Portpatrick Cliff Walk' sign at top of car park. Climb grassy path. At top, cross fence by boulders and bear left along cliffs for 1½ miles. Opposite Dunskey Castle bear right, keeping about 100 yards from fence, following gorge inland to road. Left to cross Portree Bridge (010537); left into Castle Bay Caravan Park. Follow park roads; in far right corner of park, cross stile to pass Dunskey Castle (003534). Continue along cliffs to Portpatrick harbour (999542); right up Main Street, left along St Patrick's Street to visit Old Kirk ruins (000542).

For Dunskey Glen circuit, returning to Portpatrick, download directions from *www.walkingworld.com*, Walk No. 825. For clifftop walk, continue around harbour; climb steps at far side; follow Southern Uplands Way (white thistle waymarks, yellow arrows) to Port Mora and Port Kale (990552). Retrace steps to Portpatrick harbour.

From harbour, left up Main Street; first right by Gillespie the Baker, to top of Hill Street. Beyond garage (001542) climb steep grassy bank. Ahead at top to T-junction with bridge on left; right here up gravel track; in 50 yards, ahead by bollard up narrow tarmac track. Right at top past houses to crossways (005543). Right along moor road for 2¼ miles, past caravan parks and over Portree Bridge. Pass farm by bridge over Port O' Spittal Burn (029033); in 100 yards, right to Knockinaam Hotel.

LENGTH: 8½ miles

CONDITIONS: Cliff paths; can be boggy/slippery after rain.

REFRESHMENTS: Campbells Restaurant, Portpatrick; other pubs/cafés in Portpatrick; Castle Bay Caravan Park shop.

WALKINGWORLD: This walk is an adaptation of Walks 824 and 825 from the Walkingworld website (*www.walkingworld.com*)

DUNSKEY GLEN WALK: Glen is open March to October. At other times by arrangement – tel 01776-810211.

Walk 90

Caerlaverock, Solway Firth

Winter haunt of the barnacle geese

W HEN THE BARNACLE GEESE come south from the Arctic
Circle to the Solway Firth each October, they arrive mob-
handed. The entire population from the island of Spitzbergen in the
Svalbard archipelago – some 20,000 birds – takes wing at the onset
of the Arctic winter and pilots its way southwards across 1800 miles
of coast and sea, to make landfall on the mudflats and marshes of the
great boundary estuary between Scotland and England.

The barnacles must have been following this southward impulse
for countless millennia before one particular species of hairy biped
developed eyes and fingers skilled enough to fire a flint-tipped arrow
in their direction. But the habits of the wild geese, being already
perfect for the purposes of mating, feeding and surviving the winter,
never changed.

For centuries, unable to locate the breeding grounds of the geese,
men believed that they hatched from the goose barnacles that were
washed ashore clinging to seaweed. Man got cleverer, though, and
learned more efficient ways of getting at the Spitzbergen barnacle
geese. By the 1940s, wildfowlers had reduced their numbers to about
four hundred – the brink of extinction.

In search of inspiration for a winter walk in Scotland, I telephoned
my Edinburgh-dwelling friend Dave Richardson. 'Caerlaverock, on
the Solway,' was his instant recommendation. 'It's a beautiful place
in winter, and the barnacle geese will be in.' What kind of numbers?
'Oh, thousands of 'em. Really one of the classic bird-watching sights.
Hell of a noise, too, at flighting times.'

In the past forty years the barnacles have been pulled back
from the abyss by the establishment of a National Nature Reserve,
looked after by Scottish Natural Heritage, on 20,000 acres of muds,

foreshore and merse (saltmarsh) at Caerlaverock on the Scotland shore of the Solway below Dumfries – part of the Duke of Norfolk's estates. This flat, windswept ground, carefully warded and managed, supports ducks, waders, geese and songbirds; barn owls, hen harriers, peregrine, merlin; plovers and curlews; roe and red deer; otter and badger; colonies of the very rare natterjack toad. At Eastpark Farm, in the heart of the reserve, the Wildfowl and Wetland Trust's Centre lets the public in on these natural treasures, funnelling visitors along concealed tracks to hides and towers right in among the birds.

I picked Dave up from Lockerbie Station on a crisp blue morning. Down on the Solway the long rising granite ridge of Criffel, five miles away across the River Nith, streamed white puffs of cloud like a volcano from its 1,850 ft crest. A good sign, this: the early mist was lifting, and already we could hear, faint and far-off, the gabble of the barnacle geese on their grazing meadows a couple of miles inland.

Before setting off from Eastpark Farm we looked at big display photos of the barnacles' Arctic breeding grounds – the bare islets just offshore where they hatch, the flat ground of the coast where they feed on rich grass sward, and the great curtain of wrinkled cliffs that rises sheer from the Spitzbergen shore. Life in these harsh remote regions is no summer picnic. Glaucous gull and Arctic fox are always on the alert for that one moment of parental inattention that gives them their chance to rob the nest. And there is always the possibility of a raid by a polar bear isolated by retreating ice sheets.

Dave and I splashed down a rutted cart track in the direction of the merse. Halfway along, Dave's eagle eye caught a movement in a muddy puddle – a tiny toad, valiantly doing the breast-stroke towards the shelter of a grass clump. Out in the merse, the sodden coarse grass squelched under our boots. Curlews bubbled from the reed beds, and a roe deer showed us his white scut before bobbing into cover.

In the coastal carr woodlands everything was as damp and trickly as could be. Vast ancient boles of alder, coppiced for clog-making or charcoal-burning centuries before, stood half-smothered in ferns, mosses, fungi and sedges – all vegetation that likes a drink or two. Half wood and half water, here was a wetly exhaling moistland above which coal tits, chaffinches and great tits hopped and chittered among the bare twigs.

It must have been a combination of wet malarious marshland and incursive Solway tides that caused the Maxwells in 1270 to abandon the castle they had established here only 50 years before, and build a grand new one on a triangular plan half a mile inland. Dave and I passed the green mound of the original stronghold, knotted with sawn-off tree trunks, and emerged from the woods to find the jagged sandstone walls and towers of Caerlaverock Castle reflected in their glass-calm moat.

Any castle in these troubled border regions was guaranteed a lively Middle Ages, and Caerlaverock enjoyed its full share of burnings, demolishings, sieges, hangings and slaughter. In 1300 AD, King Edward I arrived outside the walls with 87 knights and 3,000 men. The king's giant siege engines lobbed huge stone balls over the walls until Caerlaverock's sixty-strong garrison surrendered. Many were hanged on the spot for their defiance.

In the gloomy red interior of the castle Dave and I found a number of the siege balls that had been dredged from the moat. We admired 'Lord Nithdale's dainty fabrick', a three-storey mansion with wonderful allegorical carvings over the windows, built into the castle's structure in 1634. Then we steered in failing light for the Roman camp on Ward Law hill.

We never made it up to the copse at the summit of Ward Law. A wretched ewe, thrashing by the hedge with a thick briar knotted round her throat, demanded attention. By the time we had summoned the farmer, the sun was dipping in smoky gold behind Criffel's ridge.

A swift road march and a thumbed lift in a warden's pick-up got us back to the WWT Centre at Eastpark Farm just in time for the evening flight of the barnacle geese. A few decades ago this would have been the hour of the wildfowler, waiting in concealment for the geese to pass overhead between their daytime feeding grounds inland and their night roosts on the merse.

Legend tells of the local van driver who spied a Land-Rover full of men with guns. Taking them for poachers, he offered them a word of advice: 'Ye'd best tak' care – yon bloody auld Duke o' Norfolk's aboot.' To which one of the suspects replied good-humouredly, 'That's quite all right – I *am* the bloody old Duke of Norfolk.'

Squeezed into Caerlaverock's smallest hide, Dave and I peered out across a fleet of water where a ghostly full moon lay mirrored. Three thousand barnacle geese were gathered in a dense black and white mass, not 20 yards away. The noise was intense and continuous, like a mass of excited children and dogs in a schoolyard.

Suddenly the whole pack got up with a thunderous crash of wings and flew over our heads, barking and gabbling, out towards the moon-silvered Solway. A mind-numbingly beautiful spectacle, elating and other-worldly. 'Like having the Arctic right on your door-step,' breathed Dave in my ear, and that exactly caught the moment.

STEPPING OUT – *Walk 90*

MAPS: OS 1:25,000 Explorer 314; 1:50,000 Landranger 84 and 85

TRAVEL: By road: M6 to Carlisle; M74 to Gretna; A75 to Annan, then B724. Just before Clarencefield, left on B725. 1 mile beyond Bankend, WWT signed on left.

WALK DIRECTIONS: From WWT's East Park Centre (OS ref NY051656) walk up road for ½ mile. Left past Scottish Natural Heritage's information point (043659 – signed) along lane. In 300 yards left by house, through gate, along hedged track to edge of merse (042652). Right here (white arrow); left at following fence, going south for 200 yd; right along flood bank for 1 mile to corner of wood (025651). Right over stile along woodland track; in ¼ mile cross footbridge; continue past house, up lane to old castle mound (027653). Left here for 20 yd; right on duckboard trail through trees to Caerlaverock Castle (025656).

Up drive to cross B725 (025660); up track to top of Ward Law (024667). Return to B725; left for ⅔ mile; right (030669 – WWT sign) for 1½ miles along lane to WWT.

Ask advice here about which tower to ascend to view birds.

LENGTH OF WALK: 6 miles (allow 3 hours plus bird-watching time).

CONDITIONS: Merse section can be very wet – wellingtons advisable. Bring binoculars, bird book.

REFRESHMENTS: Tearoom in Caerlaverock Castle.

INFORMATION: *Caerlaverock National Nature Reserve* – Scottish Natural Heritage (*www.snh.org.uk*)
Wildfowl and Wetlands Trust (*www.wwt.org.uk*)
Caerlaverock Castle (*www.historic-scotland.gov.uk*)

Grey Mare's Tail and Loch Skeen, Dumfriesshire

From a thrilling waterfall up into bleak moorlands

AFTER TWO MONTHS OF RAIN in a wet Scottish summer, the Grey Mare's Tail was in full flow. Swishing sinuously from side to side in a rising wind, the waterfall came hissing out of the hill mist and hurtled two hundred feet down its shiny black rock funnel.

As a dramatic introduction to the remote Dumfriesshire hills, the Grey Mare's Tail is hard to beat. Most visitors are content to climb a short path above the car park on the valley road from Moffat, to stand overawed by the crash and roar of such a weight of falling water. But Dave Richardson and I had something more strenuous in mind: a high and mighty circuit of the hills protected by the National Trust for Scotland above Loch Skeen, a secret lake tucked away out of sight in a hanging valley 300 feet above the road.

'Great colour,' murmured Dave, halting on the narrow path above the Grey Mare's Tail. He swept a hand over the luminous purple of heathery braes that sloped precipitously into the dark cleft of the Tail Burn's glen. 'It's good to get out of Edinburgh for a day.'

There's not much in Auld Reekie for a hill walker, botanist and birdwatcher like Dave. My phone call had brought him down to the valley of the Moffat Water in hopes of a good walk, in spite of the mist now blanketing the hills. 'The Moffat area has the best chance of a gleam of sunshine,' the Weathercall announcer had asserted in his cheery drawl down the telephone line early this morning. That looked a vain prophecy.

Near the mistline a flicker of movement in the uppermost section of waterfall caught our attention. Through field glasses we could see a solitary sheep standing mournfully on a slippery rock ledge right in the middle of the fall, imprisoned by solid walls of water.

God alone knew how the wretched animal had got into that perilous spot. There was nothing we could do to help it. We climbed guiltily on, vowing to ask the first descending walker we met to pass on news of the sheep's plight to the NTS rangers in the car park now far below.

Up in the hanging valley, all was silent. This was a world of mist-pearled grass and sedge. The Tail Burn cascaded through a landscape strewn with mounds of flood-washed rubble left behind by glacial meltwaters, weathered over ten thousand years into rounded hillocks. Wind-stunted bushes of willow, hazel, birch and rowan hugged the heather.

The steel-grey wavelets of Loch Skeen lapped dark peaty banks. 'Hmmm,' said Dave, fingering bushy green tufts by the water's edge, 'viviparous fescue, I think.' I must have looked blank – not an uncommon state for me, when faced with Dave's bottomless well of botanical information. 'Viviparous means giving birth to live young – see these new seed heads, germinating on the parent plant?'

Sulphurous yellow sphagnum moss made a dayglo splash against the dull greens and browns of the sunless upland bog. We splashed and squelched our way from the loch across to the drystane dyke – a dyke is a wall, not a ditch, hereabouts – that would serve as our guide over the next few mist-obscured miles.

It was a stiff old haul from the boggy collar of land around the head of the loch up to the heights of the grassy hills beyond. Sheep scuttered away into the mist. Pipits cheeped on the lichened stones of the dyke. At the top we took on oxygen like the Flying Scotsman takes on water – wheezing and steaming – before striding away over the peat hags on a path that dipped and swooped rollercoaster style beside the wall.

These roadless hills have always been a refuge for rogues and reivers, a lawless area in times past where cattle-rustlers would hide their stolen beasts in secret clefts and hollows. When King James V came down on the hills with twelve thousand men in his 'Great Hunting' of 1528, he slew eighteen score of harts. But the real purpose of the king's visit became clear when he hanged several Scotts and Armstrongs and threw the Earl of Bothwell and Lord Maxwell into jail, along with dozens of other local lordlings who had overstepped the bounds of autonomy.

Wild men in a wild land. Feuding, raiding, backstabbing and thatch-burning were the natural order of things up here, until

General Wade and his military roads rolled through after the Jacobite rebellions of the 18th century.

Dave and I forged on up and down the slopes, stopping to admire the olive-green frogs that leaped muscularly away from our descending boots to freeze like tiny carvings beneath tussocks of wet grass. Thick vapour rolled across as we reached the final kink in the dyke and turned east towards the Tail Burn once more.

Off to the south, smothered beyond sight in the mist, the Carrifran Glen fell away towards the valley road. When hill-walker Dan Jones found a 6,000 year-old hunting bow in a peat bog at the head of the glen in 1990, he fired academic imaginations. Pollen samples taken from the bog showed the richness of the post-glacial species that had colonised the now treeless valley: ash, elm, birch, cherry, oak, holly, willow, alder, hazel.

Scotland has lost almost all its native wildwood to over-grazing by sheep and cattle. Here was the chance to recreate a sizeable slice of that leafy lost world. The Carrifran Wildwood Project was set up, and over the course of several years raised the money to buy up the whole 1500 acre glen. Saplings were grown in their tens of thousands in the back gardens of volunteer enthusiasts. The process of reforesting Carrifran Glen with its original species is well under way now, thanks to a leap of imagination and a huge deal of sweat and hard labour.

On the slopes above Loch Skeen we found a shaggy carpet of dark green leaves. 'Now what the hell is this?' pondered Dave, bent double. 'Dwarf cornel, I'm pretty sure. I've seen it further north in the mountains, but I didn't know it grew on these hills. It's really an arctic or subarctic species – must be right on its southern limit. Very scarce.' He straightened up, grinning with pleasure. 'Well – that's made my day.'

A short sharp scramble down the rocky face of Rough Craigs, a bit of heather-bouncing and a boot-filling splash through the Tail Burn, and we were heading back down towards the Moffat Water. The waterfall sheep had somehow scrambled to a ledge, out of immediate danger. The Grey Mare's Tail thundered below, a ghostly vibration as we picked our way down out of the mist into late afternoon light washed clear and luminous.

STEPPING OUT – *Walk 91*

MAP: OS 1:25,000 Explorer 330; 1:50,000 Landranger 79

TRAVEL: M6/A74 to Moffat; A708 Selkirk road for 10 miles to car park on left at OS ref. NT185145.

WALK DIRECTIONS: From car park, cross Tail Burn over A708 road bridge and turn left up wooden steps; then on up along hill track with Grey Mare's Tail on your left. Follow Tail Burn up for 1 mile to reach Loch Skeen (175160). Skirt loch on right bank; halfway along lochside, bear right over wet heather to fence (175165).

Fence soon becomes wall (this stays on your right for 4 miles until it returns you to the Tail Burn). Follow it uphill from Loch Skeen, at first over sodden peat bog, then steep climb on grass. In ¾ mile wall turns left (171176); continue another ¾ mile WSW, to left turn on Firthybrig Head (158172); 1 mile SSW by Donald's Cleuch Head to Firthhope Rig (153154). Main wall continues 50 yd (little cairn just beyond); but turn left along a wall which has been reduced to a line of stones at ground level.

Follow E for 1 mile to steep stony slope of Rough Craigs (171152). Descend carefully. At foot, wall trends away to right; but keep ahead (E) to ford Tail Burn. Turn right to return to car park.

LENGTH OF WALK: 7 miles (climbing 2,000 ft) – allow 4–5 hours.

CONDITIONS: A safe walk in wild country, if you take proper care. Very steep slopes fall from path to Grey Mare's Tail. Some bog-hopping above Loch Skeen; steepish climb out of the loch valley. Short steep descent at Rough Craigs, followed by fording Tail Burn (could entail wet feet). Wear full hillwalking gear.

REFRESHMENTS: Take picnic, water, hot drink.

CARRIFRAN WILDWOOD PROJECT: Donations and information – *www.carrifran.org.uk*

Walk 92

Black Law and the Covenanter's Grave, Pentland Hills

An ancient feud and a modest hero in the rolling Pentland Hills

'AWFULLY SORRY, old chap,' said Dave Richardson, wincing in his bed, 'hurt my dashed back, and can't jolly well move.'

Actually, those were not quite the words that Dave employed. It's mortifying enough to rick your back painfully in the unheroic act of tying up your shoelaces. Far worse for the recumbent musician to look out on a gloriously clear autumn day spread over Edinburgh, and be unable to move as far as the door – let alone go striding the Pentland Hills with me as he had been eagerly anticipating.

Unexpectedly alone, I set off an hour later from Dunsyre Kirk, twenty miles south of Edinburgh, in air so clear that each individual sheep on the side of Dunsyre Hill looked as if it had been outlined with a fine artist's pen. I knew such perfect visibility in the Pentlands usually presaged an afternoon downpour. So it turned out today, but I made the most of the peerless morning.

I walked fast along the stony moorland track above Medwyn-bank, taking it all in – the rounded hills of Black Law and Bleak Law, the head-high sedges, pipits calling from the tops of heather clumps, and the astonishing, psychedelic purple of the heather itself. Giant white clouds were hoisting themselves above the skyline, riding on the backs of dove-grey rain bands falling on other hills and other walkers. That was good enough for me.

Above the lonely farm of Medwynhead I turned aside into the narrow valley of the upper Medwin Water, looking for *asplenium viride*. 'You should find it thereabouts,' Dave had told me over the wine glasses the previous evening. 'Little fern, quite rare – like maid-enhair spleenwort but with a green spine.' After some fossicking about I found the fern under a rock, a few tight little fronds with tiny round greeny-red leaves.

'Roger's Kirk,' the map named this isolated spot. During the late 17th century Presbyterians who refused to accept a Church of Scotland ruled by bishops would gather in hidden valleys and secret hollows in the hills for illegal open-air services, known as 'conventicles'. Attendance at a conventicle laid a worshipper open to persecution that might include fines, beatings and imprisonment. Any minister who was caught preaching at a conventicle was liable to be executed.

These 'Covenanters' – some of them had signed a declaration or National Covenant in their own blood back in 1638 – were determined to resist outside interference in their religious lives. Crown and Parliament were equally set on crushing what they saw as treasonable rebellion. There were skirmishes, ambushes and murders on both sides.

On 27 November 1666 a battle took place at Rullion Green, a few miles north of Dunsyre. Against the heavily armoured dragoons of the government forces, a peasant army lined up:

'Some had halbards; some had durks;
Some had crooked swords like Turks;
Some had guns with rusty ratches;
Some had firey peats for matches;
Some had bows but wanted arrows;
Some had pistols without marrows ...'

As they would one day do to the Highland clans at Culloden, and later still to the Duke of Monmouth's peasant army at Sedgemoor, the dragoons simply mowed the countrymen down. Fifty were killed on the field; many more were hunted and slaughtered, hanged or transported over the following weeks.

At Blackhill near Medwynhead I came across the broken shell of a stone-built house. It was here that the shepherd Adam Sanderson answered a thump on his door on the night of the battle. It was a desperately wounded fugitive from Rullion Green, John Carphin of Ayrshire, who wanted help but would not come into the house in case his presence should bring trouble on the occupants.

The shepherd helped Carphin to stagger a few hundred yards up the West Water. 'Bury me within sight of the Ayrshire hills,' was the Covenanter's last request before he died. Sanderson carried his body up Black Law and buried it near the summit with a view across to the Ayrshire hills – an act of charity he performed at risk of his own life and liberty. Later the Blackhill herd put up a memorial stone, discreetly lettered so as to be indecipherable to unfriendly eyes.

Another stone stands on Black Law today, erected in 1841 and inscribed with the facts of the burial. The story of the buried Covenanter had persisted in the area, taking on the aura of a legend as the years passed. In 1817 one young farmer's son went so far as to dig up John Carphin's skull and coat buttons. This desecration of the martyr's grave earned the lad a good belting from his outraged Presbyterian father, by all accounts.

I sat for an hour or so beside the Covenanter's Grave on top of Black Law, looking west through a gap between Bleak Law and The Pike towards the hills of Ayrshire, lying low under the march of distant rain. Not a hum of traffic or growl of a jet in all the wide world; the only sounds were the bleating of sheep, rush of wind in heather and the occasional sharp buzz-saw passage of a fly.

Down below John Carphin's grave I came across another memorial. 'James Cumming, MC. 15-8-20 – 21-10-90,' read the lettering. MC – Military Cross? He would have been the right age to have earned one during the Second World War. No other clue about the man. The questions came welling up. Who was he? Did he love these wild purple moors? Was this a memorial to a man buried elsewhere, or was James Cumming at rest below my boots, under these sedge clumps? How many more informal graves lie in the remote corners of the Pentland Hills?

It was a thoughtful hour's walk down the track to Easton Farm, with tumbled Border country stretching away ahead. On the windowsill in Dunsyre Kirk, a plain little building in shaky repair, I found the Covenanter's stone originally set up on Black Law by Adam Sanderson. 'UNON COVENANTER 1666' was all the shepherd had dared to carve.

A name on a placard next to the stone caught my eye. In the kirkyard, it said, lay buried Wm. Somervil, Minister of Dunsyre and one of the original signatories of the National Covenant. I couldn't find his gravestone, though I scanned a dozen curious little memorial slabs decorated with carvings of skull-and-crossbones, hourglass and sexton.

Was the long-dead minister some stern-minded ancestor of mine, caught up in the fury and drama of those bloody times? Perhaps. It would make a good story to take Dave Richardson's mind off his crocked back, anyway.

STEPPING OUT – *Walk 92*

MAP: OS 1:25,000 Explorer 344; 1:50,000 Landranger 72

TRAVEL: By road: From Edinburgh, A702 Biggar road. 3½ miles
south of West Linton, right turn (signed) to Dunsyre. Park near
Dunsyre Kirk.

WALK DIRECTIONS: From Dunsyre Kirk (OS ref NT072481)
walk back along road for 50 yd. Where road bends right
downhill, keep ahead along lane. In 1 mile, pass foot of Easton
farm lane (086487). In another ½ mile, ford confluence of
West Water and Medwin Water (094493) and continue ahead,
following telegraph poles up sunken track through two gates.
On above Garvald towards Medwynbank. Cross Medwin
Water; right along gravel drive for 100 yd, then left through
stone gateposts. At lake (100497) bear left on track that passes
along back of Medwynbank house. In farmyard beyond, right up
stony track for 1¼ miles to Medwynhead.

Just before farm, bear right up side of copse (094513);
through gate, continue uphill to turn left on track marked
with posts. At crossing of Medwin Water (089518), detour
right beside pipeline for ¾ mile to site of Roger's Kirk (087527
approx).

Back at Medwin Water crossing, bear right along track.
Adam Sanderson's house ruin lies below (088515 approx). In ½
mile, right (082513 – double fingerpost, Crosswood direction;
NB 'Crosswood' partly obliterated) up trackless side of Black
Law, following line of shooting butts. Aim for direction post on
skyline. Covenanter's Grave (078528) lies just to right of posts,
almost at summit.

Continue on same bearing following posts for another ⅔
mile, to meet head of track (074532), clearly visible across valley.
Left down track, via reservoir (070519), for 1½ miles. Just before
Crosswood fingerpost, right (080515) on well marked track for
1⅔ miles to pass Easton Farm. In 400 yd (086487), right to
Dunsyre.

LENGTH OF WALK: 12 miles – allow 5–6 hours

CONDITIONS: Trackless heather over Black Law – watch your step!
Otherwise firm tracks underfoot all the way.

REFRESHMENTS: None en route

Ben Lomond, Stirlingshire

From Loch Lomond's shore to a sensational mountain-top view

B EN LOMOND is the Glaswegian's Munro, a fine shapely hump of high ground that beckons seductively across Loch Lomond to drivers on the Fort William road. There is a 'tourist path', broad and clear, that ascends the long, gently rising south ridge of the mountain, delivering walkers quite easily to the summit at 3,192 feet. The temptation for hill walkers who climb and descend Ben Lomond this way on a lovely sunny day is to dismiss the mountain as tame. But what appears a smiling green hill in sunshine seems to swell, darken and threaten when rain and wind are pushing across Loch Lomond.

I'd seen Ben Lomond often from across the loch. I'd promised myself I would get up onto that handsome green brow one day. Dreich weather had thwarted me twice over the years. But today I was in luck. The morning broke fine, blue and warm. The bluidy midgies were off on their holidays elsewhere, for a mercy. And I had three excellent companions for the walk – Dorothy Breckenridge, Lindsey Mowat and Jenny Glumoff, three women who between them have crunched an awful lot of heather. Dorothy runs the estimable C-N-Do guided walking holiday company. Accustomed as she is to hurdling the highest Scottish mountains in the worst of winter and exploring the remotest back corners of the Highlands and islands, today's little toddle up and down Ben Lomond would be a piece of cake for her. But to me it represented a treat long savoured in the anticipation.

All the world and its walking poles seemed to be headed for the Scottish hills. The four of us put our heads together over the map and picked out a way up the mountain that would avoid the procession going up the 'tourist route'. Our choice was a much steeper and more uneven path, hugging the steep west flank a mile or so to the west of

DOROTHY, CHRISTOPHER, LINDSEY & JENNY & THE VIEW FROM THE SUMMIT

BEALACH BUIDHE

SCRAMBLE UP 3 ROCK 'STEPS'

BEN LOMOND

LOCHANS

PTARMIGAN

'TOURIST PATH' POPULAR ASCENT ROUTE

LOCH

TOM AN FHITHICH

SRON AONAICH

CONTORTED ROCK LAYERS NEAR THE SUMMIT

LOMOND

HAREBELLS

BEN LOMOND COTTAGE

YOUTH HOSTEL

NTS CENTRE

NTS CAR PARK

ROWARDENNAN HOTEL

BEN LOMOND
STIRLINGSHIRE
SCOTLAND

VIEW OF LOCH LOMOND FROM TOM AN FHITHICH

the main ascent track. We began the climb beside a gently hissing waterfall, with Loch Lomond glowing a deep silky blue on our left, seemingly close enough to leap and dive into.

The path rose across slopes choked with bracken and broom. 'That'll be gradually cleared,' Dorothy told us, 'and it'll be replaced by rowan, birch, oak, ash and alder. It's a wonderful scheme by the National Trust for Scotland to regenerate our native woodland. It might take 300 years – which is pretty long-term thinking, I'd say, on a Capability Brown scale – but eventually these braes will look as they did before felling and grazing produced today's very bare landscape.'

The zigzag path went steeply up the flank of Tom an Fhithich, the Mound of the Ravens, a craggy nose of a hill. Across slopes bright with harebells and shocking pink lousewort, through wet patches stuck with golden rockets of bog asphodel we climbed, looking across the ever-broadening water of Loch Lomond to the hooked peak known as The Cobbler. 'Between the wars,' Dorothy remarked, 'there was this great upsurge in walking in the country, especially among poor folk in Glasgow. Even if money was really tight you could get on a cheap bus to Balloch at the foot of Loch Lomond, walk up the loch and climb The Cobbler – that was about the limit of where people with no cars could get to on a day out from the city.'

A young Lancastrian couple and their Dalmatian came bounding down the path from the heights, the very picture of rude health and happiness. 'Spent the night up near summit – so beautiful and so peaceful,' they rhapsodized. 'Opened tent flap this morning and it were wall to wall blue!' It was wall to wall blue across the mountain hereabouts, too, thanks to drifts of bluebells opening their turned-back petals to the sun among tall, serpentine fronds of bracken. 'Back home in Sweden,' noted Jenny, 'we call the bracken "snake-bush".'

We drank cold burn water from a tiny, diamond-bright rill, and climbed on, talking of fiddle music and whisky, of windfarm schemes and the empty clearance lands of the west. At the rock-scabbed head of the knoll called Ptarmigan, with Loch Lomond now lying 2,400 feet below, a sheen of mica made the schist gleam salmon pink and silky grey. Above us the head of Ben Lomond rose against the blue sky, its purple-grey screes and crags sweeping round to form a lonely corrie.

The rugged spine of the Arrochar Alps lay across a whitening western sky beyond the Lomond water. I thought of the Barra

MacNeils playing the stately air 'Maids of Arrochar', and felt a great desire to whistle or hum it. But I couldn't quite bring the opening phrase to mind. I teased at it as if enticing a hermit crab out of a shell while we tramped on past a string of lonely dark lochans to cross the saddle of Bealach Buidhe, the Yellow Pass. Now came the final ascent, 600 feet up three sharp rock steps in the nape of Ben Lomond to the crown of the mountain, an OS trig pillar rising proudly out of a sea of pale, boot-eroded rock.

After the obligatory group hug, the hundred-mile view round the compass – the Campsie Fells in the south-east as a wrinkled green wall towards Glasgow, with the Ochils beyond them running down to the Firth of Forth and the Pentland Hills; the 'Highlands-in-miniature' of the Trossachs to the east with the peaks around Ben Lawers further away; 3,852-ft Ben More in the north overlooking Crianlarich and the Road to the Isles; out west a sea of mountains parting to reveal the Inner Hebrides and the upthrust Paps of Jura.

A rattle of Swedish made Jenny's ears prick up. Mine, too. Squatting nearby was a cool blonde couple looking every inch the Nordic goddess and godling. And where were they from, exactly? 'Dalarna province – from a town you won't have heard of, but we have wonderful music there, a town called ...'

'Falun, I know!' I burst out like a smartie-pants schoolboy. Jaws dropped all round. There was some excuse for my excitement. Twelve years before, I had enjoyed a memorable week at the Falun Folkmusik Festival, an international celebration of all things wonderful in the traditional music world. I had been left with a host of mind-melting images including an Apache man in full feathers and paint telephoning from a call-box under a full moon, a session of outdoor waltzing to a wind-up gramophone, Hungarian fiddlers with smoking fingertips, and four Lappish dancers conjuring dancing magic in a deserted concert hall in the early hours of the morning.

We bade the Swedes goodbye and made our way off Ben Lomond. The long track up the southern ridge was a snake of walkers toiling in the afternoon sun. We skipped past them. In front of us, all the way down, the magnificent prospect of Loch Lomond, spattered with islets, lay spreadeagled in all its glory. I found that the mention of Falun had kick-started the rusty old 2-stroke in my skull. 'Maids of Arrochar' came gliding out of the subconscious, and I rode the lovely tune like a mountain bike all the way to the bottom of the slope.

STEPPING OUT – *Walk 93*

MAPS: OS 1:25,000 Explorer 364, 1:50,000 Landranger 56

TRAVEL: A82 from Glasgow towards Crianlarich; at foot of Loch Lomond, right in Alexandria on A811 for 8 miles to bear left on B858 into Drymen. B837 to Balmaha; minor road up east shore of Loch Lomond for 6 miles to pass Rowardennan Hotel (OS ref NS360983) and park in NTS car park just beyond.

WALK DIRECTIONS: Continue along lochside road; in ⅓ mile fork right by entrance to Youth Hostel; pass NTS centre on right, then Ben Lomond Cottage. Cross stream just beyond cottage, and turn immediately right (360995 – before fork in road) up left bank of stream on narrow path through trees. Meet fence on your right and follow it north to pass below and left of Tom an Fhithich (361012). Pass through kissing gate and continue up zigzag track over Ptarmigan (358022). Follow clear ridge path past lochans, round to right (NE) over Bealach Buidhe. At OS ref. 363031 bear right to climb some 600 feet up 3 rock 'steps' to summit of Ben Lomond (367028).

Descend by obvious southward track over Sron Aonaich, back to Rowardennan.

LENGTH: 7 miles – allow a good 5–6 hours.

CONDITIONS: Discernible path ascending, very clear one descending. One or two steep sections. Ascent (3,192 ft) could be tricky in mist for inexperienced walkers; in fine weather this is a circuit for any reasonably fit hill walker. Wear proper hill walking gear.

REFRESHMENTS: None en route; Rowardennan Hotel at start/finish.

C-N-DO WALKING HOLIDAYS: 01786-445703; *admin@cndoscotland.com*; *www.cndoscotland.com*

Walk 94

Ardmeanach Peninsula, Isle of Mull

Exhilarating scramble through a volcanic landscape to visit the Fossil Tree

'CHRISTOPHER, HELLO!' said Barry Meatyard, striding forward, hand outstretched. 'It must be thirty years.'

Thirty years it was – or very nearly – since I had last set eyes on Barry. A lot of water had flowed under both our bridges since Durham University days. On this cloudy, still morning in Ardmeanach, the wildest peninsula of the Hebridean island of Mull, it was eminent botanist and explorer Dr Barry Meatyard of the University of Warwick who was vigorously shaking my hand in the National Trust for Scotland car park.

To me, though, this trim individual – now grizzled of beard – was instantly recognisable as Barry the Black Pig. The student folk music band he'd played with had taken its name from Cap'n Pugwash's pirate ship. The Black Pig's tunes, heard in Durham folk clubs and pubs, first opened the door for me on a life-long love of traditional music.

'I'll have the mandolin and guitar at the bothy,' Barry had promised over the phone while we were planning this reunion walk. 'Bring a sleeping bag and a bottle of wine. We'll have a bit of a session.' I was looking forward to that. But first, there was the little matter of a long day's journey into The Wilderness.

The geological map of Mull looks like an explosion in a paint factory. Variegated rock types burst out of a central point – the giant volcano that erupted many million years ago – and cartwheel off to all points of the compass.

The middle of Mull's three west coast peninsulas – layer-cakes of basalt worn into dramatic ledges and crags – is as rugged as any determined walker could want. They call its western face The Wilderness, with good reason. Cliffs hem Ardmeanach, caves pierce its flanks, crystalline columns of rock prop it up. Its seaward slopes are carpeted in soft grass and crammed with scores of species of tiny, delicate wild flowers, sedges and ferns.

Feral goats crop Ardmeanach's grasses. Eagles overfly its beaches and coastal waters where seals, otters and porpoises play. To a professional botanist, organiser of student expeditions and hawk-eyed observer of the natural world like Barry Meatyard, Ardmeanach is rich in resources. To an uncritical lover of the islands like me, it is, simply, a foretaste of heaven.

With Barry's black labrador Folly wagging at our heels we set off from the car park along a stony track that wound through cool beech woods and across bracken slopes. More than 300 people farmed these braes before 19th-century clearances saw them evicted and scattered across the world. The raised ridges of the 'lazybeds', where they laboured to grow potatoes and grain, still stripe the hillsides.

We passed the tin-built former school at Scobull, and the four cairns raised in memory of four generations of MacGillivrays, the last indigenous family to live hereabouts. Christina MacGillivray – 'Chrissie Burgh', who died in 1989 – is still well remembered for the hospitality she showed all who reached her cottage out at Burgh. Now the little stone house has become the NTS bothy. Here Barry and I dumped our heavy gear; then we set out, past Chrissie Burgh's memorial cairn, for the outermost reaches of Ardmeanach.

Thirty years take some catching up with. Barry had accompanied school and student expeditions here, there and everywhere: to Iceland, to the Galapagos archipelago, to Ecuador. Now he was conducting his own research in Mull on an extremely rare and environmentally sensitive plant, Iceland purslane, and had become a passionate promoter of SAPS, Science and Plants For Schools ('We're trying to show young scientists that plants aren't boring: they're probably our greatest natural asset').

'Centaury – lady's bedstraw – milkwort,' intoned Barry, bottom up and nose down. 'English stonecrop; eyebright; cocksfoot grass. Here's sheep's fescue. And Yorkshire fog.' His hand lens travelled across a sloping carpet of blue, pink, yellow, mauve and white – forty species to a square yard. 'Wild carrot ... self-heal ... sea plantain ... whole masses of thyme here. What's this? ... umm ... *hypericum pulchrum*, the beautiful slender St John's Wort – very aptly named.'

Now the path narrowed and began to climb, a spidery track hanging between the basalt columns overhead and the jumbled rocks of the shore below. Rounding the corner of the peninsula, we looked out north-west to see shadowy islands clinging to the sea horizon – Lunga, Fladda and the low wedge of Staffa, in whose blunt westward profile we could just make out the dark open mouth of Fingal's Cave.

'Can't really carry Folly down the ladder,' said Barry. 'I'll see you on the beach.' Man and dog were off downhill in a patter of stones, while I went gingerly on between crag and sea to find the rusted old iron ladder by which adventurers into The Wilderness make their way down to Ardmeanach's famous Fossil Tree.

'Now here was a pine,' said Barry Meatyard, as we stood craning up at the Fossil Tree, 'eking out an existence, maybe ten million years ago. Suddenly the volcano goes up, lava rushes down and burns the tree. There's a hollow cylinder left in the lava, which fills up with rubble, and you've got a cast of the trunk. See the charcoal?'

This was something to get the mind round: a black sludge of burned wood and the fine grooves of pine bark 10 million years old, at the base of a forty-foot trunk moulded into the cliff. Barry spread-eagled himself athletically across the dark rock wall, collecting specimens of black spleenwort fern. Folly lapped a brackish pool, and I ran my fingers across the antediluvian tree, picturing it ablaze in that volcanic tide.

Walking home along the head-turning cliff path, I looked down through glass-clear water into submerged rock pools of weed, shells, anemones and starfish. Back at the bothy after our long walk, we felt cold enough to light the fire. Choking smoke filled the three wood-panelled rooms. Up on the roof, the capable Meatyard employed a baulk of timber to rod out the chimney.

Bothy cuisine is basic stuff. We threw everything we could lay our hands on into the pot, set pasta on to boil, and took the instruments outside for a bit of a twang. By the time that Lynne Farrell of Scottish National Heritage had joined us for dinner – another bothy-dweller, she'd been off up the hill all day, counting plants – we'd burrowed our way into a rich vein of nostalgia.

The bothy's amenities are none too sophisticated. Cold water, as sweet as a nut, comes from the burn outside. You sleep on the wooden floor. But there was enough electricity to cook on, and enough fire-wood to make a blaze for our late night chantying. Did Meatyard and I really sing our way through the entire works of the Incredible String Band, 1967–1970? I fear so.

STEPPING OUT – *Walk 94*

MAP: OS 1:25,000 Explorer 375; 1:50,000 Landranger 48

TRAVEL: *Car ferry:* Caledonian MacBrayne (www.calmac.co.uk) – Oban to Craignure, 7 days a week.

Road: A849 towards Kinloch, Bunessan and Iona Ferry. 1 mile before Kinloch (OS ref NM547292), right on B8035 Gruline and Salen road. After 4 miles, left by converted chapel (491286 -'NTS Burg' sign). Continue for nearly 2 miles, past Tiroran House, to NTS car park (477275).

WALK DIRECTIONS: Continue through gate and along track, passing old school at Scobull (468274), the Four Cairns (465273) and Tavool House (437274), to reach NTS bothy at Burgh (425266 – 3½ miles from car park). Continue on green path through bracken, at first near shore, then on steep slope, for 1½ miles to ladder (404273 approx). Descend to shore and continue for ½ mile to Fossil Tree (402278 approx). Return same way.

LENGTH OF WALK: Car park to bothy: 3½ miles (allow 1½ hrs each way). Bothy – Fossil Tree – bothy: 4½ miles approx (allow up to 4 hrs)

CONDITIONS: Car park to bothy – easy track. Bothy to Fossil Tree – clear path, becoming increasingly narrow, steep, rocky and vertiginous, though well within capabilities of reasonably fit walkers. Vertical ladder of 25 steps to negotiate.

Car park – Fossil Tree – car park (12 miles – allow at least 7 hrs) makes long, demanding hike.

GEAR: Good hiking boots; flower/bird book; packed lunch; binoculars.

REFRESHMENTS: None – several drinkable streams/waterfalls en route.

ACCOMMODATION: NTS bothy at Burgh (book through National Trust for Scotland on 0844-493-2212). Electric light and cooker: cold water. Bring sleeping bag, mat, pillow, food, drink. Leave firewood/food supply at least as well stocked as you find it, and bothy at least as clean.

Walk 95

Corrour Station to Rannoch Station,
Rannoch Moor

Across the wilds of Rannoch Moor on the Road to the Isles

A HEARTY BUNCH of Glaswegian walkers in breeches and bare legs was descending from the train at Bridge of Orchy station as I climbed on board. Laughing, hoisting knapsacks and scuffing their boots in the platform gravel, the hikers looked delighted to be out in the sharpish breeze of this beautiful clear day in the Scottish mountains. After months of inactivity enforced by a recent outbreak of foot-and-mouth disease, and consequent closure of footpaths across the land, I knew exactly how they felt.

The two-car sprinter rattled north across the eastern edge of Rannoch Moor, sending a herd of red deer bouncing away from a loch beside the railway line. Cloud shadows dimmed the moor colours to sombre tans and olives; then the sun slid through again and spread thick gold across heather and grass. The light train gave a gentle spring every now and then, a reminder that when the West Highland Line was built across Rannoch Moor in the 1890s the engineers had to float the track on bundles of brushwood. The treacherous peat, up to 20ft thick in parts, was far too yielding for any conventional hard foundation.

At Rannoch station, out in the wilds, Steve Duncan and Irvine Butterfield hopped on. I'd been keenly looking forward to walking with this pair – fresh-faced Steve from the Perthshire tourist board, bursting with enthusiasm for the hills, and stocky white-bearded Irvine, a deep well of knowledge of Scottish landscape and culture. A Skipton-born man with a rich Dales accent, author of a clutch of well-respected books, Irvine has forgotten more than Steve and I have ever learned about the mountains and moors of Scotland. By 1971, the year I left university, Irvine had already climbed all 277 of the Scottish 'Munros' or 3,000ft mountains, a feat achieved by every lycra-clad peak bagger these days, but a rare triumph back then. He wrote a bestseller about it, too – *The High Mountains of Britain and Ireland* – the bible of Munro-climbers ever since.

'Loch a' Chlaidheimh, the Loch of the Sword,' Irvine said, pointing out of the train window. 'Now there's a great story attached to that, about the time the Earl of Atholl and Lochiel of the Camerons of Lochaber agreed to meet alone at the loch to settle which of them the land belonged to. But both had men hidden in the heather. When these guys jumped up and faced each other, the chiefs declared a kind of draw. Atholl threw his sword into the loch, saying the land would belong to Lochiel and Lochaber until the sword should be found.

'Anyway, in 1826 a boy actually fished Atholl's sword out of Loch a' Chlaidheimh. But no one wanted to stir things up – especially the Lochaber people! So they took the sword off the boy and chucked it back in the loch again – where it still is.'

Corrour is the remotest railway station in Scotland, marooned below the mountains at the northern edge of Rannoch Moor, ten miles at least from the nearest tarmac road. We left the train and struck out along a rough dirt road, making for Loch Ossian in its cradle of mountains. Steve Duncan had trawled his walkingwild.com website to pluck today's peach of a walk for us – ten miles or more in some of Scotland's most bleakly beautiful country. We were heading south, back towards Rannoch station on the ancient track known to generations of cattle thieves and drovers as Rathad nan Eilean, the Road to the Isles. 'As step I wi' my cromach tae the Isles,' sang Harry Lauder in his 'Road To The Isles' smash hit song, and Irvine was wielding his own fine cromach with a carved ram's-horn crook as we crunched down to the lonely youth hostel by the lake.

The Road to the Isles left the stony lochside road and ran parallel to it before plunging abruptly away southward. The three of us trod a firm green track founded on a bed of stone, with rough stone culverts carrying burns beneath it. This was no casual cattle path wandering through the heather, but a proper moorland road maintained down the centuries by the drovers who depended on it for their livelihoods. As Irvine told the tale, these hardy men were the lynchpin that held the economics of Highland society together from medieval times until the fallout from Culloden and the coming of the railways consigned them to history.

'The owners of the cattle would have to trust the drovers, firstly to take their cattle safely for hundreds of miles from the Western Highlands down to the great trysts or markets at Crieff and Falkirk, secondly to get the best price they could from the dealers, and lastly to bring the money back home again. Sometimes the cattle would be taken on for fattening as far as Norfolk, a journey of getting on for six or seven hundred miles. Most of them became salt beef for the Army or the Navy; the Napoleonic wars did the owners and drovers a very good turn, economically.'

I looked round the bleak scene: the rolling empty moor, stripped hundreds of years ago of the great Wood of Caledon that once covered its sixty square miles; the inhospitable granite humps of the mountains; ragged edges of lonely lochs. Where would the drovers find shelter for the night?

'Oh,' said Irvine, 'there'd be stances along the way, rough-and-ready inns with a patch of grass. The men could have a dram and put their heads down while the cattle grazed. But when I see this land-scape I think of winter and other travellers on the track, in a blinding snowstorm maybe, or lost in mist. Rannoch doesn't always look like it does today, you know!'

That was a true word. When a party of engineering experts including Robert McAlpine set out in January 1889 to walk the 40 miles from Spean Bridge to Inveroran across the moor, they became separated in mist. Benighted and lost, with one of the party helpless with exhaustion, they had to be rescued. 'An inconceivable solitude,' wrote Dr John MacCulloch in 1811, 'a dreary and joyless land of bogs, a land of desolation and grey darkness.' The authors of the West Highland Way official guide, Bob Aitken and Roger Smith, remark dryly of Rannoch Moor: 'In rain or snow with low cloud driving before a gale, it tends to promote the conviction that Hell need not be hot.'

Today, though, all was sweet on Rannoch as we followed the green ribbon of the Road to the Isles. We stopped to picnic on a rock, watching sun and cloud shadows sweep each other majestically from the flanks of Carn Dearg, the Red Rock. 'I was in the glen at the back of it at the weekend,' Steve said, 'and I couldn't hear a sound. Complete silence – how rare is that nowadays?' We sat listening. The scratchy song of a pipit, a faint sigh of wind in grass – that was all.

In the afternoon we explored the ruins of Corrour Old Lodge, a wilderness of grey stone walls above the track. Then we went on, with Irvine and Steve deep in the peak-naming game. 'Garbh Meall? Well, if it is, that must be Meall Chomraidh in front.' – 'No, that's Meall a'

Bhobuir, I think.' I was more than content to walk in ignorance, with snow-streaked mountains filling every far view, and late afternoon sunshine flooding gloriously across the moor.

STEPPING OUT – *Walk 95*

MAPS: OS 1:25,000 Explorer 385; 1:50,000 Landranger 41 and 42 'Glen Garry'

TRAVEL: By rail (www.thetrainline.co.uk) to Corrour Station.

WALK DIRECTIONS: At Corrour station (OS ref NN355664) cross railway and take rough road ('Tulloch Station 15 m'). In 1¼ miles, opposite Youth Hostel (371671) on shore of Loch Ossian, bear right off road; then immediately left (372669) onto grassy track heading eastward. Pass Meal na Lice on right, keeping parallel with and above loch-side road. After 1½ miles track swings south ('Peter's Rock' on map – 393670).

Continue south, then south-west on clearly defined track, passing ruin of Corrour Old Lodge after 4½ miles (408648) and crossing Allt Eigheach on footbridge after 7½ miles (435604). In another 1¾ miles, meet B846 road by Loch Eigheach (447578); right for Rannoch station (423579).

LENGTH OF WALK: 11 miles (allow 4–5 hours)

CONDITIONS: No steep climbs or descents; some boggy patches. Wear ankle-supporting boots; take picnic, water, raingear.

REFRESHMENTS: Moor of Rannoch Hotel, Rannoch Station; Corrour Station Restaurant

CORROUR ESTATE: A courtesy call (01397-732200) would be appreciated, especially in the stalking season (Aug 1 – Oct 20)

READING: '*The Famous Highland Drove Walk*' by Irvine Butterfield (Greystone Books 1996)

INFORMATION: *www.walkingwild.com*

Glen Esk and the Falls of Unich and Damff, Angus

Springtime in the glen marked by the finger of God

T HEY SAY WHEN GOD sculpted the earth from rocks and clay, He was so enchanted with the work that before He set it spinning into space He gave it a last loving pat. It was that celestial hand-print which formed the Glens of Angus – God's thumb-mark the River Tay, His four fingers the four glens of Isla, Prosen, Clova and Esk. As the poet John Angus expressed it:

> *'Four fair green glens reach far into the west,*
> *And of them all, the loveliest and best*
> *Is Esk – Glen Esk, by loving gesture given;*
> *God's little finger left the mark of heaven'*

Amen to that on a glorious morning in spring, a day of sunshine and blue sky over the Scottish hills with curlew song bubbling like meltwater out of the moors. 'One of those days you can only hope for,' was Dave Richardson's comment as he laced his boots in the doorway of Mangey Cottage, looking out over upper Glen Esk to the sunlit humps of East Knock and Cowie Hill.

As a travelling musician with some thirty years of on-the-road experience under his belt, bringing the unrivalled charge of Celtic music to the concert stages of the world with his band The Boys of the Lough, Dave has seen a plethora of breathtaking landscapes in every corner of the globe. As a friend and walking companion since university days he has shown me more about the birds and the plants of upland Britain than I could set down if I scribbled for a month of Sundays. But neither of us had yet walked this delectable glen in the southern foothills of the Grampian range.

GLEN LEE

FOOTBRIDGE

FALLS
OF UNICH

WATER

CRAIG
MASKELDIE

WATER OF LEE

FALLS
OF DAMFF

FOOTBRIDGE

CRAIG
DAMFF

CARLOCHY

UPPER GLEN UNICH

CAIRN
LICK

SHANK OF
INCHGRUNDLE

WATER OF
UNICH

ALTERNATIVE
ROUTE

LANDROVER
TRACK

BURN OF LATCH

FALLS OF DAMFF

CAR PARK
(START &
FINISH
OF WALK)

KIRKTON
OLD CHURCH

HOUSE OF MARK

AR KIRKTON

MANGEY
COTTAGE
5 MILES

INVERMARK
CASTLE

LOCH LEE

CHGRUNDLE
RMHOUSE

GLEN ESK
& THE FALLS OF
UNICH & DAMFF
ANGUS, SCOTLAND

Last night's fun had included lots of wine, reams of blether, and a not-too-successful attempt by Dave to teach me a most beautiful jig, 'Out On The Ocean'. Having stayed afloat till the wee hours with mandolin and accordion, we were both in need of a good blow among the Angus hills.

Jane, Alexa and John, three chums of Dave's from his home town of Edinburgh, were coming along with us for the walk and the crack. Elspeth, a fourth member of the Auld Reekie gang, had opted for gentler pursuits in the lower glen today. She waved us off like a woman all set to bask in the first proper sunshine of this dreich and murky spring.

Jackdaws went sailing in and out of the windows of Invermark Castle as we crunched past its gaunt ruin on the track down to Loch Lee. The tower was built stark and strong in the bad old days of the 1520s when a Scots lord with any sense trusted neither foe nor friend. The front door of Invermark's grim stronghold was sited fifteen feet above ground level. With the ladder pulled up and the squint windows manned, you could hope to sit out a siege until help arrived or frustration drove your enemy away.

Down on the shores of Loch Lee we turned aside into the graveyard of a tumbledown church. Alexander Ross, poet and schoolmaster of Lochlee, was buried there in 1784, his feet to the loch and his head to the glen, the verse on his gravestone his sole obituary:

> *How finely Nature aye he paintit,*
> *O' sense in rhyme he ne'er was stintit,*
> *An' to the heart he always sent it*
> *Wi' micht an' main;*
> *An' no ae line he e'er inventit*
> *Need ane offen'*

Along the shore of Loch Lee we went, looking through binoculars at peregrines cutting the air in springtime display a mile above the glen. 'Frogspawn!' observed Jane, scanning the ditch beside the track, and 'Primroses!' responded Alexa, nose among brilliant yellow clumps in the winter-brown heather. 'Herbs, too – do you get that beautiful spring smell?' Wheatears were flirting their white rumps and rose-coloured breasts on the fence wires. It seemed as if spring had crashed in mob-handed all at once on Glen Esk.

Some vandalistic fool had temporarily abolished the footbridge across the Water of Lee. We splashed across the river at the cost of wet feet and made for the Falls of Unich, a skein of white water tumbling out of a shadowed gorge below Craig Maskeldie. It was the start of a thousand-foot climb past pools and rapids, stumbling upwards on a zigzag path towards the lip of the cleft.

The world of science lost a great botanist when music sank its fatal talons into Dave Richardson. I would have seen nothing on that ascent if it hadn't been for my sharp-eyed friend. 'Broad buckler fern under the rock here,' mused Dave, his restless curiosity all fired up, 'and, let me see ... yes, green spleenwort. Yellow mountain saxifrage, not really open yet of course – and purple saxifrage ... hmm, cloud-berry, *Rubus chamaemorus*, yes ...' The bare rocks seemed to flower as he pointed out their spring glories.

Up in the broad glen of upper Glen Unich we picnicked, dangling our legs from the footbridge upstream of the Falls of Damff. Tracks, rocks and open patches of moorland glittered with mica in the weak sunshine of early spring. Away to the north the three thousand foot crest of Mount Keen rose above all its sister peaks. Scuds of cloud swept up and across the steady blue field of the sky. This was spring in Angus as I had imagined it while coming north through grey weather from a stale southern city – cold, clean and entirely captivating.

We licked the last of the Arbroath smoky pâté from our fingers, swigged the remnants of the tea, and made off along the Water of Unich among stubbly peat hags and the black channels of hill burns. The map and my notes both promised a Landrover track which would carry us all the way back to Loch Lee. There were a couple of 'Where-the-hell-is-it?' moments; but soon we had zeroed in and were tramping its well drained and well surfaced course.

On our way down the steep breast of the Shank of Inchgrundle we turned aside to stare into the craggy corrie of Cairn Lick. At the foot of the cliffs lay the shadowed little lake of Carlochy, tucked away from all but hill-walkers' view on its high cushion of green glacial rubble.

There was definitely something in the Angus air. Mountain hares in snow-white coats went bouncing away over the dark heather as we descended to Inchgrundle farmhouse. A scimitar-winged shape skimmed close over the waters of Loch Lee – the first swallow of spring. I made up my mind that before this night was out, I would get Dave to help me nail for good and all that tricky turn in 'Out On the Ocean'.

STEPPING OUT – *Walk 96*

MAP: OS 1:25,000 Explorers 395 'Glen Esk' and 388 'Lochnagar'; 1:50,000 Landranger 44

TRAVEL: From Edinburgh, M90 to Perth; A90 to Brechin; B966 through Edzell. 1½ miles beyond village, left on minor road up Glenesk to Invermark. Car park below House of Mark (OS ref N0445804).

WALK DIRECTIONS: From car park continue up road, across bridge, through gate by letter box, to pass Invermark Castle (442804) and on along track. Pass ruined church at Kirkton (431801); on along north bank of Loch Lee. Pass top of drive (412796) to Inchgrundle farmhouse. Continue on track for 1⅓ miles; where it swings right up Glen Lee, bear left (395804) over footbridge across Water of Lee. Follow track to Falls of Unich (387802). Up path on right of falls; continue up steepening path in gorge for ¾ mile to pass Falls of Damff at top (385793).

In 200 yards bear left across footbridge (385792); then bear right along the left (east) bank of Water of Unich. In ½ mile, choose between 2 options: (a) turn left (383785) uphill beside Burn of Latch for 300 yards to meet Landrover track at ford (384783) and turn left along it; or (b) continue along Water of Unich for another 300 yards to turn left (379784) up Landrover track to ford.

Follow track for 2 miles over Cairn Link and down Shank of Inchgrundle to Inchgrundle farmhouse (411791). Left along drive to regain lochside track (412796); right to return to car park.

LENGTH: 10 miles

CONDITIONS: Clear paths or tracks except along east bank of Water of Unich between Falls of Damff footbridge and Landrover track/Burn of Latch. Steep upward path in gorge between Falls of Unich and Falls of Damff. Paths can be boggy and uneven between Glen Lee track and Inchgrundle. Wear hill-walking gear and walking boots.

REFRESHMENTS: None en route; take picnic

Walk 97

Abernethy Forest, Strathspey

Winter quiet in the ancient Wood of Caledon

I T WAS A COLD and very windy Scottish winter's morning, with dramatic armies of clouds marching east along the Cairngorms. The weather giants were obviously having a stamping good time up there, flattening climbers and snowholers into shelter and deluging the high tops with squally snow.

Down on Speyside, however, in the shelter of the pine trees of Abernethy Forest, it was a different sort of day entirely. As Andrew Bateman and I drove past Loch Garten whitecaps were ruffling the water, but the sky overhead and all around was the most brilliant blue. The celebrity ospreys that have made Loch Garten famous among bird-watchers the world over would not be back to build their nest and rear their chicks for another couple of months, so we had the great RSPB-owned forest and its maze of tracks virtually to ourselves.

'Where we're going,' said Andrew as we pulled on our boots at Forest Lodge, 'is a remnant of the old Wood of Caledon. It never really covered all of Scotland as the myths say, but it was a vast forest. This part of it, Abernethy Forest, was clear-felled for the timber at the time of the Napoleonic Wars, and a lot of it's been cut down at times since then. But it's regenerated itself, especially since the RSPB bought part of it. It's still a piece of real old native pine forest, one of my favourite places for a walk. The pines do well here because the Cairngorms are drier than the west of Scotland – in spite of what you might think from what's going on up in the mountains today!'

The wind roared like the sea in the pine tops, but on the forest tracks we walked in the shelter of countless thousands of trees. This was not some gloomy block of shoulder-to-shoulder Forestry Commission conifers, but a loose-knit confederation of woodland, open moorland, clearings and grassland. The understorey of the forest was spectacularly rich – great wet tuffets of red and green moss, sprigs of brown heather shaking last year's dried flowerheads, cranberry and juniper, crusts and trails of lichen, and everywhere the tender green shoots of young pine seedlings seeing out the winter under the protection of their parent trees. The cold wind brought hints of pine resin and damp smells of earth sodden with snow-melt.

Andrew walked at ease, looking around at everything with obvious pleasure. A mountain leader and adventure instructor, most of his time in winter is spent shepherding guests up and down the Cairngorm peaks and across the wilderness of the snowbound plateau. A day like this, daundering around at valley level along well-marked paths under a blue sky, was a rare delight for him. Nevertheless, we were drawn as if by magnets up a slope and out of the trees to where we could look south at the storm-capped Cairngorms in all their glory.

It was a view to catch the breath – the deep, dark cleft of Strath Nethy, running south away from us, punching its way into the face of the massif. The black strath was flanked by the triangular head of Bynack More on the east, and the great smooth whaleback of Cairngorm mountain rising into cloud on the west. Gullies, screes and corries were splashed white with snow, and the heads of the mountains were swathed in apocalyptic shafts of opaque sunlight, rain and snow, all charging east.

'Blowing a hooley up there,' was Andrew's laconic comment as he snapped away with his digital camera. It evidently was – a real storm battle, but all fought out along the high corridor of the mountains. Down here in the forest, only half a dozen miles off, it was like looking from a calm garden into the wildest of weather jungles.

We turned back into the trees and mooched along the heather-grown tracks, crunching pungent, gin-tinted juniper berries between our teeth. Soon the path left the trees and ran across a wide brown moorland, with the low, snow-free hummocks of the Braes of Abernethy on the skyline. A lone dead pine stood in a litter of its own flaky bark, trunk hammered into holes by woodpeckers, every sapless branch and twig hung with streamers of lichen. Under the scales of bark that still clung to the tree, colonies of spiders and beetles slept out the dead months. 'It's reckoned,' said Andrew, 'that one of these old dead pines actually supports more life than a living tree.'

It was good to be out of the trees and stepping it out across open ground. We splashed across the Faesheallach Burn at the cost of wet boots and went on over the moor. Soon the track swung back towards the trees again and brought us to the edge of the River Nethy opposite the old farmstead of Lyngarrie. The rotten timbers of a demolished footbridge lay scattered on the bank. Nearby were two stout iron girders for the decking of the replacement bridge, not yet in position.

Andrew and I eyed the icy brown waters of the Nethy. Hmmm … don't think so, do you? The detour to the next bridge upstream cost us an extra forty minutes and two more splashes across ice-cold burns, but we didn't really mind. The day had taken on its own rhythm, an easy and contemplative one.

Back on RSPB territory again, Andrew gripped my arm and pointed up into the tree we were passing under. A little dumpy bird was hopping from perch to perch, giving out a needly squeak of song, the back of its head combed punkily up into a tuft of feathers. 'Crested tit,' murmured Andrew, binoculars to eyes. 'Excellent!'

We passed a miniature mountain of pine needles, its summit heaving with hundreds of scurrying wood ants. Another, further along the path, seemed to have had its top ripped off. 'A pine marten,' Andrew explained. 'They dive into these ant heaps, grab as many grubs as they can, and get out quick before the ants can spray them with formic acid. A tough way to get a meal.'

The forest lay quiet, seething with unseen life, enduring the winter, making its preparations for spring. Walking through the sunlit pines, snatching glimpses into these secret lives on every side, I felt like a man with a prize in each hand.

STEPPING OUT – *Walk 97*

MAP: OS 1:25,000 Explorer 403; 1:50,000 Landranger 36

TRAVEL: By road: A9 to Aviemore, A95 towards Grantown-on-Spey. 4 miles north of Aviemore, bear right (signed) to Boat of Garten. Cross River Spey, then follow 'Loch Garten' signs to pass Loch Garten, then RSPB Loch Garten car park. Turn right ('Tulloch; Tulloch Moor' sign). In a little over 2 miles, at unmarked fork (OS ref NH998167), bear right on dirt road, soon crossing stream. In another 1½ miles, park at Forest Lodge (NJ020161 'Welcome to Abernethy Forest Nature Reserve' sign).

WALK DIRECTIONS: Start up track to left of 'Welcome...' notice (signed 'Sorry, no vehicles past this point'). In 100 yards, pass building on left. In a few hundred yards bear right across bridge over River Nethy (022163). In ¼ mile, right (05162) on good forest track. In 1 mile, bear left at junction of track (025145), and continue for ⅔ mile uphill around foot of Cairn a' Chnuic to where trees on right fall away (035140 approx.) – superb viewpoint south to Cairngorm, Strath Nethy and Bynack More.

From viewpoint retrace steps. In a few hundred yards bear right off descending dirt road on smaller, rougher track, curving right into trees (030142). In 1 mile, at boggy patch (030157) bear right onto lesser track through trees. Soon it leaves the forest (031162) to cross open moor and go through gate in deer fence. Ford Faesheallach Burn (032164) and continue on moorland track with trees close on left.

At 2 gates (032170), go through left-hand one and follow muddy track west. Soon roof of Lyngarrie house (026170) appears ahead; aim for it, to descend bank and meet track; turn right along this. In a few hundred yards, bear left off track, descending to cross footbridge over River Nethy (026172) below Lyngarrie. Follow forest edge up to left behind house to go through gate and continue along forest track to T-junction (020170).

Turn right along track through forest. In ¾ mile it begins to bend left, then runs west to T-junction by a stand of fire-beaters (014182). Turn left for 1⅓ miles to T-junction; left for Forest Lodge.

LENGTH: 8 miles.

CONDITIONS: Good forest and moorland tracks, muddy in some places. One burn to ford.

REFRESHMENTS: None – take food and drink with you.

GUIDED WALKS: Andrew Bateman, Mountain Innovations (01479-831331; *www.scotmountain.co.uk*)

Achnashellach and the Coulin Circuit, Wester Ross

Lonely lochs and waterfalls in the back country beyond Glen Carron

Fɪʀsᴛ, ᴛʜᴇ ɢᴏᴏᴅ ɴᴇᴡs. I woke up at Inchbae Lodge, drew the curtains, looked blearily out on north-west Scotland at first light – and it wasn't raining. Better still, a handsome red deer stag stood muzzle-down twenty yards away, breakfasting off the scatterings of the hotel's hen-coop. A pearly early morning in Wester Ross, the absolute heart and soul of the Western Highlands.

Next, the bad news. Scrambling my things together in haste for the morning train, I couldn't find my walking boots. *Kritziturken!* Must have left them at home, 600 miles away, at the other end of the country... Swearing like a sergeant-major, I made for the telephone.

Calmly, quietly, Jean Stewart made reassuring noises down the line from Loch Carron. She'd try and rustle up a pair of size 11s, and would meet me at Achnashellach station as planned. She was looking forward to our walk round the Coulin Circuit. OK? See you there. 'Bye.

The 9.34 from Garve groaned round the tight curves and up the steep gradients of the West Highland line. I gazed out of the window at the wild country that hems in Britain's most scenically striking railway: dark moors and cold grey lochs under humpback mountains. At this low time of year the peaks along Glen Carron had pulled thick grey blankets of cloud over their shoulders, hiding their heads. Achnashellach enjoys the unhappy distinction of being the wettest place in Scotland, with over six feet of rain falling here in a 'good' year. It looked as if a fair proportion might be fixing to fall in the not too distant future.

I found Jean Stewart waiting on Achnashellach platform with a pair of borrowed boots in her hand. As we climbed north up a forest track, Jean recalled her rapture on discovering Glen Carron ten years ago. 'I was teaching in Cambridgeshire, and just happened upon Wester Ross. I didn't choose it. I certainly didn't know it was the best bit of the north-west coast. I simply fell in love with these mountains, and thought: I've got to go.'

Our way led north from Glen Carron, climbing steadily beside the rocky bed of the River Lair. Between oak and rowan trunks we stared into the steep little gorge down which the river hissed and bounced among the boulders. High overhead rose the dark shark's-tooth peak of Fuar Tholl, the Cold Hollow, a couple of thousand feet of piled strata sloping as they soared up to a sharp point against the sky... 'There's a deer up there,' said Jean, pointing across the glen. I looked up to see a tiny figure, outlined against hurrying grey cloud, that dipped its branched head and disappeared.

Now tremendous country was beginning to unpeel itself from the skyline ahead. We reached the saddle a thousand feet above Achnashellach, and found ourselves looking west into a majestic horseshoe of tilted sandstone mountains 750 million years old – Fuar Tholl, its sharp-nosed twin Sgorr Ruadh (Red Rocky Peak), and facing them Beinn Liath Mhor, the Great Grey Mountain, three craggy humps streaked with dully gleaming sheets of quartzite that topped out more than 3,000 feet into the clouds.

Below the peat slopes and scree lay Loch Coire Lair, cradled in these spectacular mountain arms, beautiful and remote. I had climbed up here on a warm summer's day ten years before, carrying a baby in a back pack while two older children scampered ahead. That afternoon on the banks of the loch we had found sundews and orchids, bog asphodel, dwarf juniper, dragonflies and miniature frogs. On this cold, windy morning, upland nature seemed shut down for the winter. Only the juniper smell remained, a ghostly hint of gin in the air like a dowager's breath.

An ancient track went ribboning westward below Beinn Liath Mhor, on its way over to Glen Torridon. Local legend says that a lovelorn postman of Torridon, smitten by the charms of a maid of Achnashellach, would regularly ride his bicycle over this craggy and mountainous track to visit the lady, then ride all the way back. He must have been a superman

The route that Jean and I were following lay north-east, into the Coulin Forest. Jean led the way across a boggy plateau littered with square-shaped boulders, standing where they had been dumped ten thousand years before by retreating Ice Age glaciers.

Down in the open throat of the Coulin glen, venerable Scots pines stood tall and wind-tattered. Drawn up ramrod straight, they formed an Old Contemptible platoon of the decimated army of trees that once covered the Highlands of Scotland. These veteran survivors of the great Wood of Caledon attracted the admiration of John Hillaby as he travelled on foot through Wester Ross in 1965. 'Altogether a noble tree,' he wrote in *Journey Through Britain,* his account of that epic 1100-mile walk. 'Nothing else in the streets of the mountains gives such a sense of pageantry. They have about them the quality of a bugle blast.'

The peaty brown River Coulin skates down the glen over a series of waterchutes, the Easan Dorcha or Dark Falls. We passed a water-fall tumbling thirty feet down a black rock face into a dark pool. A mesmerisingly peaceful and beautiful place, where the air hung cold and still. I knelt to push my arm up to the elbow into a soft crimson cushion of moss, and felt the toughness of the roots at its damp heart. Looking up, I saw a wonderful view northwards – the hard white quartzite face of Ben Eighe lifting into cloud, its long bulk filling the far side of Glen Torridon.

Jean and I crossed a stone bridge over the fast rushing River Coulin, and turned back to the south along the long track that rises two miles to the Coulin Pass high above Glen Carron. For centuries the tough itinerant drovers brought their long strings of Highland cattle up this route, driving them steadily south and east for weeks at a time, through the glens and over the passes to the sales at Muir of Ord near Inverness. From there the cattle went south to the great trysts at Crieff and Falkirk, and then on to the fattening meadows, the butchers' slabs and household tables of the Industrial Revolution towns of England.

In the footsteps of the drovers we breasted the Coulin Pass and dropped down the long forestry road through resin-scented stands of spruce and fir. I said goodbye to Jean Stewart, handed over her kind neighbour's walking boots, and caught the late train back to Garve through a glen now smothered in the blackest of nights, out of which the lights of lonely farms shone brightly.

STEPPING OUT – *Walk 98*

MAP: OS 1:25,000 Explorer 429; 1:50,000 Landranger 25

TRAVEL: By train – West Highland line to Achnashellach (*www. thetrainline.co.uk*).

By road – From Inverness, A9, A835 towards Ullapool; at Garve, A832 towards Kyle of Lochalsh; at Achnasheen, A890 (towards Kyle of Lochalsh) to Achnashellach (13 miles). Park on A890 near telephone box (OS ref NI 1005484), and walk up track to station.

WALK DIRECTIONS: At station (003485) cross line, go through gate, up woodland track. In 100 yd, left along level forestry track, through deer gate and on. In ½ mile, black arrow points left (white stony scraping on right), 50 yd down to kissing gate. Through gate; right on clear track by river, climbing for one mile to rocky plateau. Just beyond big boulder on right, track forks at small cairn (990503). Go left here for ½ mile to view Loch Coire Lair; right to continue towards glen of Allt nan Dearcag. In 1 mile path becomes less obvious; steer NE through heather towards tall pine trees at head of glen. Cross stream on footbridge, between falls and hut (012525).

Continue on better stony track for 1 mile to turn right over River Coulin on stone bridge (024531). Ascend steadily due S on good track for 2 miles to aerial at Coulin Pass (024500). Through gate, and descend through trees on forestry track for 2 miles. Just above Achnashellach station, track swings left by 3-armed electricity pole; but keep ahead here past pole, down path between rhododendron bushes to station.

LENGTH: 8½ miles – allow 5/6 hours.

CONDITIONS: Moderate gradients; path stony, occasionally boggy. Take full hill-walking gear, including compass.

REFRESHMENTS: Take packed lunch and a hot drink. Plenty of hill burns to drink from.

Walk 99

Inchnadamph and the River Traligill glen, Sutherland

Traditional music meets acid rock

OPENING THE CURTAINS with due caution in our bedroom at the Inchnadamph Hotel, Dave Richardson and I were rewarded with the sight of a pair of red deer grazing unconcernedly on the hill slope a couple of hundred yards away. There wasn't much else to see – the mountains of Assynt had withdrawn modestly behind veils of low cloud, and spitting rain was drifting steadily across their flanks.

The hotel's fishing guests had already swallowed their porridge and kippers, and were congregating in a hallway pungent with the tang of damp booth-leather and yesterday's trout. They stamped into their waders and water-proofs, bent on a wet day's flogging of loch and burn.

You don't come to the Assynt region of Sutherland, almost as far up north-west Scotland as it's possible to go, to griddle yourself on a sun-kissed beach. This is stern country for anglers and walkers, a rain-washed landscape empty and challenging, where the mountains loom up and away from bog and moorland blanketing some of the oldest rocks in Britain.

Playing the traditional music of Scotland and Ireland all over the world is a disorientating way to make a living. The previous day Dave Richardson had flown into Edinburgh exhausted, with the applause of thousands still ringing in his ears, from the Canary Islands where he'd been giving a concert. Tomorrow he would be jetting out to Scandinavia with his band, the Boys of the Lough. Today was a rare chance to snatch a few hours of botanising and bird-watching in the blessed silence and loneliness of Assynt.

The night's rain had swollen the River Traligill to impressive height and power. A tumble of racing water, stained bottle-brown by peat, was snatching at the lichen-encrusted branches of willow, birch and rowan. Stupendous mountain vistas lay all around us as we trudged along the stony track above the river, with the crowning glory of Ben More Assynt – at 3,273 ft the highest mountain in Sutherland – standing dead ahead. So the map told us, at any rate; today wasn't the day for views. It didn't matter. There was more than enough to look at along the bonny banks of Traligill.

In steep, lumpy pastures striped with tumbledown stone walls the sheep were nibbling at grass washed by the rain into glistening greenness. The flowers shone in tiny points of brilliant colour, spattering the sward, dotting the bog, and clustering on the ledges of limestone cliffs.

'Limestone and acid rock – this is where they meet,' Dave said, sniffing the vanilla scent of a fragrant orchid. 'There's a band of limestone running through the gneiss here, so you get this amazing variety – plants of the limestone, like these orchids, side by side with plants of the acid bog and rock. Look over there, in the peat – bog asphodel … and here's lemon-scented fern. Notice the smell?'

I did. Nose and eyes were hard at work as we left the track to climb limestone crags bristling with clumps of yellow saxifrage. From near the top of the cliff I got a clearer picture of the glen's layout – the characteristic smooth green of lime-fed grass, bright with pink and purple orchids and royal blue milkwort, invaded by streams of acid peaty water that were trickling down from the heights of Ben More Assynt and its foothills. The trickles were slowly building up moist patches of bog starred with yellow tormentil and deep pink lousewort.

Until today I'd thought of sedges as no more than gloomy brown spikes in gloomy brown bogs; but down in the wet peat, drawing a stem of flea sedge ('Carex pulicaris,' prompted Dave) through my fingers to make the seeds pop off like performing fleas, I changed my mind.

'Carex panacea over here,' Dave beckoned, 'fruits like bunches of nuts, can you see? And this is star sedge – um – Carex echinata, I think – with these fruits like spiky little stars. You probably know that one,' he added, tactfully if unrealistically.

Squelching wet of boot and soaked of anorak, legs smeared with peat and knuckles well barked on limestone, I could happily have played the botany student all morning along the glen. Twenty-five years ago Dave had undergone a similar outdoor induction from David Bellamy, his professor at Durham University; now the master's enthusiasms were being handed on.

When at last we did raise our eyes from the grass and sedge, it was to see a red deer outlined in classic *Monarch of the Glen* pose on the skyline across the valley. The hill burns, gorged with rain, were crashing in chutes of white water down the hillsides, and the River Traligill foamed down its rocky bed. A young golden eagle suddenly appeared, flapping slowly along the crags, white juvenile fluff still powdering its rump.

We climbed on up the path to where the ground opened in a series of dark, sheer-sided slits hung with dripping ferns. In the depths 30 feet below, a stream roared and sluiced away through black subterranean tunnels, a mesmerising sight. The limestone of the Traligill glen, eaten into by the acid waters from above, is pocked with these swallets and honeycombed with underground cave systems.

'Traligill,' mused Dave, as he nursed his vertigo well back from the hole. 'I wonder if that means Troll's River? In Shetland they have a tale about musicians caught by the trolls and taken underground to play for 100 years. You can escape by crossing water, though.'

Water is a commodity that tends to be shunned by musicians, Shetlanders or not, but there was no avoiding it today. We forded streams and splashed through bog, climbing from the pastoral beauties of the limestone towards the harsh peat wilderness of high moorland. As the views began to widen through the trailing cloud, ornithology shouldered botany aside. Wheatears flickered their 'white-arse' trademarks from heather to rock and back again. A ring ouzel bobbed under the crags with a neat white parson's collar round his black throat, and along the rim of the glen darted the lean and purposeful shape of a peregrine.

We topped the rise and came to a lumpy plateau of wild moor. No hint of limestone's soft graces here – just peat bog, pools of water scummed with green sphagnum moss, and the steely grey sheet of Loch Mhaolach-coire lying dark and sombre at the shrouded feet of Ben More Assynt.

On the shore of the loch, before dropping back down the Traligill glen, we munched slices from a goat's cheese that Dave had bought two days before in the sunshine of the Canaries. In two days time he'd be playing for his livelihood, if not his life, in the real land of the trolls. But just now, in the absolute stillness and emptiness of the Sutherland hills, the hunted musician could stand and catch his breath for a few precious minutes more.

STEPPING OUT – *Walk 99*

MAP: OS 1:25,000 Explorer 442; 1:50,000 Landranger Sheet 15.

TRAVEL: By road: To Ullapool – from Edinburgh, bypass to Forth Bridge, M90 to Perth, A9 to Inverness and Tore, A835; from Glasgow, A80, M80, M90 to Perth, then as above to Ullapool. On to Inchnadamph – A835 north to Ledmore Junction (OS ref. NC247125 – 11 miles); A837 north to Inchnadamph Hotel (251216 – 6 miles).

WALK DIRECTIONS: From Inchnadamph Hotel turn right along A837, over bridge and immediately right up track on north bank of River Traligill. In ½ mile cross Allt Poll an Droighinn burn (260220 – footbridge and ford) and follow track past Glenbain house (264217) and below conifer wood (270211) to cross River Traligill (271210 – footbridge) and reach pothole caves (275205).

Bear right above these on narrow path that becomes more distinct as it skirts head of deep gully (276204). Cross burn and continue on boggy path, heading ESE, over lip of moorland to reach Loch Mhaolach-coire (277197). Return by outward route to Inchnadamph Hotel.

LENGTH OF WALK: 5 miles – allow 3 – 4 hours.

CONDITIONS: Rough hill tracks, upper sections wet and boggy. No steep ascents or descents. Take great care near caves – sheer drops into underground rivers. Leave details of route and estimated return time at hotel.

GEAR: Essentials are hill-walking clothes and boots, map, compass, food, hot drink; also, take flower book and binoculars for bird-watching.

REFRESHMENTS: Inchnadamph Hotel (tel 01571-822202; www.inchnadamphhotel.co.uk). NB Hotel closed from end of October till mid-March.

FURTHER INFORMATION: Hotel has selection of booklets on local history, flora and geology.

Strath of Kildonan and Suisgill Burn, Sutherland

Wild hills of the Sutherland Gold Rush

T HE STONE in the middle of the flooded burn looked a solid enough footing, but I had reckoned without its rain-slathered coat of moss. My descending boot skidded treacherously, my heels flew over my head and I landed on my back, full length in the burn, my brand-new camera under me. The omens couldn't have been clearer: this wasn't going to be my lucky day in the goldfields of the Strath of Kildonan.

As soon as I had looked out of my bedroom window at Broom-hill House in Helmsdale, I'd marked the day down as one for all-out foul weather gear. Nothing strange in that, here in the far north-east of Scotland, even in summer. A Bristolian fellow-guest at breakfast, talking of his searches for the hidden treasure of the Sutherland hill burns, had sharpened my appetite for the rainy walk.

'Oh, I've been up the strath several times, panning the Kildonan Burn. You just shake the gravel out of the pan, like this' – his hands made a circular motion, as if steering a bus round a sharp bend – 'and there's the gold, sunk to the bottom. If you're lucky.' How did he feel at such triumphant moments? 'Justified. It's a long way to come for a few flecks of gold.'

The valley of the Strath of Kildonan cuts into the Sutherland hills in a deep green bow, curving north west inland from Helms-dale. In 1868–69 more than 500 prospectors thought it worth a long journey to settle themselves in tented encampments a dozen miles up the strath, panning the burns for the seductive flecks of gold. They braved the wild weather of the hills, isolation, cold and hunger for a dream which saw no one greatly enriched and many disillusioned. All told, about £10,000 worth of gold was extracted during the Suther-land Gold Rush, most of it in poor-quality gold dust.

But the dream lives on. Driving up the Strath of Kildonan I came to Baile an Òr, the Town of Gold, a stretch of level grass where the gold-rush panners once lived in wooden shacks. From here amateur prospectors with a free permit from the Suisgill Estate still try their luck along the Kildonan Burn.

Today the rain was sluicing down on a lone tent, at whose flap a grizzled, bald and bearded face was grumpily surveying the elements. His gold pan lay on the grass nearby. So would he or wouldn't he? The prospector grimaced and withdrew his head like a dyspeptic tortoise. It's a hard life in the goldfields of Kildonan.

Red deer were grazing under the birches close by the River Helmsdale as I neared the bridge across the Suisgill Burn. The Sutherland hills were lumped together in shades of rain-swept grey from slate to ashen. This is one of the loneliest valleys in Scotland, sternly beautiful in sunshine, forbidding and challenging on a day such as this.

Nowadays the strath holds only a scatter of houses, Earlier inhabitants forced a bare living for the best part of 4,000 years out of the fertile land beside the Helmsdale River and its tributary burns. Near the bridge a square-cut chamber, stone-walled and roofed with big, flat stone slabs, ran into the slope of the hill: a souterrain, in which some Iron Age tribesman had kept his goods away from the rain and the clutches of others.

A curlew called, mournfully – *curleek! curleek!* – as I set off up the Suisgill Burn over wet heather and brilliant green and red splashes of sphagnum moss. There were other green patches on the slopes. Round ones partly walled in stone were remnants of ancient hut settlements; square ones smothered in heather and sedge once housed the cattle and families of Clan Gunn. The clansmen of the Strath of Kildonan had clung on through hard times and easy, until in 1813 and 1819 their English landlord, the Marquess of Stafford, cleared them from his lands to make way for sheep.

'The whole inhabitants of Kildonan parish, with the exception of three families, nearly 2,000 souls, were utterly rooted and burned out. Many, especially the young and robust, left the country but the aged, the females and children were obliged to stay and accept the wretched allotments allowed them on the seashore, and endeavour to learn fishing.' So recorded Donald Sage, the minister born in Kildonan, telling in outrage and bitterness a story that was to be repeated up and down Scotland in the following years.

Men gave way to sheep, and today the sheep fatten all down the strath and its side valleys. A couple of them were watching impassively as I hauled myself out of that freezing cold burn after my pratfall. Oh, well – at least I couldn't get any wetter. Stiffening my upper lip and getting a certain bloody-minded enjoyment out of the all-pervading wetness and greyness of the morning, I strode on, squelching, towards the pale loom of Cnoc na Béiste, the Hill of the Beast.

At the fork of the Suisgill Burn below the hill, the ground was hummocky with the mounds of bygone gold digging. This stretch of the burn was one of the most heavily worked during the Sutherland Gold Rush. The prospectors, fearing what locals told them of the black dog with two heads and burning eyes who haunted Cnoc na Béiste, preferred to sleep in their tents down in the broad green strath below. I couldn't blame them; this is an end-of-the-world place, ruled by wide hills and the rush of burn water and moan of wind, stripped bare of all but the most elemental sights and sounds.

With my tumble freshly in mind, I did not brave a fording of the Suisgill Burn but struck out eastwards along deer paths on the brink of the burn's steep banks. Then I made for the strath road by way of a stalker's track across the thick heather of the hills, wrapped in rain that strengthened all the way.

Tight, woolly balls of spider eggs, bound up in the tips of the heather sprigs, were anchored against the wind by long silken mooring ropes attached to other sprigs nearby. Curlews continued to call, pipits to flit across the hill. Nature seemed to be doing well out here in the rain, whatever a walker might be enduring.

Instead of gold, I had found a thorough soaking. But I was discovering, too, a gritty pleasure in outfacing harsh hill country through the foulest weather in Scotland.

STEPPING OUT – *Walk 100*

MAP: OS 1:25,000 Explorer 444; 1:50,000 Landranger 17

TRAVEL: By train: Kildonan station (next stop north of Helmsdale, 2½ miles from bridge) – www.thetrainline.co.uk.

By road: A9 from Inverness to Helmsdale; A897 Melvich road to bridge over Suisgill Burn (OS ref NC898252 – 1¾ miles beyond Kildonan, 12 miles from Helmsdale). Park by bridge.

WALK DIRECTIONS: Souterrain is 30 yards back from Suisgill Burn bridge, just above A897. From here climb stony track immediately above, across hill and under power lines, to ford side burn near circular stone sheep fank (pen) above wooden bridge over Suisgill Burn (899255). Continue for 1 mile on east bank of Suisgill Burn to junction of burns by eroded cliffs below Cnoc na Béiste (904269).

If Suisgill Burn is low, ford and continue east on north (left) bank; if burn too swollen, climb to top of south (right) bank and continue east on deer paths. Pass waterfall (913271); in another ¾ mile bear left along main burn round knoll (916272).

In another ¾ mile (20 mins) look for stalker's track climbing away to south (right bank – 931276). Follow this for 1¼ miles (½ hr), round west flank of Torr nan Gabhar, to junction of tracks (927256). Bear right on track for 2 miles past Cnoc a'Mheadhoin and Cnoc nam Féinn to A897 at Suisgill Lodge (901238). Right along road to bridge.

LENGTH OF WALK: 7½ miles – allow three hours in good conditions, more in poor.

CONDITIONS: Clear track from A897 Suisgill Burn bridge to Cnoc na Béiste. Clear on north bank going east to stalker's path; narrow deer paths, thick heather on south bank. Clear stalker's track to A897.

After rain, burns may be impassable. Care always needed, as paths rough and often slippery. In very heavy rain or mist, walk to stalker's track at 931276 and return same way. Let someone know where you are going and don't forget to check in with them on your return.

Take full hill-walking gear, hot drink, food.

REFRESHMENTS: None en route